Wise Her Still Too

One Woman's Pearls Was Another Woman's Pain

TIFFANY KAMENI

WISE HER STILL TOO

TOO

(Volume I)

by Tiffany Buckner–Kameni

Copyright

Disclaimer

This book is designed to provide information and motivation to our readers. It is sold with the understanding that the publisher is not engaged to render any type of psychological, legal, or any other kind of professional advice. No warranties or guarantees are expressed or implied by the author, since every man has his own measure of faith. The individual author(s) shall not be liable for any physical, psychological, emotional, financial, or commercial damages, including, but not limited to, special, incidental, consequential or other damages. Our views and rights are the same: You are responsible for your own choices, actions, and results.

Most of the stories in this book are fictional. Names, characters, businesses, places, events and incidents are either the products of the author's imagination or used in a fictitious manner. Any resemblance to actual persons, living or dead, or actual events is purely coincidental.

Some of the stories in this book are the non-fictional, as told by the individuals who lived them firsthand. The contributors have tried to recreate events, locales and conversations from their memories of them. In order to maintain the anonymity of the subjects in their stories, the contributors may have changed the names of individuals and details such as physical properties, occupations and places of residence. The author (Tiffany Buckner-Kameni) accepts no liability in respect of this information shared in this book by the contributors.

Dedication

I dedicate this book to the one and only true and living GOD, YAHWEH. You gave this book to me, and I'm giving it right back to you to use for your glory.

Acknowledgments

I would like to give a special thanks to the four women of GOD who submitted their stories in this book:
- B. Davinia Gordon
- Earlean Johnson
- Lashonda Moultrie
- Yolanda Tarkington

Ladies, your stories are so very inspiring, and I know they are going to bless women of GOD all around the world. You are blessed of GOD to carry your stories to the nations, and I am honored that you chose to share a piece of your history in Wise Her Still Too.

A special thanks to Davinia Gordon for not only submitting your story for Wise Her Still Too, but for proofreading this book. You are a valued friend and I am thankful to GOD for your help, support and love.

Table of Contents

Introduction...I

Successful Failure...3

Impersonating a Servant of the Lord............................23

Cry Me a River...41

Every Season Has a Reason...91

And Suddenly...127

The Strength to Restrain..163

A New Normal...181

Her Story- B. Davinia Gordon.....................................221

In Full Costume..233

The Other-Other Woman..275

One Tear Closer to You..317

The Devil's Pacifier...347

The Belly of Hell...357

Miranda's Rights...371

Her Story- Earlean Johnson..415

Friends Without Benefits..437

Seasonal Lovers...453

Man-You-Factored...501

The Sin-Finder..531

Demotion For Promotion...555

Spiritual Pedophile..579

Introduction

Where does the title "Wise Her Still" come from?
Wise Her Still was taken from Proverbs 9:9 NIV, which
reads, "Instruct the wise and they will be wiser still;
teach the righteous and they will add to their
learning." The term "wiser still" was changed to make
it more suitable for women, thus you now see "Wise
Her Still."

Wise Her Still Too is a follow-up to Wise Her Still; a
powerful book detailing stories of abuse, envy,
adultery and many of the struggles the women of
GOD face in their daily lives. Each story is written to
teach a lesson as it relates to so many women, the
struggles they are in and the battles that are before
them.

In Wise Her Still Too, you will also find four true-to-life
stories as written by four women of GOD who have
faced the storms you can probably relate to, and they
have overcome these storms to testify about the
goodness of GOD. Even though the rest of the
stories are fictional, the lessons in them are not.
When women purchased the original Wise Her Still,
many of them came back and purchased extra books
to share with their friends, daughters and other family

members who were currently in the very same situations some of the characters in that book found themselves in.

In Wise Her Still Too, the stories are longer and the lessons are clearer: the women of GOD have to change if they want to see a change in their lives.

Successful Failure

"Seed it. Don't need it."

It's not uncommon to see talented or skilled people who
never go further than where they are now. That's because
the average believer thinks that success and luck are one
and the same. Let's get one thing straight: There is no
such thing as luck. The word "luck" is believed to have first
entered the English language through gambling. With
GOD, there are no gambles. Everything that GOD created
in the Earth operates in seed-time and harvest. You sow a
seed, and when the right season comes around, you reap
a harvest.

Most believers have skills or talents, but they are not
willing to sow into their skills or talents. The majority of the
ones who do sow oftentimes sow a little but expect a lot,
and it just doesn't work that way.

Everyone applauded as Jasmine left the stage. What a
talented girl she was. Jasmine was at a business
conference in Dallax, Texas. She was an Independent Sales
Representative for a large multilevel marketing company
called AdVor-Ties. AdVor-Ties was the leading multilevel
establishment company in the nation, and their company

was designed to help people establish their own multilevel marketing companies. They would also help them to plan and host their own conferences. Jasmine's job was to talk to people who'd shown interest in contracting with AdVor-Ties, and she was to try to sell their services.

Jasmine loved working for AdVor-Ties because she'd garnered some recognition and even earned a few thousand dollars. She wasn't earning enough to make a living with; nevertheless, she had seen a fluctuation in her earnings, so she believed that she was well on her way to success. After all, there were many AdVor-Ties representatives on the conference calls and at the live conference who'd become millionaires in the company. Because of her recent success in selling forty new clients, Jasmine was invited on stage to give her testimony about the success of the company.

As Jasmine made her way to her seat, she couldn't help but feel honored. She felt that all eyes were on her since she'd just made Director and was well on her way to holding the golden microphone. Everyone working for the firm who'd earned six digits in a year was given the golden microphone at conferences. Every time someone stepped on the stage, you already knew what income bracket they fell in based on the microphone they reached for.

Jasmine still had an eight-to-five job as well. After all, AdVor-Ties wasn't paying her enough to maintain her bills, but she was able to pay her car note with what she earned. She was also able to put a little money aside for rainy days.

Jasmine was the single mother of two children: an eight-year-old boy named Carson, and a five-year-old daughter named Faith. Jasmine had never been married, and she and the children's father (Carlton Briggett) had broken up five years ago, not long after Faith was born. Carlton was actively involved in the children's life. He'd also gotten married three years after his relationship ended with Jasmine, and he'd had two more children since the breakup.

Carlton was active military, and he paid his child support to Jasmine faithfully. Jasmine and Carlton had a civil relationship with one another, but Jasmine didn't get along too well with Carlton's wife, Autumn. This was partly because Jasmine always tried to exclude Autumn from any discussions about Carson and Faith. Truthfully, Jasmine felt like Autumn would be a short-term fixture in Carlton's life; therefore, she didn't want to involve her in what she referred to as her and Carlton's business. In the beginning, Carlton had done everything to get the women to put away their swords so they could properly raise the children, but he'd finally found a way around their bickering: he would simply rush Jasmine off the phone anytime she called.

Besides selling things, Jasmine was talented in cooking, writing and singing. She had been raised by her grandmother, and she'd been cooking since she was a little girl. Cooking was a passion for her, and she often found herself watching cooking shows or visiting recipe websites trying to learn to cook more dishes. As for writing, Jasmine had always been a talented writer. She loved to write short stories and she loved to blog. Even though Jasmine had a beautiful voice, she was always ashamed to sing in front of others. Because of this, most people who knew her were not aware of the fact that she could sing, and she had the voice of an angel.

Autumn, on the other hand, was a talented cook, seamstress, singer, writer and hairstylist. It seems that Carlton was attracted to talented women. The differences between Autumn and Jasmine were their drives, plans and beliefs. Jasmine was a woman who jumped on whatever opportunity she saw as a good opportunity, but she did not tap into her talents. Autumn was a woman who saw her talents as her opportunities, so she'd hired a web design firm to create a website for her business called Hampton Mall Online. She'd gotten with some local business owners and sold space on her website. Her website listed services from catering, reserving a hairstylist, fashion, cosmetology and so on. Her company had taken off in less than a year of her opening it, and Jasmine envied her success. Jasmine worked hard at AdVor-Ties, hoping to earn her own success in fields unrelated to those in which Autumn worked. After all, they had some of the same talents, and Jasmine did not want to ride in Autumn's shadow.

It was a Friday evening, and the children had just come

home from school. They were all out for spring break, and Jasmine prepared dinner for them before heading to their rooms to pack their bags. They would be spending spring break with their father, and she'd decided that she would prefer to drop the children off at his place, rather than have him come to her place. Jasmine's home was a mess because she had AdVor-Ties materials scattered all over the place.

After the children finished eating, Jasmine loaded them into the car and took them to their father's house. When she arrived there, she noticed that Carlton's car was not in the driveway, but Autumn's was. Carlton lived thirty minutes away from Jasmine, so she didn't want to take the children back home with her. All the same, she didn't want to leave her children with Autumn. She did not want the children to bond with Autumn, even though Faith had already established that she liked Autumn and loved spending time with her and her children. Carson was loyal to his mother, so he was often quiet and stand-offish around Autumn. Jasmine decided to call Carlton's phone to see where he was.

Carlton: Hello.
Jasmine: Where are you? I'm outside in your driveway.
Carlton: I'm at the barber. Just leave the kids there. Autumn is in the house.
Jasmine: Carlton, you know I don't want to leave my kids with your wife.

Carlton: Well, take them home and I'll come by and get them when I leave the barber shop.

Jasmine: No. I have plans tonight.

Carlton: Jasmine, what do you want me to do then?

Jasmine: How long will you be at the barber shop?

Carlton: I'm not sure. Maybe an hour or an hour and a half. I just got here, and there are four men ahead of me.

Jasmine: What barber shop are you at? Maybe I can just drop them off there.

Carlton: No. Just leave the kids with Autumn. They'll be alright, Jasmine.

Jasmine: Why can't I drop them off at the barber shop with you?

Carlton: Jasmine, these men curse up here. This is not a barber shop you want to bring kids to. At the same time, I keep telling you that you and Autumn are going to have to put your claws aside to raise those kids.

Jasmine: I'm not the one with the claws. She just doesn't want to communicate with me.

Carlton: No. You want to rule our house, and she's standing her ground.

Jasmine: I'm not trying to run your house.

Carlton: Yes, you are. For example, you told her that one of your rules was that she would have to call you before feeding the children to tell you what she's feeding them. What kind of foolishness is that?

Jasmine: I'm a mother, and I'm watching out for my children.

Carlton: No. You keep trying to find a throne for yourself in another woman's castle.

8

Jasmine: Whatever, Carlton. I'll go ahead and leave them here, but if she does anything to my children, I'm going postal.

Carlton: Just leave them there and stop being so dramatic.

After hanging up from Carlton, Jasmine unloaded the children from her car and headed up to the door. Before she could knock, Autumn opened the door. She was holding her six-month-old little girl who was now asleep. Without greeting Autumn, Jasmine kissed her kids and sent them into the house. She then attempted to hand their briefcase to Autumn, but Autumn shook her head and told Jasmine to bring the bag in the house.

Jasmine: Autumn, can you please take the children's briefcase?

Autumn: Jasmine, I'm holding my daughter. Bring it in.

Jasmine: Can you go and lie her down? She's asleep already.

Autumn: Jasmine, bring the bag in the house. It's not that big of a deal. I need to speak with you anyway.

Jasmine: You can talk with me here.

Autumn: Jasmine, please come inside the house. Please. I can't keep holding this door open; otherwise, mosquitoes will get in.

Jasmine finally decided to come in. This was her first time ever entering Carlton's house. She noticed how beautiful the interior was. It appeared that Carlton was making more money than he was letting on, she thought. Autumn asked Jasmine to sit down, and after hesitating for a minute, she decided to go ahead and sit down. The children went into the toy room to play, and Autumn went and put her baby to bed.

Jasmine: What did you want to talk with me about? I have somewhere to be.

Autumn: Jasmine, you and I are both mothers. Our children are siblings, and we are both Christian women. What I don't understand is why we don't get along. I have done everything in my power to get along with you, but it seems that you are determined to make sure that we are at odds with one another. I invited you in so that I can better understand what I did to you so we can fix the problem.

Jasmine: There is no problem. I tried to resolve it with you a while back, but you refused.

Autumn: No, you tried to run my house and that wasn't going to happen.

Jasmine: How did I try to run your house?

Autumn: Jasmine, you tried to tell me what to cook, how to feed the children and how to dress them. You even had the nerve to tell me to notify you before feeding your children.

Jasmine: I was just looking out for my children.

Autumn: I love Carson and Faith as if they were my own children. What hurts me is seeing Carson trying his best to show his loyalty to you by refusing to talk to me or to play with my children. Jasmine, that's not something an eight-year-old should be concerned about. He should be enjoying his childhood.

Jasmine: So you're calling me a bad mother?

Autumn: Stop with the defensive tones. If I was going to call you a bad mother, I wouldn't mince words. What I'm saying is that I understand why you are angry with me.

Jasmine: Why do you think I'm angry?

Autumn: It's obvious, Jasmine. You're not completely over Carlton, and I understand that.

Jasmine: What? I am over Carlton. Don't let him fill your head up with lies.

Autumn: No, my dear. You are the only one lying to yourself. You see me as a woman who took your man, but you and Carlton had been broken a year before I met him. So it's not fair for you to treat me as if I took him from you.

Jasmine: Is that what you think? You think I want Carlton? If I wanted Carlton, I could have Carlton. I'm not going to let one of Carlton's women perfect her mothering skills on my children.

Autumn: You see? Listen to what you said. I'm not one of Carlton's women. Carlton dated two other women before meeting me. I am his wife. That means I'll be around for a lifetime.

Jasmine: Oh, please. I was with Carlton for ten years, and we still broke up. You've only been married to him for two years. Just give it a little time.

Autumn: That's what you wish, but there is a difference. Carlton and I got married. You were his girlfriend for ten years.

Jasmine: Whatever! I had his children first. I supported him when he had nothing! I worked two jobs so he could finish school!

Autumn: Lower your voice, Jasmine. I'm not trying to offend you. Listen to yourself. You keep talking about what you did for him. That means that you feel that you should be the one living in this house; you should be the one he's with. I understand that because you were with him for ten years. You sowed love, money, time, sacrifice and two beautiful kids into that relationship. Believe me, I understand how you feel. Now that Carlton has graduated college, is in the military and working in his field, you feel that you should be enjoying the fruits of your harvest.

Jasmine: How would you know how I feel? Both of your children are with Carlton. You didn't give a man ten years of your life, only to have him leave you with two kids over a silly argument. How would you feel if you gave a man ten years of your life and he never proposed to you, but he meets a girl, knows her for a year and then marries her? I'm not saying that I'm not over him, but I am saying that I am within my rights to be angry with how it all played out.

Autumn: Okay. Allow me to speak and please don't take offense at anything I say. I am talking with you because I want us to get along; I want us to be friends, and I want you to feel comfortable around me. Jasmine, I was with a man for seven years before I met Carlton. He was the love of my life; my first, and at that time, I felt he was my everything. I gave him everything that I had and that I was, and then one day, I found out I was pregnant by him. Everything was fine at first, until one day, he came home drunk. He beat me until

I was a bloody mess. I ended up losing my baby. I was five months pregnant with a little girl who I was going to name Mandy. A year later, I got pregnant again. I was still young and dumb, and I thought I could change him. When I got pregnant again, he seemed happy about it, and for the entire length of that pregnancy, he didn't put a hand on me. He would rub my belly, kiss my belly and tell me that he loved me every day. I thought all of my time in that relationship had finally paid off. I ended up giving birth to a little boy that I named Jason, after his father.

Jasmine: I didn't know you had kids.

Autumn: I did. Jason died when he was three years old in a drunk driving accident. One day while I was at work, his father had gotten drunk and was taking him to go and see his mistress. While on the way there, they ended up hitting a tractor trailer. My son was killed instantly, but that hoodlum survived.

Jasmine: I'm so sorry. I didn't know, Autumn.

Autumn: *Cries.* It's okay. The hardest thing I have ever had to do was forgive that man. I hated him for years. I often asked GOD why couldn't he have died, and my son lived. I was mad at GOD for so long until one day, I finally gave in to my mother, and I went to church with her. Every word that preacher preached touched my heart in the right way. I gave my life to CHRIST that day, and I had to learn to forgive the man who'd killed my son.

Jasmine: I feel awful. Here I am mad at Carlton for walking away from us, but I never thought about what it would be like to lose a child. How did you survive that?

13

Autumn: It took a lot of praying. There were days when I was suicidal, and there were days when I just sat up in a closed in room all day and stared at the wall. Forgiveness didn't come easy, but I prayed for it, and GOD finally started teaching me how to access it. I met Carlton at church. We were both members of Mount Zion Church, and he just kept watching me. At first, I did everything in my power to scare him off. I didn't want another man after what had happened to me. I thought they were all crooks, devils and liars, but he proved me wrong. I made it clear to Carlton that I was waiting on my husband, and I was not willing to date a man for more than three years, nor was I willing to sleep with a man who was not my husband. To my surprise, he hung in there, and after a year, he'd proposed. I didn't get with him to hurt you. I got with him because he was single, handsome, Christian, available and he pursued me. My children now are my pride and joy. Your children are my pride and joy. I feel blessed to know them. They are wonderful children. I just want you to know that if I have ever done anything to offend you, I am sorry. I really want us to get along. Life is too short for strife.

Jasmine: Autumn, you just gave me a new perspective on life. I am so sorry for what happened to your son, and I feel like such a moron for acting the way I did. You are right. I never gave you a chance, and I didn't realize until today that I was still harboring some things in my heart for Carlton. I will be praying to have those feelings removed, and I will be a better person to you as well. You're right. It is better for us to co-parent the children than it is for us to bicker. Will you

accept my apology?
Autumn: Of course. I wouldn't have it any other way.

The two women hugged, and Autumn continued to speak.

Autumn: Jasmine, you are a beautiful girl. Can I make two recommendations? And please don't be offended.
Jasmine: Thank you, Autumn. Sure. I won't be offended.
Autumn: My pastor gave a sermon once on seed time and harvest. What I learned during that sermon was that I was sowing seeds into the wrong things and withholding seeds from the right things. I'd sown seven years into that previous relationship, and I reaped pain from that relationship. He told us that we have to set our own prices and refuse to accept otherwise. When a man comes along in your life, set your price. Any man who doesn't have enough faith to afford you will go away, and that's the way it's supposed to be. Staying in GOD'S perfect will runs off everyone who does not serve the LORD. Set your standards. Determine how long you are willing to wait; tell the man how much time he's got and don't sleep with him. If GOD didn't send that man to you, he'll get up and run away from you within days or months. I had to learn that myself. I'd given my body to a man for seven years, and he never took me to an altar because I gave him husband privileges when he was nothing but a boyfriend. He had never even approached the altar for repentance or deliverance. I had to learn from that mistake. I believe you will be found by your GOD-appointed husband one day. When you and Carlton got together, he wasn't in

15

---

church like he is now, but he's a different man because the WORD changed him.

Jasmine: I totally agree, and I will. I've been celibate now for a year, and I'm really trying to do things the right way. Thank you so much. I feel like I've just met you for the first time, and I love you already.

Autumn: I love you too, love. The second thing is this: You're a talented girl. Don't keep burning off your oil in those multilevel marketing schemes. The Bible says your gift will make room for you and bring you before great men. You are gifted, Jasmine. Don't throw away your gifts trying to help another man earn from his skills.

Jasmine: I wouldn't even know where to start to tell you the truth.

Autumn: How about this? I'll help you by coaching you along the way. Would you be willing to receive coaching from me?

Jasmine: Why not? Of course. Thank you so much,

Autumn: You are a beautiful woman inside and out.

When Carlton came home, he was surprised to see the women sitting together civilly, in the living room. From that point on, Jasmine and Autumn got along just fine, and Autumn helped Jasmine to market her gifts. Jasmine eventually listed her services on Autumn's website, and she earned enough to make a living from her talents. The two women co-parented Carlton's kids, and when Jasmine finally got married three years later, Carlton became good friends with Jasmine's husband.

The End.

What was the issue here? It's simple. Jasmine was sowing seeds all over the place, but into the wrong things and the wrong people. Just like many women of GOD, Jasmine thought her seed had the power to change a man. All she had to do was cook for him, provide help when he needed it, and be there for him when he was down. She believed that this was enough to earn her place in his life as his wife. It didn't work because Carlton had enjoyed ten years of playing house with Jasmine. He'd lived as her husband, and he'd gotten the benefits of a husband; nevertheless, he'd never committed himself through GOD to be her husband. Jasmine had not set her price high enough, so Carlton and other men were able to remove her from her low place, use her, and then return her once they'd had their fill of her.

There are so many women out there right now who are mad at the men who abandoned them after using them. This is an error because it teaches our daughters that fornication is okay, and when the guy doesn't stick around, they should be mad at him and his new woman. It teaches our sons that women are disposable and should be disposed of every few years or months. Sure, it's easy to hand the responsibility to a man who has abandoned you, but it is better to take accountability for your own part in your situation. You successfully entered a relationship without GOD, and that relationship did what it was supposed to do: fail. If you give a man all of you when he has not committed to being your husband, you won't have anything left for him to consider marrying.

At the same time, you can never allow a man to become your everything. You shouldn't even let your children become your everything. Always remember that GOD is jealous over you, and anything or anyone you put before HIM becomes an idol and a snare to you. Idols always had to be destroyed in the Old Testament. What do you think happens to idols now? If that relationship is your idol, it will be destroyed. When you make an idol of your children, you put them in harm's way.

Finally, there is the business aspect of it all. Most Christian business owners or aspiring business owners do not invest much into their business or ideas; nevertheless, they throw money at vain things just as the world does. That's why many keep reaping the same benefits as the world. Multilevel marketing may have worked for some people, but for the large majority of people, it's a waste of time and money. In my opinion and from my experience, multilevel marketing is only good if you have a substantial investment to make into it. If you have bills that confront you faithfully each month and not enough money to pay them, multilevel marketing may not be right for you at that time. I've seen so many aspiring business owners throw money at these programs, and I've often wondered why they don't throw that money at their own businesses using their own gifts. The truth is, most people trust the lead of others rather than the lead of the LORD. If a person or a business projects success, people will flock to that person or business, but everyone's gift isn't for you or me. Too many people spend too much time throwing their seeds at other people's gifts, and they end up helping those people become successful while their own gifts rot in the ground. Just what are you good at, and why aren't you learning to perfect it? Why aren't you sowing seeds into your gifts?

Here are some truths you may not know:
1. Multilevel marketing takes about two to four years before you can earn work-at-home income. It takes about the same amount of time (sometimes less) to make a full-time career out of your own talents.
2. Whatever you are talented at, you will be passionate about. When you work in the field GOD has graced you to work in, it won't feel like work to you. Instead, you'll love doing it, and you'll be better than those who are skilled to do it but don't like doing the work. Passion always shows in the form of excellence.
3. When you don't sow into your talents, you are burying your talents.
4. When a talent is buried, the LORD will oftentimes take it from the person who buried it and hand it to someone who is faithful.
5. A talented person working in their own field can earn ten times more than a person with a job and a degree.
6. The average person quits working in their fields after a year because they don't see success, but on

average, it takes two to four years to earn full-time income from your talents. But think about it this way...you would never be unemployed again.

7. Foreigners come into the United States of America and call us stupid and spoiled because we have one of the greatest oceans of wealth available in the earth, yet most Americas settle into puddles and swamps.

8. Wealth chases the righteous, but the unrighteous foolishly chase wealth and catch chaos, lack and a bad attitude.

9. Every dollar you have will either be sown or spent. When you spend money, you get your reward immediately, and nothing else can be expected to come from what was spent. When you sow money, you get your reward eventually, and you can expect to reap increase from what was sown in faith over the course of your life. One seed successfully sown drops more seeds.

10. Most people who refuse to sow into their talents are afraid of failure. Most people who do sow into their talents are confident of success. What's the difference? One person has fear, and the other has faith. Faith is believing GOD for what HE said even though you can't see it; fear is believing what Satan said because of what you do see.

If you have a need, you likely have a seed. Sow it. As time passes, you will find how GOD will stretch you, give you more understanding and enlarge your territory as you enlarge your faith. What you see in your bank account right now is the reflection of the faith you have. If you want to see more, you have to hear more WORD of GOD. *"So then faith cometh by hearing, and hearing by the word of God"* *(Romans 10:17).*

Impersonating a Servant of the Lord

"You can't live with sin and expect GOD to take care of you."

Let's face it: Sin can be fun. Most of us don't like to admit this because we feel it'll make the LORD angry with us, and that admission will show us in a bad light. But the truth is: We were born in the flesh, and the flesh's nature is sinful; therefore, sin can be fun to us. That's why it's so hard to stop sinning, and that's why we have to be born again.

The issue is that the way GOD designed us requires seed time and harvest, sowing and reaping. Seasons of sowing are rarely seasons of joy. Sowing often requires that we press forward towards the mark, even when we are in opposition. It's similar to farming. A farmer can't neglect his field just because it's too hot outside. Even though the heat opposes him, he has to continue farming so that he can reap a harvest in the season of reaping. We work the same way. Our lives are fields, and we can't neglect living them for the LORD just because the fires of trials have gotten too hot. Instead, we have to press forward in the LORD, doing HIS will so that we can reap in due season.

But here's the thing: Whether you serve the LORD, or you serve yourself, you are going to reap in due season. Nevertheless, what you reap will be a reflection of what you've sown.

"She's asleep," said a voice coming from the other end of the telephone. The voice was coming from Mrs. Witherspoon, and she was less than friendly with her tone. The caller was named Penny, and she was beginning to get frustrated with Mrs. Witherspoon. Penny had been calling the Witherspoon residence for three days now, and every time she called, Mrs. Witherspoon answered the phone and said that Sonya (Penny's half sister) was asleep. Penny knew that she was lying, but there was nothing she could do about it.

It all started a few months ago. Penny and Sonya, both twenty-seven years old, had recently come back in contact with one another after eleven years. Their father had been a wild man, juggling multiple relationships at one time. Even though he'd never been married, he did have his fair share of children: fifteen, to be exact. He'd been living with Sonya's mother when she became pregnant with Sonya. Not long after her pregnancy, she discovered that another woman named Penelope was also pregnant by him, and both children were due to be born in mid-June. Because of this, Sonya's mother had put Rico out of her house; nevertheless, she continued to see him for another three years until he was killed in a drunk driving accident. After the accident, nine of the mothers put their differences aside and decided to make sure their children knew one another. Sonya and Penny had grown up especially close because they were the same age. As a matter of fact, their birthdays were only three days apart.

But when the girls were both seventeen years old, they became angry with one another over a boy who went to their school. His name was Diego Martinez, and he was quite a looker. They were all seniors in high school, and Diego had taken a liking to both women, even though he hadn't established a relationship with either of the girls. Instead, he would catch them alone in the hallways or during the classes that he took with them, and he would flirt with each girl. When the time for prom came, Sonya made it very clear to Penny that she wanted Diego to take her to the prom, but Penny was also hoping that Diego would ask her. After all, Diego was their local stud, and every girl wanted him. Sonya became angry with Penny because she felt that she'd been the first to make her desires known; therefore, Penny should have gone ahead to the prom with Adrian Valles. Adrian was also a looker, but he was no Diego. Adrian was really smitten with Penny, but Penny wasn't too interested in him because of his reputation with the women. All the same, she wanted to remain free for Diego.

One week before prom, Diego asked Penny to the prom, and she happily accepted. When the news got back to Sonya, she was enraged. During lunch period, she'd seen Penny sitting in the cafeteria bragging about being asked to the prom by Diego. Sonya went and confronted her sister, and when Penny did not back down, Sonya attacked her. The fight was vicious, and Penny ended up getting the best of Sonya. She'd given Sonya a black eye, and she'd even bit her on her jaw, leaving a huge imprint of her teeth. Both girls were disciplined, and Penny ended up going to the prom with Diego without a scratch on her. Sonya wasn't so lucky, however. Her black eye and bruised jaw made her the target for ridicule, and she ended up going to the prom with an outcast named Jorge.

After the fight, Sonya's mother had called Penny's mother and verbally attacked her and her daughter. She also took Sonya out of that school and put her in a private school because of the humiliation Sonya was suffering. Because of this, the two sisters ended their friendship and didn't speak to one another for eleven years.

Eleven years later, they'd met again at church one Sunday. Penny had just moved back to town with her two-year-old son, Rodriguez. She was going through a divorce and moved back home to be closer to her family. One Sunday, she decided to visit a new church in the city. She loved the atmosphere, the people and everything about the church, so two Sundays later, she joined the church. After joining the church, she was surprised to see Sonya sitting with the ministry team. She still looked the same, but of course, she'd filled out a little more.

That day, Sonya approached Penny, and the two of them shared a loving embrace. Penny introduced her son to Sonya, and she was surprised to see that Sonya also had a son, and he was ten years old. His name was Bryson, and there was no doubt as to who his father was: Diego! He was the spitting image of Diego. Penny learned from Sonya that she had been so upset with Penny for going to the prom with Diego that she'd gone out with him the night after the prom, and that was when Bryson was conceived. After hearing about Sonya's pregnancy, as well as hearing rumors of another girl possibly being pregnant by him, Diego had fled to Mexico, where he finished school at his grandparents' house.

After laughing and talking about how naïve they once were, the two women decided to stay in contact with one another. Penny even moved into a house a few blocks away from Sonya's apartment because she wanted to be closer to her sister. She was so excited that Sonya shared her faith. Now, the two of them could really be sisters, and since Sonya was on the ministry team, Penny thought she could learn a thing or two from Sonya.

One day, Sonya invited Penny out to eat. Sonya's son was at school, and Penny's son was at his grandmother's house. Sonya wasn't scheduled to go into work until three o'clock that evening. Penny, on the other hand, was not working because she was still in the process of looking for a job. They decided to meet up at Rancho's Hotwings for lunch.

Both women arrived at the restaurant at the same time. They embraced one another and then entered the restaurant. Once seated, Sonya told Penny that she had a problem that she needed help with. She believed Penny was the only person she could trust with her secret.

Sonya: I have a little secret that's been bothering me, and it's about to come screaming out in the open. You're the only person I feel I can talk to about it. I couldn't tell my mom because you know how she is.

Penny: What's wrong, Sonya?

Sonya: Well, I'm pregnant.

Penny: What?!

Sonya: Yeah. Eight weeks along so far.

Penny: By who?

Sonya: Well, that's the complicated part. Please don't judge me; okay?

Penny: Who is it Sonya?

Sonya: *Sighs.* Luis.

Penny: Do I know him? Who is Luis?

Sonya: Luis Romero.

Penny: Wait. There's only one Luis Romero that I know and he's married. Sonya! The youth pastor?!

Sonya: Yes! Please keep your voice down. People are starting to look over here.

Penny: Sonya, stop joking. You're a woman of GOD. He's a man of GOD, and not just a man of GOD, but a married man of GOD. How could you do that?!

Sonya: Calm down. I called him one evening when I was

going through a rough patch in my life. He said he was at the grocery store picking up a few things for his wife. I asked him if he would stop by and pray for me, and he did. And that's how it all got started.

Penny: But why would you ask him to stop by your house, Sonya?! You knew he was married!

Sonya: Penny, keep your voice down! I guess I was just lonely and wanted some company, but I didn't plan to sleep with the guy.

Penny: I am so disappointed in you. I felt bad hearing you say you were pregnant because I knew you weren't married, but as if it couldn't get any worse, you're pregnant by a married Pastor and you're an Evangelist?

Sonya: Penny, like I said...don't judge me. We're not all perfect. I called you here because I don't know what to do next. What should I do?

Penny: I haven't the slightest clue. Ouch, Sonya. Has he told his wife? Does Pastor Ramirez know? Wait. Does he even know?

Sonya: Yes, Luis knows. I told him yesterday, but Pastor Ramirez doesn't know. I can guarantee you that he hasn't told his wife.

Penny: Well, what did Luis say?

Sonya: He wants me to get an abortion. Can you believe that? He's supposed to be a man of GOD and he's asking me to get an abortion.

Penny: I think the act that took place that caused you to even consider an abortion should have been the time when you questioned his credentials.

Sonya: Penny, this is serious. I can't get an abortion. It goes against my beliefs.

Penny: I'm against abortions as well, but how is it that you had no reservation in calling a married man over to your house and sleeping with him, but now, you suddenly have morals?

Sonya: Oh my goodness! I forgot how judgmental you could be. You know what? This was a bad idea. Forget I even called you.

Penny: Sonya, wait. I'm sorry. I'm just disappointed; that's all. I would hate to see Grace Extended fall to a scandal like this. I mean, it's a great church, and Pastor Ramirez is a great Pastor. Situations like these can ruin a church.

Sonya: Yes, I know. What should I do? I am not going to abort this baby, and Luis still refuses to leave his wife.

Penny: Wait a minute. So, you're still seeing him? And you're trying to get him to leave his wife? Sonya, what's gotten into you?!

Sonya: You wouldn't understand, Sonya. His wife is horrible to him. I dreamed that he and I were walking down the aisle to get married. Do you think it could have been a prophecy?

Penny: No! GOD will never take another woman's husband and hand him to you or any other woman, for that matter. I think the two of you need to talk to Pastor Ramirez before this thing comes out in the open, and Luis definitely needs to tell his wife.

Sonya: Yeah, when I told him that he needed to tell his wife, he became really upset. I told him that if he didn't tell her, I would.

Penny: What did he say?

Sonya: He was upset, but he wants to meet up with me tonight after I get off work to talk about it. We'll discuss our next move tonight. Please keep me in your prayers.

After they left the restaurant, Penny headed back home. She wanted to file some more job applications online. Sonya sent her a text message thanking her for listening and being there for her.

The next day when Penny woke up, she felt awful. She got out of bed and made breakfast for Rodriguez. She couldn't get over how bad she felt, and her mind fell on Sonya. Concerned, Penny went to call Sonya to make sure everything was okay, but before she could call, she saw that she had eight missed calls. Six of the calls had come from Sonya's mother's house and two of the calls had come from a blocked number. Burdened with fear, Penny called Sonya's mother back.

Mrs. Witherspoon: Hello? Penny?! Penny, have you seen Sonya?

Penny: No. I saw her earlier yesterday. Why?

Mrs. Witherspoon: She didn't come home last night, and I'm worried sick about her.

Penny: Yeah, she was supposed to meet with someone....

Mrs. Witherspoon: Who? Please tell me.

Penny: Uh....it's no one important. Let me make a few phone calls and I'll call you back.

Mrs. Witherspoon: Please call me back as soon as you can. Bryson and I are worried sick about her. She's not even answering her cell phone.
Penny: Okay, I'll call you back.

After hanging up the phone, Penny began to dial Sonya's number, but she kept going directly to her voice mail. This wasn't like Sonya, and Penny hoped she'd just lost track of time. Somehow, she knew this wasn't true, however. She knew that something more sinister had happened. Penny decided to try and find Luis's number to see if he knew where Sonya was. She looked through the phone book and there were seven people named Luis Romero listed. After calling three of the numbers, she finally reached the residence of the Youth Pastor.

Luis: Hello.
Penny: Hi, I'm looking for Pastor Luis Romero.
Luis: Speaking.
Penny: Hey, Luis. My name is Penny. You met me a few times at church. Anyhow, I'm a friend of Sonya's.
Luis: Okay.
Penny: She didn't come home last night. I was wondering if you knew where she was.
Luis: No. Why would I know where she is?
Penny: Well, she told me yesterday that she was going to meet with you later.
Luis: I don't know what you're talking about. Hey, it was nice talking to you, but I have to go.

At that, Luis abruptly disconnected the line. From that moment, Penny knew something was really wrong. She knew that something had happened to Sonya, and she needed to relay the details to the authorities. She called Sonya's mother back and told her about the conversation she'd had with Sonya the previous day. She also told her about Luis pretending he didn't know what she was talking about. They agreed that Sonya's mother would call the police, and Penny would come by the house to tell the police what she knew.

Just as she was about to leave, her phone rang again. The call was coming from a blocked caller. When Penny answered the phone, the caller listened for a minute and then hung up. A few minutes later, the call came through again just as Penny was entering her car. It was Luis calling from a blocked number, and Penny could tell that he was now outside because she could hear traffic.

Penny: Hello?

Luis: Yes, who is this?

Penny: This is Penny. How can I help you?

Luis: This is Luis. You called my house about thirty minutes ago. Yes, I thought you said Tonya, but when I hung up, I realized you said Sonya. Yes, I know Sonya.

Penny: Do you know where she is? She didn't come home last night.

Luis: No. Here's the thing. Sonya has been harassing me. She wanted to be in a relationship with me, but I said to her,

"Hey, I'm a married man! I have children and I love my wife!" But she didn't want to hear that.

Penny: Okay.

Luis: But last night, I saw her at Wal-Mart. She was there shopping, and she started following me when I left. She kept flashing her lights and chasing me, and I was scared for my life, so I drove really fast.

Penny: And then what happened?

Luis: I don't know. I lost her. I was driving so fast that she couldn't keep up.

Penny: Okay. Well, we've already called the police because she didn't come home, and we are worried about her.

Luis: Why get the police involved? I'm sure she's somewhere with her boyfriend. Hey, did she tell you? She has a boyfriend, and she just found out that they are going to have a baby.

Penny: Luis, she doesn't have a boyfriend. Sonya is my sister.

Luis: You said earlier that she was your friend.

Penny: She is my friend and my sister. Anyhow, we have to get the police involved. What if she had a car accident? Time is of the essence in these types of situations.

Luis: Okay. Do me a favor. Don't tell the police you talked to me or that Sonya knows me. I'm a married man and a Pastor. I don't need this type of attention.

Penny: I hear you.

When Penny arrived at Mrs. Witherspoon's house, the police were already there. She told the police about the conversation she'd had with Sonya the previous day and about her suspicious conversations with Luis. The police took the report and went to question Luis.

Later that day, Sonya's overturned vehicle was found off a steep embankment. Sonya was not in the vehicle, however. After vigorously questioning Luis, the police were able to extract a confession out of him. He then led the police to an abandoned house where they found Sonya lying face down on the floor. She had been stabbed from behind multiple times. To their amazement; however, she was still breathing. She was rushed to the hospital, and she survived the attack; howbeit, she was paralyzed from the waist down because of the attack.

When Sonya was in the hospital, her mother told the hospital staff not to allow Penny or anyone from Grace Extended Church to visit Sonya. When Sonya was released from the hospital, she refused to allow Penny or anyone from Grace Extended Church to speak to or visit Sonya. Sonya's mother was Catholic and was never happy about her daughter's conversion to a non-denominational church. She blamed the church and its beliefs for the downward decline of her daughter.

Penny called the house one more time.

Penny: May I speak with Sonya please, Mrs. Witherspoon?
Mrs. Witherspoon: She's asleep.

Penny: Wait! Don't hang up on me again. Mrs. Witherspoon, why won't you let me talk with my sister?

Mrs. Witherspoon was silent for a minute, and then she took a deep breath and spoke.

Mrs. Witherspoon: You've always been bad luck to my daughter. In high school, you took her boyfriend, and you humiliated her in front of the entire school. She was okay until you came back in her life. I don't want you calling her. She almost lost her life because of you. Because of you, she may never walk again.

Penny: Mrs. Witherspoon, I apologize for what happened in high school. I did not take her man. We were both just young and dumb, and in love with the same boy. As far as me being bad luck, I don't understand how you can draw that conclusion. Sonya was sleeping with a married man, and he tried to kill her because she threatened to tell his wife about their relationship. She pretended to be pregnant, Mrs. Witherspoon. Now, that's not to excuse what he did, but Sonya had some responsibility in what happened to her as well. She started this affair before I came back into her life. What it sounds like to me is that you were okay with the affair; you just don't like how it ended. Sonya made her bed. The person who committed the crime is in prison, and he may never see the light of day again. Rather than blaming people for what happened to Sonya; why don't you just thank the LORD that she is alive?

Mrs. Witherspoon: You are a wicked woman, Penny! Just like your mother! You are a very wicked woman, and I would appreciate if you never call my house or my daughter again.

Penny: I will grant you your request, but I ask one favor of you.

Mrs. Witherspoon: And what is that?

Penny: Tell Sonya that GOD has not forgotten about her, and HE can heal her body. Also, tell her that I love her.

Mrs. Witherspoon: GOD? GOD? Where was your GOD when my daughter was fighting for her life?

Penny: HE was sitting on HIS Throne in righteousness, but Sonya went across the street to a place called Sin, and sin's wages found her there.

The End.

Sonya was an Evangelist. She went to church often, helped on the ministry team, and she wore the clothes that made her appear to be Godly, but Sonya did not have a heart of repentance. Instead, she went into a church and wore the title of an Evangelist; yet, she bore the fruit of a sinner. Instead of building the church up, Sonya was there to tear it down.

There are so many women (and men, of course) that go to churches with sin on their minds. They enter churches with the intentions of joining the ministry team, but not because they want to help the church; they do it because they want to help themselves to whatever power, glory or riches they can receive from the church. They don't have a heart of holiness; therefore, they treat the church the same way one would treat a club. They seek after men of GOD who are out of order or who can be seduced out of the will of GOD. From there, they begin to do the works of their father, the devil. They begin to devour these men by leading them into scandalous situations and then threatening to expose them. Make no mistake about it: Women like that are devil-sent and hell-assigned. If the Philistines used Delilah to bring down Samson, why wouldn't we think that the devil would send a Delilah spirit into a church to bring down the men of GOD? One thing about a Delilah spirit is it won't be attracted to a phony man of GOD. It is attracted to the authentic anointing. But some would question this statement by saying, "If the man was so anointed, and he loved the LORD, why would he commit adultery against his wife?" It's simple. Temptation seduces the flesh, and if the person being tempted does not run like Joseph did from Potipher's wife, they will find themselves in compromising positions. Samson was a man of GOD, but Samson's weakness was women. David was a man of GOD, favored by GOD, but David's weakness was women, and he ended up stumbling with Bathsheba. David even arranged to have Bathsheba's husband killed. Solomon was a man of GOD who loved the LORD, but when he got older, he married foreign women and ended up worshipping their gods. The list goes on and on.

The same goes for men as well, but this is a book for the women of GOD. Nevertheless, there are some men on demonic assignment who enter and ascend the ranks in the church for the riches, honor, glory and women. They too are on demonic assignment.

Sonya's heart was not for the LORD, and that could be seen in her lack of repentance for her actions. She wanted what she wanted, and it didn't matter to her that she'd be destroying a marriage and adding a blemish to the church she was a member of. Sonya cared for Sonya, but what about Luis? Luis obviously cared for his wife, but he'd made a foolish decision when he agreed to go to Sonya's house to pray for her. Any woman who asks a man to come to her house and pray with her has a seducing spirit. It doesn't take a rocket scientist to tell you what she wants. A woman who fears and loves the LORD would have called Luis's wife or asked Luis for his wife's phone number. Even if she did ask him to pray for her, she wouldn't ask him to come to her house or any private place and pray for her.

Sonya's mother was obviously an enabler. She never made her daughter take accountability for her own actions. Instead, she blamed others for her daughter's choices. Mothers like this always raise daughters designed for failure. In the end, she blamed GOD for not protecting her daughter instead of blaming her daughter for not staying in GOD'S protection, otherwise known as HIS will.

If we want to be protected by the LORD, we have to stay in HIS will. There are too many saints who don't take the LORD seriously until sin stops laughing with them and starts

39

laughing at them. It's sad when people don't want GOD until they need HIM. At the same time, every story like this doesn't always have a good ending, despite what mainstream media portrays. The wages of sin is death. Sonya was blessed to keep her life, even though it had been changed forever. She was given another chance to live and make peace with the LORD. Luis was given another chance to make it right, even though he'll be incarcerated for most, if not all, of his life.

We have to make choices that reflect the GOD we serve. All the same, we have to always be careful about our thoughts and desires. When you find that your thoughts and desires are ungodly, don't act on them, pray against them. Don't ponder the thoughts. If you do, they'll find their way into your heart, and you'll eventually act on them. Let's make sure that we aren't just representatives of the living GOD, but that we are good representatives of the living GOD.

Cry Me a River

"Older doesn't always mean wiser."

GOD told us to cast down imaginations and every high thing that exalts itself against the knowledge of GOD. GOD told us to guard our hearts, for it is a well-spring of life. But what happens when we are wide receivers, open to bad advice and misled leaders? *"Let them alone: they be blind leaders of the blind. And if the blind lead the blind, both shall fall into the ditch" (Matthew 15:4).*

The average person will open themselves up to more than a dozen bad counselors in a three-year span. Because of this, we are often derailed from our destinies and placed on paths that lead to destruction. The enemy knows your weak spot. He knows where lust is and where the WORD of GOD is not guarding you. It is those areas that he will attack you the most until you learn to guard them with the WORD of GOD.

River was a girl who saw life through closed eyes. In other words, River was naïve. She kept making the same choices over and over again, hoping for a different outcome.

River was twenty-eight years old, and fairly attractive. She had golden skin set off by the richness of her full pink lips. She was African-American, 5'2 inches tall and very toned. Wherever she went, men paid attention to her beautiful face, chestnut brown eyes and noticeable curves. With two children and a bachelor's degree, River wasn't just looking for any man anymore. After her last break-up two months ago, River set her heart on professional men. She was tired of dating the nobodies who didn't know how to appreciate the somebody that she was. She knew that she was beautiful, and she believed with all of her heart that she would make some man a great wife one day. The problem was, she'd kissed too many frogs trying to find her husband, but in return, all she got was two children and a few car notes paid.

Once a party-girl, River had given up on the club scene. It seemed that the only men on the scene were either thugs or married men looking to take off their rings for a few hours. River was now frequenting places where she thought the men of her liking would be. One of those places was church.

River had a neighbor by the name of Adenine, but everyone called her Denine. Denine was 45 years old, but she didn't look a day over 29. She too was attractive and shapely. In her 45 years, she'd managed to keep the figure and mindset of a young woman. Denine lived alone and worked for a lawyer's office as a secretary. She had four children, three of which were almost adults. Her youngest child was a five-year-old little boy named Idris. Denine also drove a new model Mercedes-Benz and had two more luxury vehicles parked in her driveway.

Denine seemed to have life figured out. She didn't take any slack from a man. Her last boyfriend had been a lawyer who she'd worked for a few years. They'd lived together for two years before Denine kicked him out. Denine had promptly (and loudly) thrown him out of the house after finding text messages on his phone from one of her best friends. It turned out that he had been sleeping with a woman Denine had been close friends with for seven years.

Denine didn't seem too affected by the break-up, and River was amazed at her strength. Ordinarily a woman would be heartbroken and harassing her ex, but Denine followed her same routine even after the break-up. She went to work for her ex until he fired her a month later. Nevertheless, it didn't take her long to land a job in another lawyer's office.

Denine would come outside everyday around six to seven in the evening to smoke a cigarette, and this is when River would make her way over to sit down and speak with her. She had so much knowledge that River wanted. River wanted that strength, and she wanted the knowledge of how to land professional men. After all, she'd seen Ms. Denine with a lawyer, a doctor and a well-known politician. River wanted that confidence that Ms. Denine radiated, and she wanted to be financially independent....just like Denine.

Denine knew that River looked up to her. A lot of the young

women in the neighborhood looked up to her and would come by her house whenever their relationships were in trouble. Many of the neighborhood girls had broken it off with their boyfriends after being schooled by Ms. Denine. As a matter of fact, one of the girls whose name was Rai had taken Ms. Denine's advice and landed herself a heavy-hitter. She ended up marrying a prominent lawyer and was now the mother of his two sons. She would come by Ms. Denine's house once a week to sit outside and talk with her. Rai wasn't like Ms. Denine, however. Any time another girl would come by, Rai would excuse herself and leave. It appeared that she didn't trust anyone but Ms. Denine.

River went to see Denine because she wanted to know where the "big boys" hung out. River had an apartment, where she had a roommate named Shauna. She would often leave her kids playing with Shauna's kids whenever she went over to see Denine. This particular day seemed extra nice. The sun had begun to set, and the breeze was perfect. Denine had just finished her cigarette and was sitting on her bench reading a Harlequin romance novel. When River came by, she smiled and put the book away. She had wanted to talk with River about a guy she thought would be perfect for her. He was a man named Arthur who owned a database administration company in a city nearby. He was recently widowed after his wife had been killed in a car accident. He was also a single father, raising the daughter he had with his wife. Arthur's daughter was three-years-old and a gorgeous doll to look at. Her name was

Arianne, and she was a daddy's girl by definition.

Denine began her conversation asking River about the last guy River had dated. He worked at the hospital as a nurse and had suddenly stopped coming to River's apartment two months ago. River had already told Ms. Denine the reason for the break-up. Her last boyfriend (Quinton) had broken it off with her, citing that he was beginning to feel overwhelmed with the relationship and River's two children. He wasn't ready for such a responsibility, and he was uncomfortable with the fact that River had her children calling him daddy within a few months of him knowing her. It had all been too much for him, so he'd broken it off and changed his phone number to avoid any drama.

During the conversation, Denine mentioned Arthur to River. It was clear that Denine truly believed that Arthur and River would mesh well together. River had two children, and she appeared to be loving and nurturing with them. Arthur had just lost his wife and needed help raising his rambunctious little girl. Initially, River was uncomfortable with the conversation because she didn't like to be paired up with anyone. What if she didn't like him? What if he didn't like her? Her mind flooded with all of the possibilities as Denine continued to list all of Arthur's strong points. "Are you listening to me?" Denine's voice seemed suddenly low. She'd noticed that River had become distracted and began to look away as she talked over and over about Arthur. "Yeah. I'm listening. My mind just went elsewhere," River responded. "I normally don't like blind dates, but because I know and trust you, Ms. Denine; I'll give him a shot." Denine wasn't surprised. She smiled, but she knew that River wouldn't turn her down. After all, none of the neighborhood girls would turn her down. She was Ms. Denine! Before Denine could open her mouth to say anything, a silver BMW sports vehicle pulled up in front of her house. The man behind the wheel had a medium-brown complexion, somewhat square-shaped face and was obviously pretty short. He was wearing sunglasses and had a head full of curly hair. He looked rather young, but he was somewhat handsome. His eyes were rather big and full of eyelashes. He had eyes like a woman, but he was all man; all 5'5 inches of him.

Ms. Denine smiled as he exited the vehicle. "That's Arthur," she said to River. "I told him to come by around this time because I knew you'd probably be over." As Arthur came closer, the breeze seemed to carry his cologne ahead of him. It was a sweet-smelling cologne, almost woman-like. He opened his mouth to speak, and River noticed that he had two foreign teeth that had grown on his gums. River wasn't attracted to him, but he did look like he would make a great fixer-upper. River was more into tall muscular guys with heavy voices. Arthur was the absolute opposite. He was short, and he looked somewhat fit except for that belly of his that had begun to stick out. He had obviously been married before. His voice sounded pretty girly, just with a hint of bass. His eyes looked sad, as if he'd been crying on the way there; nevertheless, he greeted Ms. Denine with a hug, and he handed her a bag that she promptly took into the house.

While she was gone, Arthur took notice of the beautiful River. Her beautiful pink links captured his attention right away. When she greeted him, he noticed her perfect teeth and beautiful smile. Her dark brown eyes met his as he opened his mouth to greet her back. "Wow," said Arthur. "I'm sorry. My name is Arthur. What's your name?" Before River could answer, a voice came from within Ms. Denine's house. "Her name is Christy," yelled Denine. "She is another one of my neighbors." River was surprised. Why was Ms. Denine lying about who she was? She hadn't thought about it too long before Arthur broke her thought pattern. "Well, Christy, it's nice to meet you. You are absolutely beautiful."

Denine exited her house and began to speak with the now mesmerized Arthur. As they were speaking, River was becoming more and more bothered by Arthur's choice of cologne. The wind seemed to taunt her as it blew Arthur's cologne up her nose again and again. She also noticed that Arthur's teeth were yellowing, but his big puppy dog eyes were attractive to her. And the fact that he was successful, plus he'd committed to one woman before was also attractive to River. Arthur wouldn't stop glancing over at the now quiet River. Her arms were crossed as she looked away, often turning around to sneeze. It was obvious that she was the feisty type, and Arthur liked that.

While they were still speaking, River's children came running out of the house towards her. Her roommate had fallen asleep, and the children had been fighting once again. Little Ria was crying and bending her arm forward to show her mother the almost invisible cut that was on her elbow. She said her brother Garrett had pushed her down onto his train set. Fearing that River's identity would be uncovered, Denine rushed Arthur off to his car as River began to scold her children. Arthur pulled away in his car, but not before blowing his horn and waving his hand at River. He was suddenly gone, but his cologne didn't seem to want to follow him home.

"He's cute," said River to Denine. "Of course, he's not my type, but he seems like a good guy. I just wish he hadn't bathed in that cologne this morning." River turned around again to sneeze as Ms. Denine sat back down on the bench and removed another cigarette from the pack.

Denine: Sit down, baby; let me tell you something. River, you know one of the hardest lessons I had to learn was that sometimes what we want don't always come wrapped up the way we want it. At the same time, sometimes the ones we do want aren't the kind of guys we need. You understand? Men like Arthur often stick around. They are good men; they just don't get a lot of chances with good women because good women like bad men. But if you're tired of going from relationship to relationship, Arthur's your boy. If you want to keep ending up with men like Quinton, then I can't help you.

But Arthur's a good man, and he's going to make some woman a good husband one day.

River: Okay, I'll give him a try. I trust you. I just think I can beat him up, and I don't usually go for guys like him. But like you said, if I want something better, sometimes I have to do something different. Thanks, Ms. Denine.

She leaned forward to hug Denine, but then suddenly thought about the fact that Denine didn't tell Arthur her real name.

River: Ms. Denine, I have something to ask you. Why did you tell him my name was Christy?

Denine: *Laughs.* Because I wanted to make sure that you liked him, and that you'd be willing to give him a shot before I told him that you were the girl I'd told him about. He's already been through a lot, and I didn't want to hurt his feelings.

River: That's cool. You know you're my other mother, so I trust you....Mom.

Of course, after Arthur learned that Christy was really River, he was super excited about the opportunity to court her. He would call her daily and take her out to some pretty high-end restaurants every weekend. River was excited because she was convinced that she had finally figured it all out. She could either have the man she desired who would likely abandon her in a few months, or she could have a guy like Arthur; a man she was not attracted to, but he would be almost everything she has ever wanted in a man.

Months went by, and River tolerated Arthur for the sake of having that professional man she so wanted. Denine was happy too. She was the neighborhood matchmaker who had put together another relationship that seemed promising. More women flocked to Denine's house to try on her pearls of wisdom so they too could land a man like Arthur.

There were times when River thought about ending the relationship with Arthur; especially after they'd become physically intimate with one another. River was disgusted with Arthur, but she stuck it out because she did not want to disappoint Ms. Denine, and she loved the fact that some of the neighborhood girls were now coming to her for advice.

A year into their relationship, Arthur decided to propose marriage to River. He was smitten by the bright-eyed feisty woman who never had much to say when he was around. The mystery of River made his heart pound and made him want to search her heart out even more. He wanted to marry her; he wanted to make her happy. She had obviously been hurt a few times and had developed a hardness about her that he wanted to break. He got together with Denine to plan a lavish proposal that would be sure to break River's hard stance. Arthur wanted to propose to River in a luxurious setting; maybe a restaurant or any fancy place where there weren't a lot of people. He knew that River was a private girl; nevertheless, Ms. Denine wanted him to propose to her at a party she wanted to throw that upcoming weekend. She knew that this would look great on her, since all of the neighborhood girls, and some of the women in her family, would be there. Arthur reluctantly agreed, but he worried that River would not like the setting and would probably give him what he referred to as her "frozen look." This is the look River gave him whenever he did or said something she did not like.

Saturday came, and River was not feeling well. She had her monthly visitor, and she was plagued by cramps and mood swings. She'd tried to tell Denine that she could not make the party, but Denine insisted, bringing River some pain medication she had that she claimed would knock those cramps out in a matter of minutes. The medication worked, and River came to the party.

At the party, many of the women hurdled around Ms. Denine as she told her "men stories", but River stayed off to herself. She wasn't in a good mood, and she didn't really feel like being bothered by Arthur or anyone, for that matter. Worried that River's attitude may sway Arthur, Denine decided to go for a short walk with River so she could find out what the issue was. She knew that River was having her menstruation, but she just did not want River to ruin this moment for her. She excused herself from the women, citing that she would return in thirty minutes. After whispering to the alienated Arthur who seemed a little nervous and fearful, Denine made her way over to River. "Let's take a walk," she said to River as she lowered her drink and placed it on the table. Sighing, River got up to follow her protégé.

As they walked, Arthur watched them get further and further away. He regretted not proposing at a restaurant like he'd initially planned. What if she rejected him in front of all of these people? What if she didn't feel the same way about him that he did about her? As she disappeared, in the distance, Arthur decided to jump into his vehicle and take a short ride to clear his head. He made a conscious decision to turn his vehicle, around so he wouldn't pass by the women and alarm them.

While walking, Denine wasted no time rebuking River.

Denine: What's wrong with you today? You have been moping the whole time. I planned this party because I wanted you to come by and have a great time, and for the other women to see how good your life has been going. But it seems that you want to project a different image. Arthur is too scared to even say a word to you because you obviously woke up on the wrong side of the bed. What's wrong, River? Did someone step on your toes?
River: *Sighs.* No, Ms. Denine. I'm just having one of those girl days. I didn't know you were throwing the party just for me, and I didn't mean to make Arthur scared. I just feel like I want to go home and curl up next to a television set. I want to sleep, Ms. Denine, and I want to stuff myself with junk food and cry my eyes out. That's what I do when I'm menstruating.
Denine: *Laughs and shrugs.* That's another thing. I keep

telling you young girls to stop calling me Ms. Denine. Just call me Denine. I don't want to end up giving away my age just in case I decide to try me out a young man next time. But jokes aside, Arthur loves you. You have been telling me over and over again about all the toads you've kissed trying to find a prince. Now, you have a man...a real man who wants to be with you. A man who adores your children as much as he adores you. If you blow this, I don't want you to cross my lawn talking about your love life. The power to change your life is in your hands. Don't disappoint me, River. I could have introduced Arthur to any of those girls at the party, but I chose you because you seemed more mature. Not everyone can handle a man like Arthur. It takes a special woman to see the value in a man like him. If I was younger, I would have grabbed him for myself, but I like men my own age. Now, I'm passing this baton to you. What are you going to do with it?

Denine reached out her hand as if she was handing River something. River smiled and reached into Denine's hands, clutched the invisible baton and then jogged up the street.

Denine: That's my girl! I knew I'd made the right choice! Now, let's get back to this party before Bryan finishes cooking those barbecue wings. Some of those girls there are vultures.

When they arrived back at the party, they noticed that Arthur's car was gone. But before they could panic, Arthur pulled back up in his vehicle and sat there for a few minutes. He looked towards River to see if she appeared to be in a better mood, and she lovingly waved at him. As he exited the vehicle, some of the women there noticed that he was carrying a bouquet of roses. A few of the women began to scream and clap as they watched Arthur heading towards the smiling River. River thought he was just bringing her flowers to show off, and she liked it. But she was amazed when Arthur dropped down to one knee and began speaking. At first, she couldn't hear anything he was saying because her heart started racing so fast, and the noise of the music was too much. Denine yelled to Bryson to cut off the music just as Arthur began to finish up his speech. Rai was there as well, but unlike the other women, she didn't appear to be happy for River. She seemed concerned; nevertheless, she stood by and watched as Arthur proposed to River. Once he'd finished uttering those words that River had waited her whole life to hear, River looked up at Ms. Denine, who was smiling and nodding her head. River looked down at Arthur and smiled. "Yes. Yes, I will marry you!" Arthur was happy, and so was Denine. Arthur stood to his feet and attempted to pick River up, but he barely lifted her from the ground because River was solid. She exercised a lot and was solid muscle.

A few days later, River received a phone call that was out of the ordinary. It was Rai. Rai had never said anything to River before. Why was she calling now? She'd gotten River's number from Arthur the night he proposed. She'd told him that she wanted to personally congratulate River by taking her out to eat. While on the phone, Rai asked River if the two of them could meet up at a restaurant in the central part of town. At first, River was her feisty self. "Why?" she asked sharply. "Rai, you don't even know me, and you've never even greeted me. Why do you suddenly want to dine out with me? What's going on?" Rai apologized for her behavior but ensured River that the meeting was innocent, and that she simply wanted to discuss some things with River. She asked River not to tell Denine about the lunch date. River agreed, and at six that evening, she headed out to meet Rai at The Mocha Escape, a restaurant in the downtown area.

When River arrived, Rai was already there waiting on her. River gestured to the waiter that she was going to Rai's table, and the waiter ushered her over to her seat. "Would you two ladies like to start off with a drink?" asked the waiter. River asked for water without ice, and Rai asked for coffee. As the waiter walked away, River glanced at Rai, who was still wearing sunglasses. Why was she wearing sunglasses in a restaurant, and why was she wearing a wig? Her thoughts were interrupted when Rai began to speak.

Rai: I know that you have a ton of questions, but I will try to get straight to the point. Just know that what I share with you, I share because I am concerned. When we walk out of this restaurant, you can continue life as you know it. You don't have to take what I say at face value, but I would never be able to forgive myself if I don't say anything.

River: Stop beating around the bush and just tell me. This is already making me uncomfortable.

Rai removed her sunglasses to reveal a black eye. She even had scratches on the side of her face.

Rai: When I met Ms. Denine, I was just like you. I wanted to meet and marry a God-fearing man. I wanted a man who could take me out of the ghetto and put me in a castle. Ms. Denine seemed like the answer to my prayers. I saw that she was church-going, independent, sassy and all of those things that most of us women desire to be.

River crossed her arms and sat back. She knew this conversation was going in a direction she didn't like. After all, she loved and respected Ms. Denine; nevertheless, she chose to listen to see where Rai was going with the conversation.

Rai: I know that I may be saying some things you don't want to hear right now, but I'm willing to have you mad at me for the sake of keeping you from making the same mistake I made. Anyhow, I met my husband through Ms. Denine; I'm sure you, as well as every other girl in the neighborhood, knows that. At first, I thought he was my knight in shining armor. I took Ms. Denine's advice throughout the course of me courting him. My husband wanted to move in with me before we got married, but Ms. Denine wisely told me not to do it, so I didn't. She said he wouldn't marry me if I did, and I'm sure she was right. When he hit me the first time, I went to Ms. Denine because my daddy always taught me to leave a man who hits me. My dad always said that a man who hits a woman is a coward, and he will keep hitting her because it makes him feel powerful. Ms. Denine told me that my dad was old-fashioned and uninformed. She told me to stick it out and just talk to Jason about it. She even called Jason and talked with him. It worked for a little while. After he spoke with Ms. Denine, he stopped hitting me. Two months later, he proposed, and against my better judgment, I accepted. I accepted because I did not want to upset Ms. Denine. I thought if I did things her way, I would end up married and happy with my life. I adored her at first.

River: Yeah, but where is this going?

Rai: River, you are a beautiful and intelligent girl. I don't have to spell it out for you. Don't marry a man you are not interested in just to boost Ms. Denine's reputation. Make no mistake about it; that's why she's pushing you to marry him. She could care less about what kind of man he is, and what he's going to do to you. Pay attention, River; Denine has never been married before. If her advice was so good, why isn't it working for her?

River: I kinda figured you invited me here to talk about Ms. Denine. Let me share something with you. I am not her protégé. I know her faults, just like I know her strengths. I know she wants to boost herself up, but I also know that she is simply sharing her wisdom with a bunch of women who don't have mothers or credible mothers to listen to. Of all the people, I would think that you would be the most appreciative of her. I understand that your husband is abusive, but you also got two working feet, girl; you can get up and leave him at any time.

Rai: Haven't you heard already? I left him months ago. I had to quit my job and go into hiding because he's been threatening to kill me and our children. I didn't call you here to argue with you or discourage you. You're a grown woman; you'll choose what you want to do on your own. But like I said earlier, I would feel awful if I didn't warn you first. Ms. Denine is not who you think she is.

River: Thank you for the warning, and I will take what you have said into consideration. I won't tell Ms. Denine about this meeting either because I appreciate you taking the time out to warn me. But I'm going to be honest with you. I'm going ahead with my wedding to Arthur, and I will be praying for you.

Rai: Thank you and let me know how all goes.

River: Wait. One question before I leave. If you were in hiding, why did you come to Ms. Denine's party the other day?

Rai: My husband was in jail for setting my mother's house on fire. He thought I was living there, so I knew he wouldn't make bail. I went there to tell Ms. Denine about the latest incident, and I hoped that she would see the light.

River: Oh wow. I'm sorry to hear that. Is your mom okay? And what did Ms. Denine say when you told her about the fire?

Rai: My mom is okay. She was hospitalized for smoke inhalation, but she pulled through. *Rai put her sunglasses back on.* When I told Ms. Denine, she said, "That's what happens when a man loves you, and you leave him." She then asked me to leave her house.

River: If it's been months since the two of you broke up, how did you get that black eye?

Rai: Today is exactly one week to the day that he set my mother's house on fire. I happened to pull up while the paramedics were there, and I was standing by my mother as they were loading her into the ambulance. All of a sudden, he came out of nowhere and started punching me. He hit me like I was a man. He managed to get three solid punches in before the police wrestled him to the ground. And you know what he kept saying as the police were cuffing him? *River could see the tear drops falling from under Rai's glasses.* He said, "Til death do us part. Remember that, Rai. Til death do us part."

After leaving the meeting, River was confused. Should she tell Denine about the meeting? Should she continue with the marriage to Arthur? After all, she was not attracted to him even in the slightest bit. She chose to keep the meeting quiet and just pay more attention.

Months later, Author and River were married at a beach near Ms. Denine's church, and River was happy. Arthur did look somewhat manly waiting on her near the pastor. His big teddy-bear eyes seemed to get even wider when he saw his beautiful bride heading his way. River was absolutely stunning. As she walked down the aisle, she gave Arthur a subtle smile that almost melted him. He was in love with this angel who had come to rescue him from himself. She would be nothing like his first wife. A woman that Arthur believed had caused her own death.

After the vows were said, they ended the night with a reception on the beach. The next day, Arthur and River flew to Jamaica for their honeymoon, and Ms. Denine volunteered to keep River's children while she was away. The honeymoon was near perfect. Everything seemed to go well until the third day. While in their hotel room, Arthur had become enraged when room service brought him shrimp instead of the lobster he'd ordered. He'd raised his voice at the room service attendant who'd delivered the food. When River cut him off and told him that raising his voice wasn't necessary, he'd gotten so upset that he'd overturned the shrimp and stormed out of the room. Later that day, he returned with roses and a warning. "River," he said with blazing red eyes. "The next time I am talking with a man about how he is handling me and my wife, don't interrupt. Remember, I am the man; I am the head of the house. You are the wife; the woman under the head of the house. Don't step out of place with me, you hear?" River was beside herself. How was this petite man standing there speaking as if he could take her? "Yeah; whatever," she replied. "One thing you will learn about me is that I'm no man's button. You can't push me on, but you can turn me off. With that said, don't ever get in my face again. That's my warning to you." Arthur laughed as River headed to the bathroom. He coached himself silently to remain cool. After all, it was their honeymoon, and he had plenty of time to tame the raging River.

Two weeks later, they were back at home, and Arthur had gone to work while River was home by herself. She'd sent the children off to school, and she was sorting through some old paperwork she had. She decided to go and store the paper with Arthur's documents. After all, they were married now. When she went to their room and pulled his suitcase from the closet, she was amazed at how heavy it was. She was even more amazed to find all of the memorabilia he had from his previous marriage. He even had his previous wife's private diary. It had a lock on it, but the lock had been broken. River put her documents into the bag and then put it back in the closet. While in the living room, she couldn't contain herself. What did his old wife write about? Maybe she could learn a lot about Arthur by reading what his first wife had to say. She went back to the bedroom and dragged the suitcase from the closet once more. She muscled it open and found the diary. After River lifted the diary, it slightly opened as if to invite her to read it. River then headed into the den to read it. She made sure that she put the suitcase back in place just in case Arthur came home early. She was nervous as she headed towards the den with something that was once so personal to another woman.

The first few entries were nice. Gladys (Arthur's first wife) seemed so happy as she wrote about all of the wonderful things Arthur had done for her. But something caught River's attention. She read it again and again, and her stomach filled with fear and anger every time she read it. On the third page, there was an entry that read, *"I'm so happy to know this man. He asked me to marry him today, and I know he is the right one for me. I love him so much, and I can't wait to be his Mrs. I have thanked Ms. Denine over and over again for this one. She is truly a matchmaker from Heaven!"* Ms. Denine had introduced Arthur to his first wife? This was all news to River, but she'd just grazed the surface. As she read on, she witnessed a tone change in Gladys. By her third month of marriage, she was sure she'd made a huge mistake. According to Gladys, Arthur had just begun hitting her. She didn't leave him because Ms. Denine told her not to, and she had just discovered that she was pregnant with their daughter, Arianne.

As River read on and on, she learned so much about Ms. Denine. Gladys' recount of Ms. Denine matched Rai's. She also noticed that Arthur was following the same pattern with her as he'd done with his first wife. Whenever Arthur became angry with River, he would point his fingers at her and shake them while laughing as if to warn her. According to the diary, he'd done this to Gladys for three months before he'd finally hit her for the first time.

River had read half of the diary before she heard the familiar sound of Arthur's car pulling into the driveway. It was time for his lunch break, and River had forgotten to cook him something. She had been so caught up in the diary that she'd lost track of time. She ran into their bedroom and put the diary under the mattress before jogging into the kitchen. She yawned as Arthur entered the kitchen looking for his meal. "I'm sorry, baby. I dozed off, but I can make you a quick salad or heat up one of those microwavable pizzas if you want." Arthur looked disappointed, but he didn't show it much. "That's okay. I'm not that hungry anyway. Just make me a salad and I'll take it back to work with me," he said. While River was making his salad, Arthur was suspicious. River didn't look like she'd just woken up. She was still dressed in the clothes that she'd worn to take their children to school, and River didn't like to sleep in her clothes. At the same time, River had not given him the eye contact that he was used to getting from her. He knew something was off, but he didn't know what. He headed into their bedroom and went straight for the closet. River peeped out of the kitchen with fear in her eyes. Did he detect that something was wrong? She then walked into the bedroom, and her heart dropped as she saw Arthur pulling the brief case from the closet. "Oh, yeah," she softly spoke. "I put my paperwork in there today. I was organizing some things and just mixed my paperwork with yours." Arthur noticed all of her documents immediately, and he felt reassured as he closed the suitcase and put it back in the closet. "Okay," he said. "Just try not to mess with anything in here. I kept this case organized because my ex-wife's family has threatened to sue me. I have the evidence I need here, so please don't mess with it." River was shocked. "Sue you for what?" The tone of her question relaxed Arthur even more. She was beginning to sound like the feisty River that he knew. Maybe she had fallen asleep. "The day my previous wife died, we had been arguing, and she left as a result of the argument. They are saying that I am responsible because had we not argued; she wouldn't have left, and she would have never gotten into that car accident." A tear dropped from Arthur's eyes as he lifted his dead wife's picture from the suitcase. Worried that he may notice the missing diary, River sat next to him and cradled her husband. "It's not your fault," she said. "Arguments happen and accidents happen; it's all a part of life's cycle. You're with me now, and I will never leave you no matter what; okay?" Arthur's heart melted as he heard those words. He felt loved, comforted and best of all, he felt relieved. He placed the bag back into the closet and headed back to the kitchen. He picked up his salad and went to the door to leave. Before leaving, he turned around and spoke to his wife. "River, I love you. I'm not a perfect man, and I really hope I can be the husband you want and the father your children need. Thank you for holding me. It felt great to be in your arms. Just know that I will never leave you either. Never. Til death do us part, right?" A tear dropped from River's eyes as she saw her humbled husband standing there saying the words she'd waited all her life to hear.

After Arthur left, River began to beat herself up. Why was she snooping? Why had she let Rai plant such a dark seed in her mind? After all, Ms. Denine was a good person, and Arthur was a spectacular husband. Sure, he had some flaws, but what man doesn't? She decided to start cooking supper early so it would be ready when her husband returned home from work. She decided to cook beef stew, rice and make some buttermilk biscuits. Arthur loved her beef stew. She also decided to make Arthur a strawberry upside-down cake.

A couple of hours went by, and River was in the kitchen cooking when she heard the door open. She looked out of the kitchen window, but there was no car in the driveway. She clutched the knife she'd been using to cut the onions as she tipped toed towards the kitchen door. Before she arrived at the door, Arthur stood there in the door. "I decided to take the rest of the day off," he said. "Your words touched me so much that I wanted to spend time with you before the kids got home. River was amazed, but she knew in her heart that he'd come home because he was still worried about her and that bag. Thankfully, she'd put the diary back after he left earlier. "Great, you can help me prepare supper. I decided to start cooking early because I wanted to make sure that the food would be ready when you came home today," she said with a smile. "You're a wonderful wife, River," Arthur said. "But I don't want food right now. I want you." He touched River's hands with his hands and began to lead her towards the bedroom. River followed him, wondering where he'd parked the car. She didn't question him, however. She didn't want to ruin the moment.

An hour later, River's alarm went off. She sat up hurriedly to catch her thoughts. She looked at the clock and realized it was time to pick the children up from school. Arthur lay beside her, but he was already awake. He had been watching River sleep. She looked so peaceful when she slept; so angelic. As River stretched, Arthur gently touched her face. "Hey beautiful." His words were so refreshing. River knew that Arthur was infatuated with her beauty and her physique, but this wasn't an issue for her. After all, every man that met her was mesmerized by the skin she was in. She smiled at Arthur and leaned forward to kiss him. "I've got to pick the kids up from school. Do you want to come with me?" She looked like an angel as she uttered those words. She wanted him to come with her. This was new to Arthur. His previous wife had never asked him to come along with her to pick up the kids, go to the grocery store or to visit relatives. Arthur's heart was touched. They left to pick up the children, and when they arrived back at home, River went back to the kitchen to finish cooking.

Later that evening, they'd enjoyed a lovely meal and the kids were preparing to sleep when Arthur suddenly came into the living room. He was obviously upset by something, and it was clear to River that the romantic turn the day had taken was all over with. He stopped to look at River for a minute, and then he took off his belt. River sat there confused as he turned around and headed towards the bedrooms. After a minute, she began to hear screaming. It sounded like it was coming from Garrett. River's motherly instincts came in as she jumped from her seat and ran into Garrett's room. What she saw horrified her. Garrett was not wearing a t-shirt, and Arthur was beating him with the belt. The belt was striking him on his legs, buttocks and back. All the same, Arthur was nowhere near merciful with his licks. He drew back as far as he could, and struck the child with all of his might. River tackled him before he could deliver the next blow. Arthur fell across the bed and began to punch River. Noticing that his mother was being attacked, little Garrett ran into the kitchen and called 911. He was six years old, and River had taught him to call the police when an emergency arose. Before he could get to the phone; however, Arthur intercepted him and snatched the phone line out of the wall. Stunned, Garrett ran back to check on his mother. She was now lying on the floor being cradled by Ria. She was coughing and her teeth were bloody. Arthur came into the room and watched as the children screamed for their mother to get up. He closed the door and locked it from the outside and went back into his room. He'd rigged the house for occasions like this one.

River managed to catch her breath and sit up. She cradled all of the children, including Arthur's little girl Arianne. Her mind was made up. She was nobody's punching bag, and she was not going to sit around and let a man beat her children. She noticed the broken phone next to the door, but she remembered that she'd purchased a cell phone for Garrett in case of emergencies. "Give me your book bag," she whispered to Garrett. Little Garret got up and got his bag and handed it to his mother. As she was unzipping the bag, she could hear Arthur still cursing and ranting while pacing the hallway. She picked up Garrett's phone and called the police. "911; what's your emergency?" The operated sounded pretty loud to River. She whispered back, "Please send an officer to 419 Granby Road." The operator cut in and asked, "What's the emergency ma'am? Did you say 415 Granby Road?" River was agitated, but she remained calm because she didn't want Arthur to hear her talking. "No. I said 4-1-9 Granby Road. My husband just beat me and my son, and he just locked us in a room. Please send an officer quick." The operator seemed to take forever to document what was said.

Operator: Is your husband still at home, ma'am?
River: Yes. Please send them quick.
Operator: What's your husband's name, and what is he wearing?
River: Can we sort this out when they get here? He just attacked my son, and when I came to protect my son, he beat and bit me. He then snatched the phones out of the wall, and now he's walking up and down the hallway cursing and screaming.
Operator: I understand ma'am, and an officer has been dispatched to your address, but I have to ask these questions. What is your husband's name?
River: His name is Garret Caldwell, and he's wearing a white tank top and some blue boxer shorts.

While she was still speaking, Arianne realized that her dad was going to go to jail, and she began screaming. "Don't call the police on my daddy! I don't want my daddy to go to jail! You'll have an accident if you call the police on my daddy!" Her screams caught Arthur's attention, and River hurriedly hung up the phone. She put the phone behind her as Arthur entered the room. In his hand was a large butcher's knife, and his eyes looked as if he had gone mad. His puppy dog eyes weren't cute anymore; he suddenly looked like a silent, crazed maniac. Arianne began to scream at her dad. "She called the police, and I don't want you to go to jail!" She ran and hugged her dad as he stood there teary-eyed. He realized at that moment that River was nothing like Gladys. Gladys had taken the abuse for years before ever thinking to call the police, but here it was the beginning of their marriage, and she was already seeking police intervention? "Go to your room," he said to Arianne. "Daddy's not going to jail." Arianne went to her room crying as River cradled her two children in horror. Arthur closed the bedroom door and locked it. He didn't want to kill this beautiful butterfly that he'd caught, but he needed her to understand that he was the man and that she was not to question him. Afraid that he would harm her children, River mustered up the strength to stand up. She would die for her children, and she'd already told Garrett to take his sister and jump out of the window if something happened. Garrett grabbed his little sister's hand, but Ria wouldn't let go of her mother's leg. He tried to pull her hands apart, but she screamed with all of her might. She didn't want to see her mother get hurt, and neither did Garrett, but he had a job to do.

"You called the police on me? You called the police on your husband?" Arthur's voice was unrecognizable. His voice seemed low, but pitched; desperate, but calm. As he made his way towards River, Ria began to scream louder. Garrett managed to pull his sister loose and he carried her towards the window. River didn't answer her husband. She stood there stone-faced, ready to protect her kids with her life. She was convinced that she was about to die, but she was even more determined to make sure her children didn't follow her to the grave.

Arthur was beginning to feel more desperate as well. River wasn't running, and he saw no signs of fear. She had been hardened by life, and she was ready to fight it out until the end. Tears ran down her face as she took on a fighting stance. She was ready to fight for her kids; she was ready to die for her kids. At that moment, they seemed more important to her than having a man. At that very moment, she realized how much she loved them. At that moment, she realized how important GOD is. Would she die and go to hell for the choices she'd made? Would GOD forgive her? Her life flashed before her eyes as Arthur drew back the knife. He'd changed his mind. He knew that River would never come back to him if given the chance to leave him. He drew back the knife, but before he could attack River, he heard a loud noise in the house, and then he heard Arianne screaming. He lunged forward, throwing his body against the door as he unlocked the door and ran into the hallway. He was then tackled by an officer and wrestled to the ground. Officers found River and her children in the room. Garret had just gotten the window up and was holding Ria. He was prepared to throw his sister from the window, but when he saw the police, he gently lowered her to the floor.

River was rushed to the hospital, where she recovered from a broken rib and a concussion. While at the hospital, River noticed that Ms. Denine never came to see her. As a matter of fact, none of the neighborhood girls came to see her except Rai. When River woke up from surgery, Rai was holding her hand. Her mother was also there, holding her left hand and praying over her daughter. No one said a word; they all just cried together and praised the LORD. River tried to lift her head to ask about her children, but knowing her thoughts, Rai reassured her that the children were okay. They were with River's sister in the waiting room.

A few days later, River was still in the hospital recovering when the phone rang. Her mother answered the phone and began to scream. "Don't you ever come anywhere near my daughter or my grandkids again; you devil! You hear me?! Stop calling here!" River knew who it was. Arthur had obviously made bail and was now calling her as if all was well. The phone rang again. Seeing how frustrated her mother was, River gestured for her to hand the phone to her.

River: Hello?
Arthur: Hey baby. I just wanted to let you know that I'm at home, and I cleaned up the house. Arianne misses you. When do you get out of the hospital? When can I come and pick you up?

River groaned as she sat up in her bed.

River: Arthur, it's over between you and me. Don't call me anymore.

At this, she hung up the phone.

A week later, River was released from the hospital, and she decided to go back to her mother's house to recover. She was hurt that Ms. Denine had never come to the hospital or even called to check in on her. Maybe she hadn't heard about the incident. Maybe Arthur was too ashamed, so he'd never told her. There had to be some reasonable explanation for Denine's behavior. River picked up the phone to call Denine. She was sure that Denine would be sympathetic, apologetic and would come out to see her. But that's not what happened.

Phone rings.....
Idris: Hello?
River: Hey, Idris. Where's your mom?
Idris: Outside talking to Arthur. Hold on.
River was stunned, and she hung up the phone. Why was she talking to Arthur? She laid down and wept as reality began to manifest itself to her. Denine was a snake; she was nobody's friend. She'd used River, and it was now becoming more and more real.

Later that day, the house phone rang, and River answered it. Her mom was in the bathroom, and the children were still at her sister's house.

River: Hello?

Denine: Hey, someone called this number for me earlier?

River: Who is this?

Denine: Denine.

River paused.

River: It was me, Ms. Denine; this is River.

Denine hesitated.

Denine: How are you, River?

River: I'm better. Did you hear about what happened?

Denine: Yeah, Arthur told me, and Rai came by here last week trying to go off on me. Of course, I had to put her in her place.

River: Why didn't you come to see me?

Denine: I've been busy; that's all.

River: Okay. Well, it was nice hearing from you.

Denine: Wait, River. I apologize if I don't seem at all sympathetic, but I am. I am also a little disappointed. Do you know what Arthur told me? He caught your son trying to kiss his daughter, and that's why he was disciplining him. He told me that you attacked him, and he pushed you off of him. He told me that you fell and broke your rib, and then you had him arrested. Why would you do some mess like that, River? That man was trying to be a father to your son, and here you come running in.

River: First off; lower your tone. Secondly, my son did not try to kiss his daughter. Garrett told me that Arthur came into his room and started staring at him. When he started staring back at Arthur, Arthur became enraged and started beating him. There were no words exchanged; Arthur was trying to size up my son, and that, my friend, is not okay.

Denine: You told me yourself that Garrett lies sometimes. How do you believe him? Do you know Arthur has been at my house every day since the attack, and he's been crying? He wants his wife back; he wants his family back. I know that Rai has been up at the hospital swelling your head up with lies, but don't listen to Rai. Rai lost a good man, so I introduced him to Teira, and now he's talking about marrying her as soon as his divorce from Rai is settled. Rai lost a very good man trying to be stupid.

River: Denine, you're crazy. I will never let you sit here and speak about my son in such a way. You side with abusive men, and you keep introducing women to these men. I found out that you introduced Arthur to his first wife, Gladys. You knew Arthur was crazy when you introduced him to me, but you didn't care. With that said, you can lose my number and I'll do the same favor for you.

As she was hanging up the phone, River heard Denine yell into the receiver: "Stupid!"

Another week went by, and River was strong enough to get around on her own. A couple of police officers came by to accompany River to Arthur's house to get her belongings. She'd already filed for divorce through her mother's attorney, and she wasn't seeking anything from the divorce. She just wanted Arthur to leave her alone. She had been getting many calls in the middle of the night, but she could never prove they were from Arthur. The caller would block his number and just listen as River would go off.

As they approached the home, River could feel her insides churning again. She had never wanted to see that house again. It was truly a house of horrors for her, as beautiful as it was. River rode in the car with her mother, and they were led by two police cars, and followed by another police car. When they parked, Arthur opened the door and stood outside. He wouldn't take his eyes off River. She was so beautiful to him. So, so beautiful. The officers led River, her mother, Rai and her uncle into the home. One officer stayed in the living room with Arthur, while two other officers followed River and her family through the house. Another officer stood outside just in case.

While they were collecting her things, River heard an outbreak in the living room. Arthur was crying and talking loudly. "Officer, you don't understand. That's my wife! We just had an argument; that's all. It was all just a misunderstanding. Please just let me go and talk with my wife for five minutes. You can time me. Please give us just five minutes!" The officer was unrelenting and kept asking Arthur to calm down, sit down and to not make a scene. A few minutes later, the officer called out for the other officers, and they all ran into the living room and restrained Arthur. He was crying hysterically and trying to force his way back into the room. He had also called Denine, who was now in the living room yelling at the police officers. River ran down the hall to see the commotion. Fear set in as she witnessed that same monstrous look in Arthur's eyes as he looked up at her and said, "Tell them that we are still together. Tell them to let me go, River! You're my wife!!!!" Denine stood there and looked at River with disgust, but Rai came and wrapped her arms around River. "Come on, sweetie. Let's get the rest of your stuff and get out of here."

After River had packed all of her things, she suddenly remembered her papers. The officers were still restraining Arthur. River's mother, uncle and Rai were all now in the living room trying to make sure everything stayed under control. River pulled the heavy briefcase from the closet and began to remove her documents. After she removed a book that belonged to her, she saw Gladys' diary once again. Again, the diary opened slightly after all of the pressure from River's books and documents were lifted off of it. River stared at the diary, and decided to take it with her. She wanted to know what Gladys had to say. What was her life like? What was in the pages of her diary?

As they were walking towards the front door, Arthur began to cry out to River again. "Baby, don't do this. I'm sorry, baby! Please; just give me another chance. I'll never hit you or your children again. River! Don't do this! River!" By this time, he was cuffed and sitting upright on the living room couch. River walked around the coffee table to avoid him, but Denine blocked the door. She fixed her eyes on River as if she wanted to fight her. As they were exiting the door, Denine opened her mouth to say something to River, but Rai interrupted. Rai put one arm around River and pointed her finger in Denine's face. "Your day is coming," she said.

"One day, GOD will make you answer for the evil that you are." One of the officers said to Rai, "That's enough. Go ahead and get into your vehicles."

Three days went by, and River could not get Arthur's face out of her head. How did she ever give herself to a man like Arthur? He was obviously crazy; he even looked crazy to her now. What had she been thinking? Her mother got up and left for work, and she dropped off River's kids at school. She left River's older sister there with her to make sure everything was okay with her. Suddenly her phone rang, and she answered. It was obviously Arthur again, because the person didn't say a word. River hung up the phone and started back watching television. The phone rang again, and River picked it up and then hung it back up. It rung again, and River hung it up. Finally, it rung again, and River decided to answer.

River: What do you want from me?
Rai: Calm down, girl. It's just me, Rai.
River: *Sighs.* Oh, girl.... I thought you was that crazy man. He keeps calling here with a blocked number.
Rai: You can stop your phone from receiving blocked calls, you know? I know how to do it, but I don't remember off the top of my head, so I'll text you the info later today.
River: Thanks, girl; please do. What's up?
Rai: There is something I want to tell you. Can I come over? Are you busy?
River: Yeah, you can come over. Raleigh is supposed to be

watching me, but she's no star officer. She fell asleep after eating all of my junk food.

Rai: *Laughs.* Okay. I'll be there in about an hour.

River: Okay. See you then.

Forty-five minutes later, Rai arrived and knocked at the door. Raleigh was in a deep sleep and didn't hear the knocks, so River answered the door. She let Rai in and joked about her sister, who was stretched out on the couch as they passed by, heading to River's bedroom.

Rai: Remember that day in the restaurant when I was trying to tell you about Ms. Denine?

River: Yeah. I was meaning to thank you for that and apologize for being so rude. I was just so swallowed up and blinded by what I wanted that I couldn't see the light if I wanted to.

Rai: That's okay, girl; I forgive you. Anyhow, there was something else I was intending to tell you that day, but you left before I could.

River sat down on her bed.

River: What's going on?

Rai: Well, I knew Gladys, and I was there when Ms. Denine introduced Gladys to Arthur. Just like you, Gladys wasn't all that impressed with Arthur, but she went forward with the relationship at Ms. Denine's urging.

River: Oh wow.

Rai: Yeah, but wait; it gets better. Gladys and I were friends. We weren't best friends, but we were friends. We talked at least once a week, and we dined out together twice a month. Gladys had started telling me that Arthur had been beating on her, and she wanted to leave him. Every time she tried to leave him, he threatened to kill her and their daughter. Anyhow, the day Gladys died, she had called me and told me that Arthur had hit her, and she was leaving. When I talked to her, she was in her car and speeding down Highway 42. Arthur was chasing her, and she told me that Arthur was trying to run her off of the road. River, she had their daughter in the car with her. Arianne was just two years old at that time. I begged her to call the police or head towards the police station because she told me that Arthur had a gun.

River: He had a gun?!

Rai: Yep, and he kept pulling up on the side of her pointing that gun at her. Gladys had tried to leave him several times, and he knew that it was only a matter of time before she successfully got away. He'd told her that he would make sure that she was dead before she could even consider filing for divorce. Well, it didn't happen exactly that way, but close. You see, earlier that week while Arthur was at work, Gladys went to an attorney's office and filed for divorce. The day Arthur hit her was the day he received those papers.

River: But why hadn't she left him before then? I don't understand.

Rai: Arthur is a professional man, and he has a lot of high-end connections. He'd promised her that he would take custody of Arianne, and she would never see Arianne again. She wanted to file for a divorce on her own terms. She saved up some money in a hidden account to hire a big-shot attorney to go up against whomever Arthur hired. The day she died was the day she planned to leave him. The attorney had told her the papers would be delivered to him that Thursday, but she'd obviously forgotten that Thursday was Thanksgiving. She sent the papers to Arthur that Wednesday instead. Gladys had just finished packing her and Arianne's things, when Arthur arrived home outraged. Arianne was already in the car strapped into her car seat, but Gladys went back into the house to retrieve her diary. Before she could get it, Arthur came in and attacked her. She managed to get away from him, and she ran to her car. She locked the door and pulled off. I was on the phone with her while she was driving because something told me to call her. I felt something was wrong. She told me what happened, and she told me that Arthur was in his car chasing her.

River: And then what happened?

Rai: Well, while we were talking, Arthur pulled alongside her and pointed his gun towards their daughter. That's when she panicked and went off the road. When he was pointing the gun at her, she was okay. When he pointed that gun at Arianne, she screamed out, "He's pointing the gun at Ari! He's pointing the gun at Ari!" That's when I heard tires screeching and then silence. *Tears began to go down Rai's face as she recounted the event.* I called out her name again and again, but all I could hear were moans. River, I didn't know what to do. I jumped in my car and raced down the highway looking for her, but I couldn't find her. I was on the phone the whole time calling out her name. I heard the ding ding sound the car makes when a door has been opened, and I only hoped it was Gladys getting out of the car. I am SURE I heard Arthur whisper something, and then I heard Gladys grunting before she went silent. I knew...I just knew she had been in an accident; I just wanted to find her. Finally, I was going down the highway one more time, when I saw police, ambulances and Arthur standing there. The police were putting up that yellow police tape, and I parked my car and ran out. I was still on the phone with her, but by this time, she'd went silent. I could hear baby Arianne crying, and I ran into traffic trying to cross the street. The police stopped me just when I'd gotten a glimpse of my friend's car. She had ran off a slight cliff, and her car was upside down. She wasn't strapped into her seat belt, but Arianne was.

Rai covered her face as the tears ran out. River sat close to her friend and began to embrace her. Rai's voice quivered as she finished the story.

Rai: It was hard for me to forgive myself, River. I wished I'd hung up and called the police. Maybe she would be alive today.
River: Don't blame yourself, Rai. You've proved to her in her darkest hour that you were a true friend. You didn't want to leave her side, and I commend you for that. Even though

you weren't there in body, you were there with her until the very end.

Rai: Thanks. *Sighs.* Anyhow, I told the police what happened, but they didn't have enough evidence. I told them about the gun, but they didn't find a gun in his vehicle. I don't know what he did with it. The police waited a few days to ask Arianne what happened, and by this time, she'd been brainwashed by Arthur. I just could never prove what happened. I went to Ms. Denine, and she pretended to be so heartbroken and mad at Arthur. That's why I kept going around; that was, until I saw that she had linked you up to Arthur. I knew she hadn't told you the story. To be honest with you, River, I don't believe the accident killed Gladys. I think she was wounded in the accident, but Arthur opened that door and did something to her.

River: Why do you believe that?

Rai: Because I heard the ding ding sound of a door opening a minute after the accident. I heard Arthur say something, and then I heard Gladys make some groaning noises like she was fighting to breathe. After that, I didn't hear Gladys anymore. When the police arrived, Arthur had blood on his shirt, but he claimed it came from trying to remove his wife from the vehicle. But if that was the case, when he realized he couldn't remove her, as he claimed, why did he go and stand on the highway to wait for the police while his daughter was still in the car screaming?

River: You know what? When I went through Arthur's briefcase one day, I found Gladys' diary. I read it, and I was so hurt for her. I read about the abuse. Anyhow, when we went back the other day to retrieve my things, I took the diary. I just felt like I needed to take it with me. I felt like I needed to remove Gladys from that home.

Rai: Do you still have it?

River: Yeah. It's right here.

River opened the drawer on her lampstand and removed the diary. Both Rai and River sat there for a few hours reading all of the entries. By the time they were finished, they were both convinced that Gladys had been killed. They called the police and told the investigators what they had in their possession. A couple of investigators came by to retrieve the diary as evidence. As they were knocking on the door, River's sister Raleigh woke up. Thinking it was Arthur or one of Arthur's high-end friends, she began to panic. She didn't notice Rai sitting there when she came into the room and grabbed River by the hand. She stuffed her sister into the closet and then proceeded to try and get into the closet with her. "Raleigh, what are you doing?" The question came from the dark closet. Raleigh answered, "They're here to kill you. Oh darn! I forgot to bring a phone in here to call 911." Rai sat there laughing as she heard the conversation coming from within the closet. "I'll get it," she said aloud. Rai let the officers in, and led them to River's room. She opened the closet door where they saw a laughing River and her frightened sister. "It's just us, ma'am; the police." River exited the closet and left her humiliated sister still sitting in the closet. Seeing how handsome one of the officers was, Raleigh reached out, grabbed the closet's door handles, and closed herself back into the closet. The officers laughed as one of them asked River, "Please don't tell me she's supposed to be your body guard." River answered, "Unfortunately, yes. Times are hard, and she's all we could afford."

River handed the diary to the officers, explaining why she had taken it. Rai retold the story of her friend's death to the investigators, and was relieved when they told her they had been investigating Gladys' death. The coroner had reported that Gladys' hyoid bone had been broken, and this was consistent with strangulation. It was not consistent with an accident. All the same, they told River and Rai that the accident was minor and that ordinarily, Gladys should have survived it. It wasn't a steep cliff, and over the last five years, fifteen people had crashed by running off of that cliff. None of them had died or sustained the injuries that Gladys had. They were still in the process of collecting evidence.

Suddenly, River remembered something Arianne had said to her when she'd called the police on Arthur, and she told the investigators. Arianne had said to River that she would have an accident if she called the police. "She said that?" This question came from the handsome officer whom her sister was hiding from. "Yes," replied Gladys. "She screamed at me about calling the police. At first, I thought she just didn't want me to call the police because she was afraid of her daddy going to jail, but now I realize she was in fear of losing me. I feel so awful." The officers reassured the two women and were about to head out of the room, when the handsome officer remembered the humiliated Raleigh, who was still hiding in the closet. He went and opened the door and said to her, "If it's any consolation, I think you're beautiful. Maybe we'll meet again under better circumstances." At that, he closed the closet door just as Raleigh had begun to smile.

A few weeks later, the police obtained a warrant to search Arthur's residence, and they also re-interviewed Arianne. By this time, Arianne was living in fear of her dad. She loved him, but she was afraid he could make her go to sleep the way he'd done to her mother. She told the police officers what she witnessed.

Arianne: My mommy had an accident, and she was in pain. So my daddy came into the car and helped her to go to sleep.
Child Psychiatrist: What did your daddy do to help your mommy go to sleep?
Arianne got out of her seat and approached the doctor. She then put her hands around the doctor's throat and whispered, "I told you if you left me, you'd have an accident. I told you."

Arthur was arrested and eventually charged with second degree murder. He was sentenced to twenty-five years for killing his wife. He was sentenced to another fifteen years for attempted second degree murder against his daughter.

Later that year, Arthur committed suicide in prison.

As for Ms. Denine, she was never charged with a crime. After all, it's not against the law to fix up a bunch of naïve and desperate women with the men who prey on them. She did lose her street credits, however, when the news went out. She eventually settled down with a local drug dealer and ended up serving fifteen years for trying to smuggle drugs into the United States from Mexico. By the time she was released from prison, it was obvious that age had caught up with her and dealt her a bad hand.
The End.

What's the moral of this story? There are several messages to take from it.

1. Older doesn't always mean wiser. An older fool can't advise you on how to have a better life. They can only teach you how to have a life like theirs or beneath theirs.
2. Let love find you. If you go out looking for love, you'll find out why GOD wants you to remain hidden in HIM.
3. A wise woman can slump in her wisdom, but her wisdom will keep her upright. A foolish woman can remain poised in her foolishness, but her simpleness will be her downfall.
4. GOD never asked you to settle for a man you're not interested in. He asked you to settle with the Truth that you are not interested in until you learn to love HIM and see HIS beauty.

5. Never lean to your own understanding. It'll trick you every time.

There are many dark counselors out and about looking for any form of glory, and they will gladly give you the advice that has kept them in the darkness. Just because someone looks like they have their act together, it doesn't mean that they qualify to advise you. Remember, the President of the United States has his own adviser. Many politicians, government officials, royalty and well-known individuals have their own advisers, but not just anyone can qualify for the job. They take on people who have been educated to do the job they are doing. At the same time, most of them will only take on individuals who have advised other well-known individuals before, but on a lower ranking scale. They are tried and proven to be steadfast and results-driven. Now, if we are royalty, a royal priesthood in the LORD, why is it that we think we can take advice from any person who's bold enough to be publicly stupid? It's simple. We cannot receive advice from everyone, not even everyone in the church, because there are certain people who will never arrive at the heights GOD has called us to. How can someone tell you how to get somewhere they have never been?

River and Rai's story is a common one, believe it or not. There are people out there who can make failure look good by dressing it up with lies and confidently delivering it to any woman who's not wise enough to reject it. At the same time, there are actually men out there who would rather see a woman dead than to see her without them because they are driven by obsession. They can be some of the most passionate and caring individuals, seemingly. They'll hold your hand in the sunset and wipe away the tears that others have caused you, only to give you more. They'll buy you your heart's desires and challenge anyone who challenges you, but this doesn't mean that they love you. It means that they believe they deserve you, and they will do anything to prove to you and themselves that they are the best thing that has ever happened to you. The more they do for you, the more dangerous they become towards you because, in their minds, you are their property. They have paid for you with silence, gifts, and even by coming against your enemies. They will happily marry you and give you their last name, but trying to take your own name back can prove to be deadly. Sadly enough, there are characters out there who would never leave their estranged wives or girlfriends alone unless they are incarcerated or dead. They are absolutely determined to have the women they want at all costs. What's ironic is these individuals are oftentimes the worst individuals to live with. In most cases, they are physically and emotionally abusive adulterers with a hunger for power, but no wisdom to have it. Their women have to literally go into witness protection, change their name or have them arrested before they can go on and live a semi-normal life. They can never recover the peace they once had because they have to constantly look over their shoulders. This is why GOD says to us in Matthew 6:33, *"But seek ye first the kingdom of God, and his righteousness; and all these things shall be added unto you."* GOD wants you to seek HIM and righteousness, and HE will take care of your loose ends. HE will give you the desires of your heart after HE changes your mind, and what HE gives to you will not grieve you. Proverbs 10:22 reads, *"The blessing of the LORD, it maketh rich, and he addeth no sorrow with it."* GOD'S blessing is HIS permission. HE is the GOD of "yea" and "amen"; therefore, when HE permits you to have something or someone, HE will give that something or someone to you in HIS will.

All the same, looking for a man or another person to bail you out of your lifestyle is the same as rejecting GOD'S bailout. GOD has a plan for you, and your situation is often a reflection of your mindset. GOD wants to change your mind so that you can elevate in due season. In this, there is no sorrow added to your blessings, and you will know how to maintain what GOD has given you because you will know what it took to get you where you are. No man can add on to you, but he can take away from you. GOD wants to elevate and promote you so your GOD-ordained husband will find you in a state of trusting GOD. That way, you won't need your husband, but he will be an add-on to you. GOD didn't ask you to be dependent on a person; instead, HE wants you to depend on HIM. When you trust HIM, HE can trust you with the husband HE has for you because you will know how to fill the role as the wife of the man GOD has for you. You will pray for him and with him, and you won't panic any time he makes a mistake. There are millions of women out there seeking a man from within their need, or within their desire to do better, and these women often end up with seasonal lovers who take away from them more than they add to them. That's because these women searched for men from a place of faithlessness, whereas a woman after GOD'S own heart will hide in HIM because of her faithfulness to HIM. That's why the majority of women alive will never know what it's like to spend their lives with their GOD-ordained husbands; the men whom GOD has blessed or given permission to access these women.

It's simple. Wait on GOD for your husband, but don't just sit there...do something. Get closer and closer to GOD by reading, hearing and meditating on HIS WORD daily. Get busy in whatever HE tells you to get busy in, and do not accept advice from someone whose life doesn't line up with the WORD of GOD.

Every Season Has a Reason

"Just because someone is friendly doesn't mean that they are your friend."

Here's the truth. Most people don't know the difference between a friendly person and a friend. Because of this disconnect from reality, most of us often endure friendships that lead to unnecessary hardships, and we think it's normal. After all, everyone has problems. Right? That part is true, but some problems are indications that the person you thought to be your friend is actually your enemy in disguise.

It was early on a Saturday morning as the sun peaked through Grace's window. The sunlight moved across her cocoa skin, revealing her almost perfect complexion. Grace was sound asleep and having yet another nightmare. In her dream, Grace was running as fast as she could from a horribly disfigured man. The man's clothes were bloody, and his nose looked as if it had been melted on his face. He appeared to be Latino, and a hand kept coming out of his mouth, trying to grab Grace. Just as Grace was cornered by the man at a subway station, Grace's best friend Sydney came out of nowhere and began to talk to the man. He seemed to be sweet on Sydney, so he let her by and she led

Grace away to safety. Suddenly, the alarm clock went off, and Grace suddenly sat up in her bed. The sound of the alarm terrified her to the point where she considered throwing a pillow at it, but she didn't. Grace felt frustrated, and it took her almost a minute to get a grasp on her thoughts. What was that dream about? This was the second dream she'd had where this guy had been after her, and she'd been rescued by Sydney. All the same, she was very tired, but she knew she had to go to work.

The room was very cold, and Grace did not want to remove the covers from her body. She slowly lowered her feet from the bed as she struggled to stand up. The sound of the alarm seemed to be getting louder. She'd placed the alarm on her dresser because she had a bad habit of hitting it and going back to sleep when it was on her nightstand. As she turned off the alarm, a startling sound rang out that caused her heart to race. Her home phone was ringing, and she knew who the caller was. It was Sydney trying to make sure that she'd awakened on time to get ready for work. After all, Sydney rode to work with Grace every day, and she could not afford to be late again because of Grace.

Sydney had a car, but she felt that it was more economical if she carpooled with Grace since they lived on the same street and worked at the same company.

Sydney was Latino, and she was a very pretty young woman. She was about five feet tall with long blonde hair.

Grace, on the other hand, was half Latino and half Black. Grace's mother was African American, and she had very dark skin. Her skin was smooth, almost like it had been painted on her face. Grace's father was Latino. He was born and raised in the United States, but his parents were from Brazil. Grace's skin was dark, but not as dark as her mother's skin. She almost looked completely African except for her long dark hair and somewhat narrow nose.

Grace quickly made her way across the room to answer the phone. "I'm up," she exclaimed before hanging up the phone line. She made her way to the bathroom, where she began brushing her teeth. The day was going to be a long day.

Grace and Sydney had been friends for more than twelve years. They'd met in ninth grade when they were both fifteen years old. Their friendship started because of a fight that had broken out between Sydney and a girl named Jocelyn. Sydney and Jocelyn were obviously dating the same boy, and both girls had found out about it. Rather than confronting David, the object of their affections, they chose to confront one another. Jocelyn walked up to Sydney between classes to confront her about David. They began to argue, and Grace happened to be heading towards her classroom. She'd seen the confrontation from the beginning, and she rushed to Sydney's aid because she too did not like Jocelyn. After all, Jocelyn had confronted her about that same boy a year prior to that, and she hadn't been in any type of relationship with the guy. Instead, David knew her brother, so he kept coming over to their house, and while he was there, he flirted with Grace a lot. Having heard about his love of visiting Grace's house, Jocelyn had confronted Grace about him and was ready to fight with Grace had a teacher not intervened. She was still somewhat upset with Jocelyn about the incident, so she ran to Sydney's aid. After all, Sydney took a few classes with her, and she knew Sydney to be somewhat quiet.

Grace handed her books to her little sister Trinity and ran between both women. "There's no need to fight," she exclaimed. "He's a boy, and boys will do what they want. After all, Jocelyn; are you going to fight every woman that he flirts with, or every woman he dates? If he's no good, treat him like he's no good and stop going after the entire student body over a guy who obviously doesn't care for you." At those words, onlookers laughed, and Grace ushered Sydney towards her class. Since that incident, Grace and Sydney have been very close friends, and the friendship had lasted more than a decade.

On the way to work, the car was silent. There was something awkward about the silence, and Grace didn't figure out what it was until she pulled into the driveway of her job. She'd arrived at work fifteen minutes before schedule, and this was unusual to her...and then it hit her: She'd forgotten to pick up Sydney. Panicked, she made a sharp u-turn in the parking lot and sped back onto the highway. She picked up her phone to call Sydney, and she noticed that she'd missed three calls from Sydney. Grace called Sydney's cell phone over and over again while speeding towards her house, which was about twenty-five minutes away from the job, but she got no answer. She left voice mails for Sydney and continued towards her house. Maybe she was waiting outside and had left her phone in the house. Maybe she was trying to call Grace at the same time.

Thirty-minutes later, Grace arrived at Sydney's house and ran up through the yard towards her door. As she began knocking on Sydney's door, one of Sydney's neighbors came outside. "She left in her car," replied the neighbor. "She left about twenty-minutes ago." Grace was stunned and angered by those words. Why hadn't she at least left a voice mail stating that she would drive herself to work? Why hadn't she answered Grace's calls? This was typical of Sydney. Obviously, she was upset and decided not to answer the phone when Grace called her.

When Grace arrived at work, she was called to the office. This was her third tardy in a year, and her boss was fed up. As she entered the office, she could see her boss sitting at her desk. She looked angry but somehow pleased with what she was about to say.

Grace: You wanted to see me, Ms. Rhodes?
Ms. Rhodes: Grace, I regret to inform you that as of this moment, you are now terminated from MarketMedia Concepts. We have warned you again and again about your

tardiness, and today makes the third strike on your record in a year's time.

Grace: But Ms. Rhodes, I forgot to pick up Sydney and I went back to get her. I was here on time, but my morning just started off wrong.

Ms. Rhodes: Please clean out your office and exit the building in less than an hour. You are excused to go.

Grace: Ms. Rhodes, may I say something to you?

Ms. Rhodes: Make it quick.

Grace: I have worked at this company and gave it my all for more than six years, and you have treated me worse than any employee on your payroll. Mark is always late. Jason is always late. Mrs. Camille is always late, and even Sydney has been late more than three times in a year. I have tried over and over again to figure out what I could have possibly done to you to make you resent me. I now realize that there was nothing I could have done differently to make you like me, and I'm okay with that. So, I forgive you and I will continue to pray for you, even though you have done everything in your power to destroy a career I have worked so hard to establish.

Ms. Rhodes: Are you finished? Please exit my office. You have fifty-five minutes left before I have security escort you from the building.

Grace left Ms. Rhodes' office and headed towards her office. She passed Sydney's office and decided to tell her the news, but Sydney's facial expression spoke for her. She didn't want to be bothered with Grace; nevertheless, Grace spoke to her anyway.

Grace: My apologies. I forgot to pick you up this morning. I was rushing because I kept thinking about those previous tardies, and I totally forgot about you.

Sydney: No problem. I got myself to work. Thank GOD I have my own vehicle.

Grace: Yeah, about that....why didn't you pick up your phone when I called you? You could have told me that you decided to drive yourself to work.

Sydney: You didn't pick up my call, so why would I pick up yours?

Grace: Sydney, my phone was on silent! I didn't hear your call, and if I was trying to avoid you, I would have never called you back. I drove all the way back to your house to pick you up, only to learn that you had already left!

Sydney: Yeah, well...I'm here now, you're here now, and that's that.

Grace: Sydney, Ms. Rhodes just terminated me for being late! I was late trying to come back and pick up you! I knew my job was at risk, but I foolishly went back to get you, and you didn't have enough decency to pick up your phone. It's okay, Sydney. Enjoy your life.

At that, Grace stormed out of Sydney's office and rushed towards her office. Tears streamed down her face as she passed all of the familiar faces that she knew she would miss.

In her office, Grace cleaned out her desk and started down the hallway towards the employee's exit. Standing in front of the exit was Allen Pitts, one of Grace's now former co-workers. Allen was tall, dark and extremely handsome. He was so handsome that Grace had refused his offers to go on a date for more than three years.

Allen was a fitness buff, and more than that, he was a man of GOD. He was really impressed by Grace because she was a beautiful woman of GOD who seemed to be the only woman at the office with her head on straight. She didn't throw herself at the men in the office; there were no workplace rumors about her engaging in any types of relationships with the management team, and she always seemed focused when she came to work. Unlike the other women in the office, Grace did not come to work to make friends or be liked; she came to work to do her job.

Allen: I just heard what happened. Grace, I'm so sorry. If you need anything, you have my number. Give me a call.
Grace: Thanks Allen. I don't have your number, though.
Allen: I gave it to you two years ago. Don't tell me you threw it away?
Grace: *Laughs.* I probably did, but I'm okay.
Allen: Well, I came prepared. Here is my business card. Please give me a call tomorrow evening. I have something I want to speak with you about.
Grace: Allen, I.....
Allen: Listen, Grace. I'm not trying to flirt with you. I do like

you, and you know that, but this is business. You have my word.

Grace: Okay. I'll call you tomorrow around seven, but it's business. No funny business, Mister.

Allen: *Laughs.* Funny business, serious business....it's all business.

Grace rushed towards her car, and just as she was entering her car, the tears began to flow again. What had she done so wrong to Ms. Rhodes that she'd made it a point to target her? What had she done so wrong to Sydney that she could be so thoughtless?

She started her car and began driving through the parking lot. She could see Ms. Rhodes standing outside taking a smoke break. She was standing with another employee named Naomi, who also didn't like Grace, and they were laughing as Ms. Rhodes told whatever story she was telling. Truthfully, Grace knew that it was about her, but she didn't care. She'd recently started school again, and she'd saved enough money to get her through at least six months.

Grace went home, lay down on her sofa, and cried herself to sleep. She wasn't too upset about the loss of her job. She was more upset about Sydney and what she'd done, but at the same time, Grace was somewhat relieved. She had been thinking about quitting that job for more than a year now because of Ms. Rhodes, and she knew her season with Sydney had been up long ago. She just stuck around because she was used to her, and she loved her like a sister. As Grace slept, she found herself back in the subway again. The subway was abandoned, all except for one homeless man. He was sitting up against the wall, and he was wearing a hooded sweatshirt. He kept his head down, but there was something eery about him, so Grace could not stop looking at him. Suddenly, there was a tap on her shoulder, and she turned around in sheer terror. The homeless guy had managed to get behind her, and he was standing there and laughing at her. His eyes were dark, but his face was somewhat familiar. Grace could hear the sound of the approaching train as she backed away from the homeless guy and tried to make her way to the train as it began to slow down. By now, the man's back was turned, and Grace could still hear him laughing. Grace entered the train and watched from the window as the man waved her off. His face was suddenly different. He transformed into the transfigured man, and he laughed as the train slowly sped away.

Suddenly, there was a loud thumping sound and Grace sat up on her couch. It took her a few seconds to realize that someone was knocking at her door. She considered not answering the door because she recognized that pounding. It could only be Sydney. What did she want? Grace finally got up and answered the door. Standing in the doorway was a teary-eyed Sydney. She looked like she'd just started crying because her makeup was still neatly in place; nevertheless, Grace stepped aside to let her come into her apartment.

Sydney: Grace, I'm so sorry. I had a bad morning, and I let myself get in my feelings. Please forgive me. I didn't know you were going to come back to pick me up, but I should have answered the phone. I'm sorry.

Grace: It's okay, Sydney. You and I are not seeing eye to eye anymore, and I think it's time that we went our separate ways because I don't want to hinder you, and I don't need you hindering me anymore.

Sydney: Grace, I have already apologized. Don't start with that kind of foolishness again. We have been friends since we were children, and you are like a sister to me. There's no way I can walk away from our friendship. I just got in my feelings, that's all.

Grace: You're always in your feelings, Sydney. I can't keep trying to work around how you feel. I have my life, and I can't alter it to make room for your feelings. Today, you're sorry, but tomorrow, you'll be right back in that dark place again.

Sydney: No, I won't. I listened to Pastor Horatio's CD on the way over here, and he was preaching about emotions. I'm going to do better. You'll see. Anyhow, what I wanted to tell you is, I have managed to save up about three thousand dollars, and I can loan it to you until you get back on your feet.

Grace: No thanks. But thank you anyway. I have some money saved up. I'll be okay.

At that, Grace became relaxed and started talking to her old friend. She had initially felt fearful about ending the friendship, but now that Sydney had apologized; she felt a little better. They began to talk about Ms. Rhodes, church and even the guy at work (Allen) who liked Grace. Grace enjoyed watching her friend laugh, and they talked until one in the morning. Sydney ended up crashing on the couch since she was off the next day, and Grace went to bed after she realized Sydney was asleep.

The next day, Grace woke up to the smell of bacon. Sydney was in the kitchen cooking, and she'd obviously opened the blinds to let some sunshine in. The house was filled with sunlight, and the birds could be heard chirping their morning praises. As Grace entered the kitchen, she was greeted by a horrifying sight. The man with the melted nose stood in the kitchen massaging Sydney. Grace suddenly stopped in her tracks as the horrifying man turned to gaze at her. He smiled and then he opened up his mouth. That hideous hand came out of his mouth and reached for Grace. Grace screamed with everything in her, and she suddenly sat up. It was just a dream, but the smell of bacon was in the air. Sydney rushed to Grace's room to find out what the screaming was about.

Sydney: Grace! Grace! Are you okay?
Grace: *Lays back down and groans.* Yes, it was just another nightmare.
Sydney: Oh. Girl, you scared me. I thought someone was in here attacking you.

Grace: No, I have been dreaming about this hideous, disfigured man lately, and he's always after me. I've had four dreams about him so far, and two of those times, you rescued me. Yesterday, he didn't come after me, but he made himself known and just now, he was in the kitchen with you, giving you a massage.

Sydney: *Laughs.* That was probably my ex-boyfriend, Antwan. But seriously though, was he that ugly?

Grace: Yeah. *Laughs.* What are you cooking?

Sydney: Turkey bacon, grits, eggs and biscuits. The food is almost done, so go ahead and take your shower.

Grace: Okay. On it.

That day turned out to be a good day for Grace. She enjoyed the company of her friend, and they spent most of the day together before Sydney finally went home.

Later that evening, Grace decided to follow through with her agreement to call Allen. She was a little hesitant at first because she didn't want to appear desperate. She liked Allen, but she felt he was a little too handsome to get involved with. She didn't trust men who were that handsome. Her typical dating partner was handsome, tall and oftentimes dark skinned, but Allen was different. He was an African-American male, mid-toned, and he had the whitest teeth she'd ever seen. Allen was tall, standing up at approximately six foot three inches in height. His strong masculine voice fit his height, but not his baby face. His almond-shaped eyes were dark and penetrating.

Allen's phone rung three times, and Grace was about to hang up the line. She did not want to come off as desperate, and she didn't completely trust Allen. He was too handsome to be trusted.

Allen: Hello.
Grace: Hi, Allen. This is Grace. You wanted me to call you.
Allen: Oh. Hey, beautiful lady. How are you?
Grace: I'm great. Thanks for asking. How are you?
Allen: I'm good. No complaints this way.
Grace: Okay.
Allen: Yeah, well let me get straight to business. Please call the director of human resources, and tell her what happened on the job. I can't tell you what was said or who said it because I can put my job at risk, but what I will say is this: Ms. Rhodes has been wanting to terminate you for a while, and I have the evidence you'll need.
Grace: What kind of evidence?
Allen: Let's just say, thank GOD for modern-day technology. Ms. Rhodes had a meeting in her office over a month ago with a couple of women, and I overheard them saying your name. I kinda figured Ms. Rhodes didn't like you. I mean, I think everyone at the office knew that she was no fan of yours.
Grace: But why? I have never done anything to her.
Allen: I know, but hear me out. They were in the conference room, and I had just left the room. I'd set up the camera for the conference and when I came around the corner, they were in the room talking about you. Like I said earlier, I don't

want to mention what was said, and I only told you about Ms. Rhodes since she terminated you, but the rest is on video.

Grace: What does the video show?

Allen: Let's just say this. By the time the video gets out, Ms. Rhodes will be standing in the unemployment line.

Grace: Thank you, Allen. You are so nice, but I don't want you to lose your job. If you give me that video, you are going to get in trouble.

Allen: Yeah, you're probably right. I would hand it to human resources myself, but I don't want any kind of backlash, so how about this: I give you the video tape and you just say that you accidentally packed it when cleaning out your office. The video had been recorded a couple of weeks before you were fired, so it should be pretty easy to explain away. But that's lying, right? I wish there was another way.

Grace: I'm supposed to come by the office on Monday to pick up my last paycheck. I also forgot to pack a few things, including some of my own personal video tapes I'd recorded of our Christmas parties and other gatherings. Can't we just mix it up in there?

Allen: Great idea. How can we do this?

Grace: The box is already packed in my office. When I come there on Monday, I will stop to your office to tell you goodbye. There are no cameras in our offices, so you can drop the tape in then.

Allen: Great idea. See you Monday.

Grace: Thanks again, Allen. See you on Monday.

Allen: Wait. Before you hang up, let me say this to you. Grace, I really like you, and I have wanted to get to know

you better since I first laid eyes on you. I think you are a phenomenal woman of GOD, and I would be honored if you would let me take you out on one date. That way, you can see that I'm not a jerk. I'm actually a pretty good guy if you get to know me. I'm silly, but I'm decent.
Grace: *Laughs.* Okay. One date, but let's wait until this situation with Ms. Rhodes is cleared. Like I said earlier, I don't want you to end up getting in any kind of trouble.
Allen: Ms. Rhodes has no power over my division, but I truly understand, and I look forward to taking you out soon.
Grace: Thanks, Allen. Talk to you soon.
Allen: Talk to you soon. Bye.
Grace: Bye.

The next day, everything went as planned. Grace went by the office to retrieve her last paycheck and her belongings. She stopped by Allen's office, who then slipped the video tape into her box. She decided to wait a couple of weeks before sending the video tape in so it won't look like a setup. She also prayed about her decision to send the video in. She'd planned to watch the video, but she kept procrastinating because she didn't want to become upset.

Finally, the day came that Grace had been anticipating. She was prepared to call human resources and send the tape to them, but suddenly the phone rang. On the other end was SynoMarketing Research and Development, a new mega-marketing firm that had just opened in that area. They wanted to interview Grace for a high-ranking position in the firm. She would be making two times what she was making at her previous job. Grace was excited, but she didn't want to get too happy. After all, she'd been on several interviews, only to never receive a call back.

Grace was all too familiar with SynoMarketing. They had firms all over the world, and they were one of the most innovative and successful marketing firms in the world. Grace toyed with the idea of getting the job and what that would mean for her. They set up the interview for the following Tuesday, and Grace was overjoyed. Suddenly, taking revenge on Ms. Rhodes didn't seem like such a great idea. What if GOD was removing her from that job so HE could give her something better? She decided to call Allen and tell him about her change of heart. Allen confirmed to her that he'd felt convicted about the idea of getting Ms. Rhodes fired as well.

Allen: Let's just let GOD deal with her. Have you ever watched the video?
Grace: No, I will. It's just that I don't want to go through those emotions all over again. I keep saying I'll watch it tomorrow, but when tomorrow comes, I put it off again.
Allen: Yeah, well, I think you should watch it.
Grace: Why?
Allen: Just watch it. You'll see.
Grace: Okay, I'll watch it tomorrow. I'm too tired now.
Allen: Okay. Well, I will call you tomorrow when I get off work. I was off today, and management has been blowing

up my phone all day. I didn't answer it because they probably wanted me to come in to work, but I was just too tired. But hey gorgeous, I will let you sleep. It was good talking with you, and don't forget to watch the tape tomorrow.
Grace: I won't. Goodnight.

That night, Grace had a hard time going to sleep. What was so important on that tape that she had to see? Why was Allen being so vague about it? The sound of the television set began to cut through her thoughts. The news anchor seemed especially amped up about the story she was telling. It turned out that a store on Broadway had been robbed, and the store clerk had been kidnapped at gunpoint. Grace stared at the television set, hoping to get a glimpse of the robbery suspects. She always felt that she would one day recognize someone and be able to help solve a case. The video surveillance showed a somewhat blurry still shot of one of the suspects, but Grace didn't recognize him. She reached behind her pillow to grab her remote control, and just as she was about to turn the television, Sydney called her.

Grace: Hello.
Sydney: Hey, Grace. Do you have a minute to talk?
Grace: Yeah, sure. What's up?
Sydney: *Sighs.* I'm in a little trouble, and I need your help. But you have to promise me that you won't be mad at me. Okay?
Grace: What's up, Sydney?

Sydney: Promise me that you won't be mad, first.
Grace: I can't take a vow with you. You know my beliefs.
GOD is against pledges; therefore, I am against them.
Sydney: *Sighs.*
Grace: Hello? Are you still there?
Sydney: Yeah. Let me get my nerve together. I'll call you
tomorrow and tell you.
Grace: What's up, Sydney? It can't be that bad. Tell me
because I have to go to school tomorrow.
Sydney: I'll talk to you tomorrow, Grace.
Sydney disconnects the phone line.

What was going on? Now, Grace's mind was spinning even
more. She got up and headed to the kitchen to grab an ice
cream sandwich. She thought about calling Sydney back,
but decided against it because she did not want to panic her
any more than she already was. With the ice cream
sandwich in hand, Grace went back to her room and started
watching the news again. This time, the news anchor was
talking about MarketMedia Concepts, Grace's old job. Grace
stood there frozen as she watched three people being led
out of MarketMedia's doors in handcuffs. One of them was
Ms. Rhodes, and she kept her head down the whole time,
but her peppered white hair, sagging midsection and her
walk gave her away. The other girl was Ms. Rhodes's friend,
Naomi. Naomi was loud and yelling at the cameramen to
get the camera out of her face. She even tried to kick one of
the cameramen. Finally, the other girl walked out, but her
head was covered with a coat. She kept her head down, but

there was no mistaking who she was. It was Sydney. Grace could easily tell because they'd handcuffed Sydney from the front and she was holding some documents in her cuffed hands. Her pink fingernails covered with jewels gave her away. One of the cameramen managed to get a glimpse of her face as she was loaded into the back of the police cruiser. Grace didn't hear the story, because she was in shock, so she called Sydney back, but Sydney would not answer her phone. Panicked, she called Allen. Allen was sound asleep, but he picked up the phone on the third ring. His groggy voice indicated to Grace that he had been asleep, but she didn't care. Something was going on, and she couldn't figure it out.

Allen: *Snores.* Hello.
Grace: Allen, what's going on? I just saw on the news that they arrested Ms. Rhodes, my friend Sydney and that girl who used to hand with Ms. Rhodes. What's her name again? Oh yeah, Naomi.
Allen: Huh? Arrested who? What? What are you talking about?
Grace: They arrested Ms. Rhodes, Naomi and my friend, Sydney. They showed MarketMedia on the news, and they were bringing them out in handcuffs.
Allen: What?! Are you serious?
Grace: Yeah. I was hoping you knew what was going on.
Allen: No, I don't. Wow. That's probably why MarketMedia blew up my phone today. *Sighs.* Well, we'll have to wait until tomorrow to find out what's going on. If you start calling

around, they may think you are somehow involved in whatever they are involved in. My mind is racing now. I hope I can sleep.

Grace: Yeah, me too.

Allen: Wait, Sydney is your friend? Sydney Provoste?

Grace: Yeah. Why?

Allen: Oh, Grace. Sydney was one of the women in the video tape. I saw that she rode to work with you a lot, and that's why I urged you to watch the video tape, but I didn't know she was a personal friend of yours. I thought she was just a co-worker who you were carpooling with.

Grace: You're joking, right?

Allen: I wish I was. As a matter of fact, Ms. Rhodes promoted Sydney and gave her your position the very same day that she terminated you.

Grace: What?!

Allen: Ouch. Now, it's beginning to make sense. How long have you and Sydney been friends?

Grace: Since we were teenagers. You mean to tell me....

Allen: Wait. Did you tell Sydney that I had a thing for you?

Grace: Yeah. Maybe, but not in those words. I told her that you liked me and I sorta liked you.

Allen: Sorta?

Grace: Allen, this is no time for flirtatious humor; get to the point. My mind is going over a hundred miles per second, and I'm on the edge right now.

Allen: Grace, Sydney came into my office the day you were terminated, and she began hitting on me. At first, it started off as child's play where she'd throw a joke at me, but then it got too serious for me. She started joking about the color of her underwear and asking me if I'd ever been with a Latino woman before. I had to ask her not to come back to my office because I was beginning to feel uncomfortable. Do yourself a favor and watch that video tape, but wait until tomorrow. Tonight it may be too much for you.

Grace: Okay, I will. Let me go. I have a major headache right now and I'm going to take a sleep aid so I can get some rest. Call me tomorrow. Okay?

Allen: I will. Get some rest, and sorry about today.

Grace: It's not your fault. Thanks again, Allen.

Allen: No problem. Goodnight.

Grace: Goodnight.

After taking a sleep aid, Grace finally dozed off. She woke up on a subway train, seated next to a beautiful woman whose face seemed to almost glow. She was nursing a baby, and the baby seemed to be captivated by her beauty. She was humming a song, and her voice sounded angelic. Her hair was dark, and her skin looked pure white because of the slight glow that seemed to be emanating from it. Suddenly, the train came to a screeching halt, and the woman stood up to see what was going on. She looked at Grace and handed her the baby that she was holding. She then asked Grace, "Can you hold her for me? I have to arrest someone." Grace reached out and held the baby. Arrest someone? She didn't look like a police officer, and if she was, why was she holding a baby while on duty? Grace held the baby, but she couldn't take her eyes off of the woman as she made her way off of the train. Suddenly, Grace could see the disfigured man and he had an army of men surrounding him. Every man standing near him was disfigured, and they were all pointing at Grace, but the woman had no fear. She opened her mouth, and suddenly the men were all in chains, and they begin to descend into the ground. Startled, Grace looked down at the baby who was just as beautiful as the woman who'd been holding her. The gorgeous, red-headed baby looked just like Grace did when she was small. She smiled at Grace, and her beautiful eyes seemed to look into the very heart of Grace. Suddenly, a loud sound pierced through Grace's ears, and the lady came back onto the train and wrapped her arms around Grace and the baby. The sound got louder and louder, but the woman and the baby seemed unaffected by it. Without warning, Grace found herself feeling as if she were falling. With what felt like a bounce, she woke up and realized the loud piercing sound was her alarm clock. She'd set her alarm to wake up early so she could call Sydney and Allen.

Grace sat up on her bed, turned her body so that she could stand up, and headed towards the alarm clock. After turning the alarm off, she made her way back towards the bed because she was still tired. After lying down for five more minutes, Grace realized that she wouldn't be able to go back to sleep. Her mind was racing again, so she reached across the nightstand to pick up her phone. She checked her missed calls and saw that Allen had called her, but Sydney had not called. She decided to call Sydney first so she could find out what was going on, but the operator came on and said the line was no longer in service. Surprised, Sydney looked at her phone's call log, and she'd called the right number. She called Allen back, and the call went to his voice mail as well. Obviously, he was still at work and had likely called her on his first break. Then it dawned on her to check her voice mail to see if Allen had left a message, and he had. His message said, "Hey beautiful. Just wanted to call you and let you know it's worse than we thought. Ms. Rhodes was obviously embezzling money from the company, and both Naomi and Sydney were her partners in crime. They are also investigating the termination of several employees by Ms. Rhodes, including your termination. A detective was here when I came in, and he told me that it appears that Ms. Rhodes was moving around her key players in the company, so she got rid of seven employees within a year's time. Anyhow, talk with you later. There's much more to the story, and I'm still trying to get the details. Oh. By the way, don't say anything to anyone about what I told you. I'm not supposed to be sharing this information with anyone, but I figured that since you are my future wife, it's okay to tell you. Go ahead and smile. I know you're smiling. Good day, beautiful."

Grace smiled, but what did Allen want with her? After all, she was an unemployed woman who did not see herself as beautiful. She saw herself as an average-looking woman; someone who would end up with an average-looking husband or a not-so-handsome guy with a great personality.

Her brief moment of happiness was suddenly silenced by the thoughts of the video tape. She had to watch it. She was no longer afraid of what would come out of it. Grace headed to the kitchen to make herself a peanut butter sandwich before watching the tape. She toasted her bread and grabbed a cold bottle of water from the refrigerator. After the sandwich was done, she headed back to her room so she could watch the video.

After putting the video in, Grace braced herself for what she would see and hear. She had to fast-forward, scanning through the video which showed Allen setting up the room, and a few other people coming and going into the room after Allen had set it up. Finally, Ms. Rhodes entered the room, and Grace quickly played the video. Following her into the room were Sydney and Naomi. Sydney could be seen looking out the door and then locking it. The three women stood in a huddle, but their conversation was loud and clear.

Ms. Rhodes: One of the guys here is starting to make me a little nervous. You know the old guy in maintenance? I think his name is Jethro. Well, he keeps walking in on me when I'm trying to finish the job, you know? He doesn't say anything, but the way he looks at me makes me feel like he knows something.
Naomi: Why don't you find a way to fire him?
Ms. Rhodes: He's not in my department, but what I was thinking was to see if I can get him transferred over into my department, and then I could terminate him. I've noticed that

115

he seems to leave the maintenance door unlocked, so I could terminate him on those grounds.

Naomi: Well, there you have it.

Sydney: What about Grace? I have done everything to keep her from coming to my office, but she's sometimes unrelenting. She saw some paperwork on my desk one day and started asking me all sorts of questions. When are you going to get rid of her? Because I'm tired of seeing her face, quite frankly.

Naomi: *Laughs.* If that's what you do to your friends, I sure don't want to be your enemy.

Sydney: Grace is not my friend. I carpool with her, that's all. She's nothing more than a do-girl for me. Whatever I say do, she does. But dealing with her, even riding with her, is torture. I should be compensated for my pain and suffering. After all, she's little Ms. Perfect who can do no wrong.

Ms. Rhodes: Hey, y'all. We don't have time for school-girl chats. We have to focus on the issue at hand. I'll get rid of Grace. Sydney, you have access to her, so it's easier for you to trip her up. Keep riding with her to work and just make her late a few times. This will give me grounds to terminate her, and I can justify not terminating you by blaming her for your tardiness.

Sydney: Okay. Consider it done.

Ms. Rhodes: And Naomi. Stop being so careless with your computer. I came into your office the other day, and you weren't at your computer, but you had the McIntosh account wide open. Don't blow it, please.

Naomi: My mistake. It won't happen again.

Ms. Rhodes: Great. I just terminated Mrs. Wilson today. I found out that she calls home to check on her children while on the clock, so that gave me reason to terminate her. Naomi, I'll give you her position, but you have to promise me to be more careful. And like I said Sydney, once you help me get rid of your friend, I will give you her position. Is that understood?

Sydney: Yes, ma'am.

Naomi: Yes ma'am.

Suddenly, someone tries to enter the conference room, but the door is locked. They knock on the door, and Ms. Rhodes decides to end the meeting.

Ms. Rhodes: Okay. Meeting adjourned. Keep your mouths shut and your ears open. See you around.

After the three co-conspirators left the room, Allen could be seen entering the room. He asked the ladies a question, but Ms. Rhodes could be heard saying, "They are on my team, so I had a brief meeting with them. The room is all yours." Allen was obviously suspicious, and it could be seen in his eyes on the video tape. He is then seen heading towards the video camera, and then the video stops.

Grace's face was soaked with tears by now. How could she befriend such a wicked woman? Why did Sydney hate her so much? What had she done to Sydney? She also felt that familiar rush of relief. She could finally walk away from Sydney once and for all without feeling guilty about it. Suddenly, her dreams made sense to her. It was at that moment that her understanding was opened. The monster in her dreams represented Sydney. The disfiguration of his face represented the real face of Sydney, and not the one she'd shown Grace. In a few of those dreams, Sydney was able to speak to the monster, and it listened to her. Now, it made sense. It didn't attack Sydney because it *was* Sydney. It represented the two faces of Sydney and the devil lurking in her. The hand in its mouth represented the evil Sydney had been speaking of her, but the hand was never able to touch her. Finally, there was the subway station where the disfigured man would always show up. It represented the friendship between Grace and Sydney. Even though their friendship had lasted a long time, it had taken Grace nowhere but to the same old place over and over again. It was a friendship that was beneath Grace; one that kept bringing Grace back into a dark place.

Just as she was pondering her dreams and their meanings, her doorbell suddenly rang. She rushed to the mirror to make sure she didn't look as if she had been crying. "One minute!" she exclaimed. She rushed through the living room and almost stumbled over a pair of her shoes. Gaining her footing, she looked out of the peep hole to see her sister Trinity standing in the doorway. Just as she was opening the door to let Trinity in, Sydney's vehicle pulled up and came to a screeching halt in front of her mailbox. Trinity turned to look as Sydney dashed from the car and rushed up angrily towards Grace. "Do you have something you want to say to me?!" Sydney's voice was loud and quivering. "I heard what you said about me all around the office, and you can say it all to my face!" The tears welded up in Grace's eyes again. She knew what Sydney was doing. She'd done this before. Any time she was caught up in a jam, she would conjure up some lie to force a conversation upon Grace. Seeing her sister's hand forming a fist, Grace grabbed her and pulled her into the house. "Trinity, go and peel the potatoes in the kitchen. I already have them out. I'll be okay. Just go." For a moment, Grace thought about attacking her with every force that was in her, but suddenly, she locked eyes with Sydney. Her eyes were dark. They were so very dark. It was as if Grace was just truly seeing her for the first time. "Leave my home and never return," said Grace. "I already know about you and everything you have tried to do to me. But what you meant for evil, GOD turned it around for my good. Devil, you have ten seconds to get off my lawn before I bind you and send you where you don't want to be! Nine....eight....seven....six..." Sydney suddenly stopped in her tracks. Her angry expression left and she began to look fearful. She slowly backed up across the yard and got back into her car. As she started her car, she sorrowfully waved at Grace as tears went down her face. For a second, Grace almost felt sorry for her.

The End.

Let's end the story here to discuss what happened. This is a situation that happens to so many women. Oftentimes, we don't understand and don't want to understand that the people we love do not love us back. We consider others to

be our friends based on the amount of years they have stuck around, not understanding that many of the people who stayed by our sides for so long did so because it hasn't been easy to bring us down. And they'll stay right there by your side until they find your kryptonite. A friendship isn't how many years you've been by someone's side and vice versa; a friendship is based on love, respect and more than anything, the WORD of GOD. If your friends don't love JESUS, they can't love you. It's that simple. Just knowing that there is a GOD and going to church is not enough. Friendship is honor and respect, but it's not always loyalty. Let me explain. Merriam Webster Online defines loyalty as:
a: faithful to a private person to whom fidelity is due
b: faithful to a cause, ideal, custom, institution, or
product
Here are the issues:

- You can never be both faithful to man and faithful to GOD because man is imperfect; therefore, he's not always right. To be faithful to a person means to be consistently loyal to them, no matter where they stand. Your loyalty must always be to GOD, and you will have to step on your friend's toes sometimes to tell them the truth. The average person, however, does not want the truth at all times. They expect you to be more loyal to them and their feelings than you are to GOD, and this is where evil communication comes in.
- In my experience, there are women out there who expected me to be "exclusive" to them as a friend.

They simply did not like my other friends and appeared jealous when I spoke of my other friends. Of course, I had to let them go because that just wasn't normal. That is to say that you can't and won't be exclusive to a person because GOD didn't create you to become the personal property of your friends. All the same, you don't owe it to them to be exclusive to them. *"Owe no man any thing, but to love one another: for he that loveth another hath fulfilled the law" (Romans 13:8).*

- One of the words that stuck out to me is "faithful to a custom." Every friendship has its own custom, or ritualistic behavior. You have a certain way of addressing your friends, and they have a certain way of addressing you. It's your very own tradition, but this can be a prison when your friends don't give you the necessary room that you need to change. Let's face it: You will change over the course of time, but all too often, people who are enslaved into their definitions of friendships don't go far because any change they make offends their friends and threatens their friendships.
- Finally, you are not a product. It is so very easy to get distracted from who you are and what your purpose is in the earth when you are busy trying to fit someone's definition of you.

A friend has to understand that you will grow more and more, and they have to be okay with that. As a matter of fact, they have to grow with you; otherwise, you'll outgrow the friendship. At the same time, to go forth in GOD, you can never be so dedicated and loyal to a person where you feel obligated to keep them around as long as they want to stick around. Your friends have to be in CHRIST, so they can hear HIS voice as well. This way when HE calls the two of you to go in separate directions, there will be no hard feelings. Instead, you will remain friends, just not active friends.

There are so many women who have gone beneath who they really are to entertain the friendships that hinder them from becoming who GOD has called them to be. At the same time, many women who have the potential to go far in CHRIST have denied their seasons of transition trying to fit into man's definition of what a friend is and what a friend does. You will find that in many of my books, I strongly speak against being loyal to man because it robs GOD of our loyalty to HIM. I have run across many women who have the potential to go far, but because of the relationships they are entertaining, they are stuck in a certain realm and in a certain mindset. They keep rejecting their seasons of change, and they end up paying for this greatly because they have to go outside of the will of GOD to stay inside of man's friendly limits. Oftentimes, their finances suffer, their health deteriorates, and their sanity is challenged because they were supposed to be in a whole other place. If they'd followed the will and plan of GOD, they would have a new understanding by now. They would have enough knowledge to rebuke sickness when it knocked on their bodies, and they would be at peace because peace is found in the will of GOD. GOD does not like it when we place anyone or anything before HIM. For every new mindset you enter, it's okay to invite your friends, but if they don't want it, don't go back to your old mindset to keep those friends. Instead, it simply means that you have entered a new season, and a new season calls for friends of a like mind. *"Can two walk together, except they are agreed?" (Amos 3:3).*

Grace's problem was obvious. She saw that Sydney was not her friend, but she stuck it out anyway, denying herself the truth to pacify a lie. There may have been a time in their friendship where Sydney was actually Grace's friend, but a change happened somewhere at sometime and their roads was supposed to fork off and lead them away from each other. When we change, our relationships with others will change as well. When one friend changes and the other one does not, a disconnect happens because the two no longer agree. Even though they may come together in body, their minds won't be able to sync well with one another, and because of this disconnect, hard feelings start to develop. Oftentimes, it's the friend who was left behind that gets upset and tries to "humble" the other friend because she doesn't want to understand that her friend is not puffed up; she was simply elevated into a whole new way of thinking.

Do you want a friendship that lasts a lifetime? Do the math. One you plus one GOD equals everything you'll ever want.

One you plus one friend equals two people out of the will of GOD. One you plus one GOD and one friend who loves and fears the LORD equals a three-fold cord that is not easily broken. Sit down and tell your friends these truths:

- I love you, but I may not always be around. If GOD calls us to separate for a while, let's do so without being angry at one another.
- Let's always stay focused on who we are in CHRIST as opposed to who we are with one another.
- I'm not going to always agree with you, but I will never try to force my opinion on you either. Please return to me the very same respect.
- I am going to read my Bible every day and seek to get to know the LORD better and better. If you are not doing the same, it goes without saying that one day I will outgrow you and this friendship. Please understand that I will not reject my growth or my seasons of change to be your friend, or anyone else's friend, for that matter.
- I am loyal to GOD only, but I will be a friend who sticks closer than a brother to you, as long as GOD permits.
- My desire is to be your friend until we leave this earth, but GOD'S plan may be totally different.
- If watching me elevate bothers you, please disassociate from me, because I pray to GOD to humble my enemies. Don't put yourself in harm's way becoming a secret enemy.
- I will celebrate your elevation and encourage you to

go as far as you can in the LORD.

- Whenever I start to get under your skin, it is better to speak with me than of me. Remember, I cancel words every day, and I pray for the humbling of my enemies.
- Envy and jealousy are both spirits that love to enter women. If I ever detect a trace of either on you, or you are to detect it on me, we have to sit down and talk about it. If you deny it's there, even though I can see it, I have to walk away from the friendship, and I expect you to do the same should you see it on me, and I refuse to acknowledge it. Let's always pray together against those strongholds.

Please understand that not everyone will receive those statements. As a matter of fact, the majority of people will not. At the same time, those who will not receive it don't have staying power anyhow, but they will have enough power to keep you from entering GOD'S will if you give it to them. Only a mature woman of GOD will truly understand those statements and know that this means you are offering them a lifetime of friendship should they stay in the will of GOD. You are offering them a true and loving sisterhood where gossip, slander, envy, jealousy and wrongful thinking are not allowed. Friendships where a mutual respect is established are often friendships that survive the tests of time. Friendships based on people you collectively don't like, or being able to relate to one another because of a negative experience, often don't last because they are

founded on the wrong things. Friendships based on your
love for GOD or your collective desire to do the will of GOD
are oftentimes friendships that turn into sisterhoods. All the
same, please know that GOD will oftentimes warn you about
your friends through your dreams and just by speaking to
your heart. If you shut HIS voice out, you have no right to
complain when what HE said manifests to you. Be more
willing to level up in the will of GOD than you are to stay
down in the will of man. Remember, you are passing
through each realm you enter to get to the next one until you
arrive at the whole will of GOD for your life. If the enemy can
send a friendly hindrance to slow you down or stop you from
arriving, he will. But don't mistake someone being friendly
for someone who actually is your friend. The devil is patient
enough to send one of his own to act as a friend for
decades, while looking for the perfect moment to bring you
down. At the same time, he doesn't have to bring you down.
He can simply hinder you, and this is enough to wet his
palate. Love never fails; it has no time restrictions, and
distance only makes the two of you closer. Yokes, on the
other hand, show their true nature when their limitations are
crossed.

And Suddenly

"Oftentimes, we wait on GOD to change our situations gradually, but if you've lived long enough to witness the unpredictable behaviors of the weather, you should know that GOD is not always predictable."

Sometimes, the seasons of change come our way, but the weather looks threatening. If you're accustomed to living in a certain climate in your life, any other climate is one that you'll avoid. But in order to embrace the will of GOD, you have to be willing to step outside of what you know to embrace your sudden change.

Most people think that change comes gradually, and because of this, most people miss their opportunities to enter a new realm of thinking and a new way of living. At the same time, the average person avoids new open doors because they are comfortable with all the closed doors around them. But when you embrace the will of GOD, you have to be ready to make some sudden decisions in order to embrace your "and suddenly." Everything you have been praying for is on the other side of what you do not know. It's all locked up in the unfamiliar, but it takes a peculiar GOD to remove everything that's familiar to you to make you more like HIM. It is then that you can embrace the peculiar creature that HE created you to be, and then you can access new knowledge, new wisdom and new understanding. With those treasures come a new way of thinking, a new perception and a new life. Are you ready to embrace your "and suddenly?"

Lisa and Janice had been friends for almost seventeen years. Like most friendships, they have weathered their share of ups and downs, but for the most part, they were there for one another through thick and thin. Lisa was 35 years old, a brunette and a divorced mother of two children. She was tall, slender and easy on the eyes. With deep gray eyes and winter-pink lips, she was considered a fairly attractive woman.

Janice stood at five feet, seven inches tall, just a little shorter than Lisa. She was somewhat stout, but not in a bad way. Janice was very curvaceous, and she loved to show off her curves. Janice was 34 years old, and she was also a brunette. Janice had never been married, but she had three children and a live-in boyfriend that she referred to as Buck. Even though Janice could be considered attractive, it was hard for anyone to call her attractive because of her loud mouth and lack of tact. She didn't care what she said or whom she said it to.

Both Lisa and Janice were new to the church scene. Lisa

had been going to church for a little more than a year and had recently been baptized. She'd convinced Janice to start frequenting church with her, but she had yet to convince her to leave the bar scene behind. Lisa desired to please the LORD with all of her heart, and this is what led to her divorce. When she'd rededicated her life to CHRIST, her husband began to test her faith because he did not like her new-found love interest in the LORD. He would push her buttons again and again trying to make her curse, so he could convince her that she was not a real Christian. He would try to stop her from going to church on Sundays by leaving the house in their only vehicle. To his disappointment, Lisa would often catch the bus to go to church. Finally, one day he'd made his demands known. He told her to choose between him and the church. He claimed to believe that Lisa's church was a cult, and he plastered defamatory banners around the city claiming that the church was a cult. That was it. Lisa finally filed for divorce, got a restraining order on Richard (her husband), took their kids and left. Not long after the divorce was finalized, Richard moved to Seattle, Washington, where he was said to have met and married an Atheist. He cut off all communications with his children, and Lisa decided not to pursue him for the past due child support because she wanted him to stay out of their lives.

Lisa worked as a nurse at a local hospital and had recently been accepted into medical school. Lisa wanted to become an obstetrician, and her dream was finally peeking through the clouds. Janice worked at a call center where she took orders for cell phone service. Even though their lives had gone in separate directions, they felt like they could not function without one another.

One day while out for her evening jog, Lisa received a phone call that would change her life. The man on the other end told her that Janice had been in a car accident, and she'd lapsed into a coma. Lisa ran home as fast as she could, grabbed her keys, jumped into her car and raced towards the hospital. She didn't think to call anyone. She was concerned about her friend, and she couldn't stop crying as she zoomed through traffic.

Within seven minutes, Lisa had arrived at the hospital that she worked at, and she rushed to the front desk. "Janice Petri's room, please." Her voice was low, but panicked. The front desk clerk handed her a pass to room 348. Why was she giving her a pass to room 348? After all, Janice was allegedly in a coma; therefore, she was supposed to be in the Intensive Care Unit. With no time to ask questions, Lisa rushed towards the closing elevator and threw her body between it. One of the doors hit her elbow as it closed. The pain was sharp and intense, but there was no time to concentrate on that pain. Janice needed her, and she wanted to be focused.

The elevator door opened on the second floor to let a few more people in. Lisa's frustration could be seen on her face, but she didn't say a word. Rubbing her elbow, she moved towards the side to let the crowd in. Once they'd reached the third floor, Lisa and three other individuals exited the elevator. "Excuse me," Lisa said as she ran past one man. When she arrived at room 348, an uneasy feeling came over her. What was she about to see? Even thought she'd seen some of the most beat-up people before, she was not prepared to see her best friend in a comatose state. She braced herself as she opened the door, but was shocked by what she saw. Janice was sitting up on the bed holding her youngest daughter, three-year-old Alessandra. The other two children, (five-year-old Alex and one-year-old Kenneth) were seated side-by-side watching cartoons. They seemed agitated at the door opening; nonetheless, they kept quiet and politely greeted Lisa.

With tears in her eyes, Lisa hugged her friend who was now sitting up.

Lisa: Oh, Janice! They told me that you were in a coma.
Janice: No, baby. It was just a slight accident. I ran into a tree, and they are just keeping me here for observation since the car was pretty banged up. Who told you I was in a coma?
Lisa lifted up her cell phone to go through her call log.
Lisa: The call came from your house, but I don't know who it was. It didn't sound like Buck, but it could have been him, now that I think about it.
Janice: It was probably him or his brother. You know his brother Jed is in town this week. That's why he said he

couldn't make it to the hospital. He'd promised to take Jed out on the town.

Lisa: Yeah, but that's crazy. You need him more than Jed needs him right now.

Janice: Girl, that's just men for you. My injuries aren't serious, so I'll give him a pass this time. I had my brother to drop my other car off here, so I'm fine.

Lisa: I still don't understand why he told me you were in a coma. That was cruel. I almost had like ten accidents trying to get here.

Janice: Aw, sisterly hug. You love me, don't you? I feel bad that they scared you, but I feel loved all at the same time. *Laughs.* You know they are probably drunk right now, so you can't trust a word that comes out of their mouths.

Lisa: Yeah, you always knew how to pick em'.

Janice: I know you're not talking. That ex-husband of yours wasn't the pick of the litter either. I remember when the two of you let me live in your house, and all he talked about was starting his own strip club. He even asked me if I would be interested in dancing.

Lisa: He asked you that? Why didn't you tell me?

Janice: *Waves hand.* Oh, girl, I didn't take him seriously. Besides, that was such a small incident that could have been blown out of proportion, and I would've ended up on the street. He never said anything crazy like that again, but my point is, he was scum.

Lisa: Okay, you win.

Janice: Don't I always win?

Lisa: Whatever. How are you feeling?

Janice: Just a little sore, but I'll survive. The doctor said he'll likely release me in an hour or so.

With that, the phone rang and Lisa answered it.
Lisa: Janice's room.
Buck: Hey, is this Lisa?
Lisa: Yeah. Hey, Buck. How are you?
Buck: I'm good. Just a little hungry, that's all. Let me talk with Janice.
Lisa: Okay, hold on.
Lisa hands Janice the phone.
Janice: Good evening, babes.
Buck: Hey baby. How are you feeling?
Janice: I'm okay. I'm just a little sore. The doctor said he'll probably release me in an hour or so.
Buck: Great, because Jed and I are so hungry. Will you stop by McDonald's and get us the usual?
Janice: Buck, I am in the hospital. You can't get up and get it yourself? What's wrong with your pick-up truck?
Buck: Baby, Jed and I are great candidates for DUIs right now. Ask Lisa if she'll do it.
Janice: No. I'll stop by McDonald's on the way home. What does Jed want?
Buck: The usual. He gets the same thing that I get: the number four, large with a sweet tea.
Janice: Okay. Bye. I gotta go.

As Janice turned her head, she could feel the disappointing glares of Lisa. Breaking a smile, she turned to look at her friend. "You can't be serious," said Lisa. "He wants you to leave the hospital and bring him and his drunk brother something to eat?" Janice smiled and looked at Lisa. "Okay, you win," she said.

Not long after the call, Janice was released from the hospital, and Lisa followed her to make sure she arrived home safely. She'd followed her to McDonald's and then to the house. Lisa had never met Buck's brother before, and judging by the sound of him, she wanted nothing to do with him. When they arrived at Janice's house, Janice motioned for Lisa to get out of the car and visit them for a while, but Lisa wasn't up for it. "Just ten minutes!" yelled Janice. "Just come in and sit down for ten minutes....please!" Reluctantly, Lisa exited her vehicle and followed Janice into the house. The children still seemed somewhat angry, but their attitudes weren't alarming, considering that they did not like Buck.

The house reeked of cigarette smoke and what smelled like old, wet furniture. The noise from the television set was extremely loud, but a piercing sound made its way through to Lisa's ears. It sounded like the mating call of a dying horse. Startled, Lisa spun around in the direction of the sound only to find Jed (Buck's brother) standing behind her gawking at her. Jed was tall with blonde hair and ocean blue eyes. His bad hair cut looked as if it had been the result of a lost bet. His plaid shirt was open, revealing a chiseled body, but his odor somehow overrode the other awful smells in the air. He was somewhat handsome, but obviously, he was not the type of man most women would want on their arm. He looked as if he'd once been the pretty bad-boy of his school, but somehow, life had retired some of his boyish features and now, his only claim to beauty was his deep blue eyes and almost perfect smile. "I need you in my life," said Jed. Lisa could not hear what he'd said, so he extended his arm towards the television, revealing that he was holding the remote control. He turned off the television and softly repeated his words. "I need you...in my life. You're definitely the one, so let's just cut to the chase, go on to the courthouse and get married. We've got our whole lives to get to know each other." Jed's breath revealed that not only was he responsible for the stench of smoke that had consumed the oxygen in the house, but it also revealed that Jed had either eaten a decomposing animal, or he didn't believe in daily hygiene. "No, thank you," said Lisa. "But it's nice to meet you." As Lisa was speaking, Janice re-entered the living room.

Janice: What are you two talking about? *Janice's smile revealed her inner thoughts.*
Jed: I was just here proposing to my future wife, but apparently she needs more time.
Janice: *Laughs.* Let me formally introduce you to her then. Lisa, this is Buck's brother, Jed; and Jed, this is Lisa, my best friend.
Lisa: Nice to meet you, Jed.
Jed: I told you...let's cut past all of the formalities and go straight to the courthouse. How many kids do you want, and

what's your favorite color? Oh and what's your current last name? I can't wait to change it.

Lisa smiled shyly, but she was irritated by Jed's persistent and unwanted flirting. He was definitely Buck's brother, and his future looked as dark as the cavity sitting on his left canine. Janice wrapped her arm around Lisa and started pulling her towards the kitchen. "Jed, leave her alone. You don't want to scare her away, now do you?" Janice's voice sounded joyful and in control. Jed smiled and removed the lollipop from his mouth. He glared at Lisa before responding. "Okay. Since I've just met you, I'll try not to be so forward. I'll give you an hour or so to accept my proposal, and then we can decide which courthouse we want to get married in. Let me go and eat before Buck eats up my fries. Nice to meet you, Mrs. Wright." Without warning, he grabbed Lisa's hand and kissed it before making a dramatic exit towards Buck and Janice's bedroom.

Lisa: Ew. I think I need to take a rabies shot.
Janice: *Laughs.* He's not so bad, and I've never seen him act like that before. He must really like you. I think I hear wedding bells.
Lisa: That must be the anesthesia kicking in. You know that anyone related to Buck needs to be caged and possibly put down if it attempts to breed with anyone.
Janice: He's not bad, Lisa. Just give him a chance. I actually think the two of you would make a great couple. Then, we could be sisters for real.

Lisa: Janice, when have you known me to like rednecks? I am a woman of GOD, and I take hygiene very seriously. Let's not forget that I have two children to look out for, and I'm in medical school. Jed is the type of guy you'd find living in someone's trailer, always drunk and beating on his pregnant girlfriends. No, thank you.

Janice: Aw, come on Lisa. Don't be so stuck up. By the way, Jed owns his own trailer. Their sister died and left it to him, so he's no longer living with anyone. He's a great guy, and I'm actually excited at the thought of the two of you being together. It all makes sense to me.

Lisa: Have you forgotten about my current love interest?

Janice: Who? The med-school student? What's his name again? Brussel Sprouts?

Lisa: *Laughs.* No. His name is Russell Scott, and he's not a bad guy. I actually really like him. We've been on eight dates so far, and everything is looking up. He loves GOD and I love GOD. He's divorced with two children, and so am I. He wants to remarry and have two more children, and that's what I want, so we're pretty in tune with one another.

Janice: No, Lisa. We talked about this before. Russell sounds like one of those snooty, egotistical guys who say things like, "Darling, a little help please. It appears that I have managed to acquire hemorrhoids again from being so uptight. Could you do me the honor of tucking me in, shall I say?"

Lisa: *Laughs.* No, Janice. He's nothing like that. Really. He's down-to-earth, loving, considerate and best of all, GOD-fearing. He's co-Pastor at the church he attends, and he loves children. What more can I ask for?

Janice: Maybe a man without hemorrhoids.

Lisa: *Laughs.* He doesn't have hemorrhoids, and he's not uptight. Anyhow, why would you prefer for me to have a man like Jed, who likely does not have a job over a GOD-fearing medical school student who knows how to address me like a woman? Does Jed work? I can guarantee you he's unemployed. Does he work, Janice?

Janice: I just get this feeling that you and Jed would be perfect together. He's not currently employed; he's between jobs right now, but he's looking for work.

Lisa: *Interrupts.* How long has he been looking for work, and tell the truth?

Janice: Well, he's been unemployed for three years now because he hurt his back on his last job.

Lisa: Three years, Janice? That's not between jobs; that means he just doesn't work...period. Whenever he does work, he's simply between unemployment checks.

Janice: You have always been so judgmental. I just don't want to see you end up back in divorce court; that's all. Brussel Sprouts sounds like one of those guys built for divorce court. The type who falls in love easily, gets married, has children and then leaves his wife for his secretary. Why did he divorce the first one? What was his mistress's name?

Lisa: There was no mistress that I know of. His wife was from Russia, and she wanted to return to her homeland. Russell didn't want to go so she abandoned him and the kids. He said he waited two years hoping she would change her mind, but one day she filed for divorce. During the divorce proceedings, he learned that she was six months pregnant by some Russian guy. She doesn't even call her own children. What kind of mother does that?

Janice: Yeah, that's his side of the story. I still say that Jed is a better match for you.

Lisa: And I still say you're wrong, and you know it. Anyhow, I need to leave before Jed's timer goes off. He looks like one of those guys who'd throw you in the trunk of a car and drive you straight to the courthouse. I don't need those kinds of problems. *Laughs.*

Janice: Yeah. Whatever. Call me when you get home.

Lisa: Okay. I will. See you later.

Janice: *Rolls eyes.* Bye.

Lisa went to her car, and as she was starting the engine, she heard Jed's loud and unmistakable roar. He actually sounded like a dying horse. Standing in the doorway of their home, Jed screamed out to Lisa as Buck stood by him laughing. "Baby, don't leave me! I'm sorry! We can move the wedding date back a little bit until you get over this cold feet thing you've got going! Baby, please!" Lisa drove away, and she could see Buck in the rear-view mirror on the ground and laughing. Jed then chased the car for a short distance before falling to his knees and yelling something at the car.

Later on that evening, Lisa's boyfriend called. He was going to Wednesday night Bible study at his church, and he wanted Lisa to accompany him, so she could meet his

Pastor. He really felt like Lisa was the wife GOD had
ordained for him, and he hoped that his Pastor could confirm
what he already believed. Lisa agreed to accompany him,
but she insisted that she drive her own car. After all, she
wanted to remain celibate and wanted to avoid any situation
that could cause her to compromise her faith walk. Russell
was also celibate and agreed to meet Lisa at the church.

After hanging up the phone line, Lisa received a call from
Janice, and Janice seemed a little upset.

Lisa: Hello.
Janice: Are you busy?
Lisa: Yeah, studying for Mrs. Brumfield's class. After spring
break, she's likely going to give us a pop quiz, so I want to
be ready. After that, I'm leaving in about an hour to meet
with Russell at his church.
Janice: Ugh! If I hear that man's name again, I'm going to
puke brussel sprouts. Well, tell Russell that he'll have to
take you to church another day. I need to get out of this
house tonight. Buck is drunk again, and he punched me
because he claimed I was flirting with Jed.
Lisa: Wow. Janice, did you call the police?
Janice: No, he's drunk, so I don't want him to be arrested.
I'll just give him a little time to cool off and sober up.
Lisa: Janice, you need to be resting. Your body hasn't even
settled yet from the accident, and you really need to leave
Buck before he goes too far.
Janice: Lisa, hold your horses. He's just drunk. He won't

even remember hitting me tomorrow. Anyhow, I can pick you up or you can pick me up. Do you want to just pick me up? There's a bar over on 12th Street that I want to hit.

Lisa: I told you that I'm going out with Russell, and you know I don't do bars anymore. Who's going to watch your kids, anyway? You can't just leave them there with Buck and his drunk brother.

Janice: The kids are asleep; he won't bother them. Where are your kids?

Lisa: At my mom's house. It's spring break for them, so she asked to keep them during the break. Remember?

Janice: Oh, yeah. We should all be so lucky. Wait. You're dissing me for Brussel Sprouts? You're turning your back on me at a time when I need you the most?

Lisa: How many times have I told you to save your dramatics for the theater? You don't need me, Janice. You need to leave Buck, but if you're not willing to help yourself, there's nothing I can do for you but pray.

Janice: Save your prayers for someone who needs them, like yourself. Lisa, I was there for you when your ex-husband hit you. I was there for you when he tried to have you arrested. I was there for you when you needed me, but now that I need you, you are turning me away for a man? Don't come calling me when he beats you and leaves you for the babysitter!

Lisa: Janice, I can't believe how selfish you are sometimes. Look at how many times I have been there for you, even when Buck gave you two; not one, but two black eyes! But I don't keep records because that's what friends do; we are there for one another when we need help! You don't need help because you are still there. I was separated from my husband when he hit me. Get over yourself and stop trying to make me feel bad for even wanting a bright future.

Janice: Lisa, it's as simple as this. Either you spend time with me tonight, or we can call this friendship off. I'm tired of you acting snobbish and selfish, thinking that you're now some big shot because you're in medical school. So, what's it going to be...me or Brussel Sprouts? Choose wisely, girlfriend, because you're going to need me.

Lisa: I can't believe you're saying this to me. So, let me get this straight one more time. When I wanted to become a nurse, you were against it? You told me that paying back all of those student loans would eat my paycheck alive! When I wanted to go to medical school, you were against it. As a matter of fact, when I got accepted into medical school, you didn't take any of my calls for two weeks! How silly of me?! Then, you try to match me up with a godless redneck with no aspirations for the future except making children and teaching them how to fire guns and smash beer cans on their heads. Now, you're saying that I need to end my date, or even possibly my relationship with Russell because your pathetic boyfriend has hit you again? Then you add an ultimatum on top of it?

Janice: It's simple. You're either with me or against me. I told you that it's not going to work between you and Russell anyway, so why waste your time? Buck's a good man. He's not perfect, but he's good to me and my children. He's just had one too many drinks tonight, but that pain doesn't

compare to the pain and anger I feel now knowing my best friend of seventeen years has gone coo-coo over some med-school idiot. Now, I'm supposed to come second to him? That's okay, Lisa! Now I know where I stand.
Janice hung up the line.

Lisa was heartbroken. Seventeen years of friendship ended just like that? She looked at the clock and realized that she had fifteen minutes to get to the church. She could either call and cancel her date with Russell and go hang out with Janice, or she could go to church with Russell, knowing full well that her friendship with Janice was likely finished. She sobbed as she picked up the phone to call Russell to apologize to him. She had to change her plans because of Janice. Russell understood, but he could hear something was wrong. "If you can, please come by the church. I hope you feel better," he said. He didn't press her for information; however, because he knew she would tell him later, and he believed that she would come to the church. He was sure of it.

Lisa began going through her apartment and looking at all of the things that Janice gave her. She looked at the pictures of her and Janice together, and she cried all the more. She then called Janice back but was immediately taken to the voice mail, where she left the following message: "Hey. I was thinking about what you said, and you are right. You were there for me during some pretty rough times in my life, just like I was there for you during some rough times in your life. Maybe that's just it. Maybe GOD placed us together to help one another in those times, but I believe our season as friends has ended. Janice, I love you, but I have to continue to move forward. I will be boxing up everything you have given to me, including our photos, and I will rid my apartment of them. If you want them, let me know and I'll meet you somewhere to give them to you. I'm sorry and I love you." Lisa hung up the line feeling heavy-hearted. She'd just ended a friendship of seventeen years, but she knew it had to be done.

After she hung up the line, Lisa went and took a quick shower. She cried and let the water from the shower wash her tears away. She began to speak aloud to herself. "This had to be done. I loved her, but this had to be done. How can two walk together except they be agreed? We don't agree anymore. I've changed, and I can't go back to the old me to maintain that friendship. I didn't do anything wrong. I have to move forward in CHRIST." After her pep talk, Lisa felt a little better. She quickly dressed and rushed up to the church.

Lisa arrived at the church twenty minutes after Bible study started. Nervous, she paced herself as she walked towards the well-lit church. She'd planned to quietly slip in and try to make her way to Russell, but that didn't go as planned. Instead, she walked in while Russell was up conducting the Bible study. Russell suddenly stopped teaching and smiled. He motioned for Lisa to come to the front of the church, but she stood in front of the doors frozen. She gestured no with her head, and quietly mouthed no to Russell. Russell spoke into the microphone and said, "Okay. You made me do it. Kali, that girl's single. Can you help me get her?" Kali was a six-year-old gorgeous little girl who was always trying to pair singles up in the church. Her little smug face made her all the cuter. Kali sighed and then got up from her seat as she exclaimed, "My work is never done." She made her way to Lisa, who by now had turned red from the humiliation. With her little hand, she grabbed Lisa's hand and started walking her towards the front of the church. As she marched Lisa to the front, she gave the cutest little speech with a straight face; nevertheless, she did not look at Lisa. She said, "You're beautiful, but you're not getting any younger. He's a single man; you're a single girl, so what's the problem?" This was a speech that she'd given everyone she tried to pair up. She'd actually successfully paired up two couples in the church, but everyone else just went along with her attempts because she was so cute and innocent.

When she finally got Lisa to the front of the church, she turned to look at Lisa. "What do you say?" she asked. Lisa was puzzled. What did she mean? Kali repeated herself. "What do you say to the little girl who helped you?" She crossed her arms as she awaited Lisa's response. "Um, thank you," said Lisa. "No," replied Kali. "You're supposed to say, 'GOD bless you.' I can't live off thank yous, but one can never get too many blessings." Lisa was astonished. Who'd taught this little girl to speak so well? "GOD bless you," replied Lisa. "May HE continue to bless you and give you all of the desires of your heart." At that, Kali smiled and returned to her seat. The laughter in the church began to die down as one of the Ushers showed Lisa to a seat in the front, not too far from Russell.

Russell continued giving the Bible study, and when service was over, he introduced a few of the church members to Lisa. "She's pretty, Pastor," said a woman wearing an awfully big hat and some really flashy clothes. "I could give her some fashion tips, though, but she's pretty." Russell thanked the woman who he referred to as Ms. Heidi, but declined her request. Russell's Pastor walked up and said, "Russell, is this the girl you were telling me about?" With Russell's affirmation, his Pastor then went on to say, "She's very pretty, but more than that, I can see that she's blessed of GOD. She's very favored of GOD. I think she's it, my man. Good job." He patted Russell on the back before walking away. Russell smiled big, but Lisa was confused. "What just happened here?" she asked. Russell smiled at Lisa and then looked towards the congregation. He nodded his head, and everyone stood up. Lisa turned around and she could see all of the smiling faces. Some of the people were crying and wiping away their tears. Confused, she turned to look back at Russell. Suddenly, more choir members came out of nowhere and entered the stands. Music began to play and the choir started singing.

Choir: No matter where you go. No matter what you do.

Just stay right there with GOD, and He'll always be with you.
You're just one breath away from changing your whole life..
Just answer this one question.....
Russell then sings the last line, "Will you be my wife?"
And suddenly, Lisa's tears began to fall.....
And suddenly, she realized that she had been tested. She
lost an enemy to gain a friend for life in her husband....
And suddenly, Russell was holding a beautiful marquise
diamond cut ring.
And suddenly, she said yes. Lisa couldn't believe it, but she
opened her mouth and said yes. Her heart was in
agreement, her soul was in agreement, and she knew GOD
was in agreement.
And suddenly, the choir began to sing again, and the lyrics
were even more surprising than the first ones.
Choir: No matter where you go. No matter what you do.
Just stay right there with GOD, and He'll always be with you.
You're just one breath away, and all you'll have to say
is that you'll marry him, and you'll marry him today....

"What?" Lisa was shocked. She covered her mouth and
looked back at Russell, who now had tears in his eyes.
"GOD never said we had to wait years to get married. Once
HE confirms it, all we have to do is affirm it. Will you marry
me today?" Lisa stood there frozen, and suddenly, the
church doors opened. Her mother and her children, along
with her closest family members all entered the church. Lisa
could barely catch her breath. She cried and finally spoke to
Russell. "Yes," she said. "I'll marry you today." After she

spoke those words, she was suddenly taken by the hand by two women who led her towards the back of the church. Her mother and children got up to follow them. She watched as Russell waved to her, and he was suddenly surrounded by men.

And suddenly, she was sitting in a chair, getting her hair done beautifully.

And suddenly, a gown that she'd admired for years was laid before her. Her mother knew what gown she'd wanted, so she'd relayed the information to Russell.

And suddenly, Lisa found herself wearing a beautiful wedding gown, dazzling diamond earrings and some of the cutest shoes she'd ever seen. Her makeup was done to perfection, but she kept crying, so the cosmetologist had to keep powdering her face.

And suddenly, she looked so beautiful as she stood up, ready to exit the room.

And suddenly, she found herself being photographed by some of the town's most renowned photographers.

And suddenly, another breathtaking moment almost made her ruin her makeup. Her older sister, whom she hadn't seen in five years, came out dressed in a teal green dress. She was followed by six other women who were all friends and relatives of Lisa, all except one girl who turned out to be Russell's baby sister. Lisa hugged her sister and cried as she was told by her sister that she was standing in as her matron of honor.

And suddenly, Lisa was taken back to the entrance doors and the music began to play. She was so overwhelmed with joy and surprise that she felt weightless.

And suddenly, a man came to the door and interlocked his arm with hers. Lisa looked up to see her father standing there. Her dad was in the military, and Lisa hadn't seen him in two years. Overcome with love and emotion, Lisa began to sob and hold her dad. Her cosmetologist stood next to them waiting to refresh her once again before they made the grand entrance. It took Lisa five minutes to regain her posture, and it took the cosmetologist another five minutes to refresh her makeup.

And suddenly, they entered the doors of the sanctuary, and there stood Russell. He was looking so handsome that he almost looked angelic. Was this all for real, or was it just a dream? Instead of the traditional wedding music playing, the choir got up and began to hum beautifully. They sounded like a perfect melody of heaven's angels. When Lisa arrived at the altar, Russell interlocked his arm with hers. She still couldn't believe it. She was marrying a man better than the man of her dreams.

And suddenly, Lisa and Russell turned to face one another to exchange vows.

And suddenly, Lisa opened her mouth and whispered to Russell, "Pinch me. I think I'm dreaming." Not realizing that the microphone was sensitive, Lisa was humiliated when the church erupted in laughter.

The wedding was dreamy, and Lisa left church that night a married woman. As she entered the limousine, Lisa began to think. It was all beginning to make sense. That's why her mother insisted on keeping the children for spring break. But what was up with Janice? Knowing her thoughts, her mother said, "We didn't tell Janice. We all believed she would try to sabotage the wedding. I hope you're not mad at us." They didn't know the events that had transpired earlier that day. "No, not at all," said Lisa. Thank you for loving me this much. I will never forget this day. At that, her mother and father both kissed her before she entered the limousine and was taken away to the airport. The next day, Russell and Lisa flew to Paris for their honeymoon.

When news got back to Janice, she tried to ruin Lisa's life. She called Lisa's phone repeatedly and left threatening voice mails until Lisa changed her number. She went to Lisa's apartment one night with the intention of spray painting her car, but she found out that Lisa had moved, and she didn't know where she'd moved to. She went by Lisa's job, with the intention of fighting her, but she learned that Lisa had quit and they didn't have any forwarding information on her. Another day, she went to the one place she knew she could find Lisa. Of course, this was after spring break, and Janice decided to get dressed and go to Lisa's school to possibly get her expelled. She'd planned to pick a fight with her in hopes of harming her and getting her kicked out of school, but her plans were thwarted when Sheriff's deputies, along with the SWAT team, came to her house early that morning and kicked her door in. Buck and Jed had been selling drugs from that house, and Janice had been growing marijuana in her back yard. They found enough drugs to put Lisa away for eight years, and both Jed and Buck got eleven

years.
The End.

What just happened here? It's not uncommon for women to attempt to enter new seasons with old friends. Lisa wasn't elevating because she was studying to become a doctor; Lisa was elevating because she was studying the WORD of GOD. Her promotion in the natural represented her spiritual promotion. When Lisa was granted access to a new dimension, she had to make a choice. After all, she could not enter this new dimension with Janice in tow. She had to let go of that friendship or stay where she was to entertain that friendship. Sadly enough, the majority of women who reach the doors of change refuse to enter them because of what and who they are leaving behind. Do we not understand that to please man, we must first disappoint GOD? We were created to worship HIM and glorify HIS Name in all that we do; nevertheless, most women lose their identities in their friendships and relationships. It's easy to forget who you are when you're pretending to be who you are not, or when you don't know your identity. At the same time, our true identities are revealed to us in layers of faith. The more we know GOD, the more we believe HIM. The more we believe HIM, the more we learn who we really are in HIM. Sure, the world gave us an identity, and we've all tried to be the best fool that we could be for the sake of our worldly identities. Now that we are in CHRIST, we have a whole new identity, and here's the thing: Once you begin to discover who you are, you can't go back to being who you were. At some point, we have to take off the costumes and just wear ourselves as we are.

I remember going through transition, and suddenly realizing that I had closed off so many areas of my heart to GOD. But HE can still see them, so what was the purpose of me hiding them? I was trying to pretend that those blemishes didn't exist because if I acknowledged that they were there, I would have to go through deliverance to get rid of them. If you've ever been through any form of deliverance, you would know the pain associated with letting go of mindsets you're accustomed to. I was fighting generational strongholds and thinking patterns that I'd picked up during my hurt seasons in life. I was always open in my season of joy, but I was covered up with all types of armor during questionable times. I wasn't wearing the full armor of GOD, however. I told myself that I was. I studied the book of Ephesians 6 over and over again until I could quote it verbatim. As GOD opened my eyes, I learned I was wearing the breastplate of righteousness sometimes, but I'd take it off when my flesh wanted to handle a matter. I wore the belt of truth...sometimes, but I took it off and tried to beat my situations into submission with it. I wore the shield of faith...sometimes, but all the enemy had to do was turn the temperature up on my situations, and I'd take that shield off and try to handle matters on my own. And the gospel of peace? I left that behind plenty of times, especially those times when my husband stepped on my feet. He knew my peace's on and off buttons, and he liked to play with them both to study my reactions. But I had to learn to be consistent with right-doing and truly put away my flesh's deeds. I couldn't wear faith one day, and then wear fear the next day. I had to choose between doing the will of GOD and doing the will of the enemy. To enter into the next level, I had to make some hard decisions. I had to let go of the friendships I was accustomed to. I found myself crying so much as I watched people display photos of themselves out having a blast with their friends. There was a time when I would emotionally enter new friendships and bless GOD for the women. Then, the truth would come between us. I did not enter a realm to stay there; GOD was taking me forward in HIM, and I had an assignment to fulfill. I had to go through the hurts of watching those friendships end when my friends would get upset when I chose to do the will of GOD over doing their will.

Ask all of your friends what their definition of a friendship is, and what are the requirements to be their friends. Ask them what a friend is not supposed to do, and what you'll discover is that every woman has her own definition of a friend. Pay attention to yourself with each one of them. You'll likely find that you have been trying to fit into their mental mold of what a friend is and what a friend does, thus denying GOD the privilege of opening new doors to you. You'll likely discover that you are different around each woman. With one, you're more worldly; with another, you're more spiritual. With some of your friends, you are just yourself, and with others, you wear a mask. The average person would claim that they are

themselves with everyone, but I challenge you to pay
attention to yourself, and stop hiding your blemishes from
yourself. After all, GOD sees what you refuse to look at. If
you fell down and bruised your left knee, the pain wouldn't
go away just because you refuse to look at the bruise.
Instead, you may end up causing it to get infected because
you didn't see that debris in those wounds that needed to be
removed.

Janice was a typical crab in the bucket. She could have
remained Lisa's friend for life as long as Lisa stayed behind
with her. Why do you think she wanted Lisa to get with Jed?
She did not want Lisa to do better than she was doing. She
wanted her to do as bad as or worse than she was doing. In
doing so, they would remain friends. It's amazing how many
people will celebrate a lost soul because they refused to
enter the door of change when GOD opened it for them.

*"Enter ye in at the strait gate: for wide is the gate, and broad
is the way, that leadeth to destruction, and many there be
which go in thereat. Because strait is the gate, and narrow
is the way, which leadeth unto life, and few there be that find
it "* (Matthew 7:13-14).
The path to destruction and the path to everlasting life aren't
just shown to you when you die; you are actually walking on
one of those paths right now. The gate that leads to
destruction is one that the world travels, and you will find the
majority of people walking on that path....even people who
are in the church. The path that leads to everlasting life is

one that few people walk on because it's not a popular path. It is a lonely place, but you won't be alone. It is a place where you won't be surrounded by tons of friends, but the friends who are around you are quality because they are heading up the same path as you. And even then, they may have times when their straight paths fork off in a different direction than yours because of what they are called to do; nevertheless, there will be no love lost. Mature and Godly friends understand that when the seasons of separation are upon them, it's not personal; it's spiritual. Because of this, you will remain friends and continue to pray for one another.

How many doors have you rejected trying to hold on to those friendships, relationships and partnerships that GOD has been trying to call you away from? How many times have you convinced yourself that the Christian thing to do was continue on with your friends, even when they weren't acting Christ-like? How many times have you stayed in a bad friendship or relationship because you were counting all the good things that person or those people did for you, but you forgot to consider what they'd done to you? There are so many women who would be married right now to their GOD-ordained husbands had it not been for a friendship they were entertaining. There are so many women who would be living it up in their wealthy places right now, but the door of wealth had to be closed to them because they were trying to bring people in whom GOD had not given permission to enter. We all want to be somebody's blessing until we realize that we're playing GOD, and this behavior is not Godly. Instead, we have to be lights that lead others to CHRIST. How many doors will you be accused of shutting because you thought you were here to have fun, so you surrounded yourself with fun people who had no direction? How many doors have you closed because you refused to leave a church that GOD has told you to leave over and over again?

Do you know what helped me to get over my lonely stages? It was realizing that GOD was with me the whole time, and HE wanted to spend time with me. It was when I realized that I was rejecting my future trying to hold on to my past. I remember ending a friendship because it had begun to get too testy for me. My friend was becoming too argumentative towards me for no good reason. I then thought of my future with her. I could be that friend who ended up being someone's dish rag, or I could dust myself off and be who GOD called me to be. I could stay behind and argue with her time and time again, or I could go ahead and enter the narrow path where my destiny awaited me. I could be a "true friend," but I chose to be a daughter of the MOST HIGH. When I ended the friendship, I was suddenly promoted, and GOD began to give me new and successful businesses. I was so surprised, but I truly learned a lesson then: Let go, and you'll be elevated. Hold on, and you'll be anchored down. After that lesson, I had no problem letting go of anyone who stood in the way of who I am now or who I am to be. I would meet women who would quickly call me their best friends, but in less than three to six months, we had gone our separate directions. Why is that? When I saw the ankle bracelets, the shackles and the handcuffs they called friendships, I made a break for it. Some women are offended when you are elevated. They'll say you need to be humbled, when they are really saying you need to be "brought down" to their level. Some women are offended when you say "no" to them. After all, in their worlds, your opinion is only counted when it matches their opinion. Every once in a while, they may change their mind and agree with what you've said because they want you to believe that you have a voice in that friendship. Some women are offended when you don't agree with them, even when they know they are wrong. Some women are offended when you don't answer your phone or call them back in a certain amount of time. Some women are offended if you choose to speak with your other friends over them. Believe me, I've met them all, and more than likely, you have too. But you can't get to your "and suddenly" when you are constantly going in reverse. You keep going back to old mindsets to entertain the people who still have them. Yes, it does feel comfortable to re-enter those mindsets; after all, you used to live there. Yes, it does feel peaceful to reconnect with people you used to be connected with, but you have to remember that they accepted who you were. They may not take well to who you are becoming or who you have become.

Like most women, Lisa counted years and not incidents. It's sad, but we have to understand that old friends sometimes can't enter new dimensions with us. *"Neither do men put new wine into old bottles: else the bottles break, and the wine runneth out, and the bottles perish: but they put new wine into new bottles, and both are preserved"* (Matthew 9:17).

If you were like I was, you probably saw those movies where a friend suddenly became rich and began to act snobbish towards her old friends. We were mad at her because she changed for the worse. We were happy when she got humbled and went back to reconcile those broken relationships she had with her old friends. This is the Hollywood image of friendship, but it's not true friendship. After all, you will be changed, and you have to expect to be changed. *"And be not conformed to this world: but be ye transformed by the renewing of your mind, that ye may prove what is that good, and acceptable, and perfect, will of God"* (Romans 2:2). If we are not transforming, we are conforming! It's so easy to reject change when your mind has conformed and you have become complacent with where you are. Again, you will change; that is to be expected, but when you have to remain the same to keep your friends, you have just been placed in bondage....but, at least you'll have plenty of company while you're there.

Your friends have to be transforming in CHRIST along with you; otherwise, they won't be able to be promoted with you, and that's when they'll become Satan's monitoring device in your life. They will keep you leashed up to a way of thinking, and any time they sense change in you, they'll become critical of that change or critical of you.

158

Do you want to access your "and suddenly"? Follow these steps:

1. GOD never told you to stick around evil people just because they are nice to you or just because they frequent church. HE said to judge a tree by the fruit it bears. Ask yourself this question. What type of fruit is my friend (insert friend's name here) bearing?

2. Ask the LORD to remove EVERY person in your life whom HE did not call to be in your life. You'd be amazed at how many friends you'd lose after that prayer.

3. Ask the LORD to reposition EVERY person in your life whom HE did call in your life. It is very common for us, as women, to give people positions that GOD did not call them to have. In those positions, they can turn out to be worse than an enemy because they are not spiritually equipped to be where you assigned them in your life.

4. Always be ready and willing to let go of friendships that prove themselves to be ungodly, even if your friend frequents church and knows more scripture than your Pastor.

5. Tell your friends the truth. Amazingly enough, you'll lose more false friends by telling them the uncompromising truth than you'd keep. At the same time, you'd learn to discern your true friends based on the ones who tell you the truth as opposed to the ones who withhold truth from you. When you learn to be a friend, you'll learn how to discern what a friend

really is.

If you want to enter your "and suddenly," you'd better suddenly start making changes to your life. Understand that this journey isn't for the meek; it's for those who will endure 'til the end. The choice came to me one day, and this time, it wasn't wrapped up in the lies I'd told myself. The choice was clear. I could be like everyone else, surrounded by people who loved me where I was, with no hope of ever becoming who I am, or I could be the peculiar creature that GOD created me to be. I wouldn't be surrounded by people; my path wouldn't be broad and full of fun turns, but I would have GOD with me the whole way. I could have the countless friends I wanted, or I could stay focused on the path before me. I chose CHRIST, and in doing so, GOD gave me friends (maybe one or two) who could celebrate my going up, just as I could celebrate their ascensions in HIM. There was no envy there. I didn't have to put on a costume; I simply had to be uniquely and positively myself, and they loved me just like that. There were no constraints to keep me shackled into old ways of thinking. Instead, I was blessed with friends who motivated me to go to the next level.

Truths:
1. There are some friends out there who don't mind you doing well as long as your version of "well" is worse than where they are.
2. There are some friends who stick around you because your life fascinates them and gives them

something to talk about. In other words, you are pure entertainment to them.

3. There are some friends you've picked up in your seasons of misery, and they keep trying to drag you back into a miserable state so they can relate to you.

4. There are some friends who can't deal with whole people; therefore, they have to break everyone around them and attempt to fix them as a token of their friendships. They'll happily tell you what they think is wrong with you, for the sole purpose of fixing you. In truth, they broke you and reformed your mind to think the way they needed you to think. In other words, they have to reprogram you to be their friends.

5. There are some friends who were sent by the enemy to ensure that you never elevate into GOD'S will, but that you would be so weighed down by the friendship that you'll constantly reject change.

6. There are some friends who will dump all of their problems on you but refuse to be a blessing to you when you need one. To them, you are a toilet, suitable only for carrying their problems.

7. There are some friends who could love you today where you are but would hate you tomorrow when you enter a new dimension.

8. There are friends who gather servants to serve them, and they bestow the title of friend upon them, but if you pay attention to the people surrounding them, you will find that they are surrounded by servants.

And Suddenly

GOD'S will is perfect, and HE loves to bless us suddenly.
Don't exit HIS will trying to enter someone's definition of
what a friend is and what a friend does. Pray about
everyone in your life and everyone who attempts to enter
your life, and be sure to accept what GOD shows you.
That's when you'll be able to enter your sudden blessings
and your seasons of change.

The Strength to Restrain

"In the world, strength is defined by how strong your flesh is. In the spirit, strength is defined by how strong you are against your flesh."

Marrying the wrong man always has its consequences, but more than that, marrying the wrong man always proves to be a test of your strength, your faith and your character. Strength is the ability to not do what you strongly want to do. The flesh is always under siege by some stronghold, and it is actually easier to work with the strongholds than it is to work against them. A wise man or woman possesses the wisdom needed to oppose anything or anyone that is opposing them, without the use of their flesh.

Martia was a petite woman with short dark hair. She was a wife and a mother, but more than them all, she was a child of GOD. Martia wasn't beautiful by traditional standards, but she wasn't unattractive either. She was an average-looking woman, but her heart was beautiful to GOD.

Martia was married to Gregory, but their marriage was strained. There were many things about Martia that caused Greg to fall out of love with her. One of those missing traits was Martia's inability to stand up for herself. Greg had

163

watched Martia walk away from situations that other women would have turned upside down. There was the time when one of Greg's co-workers had flirted with Greg in Martia's presence. The company had thrown a mid-July cookout and the employees were allowed to bring their families. The cookout took place at a local park, and the day was going great at first. It was a typical hot day in Atlanta, and the party was beginning to wind down. Martia was feeding their two-year-old daughter when his co-worker Toni walked up. Toni was tall with a medium build and fairly attractive. She was a blonde woman with emerald green eyes and a very slender face. Toni wore her hair in a ponytail, and she looked rather friendly. That was, until she opened her mouth.

Toni: Hello, Gregster. I couldn't resist coming over here to meet your family. Why don't you introduce us?
Greg: Hey, Toni. Well, this is my wife Martia and my son James.
Toni: Your son is really cute. I guess he took that from your side of the family.

Greg looked at Martia, but Martia didn't pay too much attention to the snide comment and was still tending to their son.

Greg: Well, I guess. Hey, did you ever close the deal on the Swinson property?
Toni: Yes, I finished up on Friday.

Martia interrupted and extended her hand to Toni.

Martia: I'm sorry. Where are my manners? I'm Martia, Greg's wife.
(Toni looked at Martia's hand and then she looked at Martia.)
Toni: I'm sorry. I'm a germaphobe, and I don't like to shake hands. Anyhow, I'd better get back to my guests. See you on Monday, Greg. Nice to meet you, Martian.
Martia: That's Mar-sha. Nice to meet you too.

There were many situations that occurred over the course of their marriage where Martia should have been offended and reacted, but she didn't. Instead, she would ignore any and every woman who approached her about Greg.

It's not rocket science. Greg isn't the faithful type, and he blames his inability to maintain a monogamous relationship on his wife. Greg believes that Martia is too weak of a woman for him. Martia's family had told him about how feisty Martia used to be. She was a fighter, and she would attack any and everyone who stood against her. Nowadays, Martia stood there as a changed woman. She didn't want to fight anymore; she wanted to serve the LORD and be a family person.

In addition to Martia being a doormat in Greg's eyes, Martia was a Christian, and all she wanted to do was go to church and spend time with her family. She wasn't into drinking and partying, but Greg was.

Over the years, Greg and Martia had many arguments about Greg's lack of respect for his wife. In Greg's eyes, Martia was the problem. If she'd only stop acting like a spineless jellyfish, he could be in love with her and stop his affairs. In Martia's eyes, Greg was the problem because he did not serve the LORD, and his affairs had become an altar where he sacrificed his marriage for the sake of himself. Because of their inabilities to see eye-to-eye, they became more and more distant. They lived in the same home, but there was an invisible wall between them. Martia prayed for her husband often and tried to focus on their son so she wouldn't have to focus on their problems.

As time went on, Greg began to lose respect for Martia all the more. He didn't like the way she walked because her walk, to him, displayed her softness. He loved to see women who stepped with authority. He didn't like the way she talked because her voice, to him, sounded as if she was afraid of something. Where was her strength? Her stories about how she handled issues at work were even disgusting to him. She worked with worldly, authoritative women who would test her from time to time, but Martia always dealt with matters by the book. How in the world did she keep receiving promotions? She was as meek as a mouse, not fit for any positions of authority in Greg's eyes.

One day, Greg and Martia went out to eat at their favorite restaurant. Of course, they brought along their son, James. On the way to the restaurant, Greg and Martia did not speak with one another. Greg was upset with Martia because she'd chosen to wear that pink dress that he hated so much. Why did she always want to be so girly? To Greg, it was like Martia wanted to hang a sign on herself that read: "I'm a scared little girl. Who wants to pick with me?" Martia had learned to ignore Greg's wise cracks. She'd realized that Greg's perception of her had ruined his view of her; therefore, she felt helpless in her marriage.

When they arrived at the restaurant, Greg got out of the vehicle and started heading towards the restaurant. He did not open the door for his wife, nor did he remove little James from his car seat. It was as if he was ashamed of his family. Hurt, but undeterred, Martia exited the vehicle and went to the back of the SUV to unload their son. She'd learned to expect this type of behavior from her husband, and she'd learned not to let it ruin her days. She stayed focused on their son, because he was the joy of her life. As she carried James towards the restaurant, her love could be seen for him. She spoke lovingly to her son as she bounced him towards the doors. Little James reciprocated her love with a smile. His two-toothed grin was just so beautiful, and Martia got lost in his eyes. She loved him, and he loved her. One of the customers held the door open for Martia. He was exiting the restaurant with his family, and he'd just opened the door for his wife and children to exit the restaurant. Martia thanked him as she entered through the doors and was met by a waiter. Instead of trying to figure out where her husband was now seated, Martia followed the waiter to

an empty booth. She wasn't in the mood for Greg's antics.
The waiter brought out a high chair for little James while
Martia began to look over the menu. "I'll have the grilled fish
with a side of Caesar salad," Martia ordered. "And let me
have a sweet tea, please. For my son, I would have your
junior's meal with the hamburger, no cheese, and fries." As
she was completing her order, she heard Greg's voice as he
rudely snapped, "Oh, so you're just going to act as if you
came in here alone? Get up! I'm sitting on the other side."
Martia was embarrassed. The waiter stood in shock but
awaited Martia's response. "Go ahead and fill the order,
please. We'll be sitting right here. Thanks." Martia's voice
was soft, but authoritative. Disgusted, Greg snarled back,
"Well, I'm eating on the other side! If you're not ready when
I'm ready, you can catch a cab home." Greg stormed off as
a few of the customers stared in dismay at the unswayed
Martia. She continued to speak lovingly to her son, who was
still smiling and laughing at his mother's goo-goo talk. One
of the older women sitting nearby asked her husband to
stand up so she could go and speak with Martia.

Magdalene: Hi, my name is Magdalene and I don't mean to
impose, but we couldn't help but hear what that guy said.
Are you alright?
Martia smiled at the friendly face.
Martia: Yes, ma'am. Unfortunately, he's my husband, but
I'm used to it. We'll be okay.
Magdalene: Oh no, sweetie. Well, I pray that you enjoy your
meal, and my husband and I have just arrived here also. So

if we finish eating before you do, we will try to stick around just in case you need a ride home.

Martia: Oh, thank you. It's okay, though. If he leaves, I can catch a cab. I've done it before, and it's no big deal.

Magdalene: Wow, you seem so very poised in a situation that would make me nuts. How is it that you aren't panicking or even hurt by his actions?

Martia: One thing that GOD has taught me is that my husband's actions are a representative of the hurt and anger going on in him. I have a choice in it. I can allow his actions to cause me to feel the pain he wants me to feel and react to it, or I can let him keep running himself crazy while I focus on the things that matter.

Magdalene: Lady, I envy your strength. So let me ask you this: Does your marriage matter to you?

Martia: I would be lying if I said I didn't love my husband or that his ways don't hurt me sometimes, but I consciously and daily remind myself that GOD'S will is going to be done, no matter how I feel about it. If Greg and I divorce, my prayers are that I get full custody of my son, and he can find the woman he thinks he wants.

Magdalene: And what about what you want, dear?

Martia: I have him already. I have my beautiful son who compliments me every day with a smile. More than that, I have JESUS. That's enough for me.

Magdalene: Wow. You are blessed, baby. Really blessed. Anyhow, here comes the waiter with your food, so I'll head back over to my table. We'll be a few seats away if you need us.

Martia: Thank you. I really appreciate that.

At the other table, Greg was furious to the point where he couldn't enjoy his food. He kept thinking of ways to retaliate against his spineless wife who always had enough strength to stand up against him, but no one else. His heart filled with hatred as he thought of the embarrassment he felt when Martia insisted on staying where she was. This was it for him. He had to divorce her. After all, he was disgusted by her, and he didn't even want her raising his son. He wanted a strong woman to raise his son. Greg ate his food quickly because he was determined to leave Martia at the restaurant, but to his surprise, when he went to the car, it was already gone. Martia had obviously beat him eating and had left without telling him. Angered, he picked up his cell phone to call his wife. The old couple from the restaurant laughed as they saw him standing in the parking lot on his phone. They realized that Martia had left him there. They stood a few feet behind Greg as they were unlocking their vehicle, but they froze as they heard the flood of venom that Greg unleashed on Martia when she answered the phone. Greg snarled, "You freak of nature, come back here and bring me my car before I have you arrested for auto theft. Do you hear me, you slithering, spineless, unattractive worthless hunk of crap?! Hello? Hello?!" Martia had obviously disconnected the line, and Greg was attempting to redial her when Mrs. Magdalene's husband walked up to him. Mr. Huey said to Greg, "Excuse me. If you want, we can take you home. It's no problem for us." Greg hung up the line and thanked the World War Two veteran. He followed the couple to their car and told them where he lived. Their home was thirty minutes away, and the drive seemed endless. Greg thought of all of the cruel things he would like to do to Martia. He was going to beat her. He'd made up his mind that for the first time in their marriage, he was going to beat her, and he was going to make this beating memorable. He thought about choking her, pinching her and torturing her in any way possible. Greg wanted to see blood. Mr. Huey sensed that the situation would not improve, and that Greg was planning to harm his wife. As he looked in the rear-view mirror at Greg, he noticed that all-too-familiar look. Greg had enemy eyes. He was obviously planning an attack; nevertheless, the couple remained quiet until they arrived in Greg's neighborhood. Greg showed them where his house was, and they watched as he exited the vehicle to enter his house.

When Greg entered the house, he saw Martia holding a sleeping James. She was singing a lullaby to their son, and she didn't even look up at Greg, even though she'd heard him enter the house.

Greg: We need to talk.
Martia: Not now. I'm busy with James. Give me about fifteen minutes since he just fell asleep and I don't want to wake him up.
Greg: I think you need to put him down if you don't want him to end up getting hurt with you.

Martia looked up at Greg. His brown eyes were now midnight black. His fists were clinched, and he held his keys in his right hand as if he intended to use the keys as a weapon. Was he serious? He was planning to harm her? "Okay," said Martia. "Let me go and lay him down, and then you can do whatever you want to me."

Martia's response confused Greg. Wasn't she scared? Why was she so calm? Greg could hear James starting to cry as Martia laid him in his crib. "Shhhhhh. Mommy's here," said Martia. She began to sing again and James drifted back off to sleep. As she exited James's room, she closed his door and walked in front of Greg. She removed her eyeglasses and laid them on the coffee table. "Now, do as you please," she said. Greg looked at the petite woman who was not afraid to take a beating at his hands. He'd expected her to panic; he'd expected her to run, beg or cry, but he had not anticipated her reaction. His anger was replaced by confusion. The adrenaline-rushed rage had fled from him, and now he wondered what she was thinking.

Greg: Why did you leave me at the restaurant?
Martia: Greg, do what you want to do to me. I'm not going to stand here and answer a question you already know the answer to. If you're going to beat me, go ahead...beat me.

Greg drew back his hand to hit his wife, but she did not flinch. This further confused him. Martia stood there with her big brown eyes and looked Greg in his eyes. Greg lowered his hand and started heading towards their bedroom. "I want a divorce," he calmly said to his wife. "I'm going to file for a divorce tomorrow." Martia's response finally fueled him up. "That's fine. Goodnight." Was this a game to her? Greg had done everything he could to get a reaction out of her, but she still responded calmly. She seemed unmoved by everything he did and everything he said. As Martia turned her back, Greg charged in her direction. He grabbed her by her hair and began to pull her head back as he screamed at her. "I hate you! You're going to die tonight, you wretched and disgusting woman!" To his surprise, Martia shyly smiled and responded, "Okay." Greg punched his wife and dragged her across the carpet towards the kitchen. Martia's nose was bleeding, but she still said nothing and she did not fight back. Greg's plan was to take a knife and scare his wife, but that did not work. He threatened to slit her throat, but Martia simply stood up and looked at Greg as if nothing was going on. Blood ran from her nose, but her hands stayed at her side. Greg wanted to put fear in her, but it wasn't working. Maybe he would have to actually stab her before she would respond. He walked over to Martia and grabbed her hair again to pull her head back. "After I kill you, I'm going to kill James and bury him alongside you," said Greg. As he was yelling at Martia, he felt something cold and piercing in his side. He released Martia and watched as blood suddenly began to gush from his abdomen. Martia backed away from him and released the knife that she'd just plunged into her husband. Afraid and confused, Greg looked at his expressionless wife. Just as he stumbled towards Martia, the police kicked in the living room door. With guns drawn, they forced Greg to lie down on the floor. One of the officers pushed Martia against the wall and began to cuff her. Martia didn't resist. She simply requested that one of the officers call her mother so that she could come and pick up James. As she was speaking, the old couple from the restaurant entered the house. They spoke with the lead detective, who then ordered that Martia's cuffs be removed. The couple had called the police after leaving. They knew that Greg would attack his wife, and that's why they offered him a ride home. They wanted to see where they lived.

Greg was eventually convicted of assault with a deadly weapon and was sentenced to ninety days in jail, since it was his first offense. Martia was never charged but was granted a divorce not long after the incident. The court gave him supervised visits with little James. He decided to stop visiting his son because he felt that he would be weak just like his mother. Eventually, Greg remarried, and this time, he married the type of woman he wanted: a brawling woman. She spent five years with Greg, fighting other women over him and fighting him because of the other women. This was Greg's version of heaven until his new wife divorced him to be with their daughter's Physical Education teacher. Greg would go on to remarry three more times, each time finding another woman more contentious than the previous one.

Martia, on the other hand, remained unmarried for four more years. She was content with her life. As she'd stated before, she had GOD, and she had her son. She cherished every moment with her son, and she lovingly embraced GOD with her whole heart. When Martia did remarry, her new husband, Ted, saw the strength in her; the very strength that Greg could not see. Martia had the strength to restrain herself, and Martia had the wisdom to know when physical strength was needed. He loved her, and he loved James as if he were his own son. He and Martia went on to have three more children, and they raised their children in the LORD. **The End.**

What was Martia's issue? Martia had real strength. An unwise woman will show her physical strength at any given moment because it's all she has. An unwise woman can't fight you with the WORD because the WORD is not in her. All she has is her flesh and her knowledge of fighting. Martia's wisdom was her strength. She knew how to diffuse a situation and an angry husband. By not displaying fear, she continuously sapped the power out of her husband's raging spirit. You see, fear actually attracts danger; it does not deter it. Faith deters danger; fear is like a magnet for every evil thing.

Greg was blind spiritually. What he saw as weakness was actually Martia's strength, and what he saw as fear was actually faith unmasked. Greg was an unwise man; therefore, a wise woman was disgusting to him. He wanted a brawling and foolish woman; one who didn't mind displaying her lack of wisdom publicly. *"Can two walk together, except they be agreed?" (Amos 3:3).* This is a lesson that so many women of GOD must get and understand. An ungodly man will always do ungodly things. He won't follow you into the church and find his way to CHRIST. He is actually more likely to lead you away from the church, and sometimes, even further away from the LORD. Let me share with you what happens in a relationship where two parties are unequally yoked.

- A believing woman marries an unbelieving man and truly hopes or believes that she can change him by taking him to church, loving him like she believes no one has ever loved him and trying to reason with him about his lifestyle. Instead, what happens is the husband fights for his right to be evil and begins to rebel even more because he feels he is being dragged into a lifestyle that he wants no part of. Anytime a man fights for his right to be evil, he will always win. Anytime a woman tries to force an evil man to follow CHRIST, she is led into sin and overcome. Everyone has their own right to be as good or as evil as they want to be.

- The believing wife searches her heart again and again for the right words to change her husband's mind, but years later, she realizes that those words just did not exist. He had the WORD of GOD available for him, yet he rejected the WORD; therefore, throwing many sound words at an unwise man is what the Bible refers to as "casting your pearls to the swine."

- The unbelieving husband grows more and more impatient with his wife because she insists on being Godly when he's not attracted to Godliness. Only when she acts sinful does she get his attention.
- In noticing that sinful ways brings her peaceful days with her husband, the wife begins to become more and more sin-minded. After all, a wife desires to please her husband. 1 Corinthians 7:34 reads, *"There is difference also between a wife and a virgin. The unmarried woman careth for the things of the Lord, that she may be holy both in body and in spirit: but she that is married careth for the things of the world, how she may please her husband."* What does this mean? It means that as women of GOD, we must absolutely marry men of GOD. If not, we'll end up caring for our husband's pleasure, thus causing us to get further and further away from GOD. You can't drag a grown man to CHRIST. GOD has to invite him, and he has to accept the invitation on his own.
- Because the woman of GOD does love GOD, she begins to wrestle inwardly. Her desire to serve GOD is still intact, but she recognizes that if she dives in completely, she will likely lose her husband. Therefore, she continues to pray for him, believing that he will eventually find his way to CHRIST; all the while, she's being led further and further away from CHRIST.
- After being around sin for so long, the believing wife then starts to become comfortable with sin and

justifies her ways. After all, when she's sinning, her husband treats her like a queen, but when she starts acting like a woman of GOD, her husband treats her like a prisoner awaiting execution.

- In many cases, the unbelieving husband will eventually hate his believing wife. *"Reprove not a scorner, lest he hate thee: rebuke a wise man, and he will love thee" (Proverbs 9:8).*

Believe it or not, real strength is being able to restrain yourself when you want to move. Any fool can fight, but it takes a wise woman to walk away from a fight that her flesh considers entering. Think about it. It is actually harder to walk away from a fight when you've been angered than it is to actually go in and fight. If a man walked up to you and slapped you, how would you respond? If a woman walked up to you and spat on you, how would you respond? Like most people, your flesh will volunteer to answer that question for you. You'd want to pounce on them and teach them that "you are not the one" to be hit or spat on. That's the flesh's response, but the most difficult thing to do is to walk away, and this requires strength; real strength that can only come from GOD.

Unlike most believing women, Martia managed to keep her composure because she'd come to the understanding that her marriage was likely not going to work. Instead of running herself crazy trying to fix it, she stayed focused on what she could do. Martia understood that she simply needed to love her husband and be a good wife to him. She did not have to serve his anger, frustrations or his sinful cravings. She had a beautiful son to look out for. She had a budding career to work at. Most of all, she had a relationship with GOD that she worked at. Does this mean that she neglected her marriage? No. She simply handed CHRIST what she could not fix herself. One of the most powerful lessons here to learn is: you can't teach an Ishmael how to be an Issac. All you can do is pray for him, but please understand that if he rejects the LORD, he's going to continue to reject you when you try and serve the LORD. Eve was Adam's rib, and you are your husband's rib. When you attempt to be the rib of the wrong man, his body, mind and soul will continue to reject you. The worst part of it is: you can't get mad at him for rejecting you. After all, you had to reject the will of GOD to get with him. All you can do is repent and let GOD lead you from there.

A New Normal

"Your normal isn't always GOD'S best for you."

One thing about us as human beings, is that we tend to park ourselves in mindsets and lifestyles and we are afraid to move away from them. Somehow, we have caused ourselves to believe that our mindsets and ways of living are coveted parking spaces, and if we allow ourselves to move or be moved, we'll lose our spots. We oftentimes hold on to old things, mindsets and relationships because we have learned to depend on them, rather than taking the chance to embrace a new normal for ourselves.

One thing we often learn over the courses of our lives is what's normal today is not going to be what's normal tomorrow unless we refuse to embrace new knowledge and understanding. Unfortunately, the majority of believers do just that: they reject knowledge because it threatens their perceptions.

"You whore! When will you understand that I am the best?!" Laughter erupted as Zara threw her last card on the table. Zara was playing a game of spades with her best friend, Latreese. She'd just won another game, and their other two friends, Aubrey and Brielle, were standing by watching the

181

best-friend duo have at it again. This was their third game of spades, and Zara had won the first game, Latreese had won the second one. This third game was the tie-breaker, and the young ladies had placed a bet on the game. The loser would have to wear clown makeup to the club that night. They were planning to hang out, drink a little, and then go out to their favorite spot. The winner would have the honor of applying the makeup to the loser. The loser would also have to wear a white t-shirt that someone had written "Loser" on.

Latreese wasn't so happy about losing the game. She'd boasted of being the best, and she'd been the one who suggested they make a bet. She'd even told her boyfriend that she'd win, and he could look for Zara at the club to laugh at her. "Bring a few of your friends," Latreese had told her boyfriend. "When you see Zara, every one of you just point and laugh." But now here she was, sitting humbled at the table while Zara continued her verbal victory party. "I keep telling this slut that she can't beat me! But she don't listen! How do you want me to do your makeup? Bozo or Ronald McDonald?" The laughter continued, but Latreese did not find the humor in Zara's jokes. "Shut up," replied Latreese. "You get lucky and win two games, and all of a sudden, your mouth becomes a motor. Turn off your engine, whore-girl, and enjoy the victory for once in your life." The laughter continued, and the women continued to throw harmful words at one another; nevertheless, to them, it was all fun and games.

Zara had been raised in the church, but had strayed away from the church at the age of 13. She'd fallen into the wrong crowd, and this had become her new normal. Zara was 32 years old. She was a dark-skinned beauty with long legs and a coke-bottle figure. Her best friend, Latreese was a little shorter than Zara. She was brown-skinned, but her true beauty could not be seen because she always wore blonde weave, green contact lenses and a ton of makeup.

Aubrey and Brielle were both sisters. Aubrey was 28 years old, a mother of three children, and a woman who liked to party hard. Aubrey was a very slender woman, standing at five feet fall, and weighing only 102 pounds. Even though she was so petite, Aubrey was known for being a pretty shrewd fighter and an even better dancer. Her energy was evident anywhere she went, but her face looked so very innocent. She appeared to be no more than nineteen years old, but she was 28. Her big eyes made her look curious, and her normal attire was a mix of girly clothes with boyish shoes. Aubrey loved to show off her belly, so she often wore midriff tops and boy-cut jeans. She wasn't curvaceous, however. Her energy and charismatic personality had earned her the nickname Bam.

Brielle, on the other hand, was 27 years old, and was somewhat overweight. Also known to be a pretty hard fighter, Brielle stood at five feet, five inches tall, and she weighed in at 212 pounds. She wasn't exactly fat, but she was considered solid. Brielle always wore the cutest clothes and kept her hair looking great. Even though she was the youngest in the clique, she was the most sensible girl, often offering advice to her friends when they'd had too much to drink or made some pretty bad decisions. She was also known for standing up for her friends, once punching one of Zara's ex-boyfriends who'd made the mistake of hitting Zara in her presence. The word out was that she'd knocked him unconscious.

There were two more women in the crew. Niya was physically present, but intoxicated as usual, so mentally, she was somewhere else. Niya was always having problems with her boyfriend, so she would take a trip out of reality by getting drunk every time the ladies had "girl's night out." She knew that she would have to go home to a raging boyfriend who would then threaten to leave her and take their children away. Niya was of Puerta Rican decent. Her parents were both from Puerto Rico, but they'd moved to the United States when Niya was just three years old. Niya had three children: two girls and one boy with her boyfriend, Maurice.

The final but missing crew member's name was Donna. Donna had moved away from her crew over a year ago, when she relocated to New York to pursue her career. She was an aspiring fashion designer and hairstylist. Donna had given her life to CHRIST since she'd moved away, but she had trouble letting go of her friends and old lifestyle. She struggled to embrace a new way of thinking because the old mindset kept stalking her. A beautiful and unique-looking woman with strong features, Donna looked like a model. Most people who saw her thought she was either a model or should be a model; nevertheless, Donna wanted to be on the other side of fashion. She was very creative and was even great at applying makeup.

The women were still talking at one another and laughing when Donna called Niya's phone. Niya was still intoxicated and unconscious in the chair, so Aubrey answered her phone. This was their normal. If Niya had gotten drunk, one of the women would answer her phone in case Maurice called her. After each outing, Maurice would be called to come and pick up his stumbling bride-to-be.

Aubrey: Hello, Aubrey speaking.

Donna: Bam, don't act like you don't know who this is. Where's Niya?

Aubrey: Who is this? Donna? Girl, you know where Niya is. Sitting here passed out with gin on her breath.

Donna: *Sighs.* I don't know what I'm going to do with her. What are you guys up to tonight?

Aubrey: Just hanging out at Zara's house, and we plan to hit the spot a little later if Niya don't mess everything up.

Donna: Y'all need to go home and go to church tomorrow, instead of engaging in all that foolishness.

Aubrey: Aw, trick...shut up! You used to kick it right alongside us, and now you're acting all holier than thou because you got front-row tickets to somebody's church. Stop it, Dee. You know you're talking to the right one.

Donna: Whatever, Bam-Bam. I told you not to refer to me

as trick, whore, slut or any defamatory names. You're speaking word curses at me, and you know I don't like that. Return to sender...tramp! *Laughs.*
Aubrey: *Laughs.* Whatever, trick. I'll tell Niya you called.
Donna: Okay. I'll probably call her again tomorrow. Tell everyone I said hello, and GO HOME!
Aubrey: We are going home, Dee. As soon as we are so drunk we can't remember each other's names.

After hanging up the line, Donna was disappointed in herself. Did she just refer to Aubrey as a tramp? These were her old ways of speaking. It seemed that every time she spoke with her old crew, she would end up falling into her old ways of speaking.

Meanwhile, back on the party scene, the women were ready to head to a club, but they knew they couldn't take Niya in her condition. They discussed what to do with Niya; all the while, Zara had taken out her eyebrow pencil and started drawing eyebrows and teardrops on Niya's face. Niya kept waking up and trying to swat Zara, but she couldn't focus or stay alert for too long. Aubrey decided to call Maurice so he could come and pick up Niya.

Maurice: Hey, Niya; where are you now?
Aubrey: This is Bam, Maurice. Niya's over here drunk. Will you come and pick her up? We are at Zara's house.
Maurice: She's drunk...again?!
Aubrey: Yep. Stop acting like you don't like her drunk.

Every time you pick her drunk butt up, she ends up pregnant.

Maurice: Yeah, right. Where's your man at, Bam?

Aubrey: He got arrested for trying to sell crack to your momma.

Maurice: Oh, Bam. You really want me to hurt you.

Zara hits Aubrey on the leg.

Aubrey: What? The boy don't really know his momma, and I know he don't like her! Okay. I'm sorry, Maurice. Will you please come and pick up your drunk fiancé, because while Zara's over here acting like she's the pope and all, she's turned your girl's face into a coloring book, and it's almost my turn to color.

Maurice: I'm on my way.

Maurice was the son of a Pastor; nevertheless, he'd taken the same path his father once took before he got saved. His father had met his mother while he was in the world, and the two of them had two children: Maurice and his twin sister Maurie. Their parents never married and ended up going their separate ways when the twins were just seven years old. Their father had taken custody of the children because their mother had become addicted to cocaine; howbeit, he raised his children in the world because the world was what he knew. Now Maurice was walking the trail his father had blazed before him. He loved being in the world, and he loved his worldly girlfriend Niya and their children. At six feet, two inches tall, Maurice found his calling in playing basketball. He hoped to make it to the big leagues of basketball eventually.

When Maurice arrived to pick up Niya, he was surprised to see her looking like a crying clown. Someone had placed an unlit cigarette in her mouth and chopsticks in her hair. They had also placed an old scarf around her neck and put a bunch of plaits and barrettes in her hair. Aubrey's voice echoed from behind him. "It could have been worse," she said. "I didn't get my chance to color, so I accessorized." Maurice laughed, and said, "Well, I'm going to leave her just like that, so she can see what kind of a clown she's making out of herself falling on her butt drunk." He lifted up Niya, and as he turned around, he could hear the roar of laughter as Aubrey stood there staring at him. Her face was serious, and her big eyes made her stare all the more funny.

Maurice: *Laughs.* What?
Aubrey: I wasn't finished with her yet.
Maurice: And what else did you want to do to my baby?

Aubrey looked down, and Maurice followed her eyes with his eyes. He laughed at the cloth shower caps Aubrey was holding.

Maurice: And what were you going to do with those?
Aubrey: I figured she probably wouldn't recognize herself when she woke up, so I wanted to make scratch mittens out of these so she wouldn't harm herself. You know she's gonna still be drunk when she wakes up. I think it'll be

funny....her waking up drunk and confused and not knowing where her hands are. Come on, Maurice. Let me prop her up in the window and leave her there. I want to put a big sign over her head that reads, "How much is that doggie in the window." Just a few photos, and I'll bring her home myself.

Maurice: *Laughs.* There is something wrong with you, Bam, and no....I'm not going to let you do any more damage to my wife.

Aubrey: Aw, man. You're no fun. Okay. I'll tell you what. I'll trail you back to y'all apartment; you can put the children to bed, park your wife in a closet, and I'll show you why they call me Bam.

At that, Aubrey started to dance and Maurice laughed as he headed out the door with Niya in tow. The laughter from within the apartment could be heard from the outside as some of the women declared to Aubrey that she was a fool.

Brielle decided not to wear the clown makeup to the club that night. She promised to do it the following Saturday, because she'd planned to leave the club early with her boyfriend. The plan was for them to get a hotel that night, and Brielle didn't want to ruin her near-perfect makeup.

That night, the four friends went to a local club called The Peak. There, they ran into three other friends whom they often partied with, and they were having fun at first. That was until Brielle got up to head to the bar. Zara turned around and noticed three women standing in Brielle's face yelling. One of the women was obviously the aggressor; nevertheless, Brielle stood there arguing with the women. The aggressor was a little taller than Brielle, and she had somewhat of a masculine build. Zara recognized her immediately. Her name was Erica, and she and Brielle were seeing the same guy. The guy's name was Rovy, and Erica had a one-year-old son with him. Even though he was no longer officially with Erica, he was still seeing her whenever he could. Zara tapped the other women and pointed at the arguing duo. Before she could stand up, Aubrey had already grabbed a beer bottle. She squatted as she made her way through the crowd. Suddenly, Erica and Brielle began fighting, and one of Erica's friends named Maxine grabbed Brielle by her hair. The other friend ran off into the crowd. Aubrey suddenly stood up and broke the beer bottle on Maxine's head, and she went to the floor immediately. Soon, all of the women were involved in a group fight; all except Erica's friend, who had run off into the crowd. This was normal for the crew. They partied together, they drank together, and they fought together.

The next day, Donna surprised the women. It was nine o'clock in the morning, and Donna had just arrived in town. She knew the women had all likely crashed at Zara's house, since that was their norm, especially if they were intoxicated. Donna rang the doorbell and waited, but no one came to the door. She rang the doorbell again and again, and finally, she decided to call Brielle's cellular phone. She knew that of all the women, Brielle was the one who didn't really get drunk. She would always drink one beverage each outing. After making two calls to the number and getting no answer, Donna decided to go in through Zara's bedroom window. After all, Zara always kept her window up. Just as she was reaching for the screen, her phone rang. It was Brielle.

Brielle: Hey Dee, you just called me?
Donna: Yeah. I'm outside. Come and open the door.
Brielle: I'm at Zara's house. We slept here last night.
Donna: I know. I'm outside.
Brielle: Oh, okay. Here I come.

Donna made her way back to the front of the apartment, and in the doorway, she saw Brielle standing there. She had a split lip and scratches on her face.

Donna: Brielle, what happened to you?
Brielle: Erica Ramsey. Need I say more?
Donna: Ow. It looks like she worked you over.
Brielle: Girl, please. I am officially her dentist. She spit out at least two teeth last night.
Donna: Y'all need to stop that, Brielle. That guy is not worth you getting hurt over. Where's everyone else?

Brielle pointed to the den where Donna could see the rest of her sleeping friends.

Back at Niya's house, it was now morning, and Niya was just

waking up. Confused, she sat up and realized that she was at home. Her mother sat opposite of her on the chair, and Maurice sat at the foot of the couch staring at her. Niya's mother was a Christian woman, and she hated to see the condition of her daughter. Even though it ached her heart to see her daughter stretched out on the couch intoxicated, she couldn't help but laugh at the makeup job that had been done on her. Zara had drawn what looked like open eyes on top of Niya's eyelids, so even when she was asleep, she looked awake. When her eyes suddenly did open, it humored her mother. Maurice had called her once again to tell her about Niya's drinking and partying. Mrs. Vanessa had cried the entire drive to Niya's house. She lived just a little over one hour away from her daughter, but she was very concerned about her well being. She'd lost her only son three years ago to gang violence, and Niya was her only surviving child. Niya's father was so disappointed in her choices that he often refused to visit her. She was surrounded by people who loved her; nevertheless, Niya did not love herself. The anger over her brother's death and the fact that the killer had never been charged with the crime was one of the factors that contributed to Niya's anger. The police knew who the shooter was, but they were never able to obtain enough evidence to arrest or convict him. At the same time, Niya had carried so many hurts with her. She'd never truly forgiven her dad for having an affair on her mother. During the affair, a child was born to her dad and his mistress. The child was a little boy named Evan, and he was now ten years old. Even though her parents stayed together, Niya had witnessed the hurt her mother had to endure because of her father's indiscretions. Then, there was Maurice's affair two years ago. Maurice played college basketball at that time, and this made him a magnet for women. The other woman's name was Natalia, and she was also Puerto Rican. Obviously, Maurice had a thing for Puerto Rican women. Niya had learned about the affair when Natalia had called Maurice's cell phone and left him a voice mail saying she thought she was pregnant. Niya often listened to his voice mails because she did not trust men. After all, if Daddy can cheat, all men had to be just as weak, in Niya's eyes. At that time, Niya was seven months pregnant with their last child, and the news stressed her so badly that she had to be hospitalized. It turned out that Natalia was not pregnant but simply had a pregnancy scare; nevertheless, Niya's relationship with Maurice had never been quite the same since then. He'd done everything in his power to get her to forgive him, but Niya felt especially betrayed because she'd shared with Maurice the pain she saw in her mother's eyes when her dad had his affair. She'd even told him how hurt she was and how angry she was with her father for his reckless behavior. To take revenge against Maurice, she'd changed her mind about naming their one and only son after him. Instead, she named their son after her deceased brother.

Because of her anger, Niya was now rebelling against the men in her life. She wanted them to hurt because she was hurting. Her pain had been seven years in the making, and it had been intensified by Maurice's affair two years earlier. Because of this, hurting people by hurting herself had become Niya's normal. But it hurt Niya to hurt her mother; after all, her mother was her world. She'd done so much for Niya, including helping her to cope with Maurice's affair. She felt very connected with her mother and could not bear the sight of her crying.

As Niya stumbled towards the bathroom, she noticed her children sitting in the dining room eating breakfast. Her oldest daughter's name was Mariah, and she was five years old. Then, there was three-and-a-half-year-old Vanessa, who Niya had named after her mother. Finally, there was one-and-a-half-year-old Yadriel, who looked just like his deceased Uncle, only darker. Yadriel was in his booster seat, and Mariah was seated next to him, and she was feeding him. Not recognizing his mother, Yadriel began to scream and cry, but Niya didn't know why. She tried to go closer to him, but he screamed even louder and appeared to be trying to get out of his booster seat. Knowing that her brother was in distress, Mariah stood up and got in front of him. "Go and look in the mirror, mother." Niya reached up and touched her face. When she looked at her hand, she saw a black substance. Niya's mother rushed to the dining room to comfort Yadriel as Niya went to the bathroom. Niya's head was hurting and her stomach felt weak. When she looked at herself in the mirror, she became enraged. Niya did not like anyone touching her, and to know that her friends had painted her was enough to make her vow to

that house. Niya smiled. She knew her mother would be very pleased with her announcement. When Mrs. Vanessa saw her beautiful daughter coming towards her, she began to weep again. "My beautiful baby. Why do you do this to me? Why?" The pain in her voice hurt Niya more than she'd ever been hurt before. Here she had been angry with her dad for hurting her mother, but she was hurting her mother continuously. Niya hugged her mother and told her that everything would be okay.

Niya: Mom, stop crying. I'm sorry, Mom. I'm really sorry for hurting you. Please forgive me. I never wanted to hurt you.
Mrs. Vanessa: Why? Why do you do this to me, baby? Why? Do you want to kill me? I don't want to bury my baby. You're all I have left, Niya! If you die, I'll die!

Vanessa's words cut Niya to her soul. Niya fell to her knees and began to sob. The pain was so great. How had she been hurting her mother like this and not noticed? How had she been hurting her kids like that and not noticed? Her eyes were now open, and she could see all of the pain she'd been causing them. Maurice also stood by crying. He'd borne the guilt of having hurt Niya, but now the guilt was gone and replaced by a humbling disappointment in his fiancé. He glanced over at the children, who were now walking towards the living room. He'd already removed Yadriel from his booster seat and carried him towards the sofa. Mariah took Vanessa's hand, and they walked over to the couch and sat next to their father.

Niya: Can everyone sit down please? I have an announcement to make. Please sit down.

Maurice picked up little Yadriel and held Mariah's hand as they walked towards the couch. Everyone feared what Niya was about to say. After everyone was seated and the house was quiet, Niya began to speak.

Niya: Anger is what I know. I don't know how to be happy anymore. This is not an excuse; this is my truth.
Niya turned toward her mother.
Niya: Mom, I went for years hating Daddy for what he did to you. I hated him! When I saw you cry that day you found out about his affair, something in me changed. I let that anger mold me. I let that anger direct my steps and my thoughts.
Niya turned to Maurice.
Niya: Maurice, the worst time of my life was the day Natalia called me. Please don't interrupt me. Please hear me out. That day, any little hope for a future that I had in me...it died. I feel like I died that day. Every choice I made from then on out was about myself. I didn't care what happened to me, but now I realize that my pain made me selfish. I started hurting innocent people. I hurt my children, I hurt my mother, and I hurt myself. *Sobs.* I'm sorry. I'm really sorry. Mariah, I'm sorry for taking away a very special time in your childhood. You were more mature and more responsible than I was, and I thank you for looking out for Yadriel and Van for me. You are my angel, baby. Mommy's sorry, and

Mommy's going to do better starting today. You have my word on that.

I can't hurt you guys anymore. Please forgive me for everything I've done. Momma, you're right. I can't live without JESUS, and we will come to church with you every Sunday from here on out.

Maurice, baby, I know you said you wanted to answer the calling on your life, and I support you one thousand percent, but I need something from you.

Maurice: What's that, baby?

Vanessa: Last year, you told me that you wanted to go to the courthouse and marry so we can get our lives in line with the WORD of GOD. I told you that I wanted to wait two or three years because I wanted to have a big wedding. Is that offer still on the table?

Maurice goes to his knees in front of Vanessa and holds her hands.

Maurice: Of course. You and my children are my world. I'm sorry for what I did to you, baby. It was a dumb mistake, and it took me a long time to forgive myself and stop making excuses for my actions. I don't plan on ever leaving you, and I hope you don't plan on leaving me. I will never hurt you or my children like that again. Never.

Vanessa: Okay. Let's do it. Let's go and get married next week. Forget about a wedding. If I'm going to live for CHRIST, I need to start wholeheartedly right now.

Maurice hugged his beautiful bride-to-be as her mother sat next to them cradling little Yadriel and crying. Mrs. Vanessa was happy. She felt like she'd gotten her daughter back. She smiled and held Vanessa's hand as she said to her, "I love you, Niya. I really love you."

Over at Zara's house, the atmosphere was different. Everyone was now awake and sharing the details of the previous night with Donna. Donna had a combination of thoughts flooding her mind as the events of the story unfolded. On one hand, she wanted to minister to the lost souls standing before her. On the other hand, she wanted to join them in their plans to find Erica once again and fight her for attempting to attack Brielle. Her thoughts were conflicted, but she managed to push through her flesh to speak to her friends.

Donna: Listen, ladies. I'm about to tell you some truths, and I pray that you don't get angry with me. I really love all of you, and I was kinda wishing that you would all get saved so we could still be the best of friends. I have never pictured my life without you, and now, doors are opening for me that I have been afraid to go through because I didn't want to leave you all behind. Listen; it's time out for this foolishness. Fighting over no-good men, clubbing, drinking, gambling; what's it all for? Listen, Brielle. You're a pretty woman. You're loyal, intelligent, and you're not afraid to be who you are, and that's what I like about you. Rovy is not the one for you, and you know it. Don't let that man ruin your life.

Before Donna could finish talking, Brielle became angry and

began to speak.

Brielle: Listen, I didn't ask you for your opinion about my life! You do you, and I'll do me! If I want to be with Rovy, that's what I'm going to do; I'm gonna be with Rovy! I don't need you or no Bible-thumping preacher to tell me how to live my life! You don't like how I live? Don't call me then! Don't visit me and don't speak my name, whore! Because at the end of the day, everything that I am, you was!

Aubry: Yeah, that's what I'm saying. You want to go to church and "pwaise the lawd", you do just that! Don't come around here acting like you better than us! If you're so much better, why do you still come around?

Donna: I wasn't trying to sound judgmental. I love you ladies like sisters, and I guess I was just hoping that what we had would last.

Brielle: Nope. You need to go on back around yo-kind! I'm not sure if I even believe all that Bible stuff y'all be talking anyway. I'm happy with my life, fights and all! This is me; this is what I know!

Donna: Okay. Well, you have my number. I love you all, and I'll talk to you soon.

Donna got up to leave.

Zara: Donna, I understand what you are talking about. I was raised in the church. Do you remember what I told you about what happened to me at church?

Donna: No, you never told me anything happened. What happened?

Zara: My family used to go to church faithfully. My mom

sang in the choir, and my dad was a deacon. My mom and I
went to church one Tuesday evening for choir rehearsal, and
you know, my mom was the type of person who believed
everybody but me. Anyway, one of the choir members told
her that I'd licked my tongue out at her, but she was lying. I
was twelve years old, so I was way past that licking-out-the-
tongue stage, but my mom believed her anyway. Donna, I
was just twelve years old. My mom told me to go outside
and bring her the strap she kept in the glove compartment of
her car. I tried to reason with her, but she wouldn't listen.
She got angrier and angrier as I tried to tell her that I hadn't
done anything. You know, it was a really bad thing to even
insinuate that an adult was lying at that time. Anyhow, that's
when that lying choir member, Ms. Lucinda, spoke up and
told her fifteen-year-old son Kurtis to follow me out to my
momma's car. I'm not lying when I say I saw a smirk on her
face. She knew she was lying, and she knew I was about to
get beat down for something I hadn't done. Kurtis grabbed
me by my hand and started pulling me towards the door.
Kurtis was a huge boy. He was fat and just disgusting. Big
guys are okay, but Kurtis was one of those big lazy guys who
smelled like sewerage. Anyhow, we got out to the car, and I
remember I could hear the piano guy playing and the choir
started rehearsing. Kurtis grabbed me and started touching
on me, and I told him to stop. He wouldn't stop. He
punched me, dragged me behind the building, and he raped
me. That dog raped me. That fat nasty dog took my
innocence.
When we got back in the church, I was covered with grass

and I was bleeding. I tried to explain to my mother what had just happened, but she wouldn't listen at first. Kurtis's mother kept telling her to beat my behind for being so disrespectful, and that's what she did. On top of that rape, my momma beat me like I'd never been beaten before. After choir rehearsal, when we got in the car, I told my mom what had happened again, and this time she listened. When she wasn't around anyone, she listened, but she never apologized. She called Ms. Lucinda, and of course, Ms. Lucinda accused me of lying. She told my mom that Kurtis said I'd came on to him, but he'd resisted me. Here I was, covered in grass and bleeding, and no one could put two and two together? My momma never called the police. Instead, she thought she could handle it in the church. She was more concerned about her membership than her daughter. She told the Pastor, and he spoke with Ms. Lucinda, but they didn't do anything about it. I was told to hush up about it, and we kept going to that church. Ms. Lucinda would always roll her eyes at me after that. She would stare at me and wait on me to look at her so she could roll her eyes. I don't know why that woman hated me so much. Anyway, it wasn't until Kurtis tried to rape another girl at the church that action was taken against him. The second girl was seven years old. It was during another choir rehearsal when she said she had to use the bathroom. Ms. Lucinda, as always, volunteered Kurtis for the job of taking her to the bathroom. I don't know what kind of woman would suggest her teenage son to take a seven-year-old girl to the bathroom. Even worse than that was the mother who agreed to it. Thankfully, the choir had messed up and the music had stopped. The mother could hear her daughter screaming no from the bathroom, so she got up and ran into the bathroom. Kurtis was in there just about to expose himself, when the mother came in and beat him. She beat that boy like he'd never been beaten. Of course, Ms. Lucinda came in and tried to fight her off her son, but it didn't work. She beat and bit that boy up, and they had her arrested. Kurtis was arrested, and the little girl's mother was kicked out of the church. They said the matter should have been dealt with in the church. We kept going there, and no one ever thought to acknowledge that I had to be telling the truth.

So, do I believe in GOD? Yes, I believe in HIM. I just don't like church people. I'm proud of you for taking that leap of faith and I hope one day, I'll take that same leap. But right now, I'm not ready. I'm not ready to deal with judgmental church people and their cliques. I'm not ready to deal with any holier than thou personalities. I'm just not ready.

Donna: Zara, I'm sorry you went through that. I'm really sorry, and I can truly understand your resistance right now, but don't blame GOD for what happened to you. Zara, there are some really evil people out there who have churches, but they are not representatives of GOD, even though they say they are. That's why GOD calls us to know HIM so we will know which churches are dark establishments, and which churches are established on HIS WORD with HIS permission.

Aubrey: I don't mean to interrupt, but you two are really killing my buzz right now with all this religious talk.

Donna: Sorry, Aubrey. Anyhow, Zara, call me and we'll discuss this a little more. I need to hit the road and head back home.

Aubrey: There is a GOD.

Brielle: A-men!

Donna left, but she was hurt by the behaviors of her friends. She knew that she would be the hot topic of conversation, besides last night's brawl with Erica.

Donna had to finally remove herself from that clique. She had a new normal, and it did not match their normal. Zara continued hanging out with Aubrey and Brielle for another four years, until Aubrey and Brielle attacked her over a guy that Aubrey had once slept with. The guy was referred to as Brown, which was his surname. He was in the military and had become accustomed to being called by his last name. He'd met Aubrey in a club one night, and the two of them ended up sleeping together that night. It was a one-night stand, and he never called Aubrey or returned any of her calls.

Brown had met Zara a year later, and they exchanged numbers. Zara didn't know that he was the one-night stand that Aubrey spoke so highly of. After all, Aubrey was so drunk she couldn't remember his name, so she referred to him as the guy in the uniform. When he'd met Zara, he was smitten by Zara's good looks and charm. By this time, Zara had slowed down on the club scene and had just enrolled back in school. They went out together to the theater one night, and Brielle spotted them together. She remembered Brown and told Aubrey about Brown and Zara's date. By this time, Brown and Zara had been seeing one another for more than six months, so they were pretty stuck on one another. When Brown dropped her off at home that night, they didn't know that Brielle and Aubrey were standing on the side of the house waiting to ambush Zara.

Brown drove up in front of Zara's apartment and they leaned in to kiss one another. As Zara exited the vehicle, she was hit by Brielle, and then Aubrey began to drag her into the middle of the yard, where the two women proceeded to beat her as if they didn't know her. Brown had run from his vehicle and was able to restrain Brielle, but could not get his hands on Aubrey because of how fast she moved. Fortunately, a neighbor who was an off-duty police officer ran over and was able to restrain Aubrey. When Brown recognized Aubrey, he was angry and confused. Had she just attacked a woman that he liked over a one-night-stand? He later learned that Zara and Aubrey had been friends. Brown and Zara continued their relationship for another year before breaking up.

Zara reached out to Donna, who was now married with one child and pregnant with another one. She helped Zara to relocate to New York, where she continued her education and rededicated her life to CHRIST.

Aubrey and Brielle never got saved. They didn't want to be saved. Aubrey was a great dancer and a great fighter, and this was her claim to glory; this was her normal. Brielle was a good fighter and a good speaker. This was her claim to fame; this was her normal.

Niya made good on her word, and she returned to CHRIST. She and Maurice married a week after she'd told him and her mother that she was going to change. She disassociated from Aubrey, Brielle and Zara because of their lifestyles, but she stayed in contact with Donna. When Zara gave her life to CHRIST, she reconnected with Zara, and the three ladies remained good friends.

Niya also reconciled with her dad and apologized for her behavior towards him. He became a proud father once again, and they became very close once again.

There's a message behind each character's story.
Zara: Zara had been hurt while in a church building. Like so many fallen souls who'd gone before her, she allowed church hurt to drive her away from the church. Like so many fallen souls who'd gone before her, she did not understand that the very devil who'd hurt her was the same devil she was running to for protection. Make no mistake about it. A devil doesn't become a saint when it stands up in a religious building. There are many religious institutions that are full of devils because the leaders that hold services in those buildings have absolutely no power. They too are

demonically led and devil-filled.

GOD told us to get to know HIM more. HE told us to trust
HIM. But so many believers end up believing their leaders
and not the Almighty GOD. What does this mean? If you
don't know GOD for yourself, anyone can come along and
tell you who GOD is and what HE does, and you would
believe them. Personally, in my own walk, I have met so
many religious devils impersonating saints that I have
learned not to trust every word that falls from a person's
mouth. I have learned not to trust the titles that they bear. I
have learned not to become distracted by the religious
uniforms that they grace their bodies with. I had to learn to
look at a man or woman's fruit. What type of lifestyles are
they living? What types of deeds are they doing? I could
not determine if they served GOD, Satan or mammon until I
began to truly serve GOD. There are times that open eyes
don't see so clearly; therefore, we have to rely on GOD for
answers. When I first entered church, I had a "church lady"
basically robbing me of my money, but did she reflect the
church? No. She reflected her own darkness, but she was
and is not an uncommon fixture in many of the modern-day
churches. My problem was I didn't know GOD'S voice at
that time, so I was easily swayed by what I heard and what I
saw to the point where I was deafening myself to the voice of
GOD and covering up my spiritual eyes so I could see what I
wanted to see. I remember meeting a woman who claimed
to be a pastor, and she had one of the darkest spirits I'd ever
met. When I pulled away from her, she told me directly over

the phone that she was going to lie on me. Why? Because I did not want to associate with her anymore, once I'd gotten a whiff of her ways. I even met a guy who would shout "hallelujah" every time I opened my mouth. He kept saying the LORD was speaking to him; nevertheless, I later learned that he was robbing churches, pretending to sell them a service, but giving them absolutely nothing in return for their money. I met a married Apostle who tried to hit on me. There were many dark souls that I met in my walk, but again, they do NOT reflect the church. They are a reflection of the enemy and proof of how far he'll go to deceive the very elect of GOD, if he could. At the same time, I have met some beautiful, anointed men and women of GOD who have a true heart for GOD, and they fear HIM.

The parable of the tares and the wheat is a profound story of how the enemy of a man sowed tares in his wheat garden. The story represented how the enemy sowed evil people amongst GOD'S people. I decided to see what tares looked like, so I searched the Internet and found that tares look just like wheat. The enemy was unable to deceive the LORD with his attempt to sow tares amongst the elect of GOD, but the people of GOD can't tell the difference without the presence of GOD. We'll believe what we want to believe, but we'll oftentimes reject the truth because the lie sounds better.

If you never get to know GOD for yourself, you'll learn to know the difference between Him and the enemy. Satan doesn't mind you going to church. He doesn't mind you shouting and screaming up and down the aisles of the church. As long as your mind doesn't change, he will gladly let you be as religious as you want to be. But when you let GOD in, your mind will begin to change, and it is then that you will become a threat to the enemy.

The enemy sends people into the church building with the sole purpose of driving souls out of the church and back into his arms. You'll find souls like Ms. Lucinda littered throughout many churches today. With no light in them, they'll devour whomever they can. They recognize truly anointed people, and they will try to befriend those people with the intent of eventually humiliating, exposing or accusing them.

Zara was a typical saint-to-sinner story. She got hurt, and she let the devil scare her into submission to him. Eventually, she came back to the LORD and learned better.

Aubrey and Brielle: These two were likely never raised in church; therefore, they never had the WORD as a foundation in their life. Because of this, they had no desire to serve the LORD. They'd found something they were good at, and they'd found identities that they were comfortable with. Sin was their normal, and righteousness did not make sense to them. To come to CHRIST meant they would have to give up their normals. They would have to give up the things they were good at. Aubrey was a great dancer. She couldn't perform her dance moves in anybody's church. She was also a great fighter, and there are no boxing rings in church for her to show off her skills. Brielle was a great fighter and reasoner. She was the type of woman that many women flocked to for worldly advice.

When a sinner makes his mark in the world and establishes an identity in the world, it's very hard for them to give up their identities to follow the LORD. Now, someone who is a nobody in the world may consider church, because they may become a somebody in the church. A person who is honored in their foolishness is likely to stay in their foolishness. *"Like snow in summer or rain in harvest, honor is not fitting for a fool" (Proverbs 26:1 NIV).* The funny part is, the ones who do actually turn away from sin still have a hard time turning away from their glory days. That's why you'll find that old deacon, for example, who'll happily tell you how he used to have seven girlfriends at one time, and how many men he'd beat up in his youth. It's really hard to let go of glory. All the same, it's very dangerous to withhold glory from GOD, and it's very foolish to glorify sin.

Did you notice that Aubrey and Brielle did not confront Zara about Brown? Why was that? Obviously, there was an underlying issue already present, and Brown was an excuse for them to attack her. More than likely, the sisters recognized that Zara was not like them and wouldn't be around them for long.

Niya: There are so many people like Niya in the earth. Let's face it: We've all been hurt in our lives by people we know and love. But we can't allow the actions of another human being to weigh us down into unforgiveness. With our parents, we have to love and forgive them. At the same time, we have to recognize the fact that they are imperfect beings. Just like we struggle to stay on the straight and narrow, they struggle in their faith walks as well.

As for the wedding, there are so many women who are engaging in fornication with a man, and they keep putting off the wedding date because they want a big wedding. First off, fornication should never be a part of your life, but if you find yourself acting like a wife, go ahead and exchange vows with the man who has uncovered you so he can properly cover you. You can have a wedding ceremony or celebration later, when you can afford the one you want. It is better to give GOD what HE requires of you than it is for you to give yourself what you want for you, and then tell GOD to stand behind your flesh. Always remember that GOD is Alpha and Omega; the Beginning and the End. HE won't come second in line to anything or anyone. Many people will gladly claim that HE'S Alpha, but is HE Alpha in your life? Or is HE just Omega in your situation, but you have made yourself the Alpha or the first?

Niya had to open her heart to see what she was doing. Her unforgiveness was hurting the people around her. Getting drunk is a form of daily suicide. Doing drugs is a form of daily suicide. It's when people kill themselves by killing their own will for a period of time. This is a time when they allow devils to drive them; a time when they rob themselves of the dominion that GOD has given them. People often drink to escape their own realities or to experience a careless existence where they can finally hold a moment's worth of happiness and not face the struggles that we all have to come face-to-face with. It's an admission of weakness, and a declaration of one's refusal to allow life to make them stronger. Getting drunk or doing drugs is a cop-out; the soul's cry out to the world that wisdom is not present in it. *"Wine is a mocker, strong drink is raging: and whosoever is deceived thereby is not wise" (Proverbs 20:1).*

Niya could have lost it all; ruined her children's life and killed her mother with worry, but she chose to turn her life around for the better. Sadly, many women don't make this choice, but they continue to blindly head down the wrong path looking for a blessing in sin.

Donna: Donna could have lost herself trying to hold on to who she was, all the while trying to embrace who she is. Trying to hold on to old friends is very common for a baby Christian, because when we are young in CHRIST, we want to believe that we can bring the ones we love with us. But GOD gave everyone free will, and HE didn't drag you into HIS will when you didn't want to be there. HE wants you and me to want HIM because through CHRIST JESUS, HE has already said HE wants us. Most of us tried to convince our old friends to come to church with us, stop drinking, stop clubbing, stop cursing, stop hanging around certain people, and on the list goes on. But they chose to continue on the paths they were on because that was their normal. We were trying to or had already embraced a new normal, but we sometimes want to merge our old ways of living with our present ways of living, and this just does not work.

Donna found herself falling in and out of the arms of sin. That's what happens when you hang around sinners; you will eventually pick up their ways. Anytime we start hanging out with people who love sin, we'll start to get more and more comfortable with sin. Sin will slowly drag a woman back into her old way of thinking, where devils are waiting to make sure that she never leaves again. *"When the unclean spirit is gone out of a man, he walketh through dry places, seeking rest, and findeth none. Then he saith, I will return into my house from whence I came out; and when he is come, he findeth it empty, swept, and garnished. Then goeth he, and taketh with himself seven other spirits more wicked than himself, and they enter in and dwell there: and the last state of that man is worse than the first. Even so shall it be also unto this wicked generation"* (Matthew 12:43-45). Always remember this: Once the face of sin is shown around you again and again, you'll eventually get used to it. It'll become familiar to you, and you'll slowly become so comfortable with it that you will no longer recognize it as evil. This is what the bible refers to as darkness. You will slowly become blind to the truth and drunk with lies.

Had Donna not finally understood that she could not continue her friendship with her old friends, many doors would have closed in her face because she chose to walk in the familiar and not the peculiar. Thankfully, she finally embraced the truth and made the best of her life.

Please understand that your normal is not someone else's normal. For example, some of the places we lived growing up had cockroaches. Even though they were irritating, this was our normal, so we learned to stomp them and keep on living. We learned to put away food properly and stir our cereal to make sure nothing floated up to the top. Many people had this very same childhood, so this was their normal. There were some occasions when we had friends over who did not have cockroaches and had never lived with them. Then tended to react strongly to the sight of a cockroach, and we found it funny. As an adult, however, I can't live with insects. It's not my normal anymore. A child who grew up in a wealthy home doesn't see their wealth as a big deal. Their lifestyle is their normal. Because they are accustomed to living in luxury, they aren't often moved when their parents buy them things. Because of this, many people refer to them as spoiled. It's not always that they are spoiled. Sometimes, the issue is they are just accustomed to having nice things and receiving nice things. A child who grew up in poverty oftentimes does not know that they are poor. Their way of living is their normal, and they aren't bothered by it. Hand them the keys to a new car, and they'll likely react very strongly, because this is not normal for them.

I remember staying at a cousin's house one weekend when I was a child. Even though we were poor, we always had something to eat, even if it was just a sandwich. During that time, I couldn't go without eating; I'm not sure why. If I got too hungry, I would start to feel weak; I would get a migraine headache, and eventually I would fall asleep. My body was used to eating.

At this cousin's house, there was no food to eat. The first day was okay, because I'd arrived there in the evening. But the next morning, I was in agony. I kept asking for food, and I could not understand how my cousins were outside playing as if nothing was wrong. Here I was in the house, trembling and crying. Three o'clock in the afternoon came, and we still hadn't eaten anything, but the other kids weren't phased by it at all. I finally couldn't take it anymore, and I ended up calling my mom and begging her to come and pick me up. Why weren't they bothered by their hunger? They were used to it. It was their normal. They knew they'd eat eventually, so they learned to focus their energy and thoughts elsewhere.

Oftentimes, the people in this earth judge one another because their norms are different than the norms of others. It's absolutely foolish to judge others who are unlike us, because we rob ourselves of the opportunity to learn something new. I met a few African women who'd grown up in polygamist households. They told me about their experiences as one of the children of one of their dad's wives. It was normal for them, but I was amazed at their stories so much that I was more focused on what they were saying than the other people who saw the polygamist lifestyle as normal.

Anytime we come into CHRIST, we are required to let go of our old norms to embrace new realities, and this isn't always easy. At the same time, the heart of GOD is without limitations; therefore, we are always traveling in HIM, trying to get closer to HIM. This means that even in our Christian walks, we have to constantly give up old ways of thinking and old lifestyles to embrace new ones.

Fact: The average person called by GOD does not answer the call, or they'll answer the call to a certain extent and then turn back to their old lifestyles.

Fact: It's hard to walk away from what you know, and the people you love, but know this: Elevation is not GOD giving you a bunch of stuff so you can finally be happy. Elevation is you walking through doors that GOD already had opened for you in your due season. It is you coming into position to do HIS will and glorify HIS Name. Elevation has nothing to do with you, and everything to do with the glory of GOD. That is to say if you want to elevate in GOD, you have to join hands with the already declared WORD of GOD and walk in obedience to where HE called you to arrive. Many people will never see elevation because they somehow convinced themselves that their lives were for them and about them. They reject new knowledge, causing themselves to be rejected by GOD. *"My people are destroyed for lack of knowledge: because thou hast rejected knowledge, I will also reject thee, that thou shalt be no priest to me: seeing thou hast forgotten the law of thy God, I will also forget thy children" (Hosea 4:6).*

Never get comfortable in a mindset, no matter how far you've gone in CHRIST. Even if you were some mega-ministry millionaire, you should never get too comfortable in what you know, because there is always new knowledge to be had. The more knowledge you acquire, the more people you can minister to, and the more souls that will come to CHRIST after hearing the knowledge of HIM in you. After all, anytime you reject knowledge, you are rejecting the opportunity to know HIM better.

Finally, there were the word curses spoken at one another. Why do some women do this? It's simple: People speak of you whatever is in their hearts for you, but they know you won't receive it if they were to take off the smiling masks. Luke 6:45 reads, *"A good man out of the good treasure of his heart bringeth forth that which is good; and an evil man out of the evil treasure of his heart bringeth forth that which is evil: for of the abundance of the heart his mouth speaketh."* As you go forward in CHRIST, one thing you'll learn is that some women can hang out with you, fight for you and pay your bills when you don't have the money to do so, and still hate your guts. Why would they help you out then? Because they are investing in something they see in you. It's not love that makes them give. Sometimes, envy can drive a woman to do more for you than a true friend has done for you. You have to check the spirit behind everyone's giving.

What's your normal, and what would you like to see changed? Pray about it and embrace new ways of thinking and living, and your normal will change to line up with your new mindset.

A true friend won't curse you; they will speak blessings over you. Remember, every friendly person is not your friend, and every person you call a friend today may be a friend for you now, but as you level up in CHRIST, they may become an enemy later. Some friends are just people who are at the same level as you, and because the two of you can relate to one another, you befriend one another. But when your mind changes, and you are not able to relate to one another anymore, chances are, you will separate. Please understand that if you intend to grow in the LORD, with no plans to stop growing in HIM, you can NEVER TRULY have truckloads of people to call friends. This includes believers whom you see as further in CHRIST than yourself. The reason is some people get to a certain height in CHRIST, and they refuse to grow any further because they feel they've come far enough. If you continue to grow without restrictions, eventually the two of you will no longer agree because your understanding will supersede what they know. That's when your friends will start referring to you as "holier than thou" and saying things like, "Well, I don't understand all that you keep talking about, but what I do know...." In order for you to remain close to them, you will have to reject new knowledge. In other words, you will have to reject what GOD is trying to give you. If your friend is a mature believer who loves the LORD, and they witness you go forward in CHRIST, whereas they have stopped moving out of fear, they will celebrate your elevation in HIM. All the same, they will watch you grow forth and go forth in HIM first, and they will use your story to get over their fears so they can advance in HIM as well. In such a case, the two of you will find yourselves agreeing and then disagreeing, only to agree again. This means the friendship will stay intact as a brotherhood, whereas you will serve as the older sibling, but only if GOD allows.

Never reject new knowledge, new understanding or wisdom. Embrace them all, but make sure that anyone who comes near your life and your anointing has permission by GOD to do so. Additionally, inform your friends that you are growing in the LORD and you intend to keep growing in HIM, never getting comfortable in a certain realm of understanding. Make sure the people who are close to you are people who love and fear the LORD; souls who are advancing in HIM, just as you are. If someone is parked in a mindset, your job is to minister to them, sharpen them and encourage them to go forward. Your job is not to park there with them and retire.

Her Story- B. Davinia Gordon

"A woman who waits for her husband ripens into being a wife before she's picked."

The truth is, the large majority of women want to be married, even the ones who say that they don't. The purpose of the wait is to teach us long-suffering. After all, no marriage will survive without long-suffering; nevertheless, the average believer eventually stops waiting and starts pursuing the desires of their heart. There's a problem with this, however. Jeremiah 17:9 sheds light on this problem for us. *"The heart is deceitful above all things, and desperately wicked: who can know it?"* Because the heart is wicked, it sends forward wicked imaginations, but it passes them off as good. That's why GOD sent us a warning in 2 Corinthians 10:5, which reads: *"Casting down imaginations, and every high thing that exalteth itself against the knowledge of God, and bringing into captivity every thought to the obedience of Christ."*

Nevertheless, the thoughts persist, and it's easy to get caught up in imaginations that seem pleasurable to us now. But GOD has created everything to start off as a seed and grow up as a harvest in its due season. Anytime we become impatient, we can easily cancel the process and forfeit the promises of GOD for our lives.

Below, you will read B. Davinia Gordon's story detailing her wait for her GOD-ordained husband and the struggles that followed. The story below was written by B. Davinia Gordon and is told in her own words.

When I first received word through a prophecy that God has prepared a husband for me, I was 23 years old. I was ecstatic! Finally, my dreams of being married and having a family were going to come true. However, my Bishop said something that I will never forget. He said, "Do not fall for Ishmael. Wait for Isaac. Ishmael is the counterfeit; Isaac is the promise. You won't have to look for him; he is going to find you."

During that time, I was the other woman in a relationship for four years. I just KNEW that I was going to marry this guy, and I was determined to MAKE him the one. Needless to say, God did not approve of this relationship, and subsequently, we went our separate ways.

At first, I was relieved to be free of a man. It felt great to know that for once, I could live my life without it revolving around a man. I was happy, confident, and feeling wonderful about myself. Then Facebook happened. I started to see family, friends and other women getting engaged, married, pregnant and having kids. At first, I was genuinely happy for them. My joy for them was because I believed that any day now, my husband was going to find me and I could gush with joy along with them.

That year passed. No husband.

I was disappointed, but I kept encouraging myself in the LORD, knowing that in time, HE was going to deliver.

Some more time passed. Still no husband.

At that point, I was beyond anxious. That joy I felt for all those women getting married and starting families turned to envy. I went to church and saw all of the married couples with their children and coveted what they had.

Another year passed. Still no husband.

Then came the questions.

Why are you single? When are you gonna get married? Why don't you have kids yet?

Meanwhile, my responses were like a broken record of the most annoying song ever: "I haven't come across the right guy yet", "I desire to abstain until marriage", "I am waiting on the Lord to send my husband", "I don't have kids, because I am not married yet."

Their response was often, "Girl, it don't take all that! You need to go ahead and give it up already!"

Then, the dreaded coup de grace statement: "You are gonna be single for the rest of your life if you don't loosen up!"

So basically, the general consensus was that me being a Christian who followed the Word of God, refusing to lie with a man until marriage, was the reason why I didn't have a man.

Got it.

At first, I was able to brush off the feelings of anxiety and cling to God's promise to bless me with a family. But as time continued to pass, without any real prospects of a husband, I slowly began to doubt that it was ever going to happen for me - at least happen for me God's way.

Let's face it. Practically everyone that I knew who was Christian and in a relationship or had gotten married was fornicating. The guys that I did attract were either not saved, unattractive, or they ran for the door as soon as they knew that I was serious about waiting until marriage for sex. And yes, these were 'Christian' men.

Meanwhile, I and countless other women got to watch compromising women who were shacking, fornicating and having children out of wedlock get married to those same 'Christian' men. Fantastic. So, if my understanding is correct based off of the continuing trend; the only way that I can be with someone is if I settle for an unequally yoked, unattractive man who I will have to lay with before marriage.

Needless to say, I was furious. It seemed like a swift slap in the face to see people who were not in the will or obedience of God being able to enjoy the very thing that I so passionately desired: A husband and a family.

They were living their lives; they were happy, and they have all the pictures and videos to show for it. In fact, from where I was sitting; it looked like they were successfully able to sin their way into a blessing after all.

Suddenly, I started to question myself and the strong stance that I took to serve and obey the Lord. Most of my days were spent longing to feel complete, needing to feel loved and have that companionship. At the same time, that blasted ticking time-bomb of my biological clock seemed like it was taunting me with an everyday reminder that I didn't have children. Truthfully, I felt bitter, disappointed, abandoned, lonely and forgotten. I felt like it was impossible for the right man of God to come along, because there were so few single ones left.

After years of still having no husband, I started to believe that it just wasn't going to happen for me. I began to think that my obedience to Christ was the reason I wasn't going to get married. It seemed like each prospect would get better and better, but they were all missing the one thing that was the most important thing: the ability to lead me in obedience to CHRIST and maintain our purity until marriage. It is truly amazing how the devil almost convinced me that my obedience to CHRIST was the reason why I was so 'unattractive' to all these men and that something was 'wrong' with me. Lies!
But after spending some quality time with GOD, He opened my eyes to the truth. First, you can NEVER sin your way into a blessing! Sure, people will make it seem like it is

possible; but always remember that just because the consequences of sin are delayed, it doesn't mean that it's denied. The only way that you will get to what GOD has for you is to love Him and obey His WORD. You can't build a Godly relationship using the devil's tools.

Secondly, when JESUS lives in you and you walk in obedience and the love of GOD, you will be 'unattractive' to all of the WRONG men that come your way! In fact, I was experiencing James 4:7 come to pass in my life!
"Submit yourselves therefore to God. Resist the devil, and he will flee from you" (James 4:7).
Also, I had to humble myself to the fact that I wanted to be married for all the wrong reasons. I desired marriage so that I could cure my loneliness, fulfill my sexual desires and to feel complete. GOD began to minister to me that HE needed to come first in every area of my life and that I needed to be content with HIM and HIS will for my life before HE would fulfill HIS promise to me.
"But seek ye first the kingdom of God, and his righteousness; and all these things shall be added unto you" (Matthew 6:33 KJV).

It was then that I realized that by desiring the love and validation of a man, I was rejecting the love and validation of JESUS. I became so wrapped up in the idea of being married that I had turned marriage into an idol. Yes, I became 'married' to the idea of being married. It was all I thought about. I was excited about the prospect of becoming a wife, and at the same time, frustrated that I wasn't a wife already.

Then I came across this scripture:

"For thy Maker is thine husband; the Lord of hosts is his name; and thy Redeemer the Holy One of Israel; The God of the whole earth shall he be called.

For the Lord hath called thee as a woman forsaken and grieved in spirit, and a wife of youth, when thou wast refused, saith thy God.

For a small moment have I forsaken thee; but with great mercies will I gather thee" (Isaiah 54:5-8).

At that moment, all the feelings of despair, sorrow and rejection made sense. God was there all along, covering me as my Husband. His love for me became more real than ever before. His words were a healing balm to my grieved spirit as I drew closer to Him.

Now, I am 27 years old, and I am married. I get to be the imperfect wife to a perfect Savior and have the best Lover alive to teach me how to be a Godly wife and what to expect out of the man He is going to send for me one day.

I am content, I am complete, and most importantly; I am loved by the greatest man in the world: Jesus.
The End.

As told by B. Davinia Gordon

What happened with the author is common amongst the

women of GOD. Let's be honest with ourselves. It's not easy to wait when there are needs and desires present. Oftentimes, the real issue is that there is a void on the inside of us, and we have learned to associate relationships as a cure for these voids. After all, when we were in relationships that felt like they were going somewhere, those voids seemed to vanish. But once we were alone again, those voids came screaming out of our heart's closets. There are reasons GOD won't give you a husband when there is a void present in you.

1. GOD is the only GOD, and HE won't share HIS throne with any man. We are created by GOD. HE is our CREATOR; therefore, only HE can fill a void in our lives. Placing a man or a thing where GOD should have been is the same as taking an idol for yourself to worship. Putting a man where GOD is needed is like pouring dishwater in your gas tank.

2. Anyone who fills a void in our lives ends up having power over our lives. This power belongs to GOD and should never be handled by man. What does this mean? Pay attention to stalkers who have been arrested for murdering the person they were stalking. What was their issue? They'd put a person in a place in their lives and in their hearts, and they gave these people some GOD-sized responsibilities that they could not fill. In many cases, the predator was so enraged by their partner's inability to fill GOD'S shoes that they became verbally and physically abusive. Most predators who stalk their prey abuse narcotics

or alcohol as well because they are looking for something to fill that void in their lives. A person who is given power in another person's life, power that they were never supposed to have, will abuse that power. Such characters have the power to determine the weather for the person they are preying on each day. They can determine if that person has a good day full of sunshine and smiles, or if that person has a bad day full of storms and chaos. GOD never intended for a man to have this kind of power over another human being.

3. A person who has voids won't be stable in a relationship. They would be driven by the fear of losing the very person they feel completes them. This would make them a danger to themselves and the person they are in a relationship with.

4. A person with voids will eventually walk away from that relationship and enter one relationship behind the other once they discover that their partners are unable to fill the shoes they are trying to get them to wear.

5. A person with voids would be led by their flesh in most of their dealings. They may be calm when everything is going well, but they'd be highly emotional any time their fear is triggered.

At the same time, any time we marry a person and try to use them to fill those voids in our lives, we become a stumbling block to that person. *"But take heed lest by any means this liberty of yours become a stumbling block to them that are weak" (1 Corinthians 8:9).*

Unlike the large majority of believing women, the author decided to wait on GOD. There is no doubt in my mind that she will end up in the arms of her GOD-ordained husband and not in the deceitful claws of an Ishmael. She chose not to be led by her lusts anymore. She chose to be led by the SPIRIT, and we know that HE can never mislead us. Needless to say, there are countless women out there who will not adhere to this message because most women recognize their own uniqueness and feel that their circumstances are different than the circumstances of other women. The enemy is able to convince many women that GOD will turn a blind eye to their iniquities (the hidden sins of their hearts) and HE will understand them when they enter relationships that HE did not ordain. After all, they plan on bringing the man to CHRIST. They don't plan on walking away from the LORD, so in their minds, there is nothing evil about pursuing the relationships.

I remember a girl wrote me one time to complain about her family. She was a believing woman, and she'd just reconnected with a man from her past. Of course, the man was an unbeliever, and the two ended up dating again and decided to get married. Her family had been against the relationship and were definitely against the marriage. She was pretty upset with her family, and she wanted me to weigh in on the matter. I told her the truth. The Bible did say not to be unequally yoked with unbelievers. She'd even told me some of the things the man did and said that served as red flags to me. Nevertheless, she would not hear the truth from me either. She was looking for someone to tell her that her marriage to him would work out, and she'd win his soul for CHRIST. I couldn't lie to her. The Bible asks us how we know if we will win our husband's souls. *(See 1 Corinthians 7:16)*. That is to say there is no guarantee. The book of 1 Corinthians also tells us that if the unbelieving want to leave, to let them leave, for GOD has called us to peace. What this is telling us is that we can expect our peace to be challenged, attacked and ran off if we marry unbelievers. Sadly enough, the girl closed the chat message and wanted to hear nothing more from me because I did not say to her what she wanted to hear. One thing about the Truth is HE doesn't go away just because we want to deny HIM or just because HE doesn't fit into our plans for ourselves. We can make plans with the wrong men every day for several years and still watch those relationships crumble in a matter of seconds. *"There are many devices in a man's heart; nevertheless the counsel of the LORD, that shall stand"* *(Proverbs 19:21)*

It is always a blessing to see one more soldier for CHRIST standing for HIM against all odds, opinions and natural logic. Nevertheless, anytime we come across that one who will wait on GOD; eventually we get to stand in awe at the glorious gift that person will hold. After seeing them blessed with their GOD-ordained and loving husbands, many women

231

will turn to look at the Ishmaels they'd chosen for themselves in utter disgust, and they will whisper in their hearts, "GOD, just give me one more chance. This time, I will obey you. This time, I will wait."

In Full Costume

"When the character you display on the outside doesn't match the character you are on the inside, you will become best friends with rejection. After all, it was you who first rejected yourself."

It's not uncommon these days to see women covered from head to toe in full costume. Nowadays, the norm for many women is to pack on the weave, hide behind the makeup and wear outfits that make them look like plastic super heroes. That's because Hollywood has become the dark shepherds of so many lost souls.

Don't get me wrong. A little hair here, and a little makeup there doesn't hurt sometimes, but if you couldn't recognize yourself in a lineup if those things were removed from you, you need to get to the root of the issue.

"It's my face and I like it just the way it is, so let's continue, please." Ebony was unrelenting and unapologetic. Ebony was a beautiful girl with gorgeous cocoa skin and naturally thick hair. She was totally against makeup, chemicals being put in her hair, and she loved to wear Afrocentric clothing. She was at a photo shoot, and her new photographer was beginning to get under her skin. She'd hired the photographer after hearing about her through some of her professional friends. Ebony was one of those women who considered herself pro-black, so she was always trying to support African-American owned businesses. She didn't like her new photographer too well and planned to never use her again.

The photographer's name was April, and she had her own studio in Los Angeles, California. April was a nice woman, by all accounts, but on this day, she felt as if she kept saying the wrong things. April was medium-complexioned and the total opposite of Ebony. April wore her hair permed, and she loved makeup. She almost didn't look as if she was there to photograph anyone; she looked as if she was there to be photographed. She wore a peach, one-piece jumpsuit that had a slight flare at the legs. The peach jumpsuit set off April's beautiful skin-tone, and Ebony loved the outfit. It wasn't fitted. It made April look like a professional woman, but her words were irritating to Ebony.

Ebony had her own magazine for African American women, and she needed some photographs done of herself. She'd just fired her old photographer because he was a no-show on some of the photo shoots. Now, here she was trying out a new photographer, and she was stepping on her toes already.

The incident was a minor one, but Ebony was being a little too snippy with April. Ebony felt that any woman who wore

weave, makeup or perms were self-hating, and she hated to
see what she referred to as "African queens being caught up
in a system that glorified European features." April noticed
how beautiful Ebony was and didn't understand why she
wasn't wearing any makeup. She felt that a hint of green
eyeshadow would compliment Ebony's colorful African gown,
and a little blush would highlight her high cheekbones.

April: You are such a pretty woman, but may I make a
suggestion?
Ebony: Sure.
April: I think you have some really beautiful features. I also
do makeup and I would love to.....
Ebony cut her off.
Ebony: No. I don't wear makeup.
April: But why? I think a little makeup would really set off
what you are wearing and highlight your features.
Ebony: Thank you, but no. It's my face, and I like it just the
way it is, so let's continue, please.

April was surprised, but she'd obviously never read Ebony's
magazine, which was called Sans Visage Magazine. Sans
visage is French for faceless. Why did such a beautiful
woman not want to be even more beautiful? The truth was
that April was excited about photographing Ebony. She'd
heard about her magazine but had never read it. When she
heard that Ebony wanted to try her on as their new
photographer, she went out and purchased a copy of the
magazine but hadn't gotten around to opening it. After

seeing Ebony, she thought she could offer a few pointers to help out the natural beauty. She knew her work would be featured, and she wanted everything to be perfect.

April: I apologize. I wasn't trying to imply that you weren't beautiful, because you are beautiful. You are absolutely gorgeous.
Ebony: No harm taken. Thank you.

The session lasted over an hour, and everything seemed to be going smoothly until five minutes before the session ended. April still wasn't fully satisfied with the session. Most of her clients would bring a change of clothes, and they would change their hair during the sessions, but Ebony wore the same clothing with the same hairstyle. Her hair was twisted in Bantu knots. April remembered a new wig she had and thought it would look great on Ebony. Again, her intentions weren't bad, but she didn't know what Ebony stood for.

April: You take beautiful photos.
Ebony: Thanks.
April: Please don't get offended. It's just a question.
Ebony: Ask away.
April: Most of my clients bring a change of clothing and wear versatile hairstyles so they can switch it up.
Ebony: Okay.
April: Did you bring anything with you, like a wig or any extra clothes?

Ebony: Why would I need a wig?

April: Ebony, your hair is beautiful, but I guess what I'm looking to do is show you in different styles.

Ebony: April, I am just fine as I am. Now, let me speak to you. Why is it that you feel makeup makes you more beautiful? Why do you feel wearing a weave makes you more beautiful?

April: I'm not wearing a weave. This is my natural hair, and I don't feel like makeup makes me more beautiful. I feel that it enhances my beauty. I'm an artist, so I use myself as a canvas.

Ebony: Why? You're a pretty girl I'm sure, but I can't really see you behind the mask you're wearing.

April: Okay, Ms. Ebony. I'm sorry. I did not mean to offend you.

Ebony: I wasn't trying to insult you. You see, when you imply that I need a wig, that's offensive. When you imply that I need makeup, that's offensive. Just like when I imply that you need to remove the mask and be your natural self, that's offensive to you.

April: I understand. My apologies.

Ebony: You've obviously never read my magazine, have you?

April: No. I picked up a copy the other day, but I haven't read it yet.

Ebony: Well, you should. I mentor many women about going back to their roots and finding who they really are.

While Ebony was talking, April's older sister Amber walked

into the studio. She had a lunch date with her sister and sat down to let the women finish their conversation. April's sister Amber wore her hair natural as well. She was wearing an afro, but she also wore makeup, and her attire was very European yet fashionable.

Ebony: Our ancestors were brought here as slaves, and we were taught that our black was ugly. Our lips were too big; our hair was freakish, and our bodies were deformed. We looked to the white man for a definition of what beautiful is and what beautiful does. My magazine encourages sisters to find their way back to their roots and stop trying to look European.

At that, April's sister could not hold her peace.
Amber: Excuse me, what's your name?
Ebony: It's Ebony. Why do you ask?
Amber: Okay, I ask because I want to address you formally. Ebony, have you ever been to Africa?
Ebony: No, I haven't, but I plan to go someday.
Amber: Okay, I've been to Africa three times. I went to Nigeria, I went to Kenya, and I went to Egypt. Do you know what I found out?
Ebony: No. What?
Amber: Every country in Africa has its own culture. Every village has its own dialect. The people are very diverse. You can actually walk fifteen minutes up the street from one village and enter another village where the people are speaking a totally different language than their neighbors.

They dress differently than their neighbors. As a matter of fact, many of them are able to determine what village a person is from just by the clothes they are wearing. So, I ask you, since you are so root-oriented, what country are your ancestors from, and what people does your clothing represent?

Ebony: I have no idea. Like I said, I've never been to Africa, but I know my ancestors are of African decent; therefore, I honor them by honoring who I am.

Amber: Okay. Since you are honoring them, what religion do you follow?

Ebony: I'm not a religious person.

Amber: More than likely, your ancestors were religious. As a matter of fact, a large number of African tribes practiced ancestor worship, voodoo or other forms of witchcraft. It wasn't a religion for them; it was mostly a lifestyle of superstition. So, why is it that you are pro-African, but you've never been to Africa? Why is it that you are pro-African, but you don't practice their religious beliefs? Did you drive a car here? Are you living in a hut or a house? Look at your nose. It's not that wide; it's more pointed. Don't you realize that you have multiple heritages, but it's hard for you to identify each heritage; therefore, you identify with the obvious? Your skin is dark; therefore, you are black.

Ebony: I understand everything you are saying, but you are missing the point. I'm not anti-white, I'm just pro-black. I am coming against self-hatred, and the downward spiral of the African-American woman.

Amber: Why do you call black women African-American?

Caucasians don't call themselves European-Americans. They call themselves Caucasians. Referring to yourself as an African-American can be seen as you acknowledging that the country you were born in and you live in is not your country, but that's not true. No color can stake claim to this country. America is a mixing pot, and if anyone had the rights to claim this place, it would be the Native Americans. *Amber turns to her sister, April.*

April, let me ask you this: Why do you perm your hair? Is it to make you more beautiful?

April: No, I love the afro-look more. It's just too hard for me to manage, so I perm my hair. I tried to go natural once, but my scalp is tender, and it hurt me to comb my hair.

Amber: So you would say that your choice to have a perm has nothing to do with self-hatred?

April: Of course not. When I wore my hair natural, I felt beautiful, just as I feel beautiful wearing it straight.

Amber: And that's just it. Ebony, in this place we call America, there are multiple races, cultures, beliefs and preferences. True, some people hide themselves under hair and makeup because they think European features are prettier; nevertheless, not every black woman wearing a weave hates herself. I wear my hair natural, but I still wear weaves and wigs from time to time. I love the fact that I can switch it up, but I choose natural hair because I know my hair. I know how to manage it, and I have learned its personality; nevertheless, I don't judge other women who don't know their hair. So until you take off your costume, you can't tell anyone else to remove theirs.

Ebony: And what is my costume, may I ask?

Amber: You're impersonating an African woman, but you've never been to Africa. You are wearing clothes from a particular village or country, and you have no clue where or what your clothes represent. You are teaching people about their skin, yet you don't teach them about their spirit. The flesh will die, and you won't be black once it falls away. What remains are dusty, off-white bones. Do you identify with your skeletal remains? After all, that's the part of your natural man that will likely stay around for thousands of years, but that beautiful black skin of yours will fall away from you once you're dead. Those beautiful full lips of yours will rot. It's the same thing with Whites, Latinos, Asians...you name it. The flesh will die someday and it'll turn back to dust, so until you can teach someone about their roots in JESUS CHRIST, you are misleading them to believe that their color is who they are, when it is not. I'm all for empowering my race, but look at my skin. I'm light-skinned, so should I help empower the white people as well? Then again, I can't truly say that my light skin comes from a European being in my lineage. After all, not all Africans were or are dark-skinned. In Africa, you will find that the more northeast you go, the lighter the skin will be and the narrower their noses are. That's because of the position of the sun there. Those who are closest to the equator are often the darkest. At the same time, America has been a mixing pot for a while; therefore, my light skin could have possibly come from an Asian being in my lineage; a Latino being in my lineage, or I may have a great-great grandfather

who was Middle Eastern. The point is, I don't know who they
were, and I don't know where they all came from. What I do
know is that I identify myself as a black woman because just
like you, that's what I was told that I am, even though my
skin isn't black. I love my heritage, but more than that, I love
my GOD, so I don't get caught up in these pro-movements
about what color my skin is and how I should embrace my
roots. How can I embrace my roots when my ancestors are
more than likely a mixture of people from several different
races and cultures? Do I identify with the color that I see, or
do I identify with my African ancestors because they were
oppressed and need my help the most?

Ebony: I like your reasoning, and I wasn't trying to be
offensive to you or Ms. April here. What I am defending is
my right to be me, just as I am. I don't need a wig; I don't
need makeup, and I don't have to wear European clothes. I
love who I am as I am.

Amber: And that's great. But think about this. April has her
right to be who she is, and as she goes further in the LORD,
her identity will continue to change. At the same time, we
wear costumes to fit the times we are in. Your costume is
more obvious than hers because you are going out of your
way to promote yourself as separate from other blacks. You
see yourself as superior, more educated and more
enlightened. But the truth is, your real identity is wrapped up
in JESUS CHRIST, and if you never know HIM, all you will
ever know about yourself is that you were once a black
woman before you died, but know this: There are no Whites,
Blacks, Latinos or Asians in Heaven; we leave that mess

behind. In addition, hell doesn't care what color you are, because crispy looks the same on everyone. If you want to help someone, tell them how to find CHRIST. Look for that woman whom Hollywood told that her dark hair, her brown eyes and her dark skin is ugly. Instead of trying to take her back to her African roots, try leading her to CHRIST; otherwise, you are only taking her from one prison into another one. When you see a Caucasian woman with collagen in her lips and silicon in her breasts, try ministering to her instead of trying to teach her about her roots. The only roots we need to focus on are the wicked things that have taken root in our hearts and in the hearts of GOD'S children. When you see a woman with her derriere hanging out, try leading her to CHRIST and covering her with the Blood of JESUS until she learns to love herself and cover herself naturally. Let me ask you this: Are you married?
Ebony: Yes, I am.
Amber: How many wives does your husband have?
Ebony: What are you talking about? He only has me.
Amber: Okay, that's against many African cultures, especially ancient Africa. Many Africans believe in polygamy; therefore, if you want to honor your dead ancestors, you may need to help him find a few more wives, especially if he has some ranking. Also, many African people worship or pray to their dead ancestors, and they believe they can pray and speak to them to remove curses. Additionally, a lot of Africans don't inherit the last names of their mothers and fathers. In many African countries, a child takes the last name of whomever that child's parents chose

to name them after. So, if you want to get back to your African roots, you have a lot of work to do.

Ebony: That's all interesting. May I ask you, what do you do?

Amber: I am a forensic pathologist. I conduct autopsies on dead people, and let me tell you one thing: I have never seen a dead woman complain about her hair, her makeup or who she's lying next to on the table. Our color is only smoke and mirrors; it's here today, gone tomorrow. But what lasts forever is our spirit man, and that's who we need to focus on grooming. Sure, there are many racist devils out there who point to our brown and black skin and tell us that we are beneath them, but that's only because there is no wisdom in them. In order to address them, you have to go to their level. But to prove them to be the blind liars that they are, you simply show yourself as a GOD-fearing woman who is not defined by their limitations. They have no choice but to see that you are black because they are blind, and every form of success you garner, they will attribute it to themselves. Just as every failure you have, they will attribute to your color because that's all they can see. But why focus your life on dead people? Anytime I conduct an autopsy on a dead person, I have to finish the job and leave them at the station. I can't take them home with me. Well, life works the same way. There are many dead people walking, and the only thing you can do is cut them up with the WORD of GOD, but you can't bring them home with you. **The End.**

Let's end this story here.

Self-hatred is not a black thing; it's a people thing. You will find self-hatred in all races. So, what was Ebony's issue? Ebony found a calling, but it wasn't from GOD. She was trying to help women identify with their flesh, whereas GOD tells us to not be led of our flesh, but of our spirit. When a person does not know GOD, they will always try to take the place of GOD. Someone who does not fear or love the LORD will glorify their knowledge or another person's knowledge. Ebony saw a problem, but she was trying to fix it from a broken state of mind. She was trying to tell black women how they ought to look. She too was in full costume because she dressed the way she felt Africans would dress, but she did not give herself the freedom of developing her own unique identity. Instead, she joined a movement in the flesh, for the flesh and with the flesh.

What was April's issue? April really didn't have an issue, except she didn't know when to exercise tact. She was so focused on making sure that her work shined in the magazine that she forgot to consider what her customer wanted. As a business owner, I have many customers with many preferences. I remember how one of my customers had ordered a logo from my website that I did not like. It was a logo that I'd designed when I was a new designer, and it was priced at the same price as many of my newer and more advanced designs; nevertheless, he purchased the one I did not like. I understand that everyone will not like what I like, but I couldn't grasp what he'd seen in that particular logo; nevertheless, I had to learn to respect the uniqueness of every individual that I meet. At the same time, I had to learn to command respect from people who I met; people who were looking for characters to fill roles in their lives, when I'm an individual with my own life to live.

There was another time when I met a woman who didn't like my style of clothing. If I wore a red and tan shirt and some blue jeans, I would likely carry a tan purse to compliment what I was wearing. I may even put on some tan or red earrings, so it's safe to say that I'm a matcher. Like me, there are many out there who like to match their clothes; then again, there are those who don't. Everyone has a style that they identify as their own. All the same, I'm not an extreme matcher. I won't wear a red and tan shirt, blue jeans and red shoes because I think that's too much. But I do accessorize what I wear. Anyhow, this woman was telling me that she wanted to go shopping with me the next time I went so she could show me what she felt would look good on me. Now, her request isn't totally offensive because I get it: She has a style, and she believes that her style would work for me as well; nevertheless, I have what I like, and I'm happy with it. Am I open to change? Yes and no. I'm open to the idea of adding a new style to the one I already have, and I'll stop wearing what I like to wear when I no longer like it. What does this mean? It's simple: I am me, and I am happy being who I am. I won't throw away what I like, but I am willing to embrace new things IF I like them. All the same, it is never a good idea to attempt to change anyone's style or even recommend a change to their style UNLESS you and that person have a personal relationship (family member or close friend).

Another story happened in mid-March in a small town in Connecticut. A petite and somewhat quiet woman walked into a bar. Her name was Emily, and it was often said that she had the face of an angel. Her long blonde hair flowed down her back and touched her waistline. Her smoky gray eyes had green undertones that were set off by her emerald green sweater. It was somewhat cold outside, but it wasn't unbearably cold, so Emily wore short black pants and snow boots. Her shorts were very short and so tight that they almost looked like underwear. Emily's objective was obvious: she was looking for a man or at least to attract some attention. Even though she didn't smile outwardly when men salivated over her, inwardly, she would be grinning. She didn't want to appear too desperate or easy. Her goal was to be beautiful and appear confident. She wanted the men to see how well-built she was. After all, she was always receiving stares and compliments.

It was a Friday night, and Emily was feeling especially pretty that night. Underneath her sweater, she wore a midriff top with what appeared to be shredded edges. She knew that after a few drinks, she would want to remove her sweater. After eleven every Friday night, the bar would be full, and every inch of cold air would be absorbed by the warm bodies that filled the bar.

Just a little after eleven o'clock, three men wearing all black came into the bar. They were obviously members of a biker gang. The one who appeared to be the leader was tall with dark hair and dark brown eyes. He wore a sleeveless leather vest and blue jeans. The fingers of his leather gloves had been cut off, and the black bandana on his head made him look especially cute to Emily. He was nicknamed Sinister, but some people referred to him as Sin because of his dark past.

This was not the first time that Emily had seen Sinister. She'd spotted him two weeks prior in that very same bar, but before she could get his attention, he'd received a phone call and rushed out of the bar. That's why Emily wanted to be especially cute to him on that night. She headed to the bathroom where she removed her sweater and freshened up her makeup. "Tonight's the night," she said to her reflection. "You're about to show him what a real woman looks like." As Emily exited the bathroom, she forgot to take her sweater with her. She made her way back in front of the bar, but for a while, she did not see Sinister. She'd purchased that outfit especially for him, so there was no way she was letting good money go to waste.

Just as she was about to turn around and order a drink, a voice came from behind her. "Looking for me?" said the voice. Emily smiled. Could it be Sinister? She turned her seat around only to be disappointed. It was one of Sinister's crew members. He was an overweight guy who looked like he could kill a man without much effort. His tattooed up arms made him appear to be immortal. The earring in his bottom lip sparkled as he spoke. "I see you looking around," he said. "And I saw you watching me when I came in. Let's get out of here and get a room." Emily was repulsed. Did he truly think a woman as beautiful as Emily would be interested in him? At the same time, Emily was upset because she knew gang rules. If one of the guys was to show interest in a woman, she would be off limits to the other gang members. As disgusted as she was, she didn't want to offend her admirer because they were known to be pretty ruthless when rejected. "Hi, handsome," said Emily. "Thank you for the compliment, but to be honest with you, I was really looking at the other guy. I think they said his name is Sin. No offense. I didn't get your name, though. I'm Emily." Emily stretched out her hand to shake the biker's hand, but he simply looked at her, puffed and walked away. Emily was disappointed. Had she went out of her way to be noticed, only to have it thrown away because some arrogant over-tattooed man was throwing a temper tantrum? Just as she was about to give up hope, she noticed Sinister heading in her direction. Was he coming to offend her for rejecting his friend? Or worse, was he coming to hit her? Emily sat straight up and braced herself for what was to come.

Sinister: Hey you. My friend told me that you were checking me out.
Emily: Yeah. I was. Hey, tell him that I'm sorry. I didn't mean to offend him; it's just that I was already eying you.

249

Sinister: That's no problem. He looks threatening, but he's just a big sensitive teddy bear. Look at him. He's already found another lady to heal his shattered ego.
Emily: *Laughs.* Well, I feel better already.
Sinister: Look, we're throwing an after-party in my hotel room. It's going to be me and a few friends. I'd love to bring you as my date. You'd be the baddest woman in there.
Emily: Sure. What time does it start?
Sinister looked Emily in the eyes, and said, "Now. The party starts now."

Emily smiled at what she hoped to be her new boyfriend. She reached for her drink and tossed back what was left of it. "Wait. Let me grab my sweater," she said looking around. "Oh, crap. I think I left it in the bathroom." Anxious, Sinister grabbed Emily by her hand. "Don't worry about that sweater. I'll keep you warm." Not wanting to disappoint Sinister, Emily followed him out of the bar and got on the back of his motorcycle. The other two men were already on their bikes, but neither of them had a woman with them. Maybe their women had their own vehicles and were going to meet them back at the hotel.

As the bike rolled off, Emily leaned her head on Sinister's back. His cologne was strong, but it smelled so manly. Mixed with his natural body odor, his cologne made the moment feel even more dreamy. What was going to come of this night? Emily was excited and scared at the same time. What would she say to him? What if he wanted to have sex? Emily didn't want to go that far on the first date, but she knew biker gang members could be somewhat impatient and upset when they didn't get what they wanted. But maybe Sinister was different. After all, he'd already broken biker rules by talking to her after she'd rejected his friend.

They pulled into a seedy green motel. Sinister parked his motorcycle next to three other motorcycles that were already parked there. His two friends pulled in and parked on the other side of him. As they got off the bikes, Emily noticed that the gang member who'd initially hit on her appeared to still be upset with her for rejecting him. He got off his bike before anyone else and headed straight into the hotel room. Emily could hear the sound of loud music and people talking coming out of the room. The other gang member did not get off his bike, however. He looked at Sinister and said, "Hey man. I forgot that Ben told me to bring some beer back, so let me run up to the corner station and grab some beer." Sinister agreed. "No prob, Schwartz. Hey, can you bring me back some cigarettes as well?" Schwartz agreed and pulled away on his bike with his legs extended as if to show off.

As they entered the hotel room, Emily began to become uneasy. There were anywhere between ten to twelve men in the room, but there were only two other women there, and they appeared to be biker chicks. One of the women was named Samantha, but everyone called her Sam. Sam wore goth-like clothing and had piercings in one of her eyebrows, her nose and one piercing just above her lip. Both of her arms were tattooed so much that her bare skin was no longer visible. The other woman was overweight and appeared to be masculine. Her Kool-aid dyed red hair made her appear to have killed someone and washed her hair in their blood. Her skin seemed to be a little too white, as if she was sick; nevertheless, she was wearing white powder on her face. Her name was Priscilla, but everyone referred to her as Raven because of her red hair. Raven wore manly clothes. Her baby blue eyes looked almost as if they didn't have any color except for her dark pupils.

As Emily entered the room, Sam got up and excused herself. She didn't greet Emily, nor did she appear to be happy at the sight of another woman. Raven remained seated, however. "Excuse me for a moment," said Sinister to Emily. "I need to go and tell my brother something right quick. Make yourself comfortable." By this time, Emily was really uncomfortable, and it could be seen in her eyes. She made her way to the sofa that Raven was seated on, and she sat next to the flaming redhead. She wasn't sure if Emily would be nice to her or not. After all, Sam had excused herself at the sight of Emily and now, Raven was the only woman left in the hotel room. Just as Emily was about to greet Raven, someone called Raven's name, and she got up and walked to the front door of the room. One of the men began speaking with her, but she had to lean in to hear him because of the loud music. Raven was carrying a beer in one hand and keys in the other hand. She nodded as the man spoke to her and then left the room. Now, the only woman left in the room was Emily, and by this time, she was sick with worry. What had she gotten herself into?

Her worry was short-lived, however, when she noticed that all of the men were leaving the room; everyone except Sinister. Obviously, he'd requested to be alone with Emily, and Emily was okay with that.

After everyone left the room, Sinister began throwing away some of the trash in the room. "Give me a minute or so," he said. "I want to make the room a little more comfortable for you." Emily smiled. "Do you need my help?" she asked shyly. "No," said Sinister. "You stay right there, looking sexy and all. Nope, don't move."

After a few minutes, the room was now presentable, and the smell of beer began to fade after Sinister took some of the trash outside to the dumpster. Seizing the moment, Emily reached into her purse and pulled out some perfume. She rushed around the room and sprayed the perfume and then hurried back to her seat before Sinister re-entered the room. She was happy. Here she was in a hotel room with a man who seemed so dreamy to her. Emily loved bad boys, and Sinister appeared to be made-for-movies handsome. If she could nab him, she'd be the envy of all her friends.
As Sinister walked into the room, he could smell the perfume. "Oh, alright," he said smiling. "I like you already." He made his way next to Emily on the sofa and without saying a word, he leaned in to kiss her. Emily was surprised.

Why was he not trying to get to know her better? This was not what she'd planned.

Emily: What are you doing? I thought we'd get to know one another a little better.
Sinister opened his eyes.
Sinister: That's what I'm trying to do here.
Emily: No, you're trying to round first base before the game even starts.
Sinister: Don't do that. Don't ruin this moment for me. I brought you back to the hotel room. I made all of my friends leave. I even cleaned up the room. Don't do that.

Emily didn't know what to do. She'd pictured the two of them having a long conversation where he'd find out just how "cool" she was. She didn't want to be the whore whose name he wouldn't remember when the alcohol wore off. At the same time, she didn't want to upset him. Her mind was racing as she sat there, realizing that she didn't have thirty seconds to respond. She needed to give him an answer quick. If she said no to sex, she knew he'd be angry. If she gave in, he would probably never talk to her again. Sensing her discomfort, Sinister leaned away from her and said, "If you want, I can take you back to the bar and drop you off. I thought you were feeling me like I was feeling you." Emily's mind was still racing, so she decided to just give in to Sinister's desires. He didn't appear to be intoxicated, and his big puppy-dog eyes were burning right through Emily. "Kiss me," she said. At that, he began to kiss Emily before reaching up to turn off the lights.

The event was less than romantic. Sinister was nowhere near gentle with Emily. He'd even called her profane words. After the sex was over, Sinister began to put on his clothes. "I'll be right back," he said. "I need to run by my buddy's room to get a cigarette." Emily felt horrible. She knew she'd been used, and she felt that she no longer had any future with Sinister. She couldn't see him anymore because the room was so dark, but his voice sounded less than loving.

After Sinister left the room, Emily sat up a little and began to bite her fingernails. This was something she did when she was nervous. Hopefully, he'd hurry up and take her back to the bar. Suddenly, the door opened and a shadowy figure entered the room, but his silhouette did not look like Sinister's. It appeared to be the guy she'd initially rejected. His name was Seard, and his role in the gang was obvious. He was the muscle; the crazy one. He entered the room and closed the door. With fear in her voice, Emily asked, "Where's Sin? Who are you?" Seard didn't answer. He began to disrobe himself as Emily sat there frozen, continuously asking him what he was up to. As Emily tried to get out of the bed, she was thrown back onto the bed. He was so strong, and he reeked of alcohol. Emily shouted no over and over again before Seard covered her mouth and raped her. Like Sinister, he was nowhere near gentle. He treated her even worse than Sinister, even pulling her hair a few times. After he was done, he stood up, put his clothes back on and left the room. Emily sat there crying. What would become of her this night? Why had Sinister done this to her? Before she could gather her thoughts, another man entered the room and did the same thing. By the close of the night, Emily had been raped by five men. Seard had even come back and raped her again. He was the final man to rape her. After the rape, he threatened Emily before leaving the room. "Dead birds don't sing," he said. "Keep your beak closed or else." At that, he left the room.

Emily sat there crying and trembling. She didn't know if it was okay for her to get up and put on her clothes, or if another man was going to come in. She didn't want her clothes to be ripped off her, and she didn't want to be killed. At this point, she feared for her life. Suddenly, the door opened again and the lights came on. It was Raven. "Put on your clothes, and I'll take you back to the bar," she said. "I'll be back in five minutes for you." Emily nodded her head and sobbed. She got out of the bed and picked up her clothes off the sofa. She headed into the bathroom and was horrified at what she saw. Her nose was bloody and so was her mouth. She had teeth marks on her chin and her neck was scratched pretty badly. She couldn't cry loudly. What if they got fearful and decided to silence her? She told herself to remain calm as she began to wash her face. She put on her clothes, and it was then that she noticed how sore her entire body was. She could barely lift her leg to put her pants back on, so she went back into the room, sat on the bed and then put her pants on while lying down. She then headed back into the bathroom where she put her hair in a ponytail. She could hear Raven re-entering the room, so she left back out of the bathroom fearing that Raven may go into her purse and take the money that she had.

Raven was driving a tan '87 Buick. She got in and started the engine. Sore, Emily entered the vehicle slowly and wiped away the lone tear that had found its way down her face.

Raven: Get in. I don't have all night.
Emily: I'm sorry.

Emily tried to move quicker. She sat down and closed the door. As they pulled away, she could see the guys standing outside of a neighboring hotel room. Sinister wouldn't even look at her, but Seard looked her in the eyes and covered his mouth to gesture that she remained silent. He then made another gesture, taking his finger under his throat as if to cut it with a knife.

Raven: Don't pay him any attention. He's still ticked off that you rejected him, you know? Those kind of men aren't used to rejection. Seard is a lady's man. He can usually get whatever woman he wants. It wouldn't have been so bad if you hadn't turned him down. Just go home, take a shower and forget it even happened to you.
Emily: Okay.
Raven: You seem like a nice girl. Almost cheerleader-like.

Why would you be in a bar dressed like that? I mean, I'm
not saying what happened tonight was a good thing,
but...don't you think you asked for it?

Emily was feeling her mouth to make sure all of her teeth
were still there and none of them were loose. Her mouth
was bleeding and the pain was almost unbearable;
nevertheless, she answered Raven.

Emily: No. A woman should be able to wear what she wants
to wear and not fear being attacked. I just wanted to get to
know Sinister; that's all.
Raven: Okay. Let me ask you this question. When you look
at me, what do my clothes say? And be honest. I won't get
offended; I promise.

Emily hesitated. What if she would get offended? After a
minute of silence, she took a deep breath and answered.

Emily: You're gay. That's what I take.
Raven: Right. That's the image I was going for, but I'm not
gay. My clothes say that I'm unapproachable, unavailable,
and I'd kick a dude's rump roast if he touched me.
Sometimes, we don't always get what we put out, but when
we do, what can we say?
Emily: I've dressed like this for years, and I've never been
raped before.
Raven: You weren't raped tonight. Okay, technically, if you
go by what the law says; yeah, you were raped. But think

about this. You head into a bar half-naked, and you go home with a man you don't even know? Sure, you can say that you didn't know that you'd become a free-for-all, but did you stop to consider the risks involved, or did you really convince yourself that Sinister was the marrying type?

Emily was silent. She didn't know how to answer the question, and they were pulling back in to the bar's parking lot. Emily finally spoke because she didn't want to upset Raven.

Emily: Well, I was wearing a sweater earlier, but I accidentally left it in the bathroom at the bar.

Raven: A sweater? Sweetie, a sweater would not have made a difference. When I saw you, I thought your pants were underwear. No kidding! You look like you came out for sex. Oh my goodness, I've seen prostitutes wear more clothes than that! *Laughs.* Where's your car?

Emily: I don't have a car. I walked here.

Raven: Walked? Well, from where? I can take you home if you want.

Emily: No, I'll be good here. I think a couple of my friends should be here by now. They said they were coming.

Raven parked her vehicle in the parking lot and let Emily leave with some parting words she would never forget.

Raven: If I were you, I'd keep quiet about what happened. If you called the cops, the guys would be arrested, but they'd bail out, and you'd disappear. Just take the lesson from it.

You'll be okay.

Emily didn't know what to do. She wanted every last one of them placed behind bars, but what if Raven was telling the truth? What if they bailed themselves out and came after her? "Okay. I'll be quiet," she said to Raven as she exited the vehicle. As she was walking away, she heard Raven screaming at her. "Hey! Hey!" Emily turned around and noticed that Raven was holding something out the window. It was her purse. She walked back to the vehicle on the driver's side to retrieve her purse. When she gripped the purse, Raven held it even tighter and released it only after warning her one more time. "Dead birds don't sing."

It was now almost three o'clock in the morning, and the bar was preparing to close. Emily entered the bar hoping to see one of her friends, but no one she recognized was there. She headed to the bar to gather her thoughts. The bartender was a forty-five year old woman named Ruth, and she could see that Emily was pretty beat up. She had a black eye forming, and she didn't do such a great job cleaning the blood from around her nose.

As Emily sat down, she opened her purse because she wanted to buy herself a drink. To add insult to injury, she was horrified when she saw that her money had been stolen. Fifty dollars was gone....just like that. Raven had obviously charged for her advice. Tears began to well in her eyes again as she searched for her cellular phone. It turned out that they'd taken the cellular phone as well. The tears ran down Emily's face as she searched her purse frantically. Ruth looked at her and said, "Whatever you're looking for, it's gone. You left with Sinister, right?" Emily was surprised. How did she know she'd left with Sinister?

Emily: Yes, ma'am.
Ruth: Then, it's not there. Whatever you're looking for; it's not there. You look pretty beat up. Do you need a ride home?
Emily cried for a little, and nodded her head.
Ruth: Do you want me to call the police for you?
Emily shook her head as if to say no.
Ruth: Okay. We're closing up here, and it'll take me about thirty minutes to clean up. Then I can take you home.

After Ruth closed the bar, she and Emily headed towards her car. Emily was still a little shaken up and kept looking over her shoulders to make sure she wasn't being followed. "Relax," said Ruth. "They've had their fun with you, so now, you're the last thing on their minds. They know you won't call the police, so they aren't thinking about you." Ruth's words got Emily's attention. How did she know what had transpired? As they entered the car, Emily realized that she was even more sore than before. She grunted as she attempted to sit down. Her neck had started to become stiff, and her hands were swollen from being pinned above her head. She finally managed to sit down. She felt three times heavier than she was. Ruth looked at her and asked her again, "Are you sure you don't want to call the police or at least go to the hospital? You look really banged up. They worked you over pretty bad." It was out of the question for Emily, however. She wanted the night to just go away, and she wanted to forget about the incident, but Ruth was concerned for her well-being, so she took a mirror out of her purse and handed it to Emily. Take a look at yourself and if you still don't want to go to the hospital, I'll take you straight home."

Emily was afraid of what she would see; nevertheless, she reached for the mirror, almost dropping it because of the swelling in her fingers. When she saw her reflection, she was even more afraid than before. Her left eye was now black and blue, and blood had filled the bottom of that eye. Her lip was split, and what looked like a bubble was bulging from it. Her arms were swollen, especially around her wrists and hands. What she saw made her realize that the attack wasn't so much about rape as it was about power and anger. For them, sex was just the bonus, but what they had really been seeking was revenge. They wanted to really hurt Emily for rejecting Seard. At the sight of herself, Emily became enraged. They were going down. They weren't going to get away with this. "Yes, take me to the hospital," she said. "I'll call the police from there." Emily's voice sounded strong, and Ruth felt relieved. "Good girl," said Ruth as she started the car and pulled out of the parking lot.

The hospital was a little over thirty-minutes away, and Ruth decided not to press Emily for details. She decided to remain silent so she wouldn't scare Emily into changing her mind, but Emily wanted to talk about it. After making sure all of her teeth were intact using the mirror Ruth had loaned her, Emily began to cry and speak.

Emily: Am I stupid? I mean, what was I thinking? I left the bar with a guy I didn't know whose name is Sinister. Who does that? I mean, what did I expect? Here I was thinking that he liked me, and I liked him, and we could possibly have some sort of future together. Boy, was I wrong! I didn't know they'd beat and gang rape me. I thought I was safe with him. I mean, am I stupid?

Ruth: I worked on the bar scene for twenty-five years now. I've seen this kinda thing happen so much that it doesn't even surprise me anymore. About six months ago, I finally gave my life to CHRIST, and tonight is actually my last night at the bar. I turned in my resignation two weeks ago because I know better than to work in a place like that now. Are you stupid? I don't know how to answer that question, so I'll try to answer it the best way I can. You're not stupid; you're just naïve. You haven't matured yet. Sure, it's pretty stupid to come to a bar half-naked and leave with a man you don't know, especially a guy named Sinister. But, hey....we've all done something pretty stupid things in our lives at some point. What doesn't kill you teaches you not to put yourself in the same situation again because you can only get so far being naïve. Nevertheless, you did not deserve what happened to you tonight. No means no. You did say no, didn't you?

Emily: Over and over again. Yes, I kept saying no, but no matter what I said, they kept beating me and raping me. It was like I was nothing but waste to them. After the second guy, I pretty much felt like I was having an out-of-body experience. I didn't want to be in my own body anymore. I just begged each guy, but the third guy was the most monstrous. He took a pocket knife and cut the side of my face with it. I didn't feel the pain, though. I thought he was just running it alongside my face to scare me, but it wasn't until I looked in the mirror that I realized that he'd actually sliced me. And can you believe that the woman who dropped me back off at the bar implied that I deserved what happened to me because of the clothes I was wearing?

Ruth: Uh...well, I don't think you deserved it. But I will say this: We live in a society where mental illness is slowly becoming the norm. People are filled with devils these days. Rape is not new, but nowadays, women do promote sex by the clothes they wear. Do they deserve to be raped? No. I had a brother who was on crack cocaine back in 1995, but I trusted him. After all, he was my brother. Sure, he'd steal from just about anyone, but I thought he would never steal from me. I'd just gotten my paycheck, and I went home to shower before going back out. My brother came by just as I was getting out of the shower. I put my clothes on and I let him in. Mind you, I hadn't seen him in months, and he always managed to come by on my payday whenever he did visit, but he'd never taken anything from me before. He sat on the couch not far from my purse, but I didn't think anything of it. I had a little over five hundred bucks in my purse, and I was going to pay my rent and get some groceries. That was the plan. He asked me if I would make him a sandwich, and I headed to the kitchen without thinking twice about it. I was happy to see my brother, and I wanted to take care of him, just like I did when we were children. Anyway, I kept calling his name trying to ask him if he wanted mustard on his sandwich, but he didn't answer me. When I went back into the living room, he was gone and my wallet was lying on the couch. My heart dropped and so did the plate I was holding. He took all of my money. All of it. I was so hurt and angry. After all I'd done for him, I felt I didn't deserve what had just happened to me, and I didn't deserve it. But, you know what? I should have known better. It was like leaving a piece of chicken on the floor in front of a hungry dog and expecting him to behave.

Emily: That makes sense, but no still means no.

Ruth: Yes, and that's the national anthem for rape victims. No means no, and it's true. Let me ask you a question. Would you let a known rapist babysit for you?

Emily: No, of course not.

Ruth: Why not? What if he hadn't raped anyone in ten years?

Emily: Still no because he may relapse. I wouldn't put my children in harm's way intentionally.

Ruth: Exactly. Then why would you put yourself in harm's way and not expect to be harmed?

Emily and Ruth arrived at the hospital, and the police were

called. All of the men who'd raped Emily were arrested and
eventually found guilty of rape and battery. Sinister was
convicted and sentenced to eleven years in state prison.
Seard was sentenced to two counts of rape and assault. He
was sentenced to twenty-five years to life for his crime. The
other men were sentenced anywhere from five to fifteen
years.

Ruth moved with her husband to a ranch in Tennessee. She
kept in touch with Emily and introduced Emily to her Pastor.
It took years for Emily to recover from her attack, but after
much needed counseling, she did recover and became a
victim's advocate for rape victims. She went to church
sometimes, but she never got into the LORD like she should
have because she still preferred the lie over the truth.
The End.

What's the message in this story? Let's first review some of
the costumes that were worn.
Emily: Emily's costume gave off the appearance that she
was some exotic woman from the jungle. Nowadays,
women love to wear short shorts with midriff tops and fluffy
snow boots. The image they are going for is the Jane of the
Jungle look.
Sinister: Sinister, like most bad boys, wanted to look like a
bad boy. Black leather is like a bad-boy's logo. His image
was shaped by modern-day television. Just like every
follower who rises up to become a blind leader, Sinister
channeled the bad boy image that was promoted in

Hollywood.

Seard: With all of the tattoos and bandanas, Seard wanted to look invincible. He went for a more intimidating look; one where he'd stand out more. This look is very common amongst men who want to send a message to anyone who sees them, and the message is that they are mentally unstable but physically powerful. This is supposed to be a lethal combination. They're the very same spirits (Legion) that were mentioned in Luke 8. *"And when he went forth to land, there met him out of the city a certain man, which had devils long time, and ware no clothes, neither abode in any house, but in the tombs. When he saw Jesus, he cried out, and fell down before him, and with a loud voice said, What have I to do with thee, Jesus, thou Son of God most high? I beseech thee, torment me not. (For he had commanded the unclean spirit to come out of the man. For oftentimes it had caught him: and he was kept bound with chains and in fetters; and he brake the bands, and was driven of the devil into the wilderness.) And Jesus asked him, saying, What is thy name? And he said, Legion: because many devils were entered into him"* (Luke 8:27-30).

Samantha aka Sam: Samantha's goth-like look is often worn by women who don't feel attractive as they are, but in goth-like clothing, they feel more appealing. This costume is oftentimes used to attract a certain type of man, namely other Gothic types. It is also used to display rebellion or non-conformity to modern-day practices. People who wear goth-like clothing are often into vampire movies or other dark films. They are oftentimes attracted to anything and anyone dark.

Raven: Raven's costume was designed to make her fit in, but to take away from her sexuality. She wanted to hang out with that group, but she did not want to be viewed as a woman. She preferred to be seen as one of the guys. Raven didn't see herself as a beautiful girly-girl; therefore, she tried to take attention away from her femininity so she wouldn't be looked down on. In gangs, women are often seen as nothing more than tools of sexual gratification.

Everywhere you go, you will see people in full costume. What we wear is directly linked to what we are trying to obtain. When I was in the world, I used to wear skimpy clothes because I wanted to show off my body. I was skinny then, and I used my body as bait. Now, had you asked me if I was trying to attract men back then, I would have told you no, because I was too prideful to admit that I was on the prowl. I had worldly friends who did the same. That's why we hung together. We were a group of women who all wanted to be married someday, but we didn't know how to go about getting husbands. We noticed that we attracted more attention walking around half-naked, so we did. Like many women, we thought we had to sift through the bad guys, and eventually, we'd pull out a good one. We wore many costumes and snagged many characters, each one auditioning for a role. In most cases, the men were auditioning to be cast in bedroom scenes. After all, we dressed like whores, so what did we expect? Truthfully, we expected to be treated like respectable women, but you get back what you give out.

Nowadays, it's easy for me to pick out the character a person is pretending to be. What's funny is, most men don't marry characters. It's so easy to see a super-beautiful woman in full costume with several children and no husband. Why is that? Because she never got to know herself well enough to introduce who she really was to men; therefore, she introduced herself as who she wanted to be. What I've learned is you never really get to know much about yourself until you get to know the LORD. At thirty-six years old, I can say that I am still finding out things about myself that I did not know. Puzzle pieces are still coming together, and every time I get to know me more, I discover a costume that I'd been wearing. It is then that I begin to strip away that costume to reveal who I am underneath. I used to wear layers of makeup and I had every exotic hairdo one could have. Now that I look back, I realize that I was trying to find out which character worked. I was trying to show men that I could be a variety of characters. I would be perfect for marrying because I could cook and be whoever he wanted me to be.

What many women don't realize is that someone can meet you and eventually marry you while you are in full costume, but you will never be able to be yourself and stay married to them. You will have to wear that costume for the rest of your life, and your character had better find some new super-powers to hold on to the man who married your character, and not you. Over the years, the marriage is more than likely going to end because who you are cannot be hidden for too long. Eventually, your ways will show through your costume, and your husband will accuse you of changing. Divorce is always sitting in the backseat of a character's marriage asking, "Are we done yet?"

I've met so many women who have said to me, "I don't understand why he was with me for _____ years, but he met and married her after a few months, and she's not even as pretty as me!" This is very common for women to say, because a lot of women measure their beauty and not their brains. Go and ask ten different men this question, and tally the results. Ask them: If you had to choose between a super-beautiful woman with a perfect shape but she wasn't that smart, or a woman who wasn't so beautiful or shapely, but she was intelligent, loving and logical, which one would you choose? I can almost guarantee you that the not-so-shapely sister would win hands-down. Men are visual creatures, but beauty is fleeting, meaning it only lasts for a little time. That's why men only stay a little while with women who are beautiful to look at but a disappointment to the ears.

And people don't just wear costumes on the outside; many people wear costumes as their personalities. They put on fake confidence and present themselves as untouchable, but in the quiet of their own homes, they weep. That's because GOD said it is not good for man to be alone, and that's why HE gave Adam a gift called Eve. When a woman continuously fails at snagging a man, she will often resort to words like, "I don't need a man. I'm content with me and my children." She doesn't mean it. She's speaking from a hurt place, and in that hurt place, she is afraid of having a man because she doesn't want to be hurt anymore. But truthfully, she wants a man; she just wants a good one. She may have lost faith in men or faith in her own abilities to find good men, but you will never see her give up on looking unless she gives her life totally to CHRIST. We attract what we put out.

Emily went after a bad boy because she was not a wise woman. Let's face it; any man or woman who purposely goes after a rebellious character is not wise. Now, there are some people who unintentionally go after rebellious characters, but they aren't necessarily simple-minded. Sometimes, they are just young in the faith and still growing up. But a woman who intentionally tries to snag a bad boy is by all means unwise. Like most women, Emily formed a thought, and she pursued what she imagined. Women often enter relationships first in their minds, and then they pursue these relationships outwardly. How many times have you told yourself that the man you were with was a loving, strong character who adored the very sight of you, only to find out that he was a lusting, weak character who loved the sight of you naked? When you weren't satisfying his flesh, you were grieving his soul. How long did it take you before you realized that the relationship just wasn't going to work? On average, most women know early in the relationship that it won't work, but many women put more layers of costumes on trying to make it work because they want it to work.

Get to know the LORD better, and HE will introduce you to yourself. It's such an amazing feeling to peel back layers of revelation, only to discover answers to some of your oldest questions. At the same time, the more you know the LORD and you get to know yourself, the more you'll learn to be content in the LORD and wait on your husband. That's not to say that you won't desire to have a husband anymore; instead, you won't be desperate to have one anymore. Most women would say that they aren't desperate to have a husband, but if you are fornicating with a man, you are desperate. If you're walking around half-naked, you are desperate; you just don't know how to go about getting a decent guy.
If you let GOD change you inwardly, your world will change outwardly. Everything looks so amazing when you have sight. Not just the ability to see in the natural, but the ability to see in the spirit. What I've witnessed with myself is the more I get to know and love the LORD, the more I get to know and love myself, for HE is in me and I am in HIM. One day, I lost interest in wearing brown contact lenses, or any colored contacts. I like my own eyes. I stopped wearing so much makeup; I like my own face. I wear makeup sometimes, but it's not for beauty. I don't think I look better with it or worse without it. My face is my face, and GOD is the Artist who designed it. Any makeup I wear now is an expression of the creative creature that I am. I love colors. I have always loved to play with colors. As far as hair, I wear

mostly braids because I don't like to style my own hair. I don't even know how to style my own hair because I wore weave for decades. Initially, I wore it because I thought I looked good with it, but now, I wear braids for convenience. Is it wrong to wear weave? No way. If I see a hairstyle that I want, and I think it'll last a long time, I'll get it with no apologies. Nevertheless, the point is, I have learned to love myself, just as I am, and the more I learned to love me, the less of a costume I wore.

My dare to the single woman would be....just be yourself. Remove the costume outwardly and the inward costume, and just let the LORD have HIS way with you. If you want to wear your weave or your makeup, do so. But don't let it be because you think you're not beautiful without it or you think you're more beautiful wearing it. Don't go looking for a husband or a companion; seek the LORD and study HIM like you were studying for a big exam. That's how you will find who you are, for your identity is in HIM. Study the WORD of GOD and ask the LORD to change your heart. It may take a little while; it depends on how you resist or don't resist what HE starts to do in your mind and life. But no matter what, do not give up on HIM, and don't give up on you. Sure, you can't do it on your own; that's why you need the LORD'S help. HE is your CREATOR; therefore, HE is the only Repairman who can reach into your heart and repair the broken places. Take off your costume and put on the truth. Whatever you find wrong with you, confess it to the LORD. Stop hiding your hurts behind your pride, and show GOD every broken piece of you. HE sees it anyway, but until you hand it to HIM, you will remain broken.

- If you find yourself attracted to bad boys, seek the LORD and ask HIM why. Then, ask HIM to change your heart.
- If you find yourself feeling more beautiful underneath layers of external things, seek the LORD and ask HIM the reason. Then, ask HIM to change your heart.
- If you find yourself feeling intimidated by another woman's beauty, seek the face of the LORD and ask HIM to change your heart.
- If you find yourself competing with other women, seek the face of the LORD and tell HIM what you see. Ask HIM to change your heart.
- If you find yourself morphing into a character you saw on television, or off television, go on a fast and seek the face of the LORD. Tell the FATHER what you see and ask HIM to deliver you from anything that has been binding you.
- If you find yourself in a situation where it's hard for you to tell a man you like "no," remove yourself from that situation and seek the LORD. That's usually an indication that the man you're infatuated with has some ungodly power over you. Oftentimes, the issue is you have bewitched yourself into believing that he could be the one; therefore, you will struggle and strain to please him. Men rarely ever marry women who are afraid to share their opinions.

The Other-Other Woman

"One woman's Ishmael is not necessarily another woman's Isaac."

The most popular movies in Hollywood nowadays are the ones dealing with romance and relationships. As the morals of this nation continue to decline, immoral movies continue to rise to accommodate a Godless people. In addition, Hollywood has begun to give life lessons to the blind and the hungry. It now teaches women that it's okay to be promiscuous; it's okay to be someone's mistress, and any man who doesn't stick around with them has some force named "karma" after him. But the truth is: GOD is for marriage, not promiscuity; it's never okay to be someone's mistress, and a man who doesn't stick with a promiscuous woman is not being pursued by "karma"; he is being led by wisdom. All the same, "karma" does not exist. The word "karma" comes from the non-Christian sects of Hinduism, Jainism, Buddhism and Sikhism. Remember, as Christians, you cannot delve into other doctrines and then head back over to Christianity when it suits you. If you want to be a wife, you have to marry the LORD and hide in HIM. Rest assured that if you do, your husband will find you. But if you are first married to yourself, yet you claim the LORD, you're not going to hide in HIM because you'll be hiding behind your own pride. This puts you in plain sight of any and every Godless man who wants to take you for a spin.

"Where is she now, Tony?" asked Felicia. "Is she home or out again?" Felicia's voice sounded muffled. She wanted to make sure that she wasn't speaking loudly just in case Anthony's wife was at home. Anthony's voice was equally muffled. "She's in the kitchen complaining about the dishes. My goodness, you would think that she would be happy having a man who provides for her, gives her whatever she wants and takes care of a child who is not his own. Let me call you back before the wicked witch comes in here."
Sighs. "I can't take this too much longer, Felicia," he said. Felicia let out a sigh as well. What a stupid woman his wife must be. "Okay, baby. Stay strong, okay? Call me when you can. Wait. Are you still coming over tonight?" Felicia's voice sounded concerned, but inwardly, she was all smiles. "I don't think so. Not tonight, baby. I gotta go. Bye." At that, Anthony disconnected the phone.

Felicia had been Anthony's mistress for three long years, and things were now beginning to look up for her. Anthony really seemed to be getting tired of his wife; he was calling Felicia more, and he'd even expressed interest in having children with Felicia. She'd been pregnant by Anthony before, but Anthony convinced her to abort the baby. She had been pregnant the previous year, but Anthony said that if the baby was born, his wife could get a fault divorce, and in this, he would lose more than half of what he owned. Felicia did not want that to happen because his well-to-do lifestyle was one of the perks of having him. He told Felicia that he believed his wife was having an affair, and he'd hired a private investigator to catch her. That way, he could keep the house, get custody of their two children, and he wouldn't have to pay alimony.

Anthony was a professor at a large university. Even though he wasn't rich, he was considered well-to-do. According to Anthony, he owned a small software creation company where he earned just over three hundred thousand dollars a year. Additionally, he boasted of being an author of four somewhat popular books. He and his wife, Victoria, lived what many refer to as the "good life." Victoria did well herself. She was a teacher at a local high school, and she worked with Anthony at the software creation company. She'd also authored four books, which had all done pretty well. Victoria was a preacher's daughter, and she lived her life by the Book. She was the mother of three young girls, two of which were Anthony's daughters. The oldest girl was seven years old, and she had been the product of a one-night-stand Victoria had engaged in when she was a sophomore in college. At that time, Victoria had gone away from the church and started hanging with the wrong crowd. While six months pregnant with her oldest daughter Alyssa, Victoria had met Anthony. At that time, the two of them hit it off well, and Anthony was pretty smitten with Victoria; but nowadays, everything seemed so monotonous. Anthony and Victoria had two girls together: five-year-old Savannah and two-year-old Kaleigh, both of whom were the apples of their father's eyes.

When Anthony met Victoria, she was a wild party girl who lit up a room when she entered. Even though she was pregnant, she was the life of the party everywhere she went. Men wanted her, and women envied her. Victoria and Anthony dated for two years before getting married. They'd gotten married when Victoria discovered that she was pregnant, and at first, the marriage was good in Anthony's sight. They partied hard and lived out loud. A year after the marriage, however, Victoria couldn't ignore the calling on her life anymore. She could no longer ignore the voice from within. She felt as if her lifestyle was eating her alive, and she did not want to raise her daughters in that lifestyle. After all, she hadn't been raised in that lifestyle. Even when she'd gone into the world, she always had plans to return to the LORD, but she wanted to have a little fun first. Worldly men looked like strong leaders who didn't fit into the church's mold of what type of man she should marry, and this was fascinating to Victoria. She was tired of being measured by her title; she wanted to develop her own identity, and Anthony seemed like just the man to help her out. But after running from the LORD for so many years, she wanted to return to the church with Anthony and her then two children in tow, but Anthony did not want to be a man of GOD. He loathed the idea of sitting in a church; he didn't like the whole church image at all.

When Victoria had become pregnant with their second daughter, Kaleigh, Anthony had just started an affair with Felicia. The pregnancy came as a shock to Anthony, Victoria and Felicia. After all, Anthony claimed that he and his wife were no longer sleeping in the same bedroom together, but of course, he was lying. Even though it was tough, Felicia managed to forgive Anthony for sleeping with his wife. *(Insert blank stare here).* After all, he'd told her that his wife had waited until he was drunk one night and had obviously taken advantage of him. It took a long time for Felicia to recover from the news of Victoria's pregnancy, but she was determined to win Anthony's hand. After all, according to Anthony, Vicky, as he called her, suspected that Anthony was seeing someone else and had intentionally gotten pregnant to deter the other woman. Felicia was determined to show her that her plans had not worked.

Felicia was a member of a local church as well. She was even on the ministry team at her church. She was a praise dancer, and she'd taught a few Bible study classes, so she was fully aware of what was right and what was wrong; nevertheless, she drew near to GOD with her mouth, but her heart was far from HIM. *(See Matthew 15:8).*
Felicia was also a party girl. She loved to drink, and she partied harder than she praised the LORD. She would always say that GOD knew her heart; therefore, she was in

right-standing with HIM. *"Such is the way of an adulterous woman; she eateth, and wipeth her mouth, and saith, I have done no wickedness" (Proverbs 30:20).*

Anthony loved the fact that even though she was a church member, she'd always leave church at church, and she didn't pressure him to serve the LORD. After all, he didn't mind his wife going to church; he just wanted no part of it. Additionally, he wanted his wife to be as sinful as she was when she'd snagged him. In a way, he felt betrayed. How could she make him believe they'd have this wonderful party of a marriage, and then trade in her beer cans for a Bible?

An hour after the phone call, Anthony called Felicia back. He was noticeably upset, and he asked if he could still come over and stay the night. He and Victoria had argued, and he didn't want to be under the same roof as her. Felicia happily agreed and began to clean up her house for her lover. She wanted everything to be perfect when he came over. He lived almost an hour away from her, so she utilized that time to organize her home and put some food in the oven. She wanted to appear domesticated; a woman worthy of being a man's wife.

When Anthony arrived, he came into the house carrying a small garbage bag with some of his clothes in it. He looked disheveled and somewhat confused, almost as if he hadn't slept for a few days. Felicia kissed him took his bag from him, and headed into the bedroom with the bag. When she re-entered the living room, she noticed that Anthony was now lying on the couch in the fetal position. Sounds coming from him let Felicia know that he was crying, and this infuriated her. Felicia ran over to the couch and sat next to Anthony.

Felicia: Baby, what's wrong? What happened? Baby, I've never seen you like this. What happened?

For a while, Anthony said nothing. He wept and laid his head on Felicia's lap. Finally, he spoke.

Anthony: That evil witch is talking about taking my children from me. I told her the truth about you. I told her that I was in love with you, and I wanted to be with you, and now she's saying that if I leave her, she's going to take my kids away. My babies are my life, Felicia! *Sobs.* My babies are my life! I can't live without them! I can't!

Felicia: Baby, don't cry. I'm here for you. Don't cry. You know I work at an attorney's office. He's the best in the state. If you want, I can talk to him for you. Maybe just ask some general questions to see what your options are.

Anthony: No, I already talked to three attorneys today.

Felicia: You did? What did they say?

Anthony: They all said the same thing. She'd likely get the house and full custody of the children. She'd get everything! She'd get everything I've worked so hard for!

Felicia: Oh wow. That's pathetic. Don't worry, Tony. We'll figure this all out. You'll see.

Anthony: I built that company from the ground up, and now she can just take it away from me, just like that? Because I don't want to be with her anymore?

Felicia: She won't take it. Just calm down, baby. Relax and let her cool down. She's just angry, that's all. Once the both of you have cooled off, you can talk about the division of your property with clearer heads. Right now, the both of you are just emotional. She's upset because she knows she'll be losing her lifestyle, and probably her kids, and you're a little worried. That's normal. Just relax and think positive. Everything will be over with soon.

At that, Felicia began to hum lullabies as she stroked Anthony's hair. Comforted, Anthony began to doze off, and when Felicia saw that he was asleep, she let a few tears drop. How dare his wife be so evil! Why won't she let him leave with dignity? After all, she only wanted him for his money; that's what Anthony told her, anyway. Felicia considered every possible thing that could happen to Anthony's wife. If she were to disappear off the face of the earth, Felicia felt things could be easier, but Felicia was no killer, at least outwardly. She could never kill anyone with her own hands, and she wasn't going hire anyone to harm her either; nevertheless, she silently wished Anthony's wife was dead. She wished mother nature would do her the honor of killing his wife so that she and Anthony could finally be together.

An hour later, Felicia had dozed off with Anthony lying across her leg. It was now one o'clock in the morning, and Anthony's cell phone began to vibrate. The phone was in Anthony's pocket, and the vibrations from the phone woke him up. It was his wife, and even though Felicia was awakened by Anthony answering the phone, she pretended to be asleep.

Anthony: Hello?

Victoria: Tony, where are you?

Anthony: I told you. I got a hotel room. Why are you calling me? We've said everything we need to say.

Victoria: Tony, I've been crying all night. What do you want me to do? I'm supposed to be okay with the fact that you're seeing someone else?

Anthony looked at Felicia to make sure she wouldn't hear his response. Seeing that her eyes were closed and her mouth was still somewhat opened, he thought she was still asleep.

Anthony: I told you that I'm not seeing anyone else. I told you that girl was just an obsessed student. I didn't know she was going to call your phone and make all of those accusations. More than that, I didn't know you would believe another woman over your own husband. That's why I left, Vicky. I can't take not being trusted.

Even though Anthony attempted to muffle his voice, Felicia could still hear him loud and clear. After all, he was lying across her lap. Hurt and angered by his words, Felicia

283

decided to slyly make herself known. "Tony, baby; who are you talking to? Come back to bed," she said. Anthony froze and looked at Felicia. Her eyes were still closed, but he knew this was it. His wife heard everything and he couldn't deny it anymore. At that, he leaped from the couch and ran into the bathroom while Victoria started firing off at him.

Victoria: Who was that, Tony?! Huh? So, you want to tell me that the hotel rooms come with live-in staff now?! Tony?! Who was that?
Anthony: That was the television set. I was watching a movie, Vicky. Look, I can't take all of this yelling and your insecurities. I'll see you tomorrow!

Before he could hang up the phone, Felicia stood in the door and asked him once again, "Anthony LaMarcus Ferguson, who are you talking to?" She wanted it to be known that Anthony was with her. If he wasn't going to leave his wife, Felicia wanted to make sure his wife left him.

Anthony was infuriated.

Anthony: Why would you do that, Felicia?
Felicia: Do what? You told me that you have already told your wife about me and you, so it's not a secret anymore, right? We can bring everything out in the open now.
Anthony: Yeah, but I didn't want her to know that I was here with you! Felicia, I'm actually trying to win custody of my children if my wife and I are to divorce; not lose them!

Felicia: What do you mean "if" you and your wife are to divorce? You told me that you asked her for a divorce tonight.

Anthony: You know what? Let me go and get a hotel room for real because I didn't leave one nagging woman to come and get castrated by another one. I'll talk with you tomorrow. Where's my bag?

Felicia was hurt. After all she'd just heard, she realized that there was another "other" woman and now, here was Anthony lying and speaking harshly to her. She didn't want him to leave like that. She had so many questions she wanted answered; nevertheless, she knew that Anthony was in no mood, so she pointed to her bedroom. Tears went down her face as she watched him storm out of the house. Her hurt slowly turned into anger. This was it for her. It was now or never. It was time for everything to be put on the table so that Anthony could decide who he wanted to be with once and for all. She'd waited three years for him to leave his wife, and she didn't want to wait anymore. After all, another woman was now staking claim to him as well. She didn't want to behave like his wife, however, because she feared that would scare him off for good. She wanted so much to call him, but she decided to email him instead.

Back at the Ferguson residence, Victoria was beside herself with grief. Even though she wanted to go and find Anthony, she had three beautiful daughters to watch over, and she couldn't leave them at home all alone. They were all sound asleep, so Victoria stumbled into the living room, holding on to the wall as she let her soul cry from within her. The pain was so great that Victoria fell to the floor. Her tears blinded her, and the pain from within numbed her senses. Suddenly, she felt a small hand on her back. She looked up to see her seven-year-old daughter, Alyssa, rubbing her back. Alyssa didn't understand everything, but she'd heard her mother and Anthony arguing earlier, so she hadn't gotten much sleep. This wasn't the first time she'd seen her mother hurt, but this was the first time she'd seen it break her down to the floor.

Alyssa: It's okay, Mommy. Don't cry. Remember, you told me that everything will always be okay if you trust GOD. I don't want to see you crying, Mommy.

Alyssa began to cry, and seeing her hurt made the pain that much greater for Victoria. Here Anthony was hurting her again and again, and she was hurting her children by letting them see her hurt.

Victoria: Mommy's okay, Alyssa. I love you, baby. Please go back to bed.

Alyssa: I don't want to leave you like this, Mommy. I don't have to go to school tomorrow, because tomorrow is Sunday. Please let me stay awake with you. At least let me hold you until you fall asleep. If you say no, I won't be able to sleep. I will worry, Mommy.

Victoria: Okay, Snuggle-bugs. Let's lie down on the couch and get some rest. Okay?

Alyssa: Okay, Mommy.

Victoria and Alyssa were just beginning to doze off when the door suddenly, but quietly, opened. It was Anthony. He was now humbled from the fear that was within him. Anthony knew he had a wonderful wife, but he was just not the type of man who could be faithful to a woman. At the same time, he didn't want a woman of GOD. He wanted a party-girl, and Victoria was now far from that. He wanted a wife just like his best friend Joel's wife. Joel had several affairs, and even though his wife was upset by the fact that he'd had affairs, she often blamed the other women and would stick by her husband throughout every new revelation. Once a woman had called his wife and said that she had spent the night with Joel, and his wife had replied, "That's good. Next time he comes over, why don't you invite me and we can all have a little fun with it, eh?" Anthony admired Joel's life. He had a nice house and a beautiful worldly wife who had all but given him permission to cheat. Why didn't Victoria just sit back, relax and let him have his own way?

As he entered the living room, Victoria felt her emotions building up from within, but she contained them for the sake of Alyssa. As Alyssa lifted her head, Victoria gently put her hand on Alyssa's head and pulled it back onto her chest. She opted to remain silent so she wouldn't upset Alyssa or wake up Savannah or Kaleigh. She angrily watched as Anthony headed towards their bedroom and closed the door as if all was well at home. Victoria kept quoting scriptures to silence her anger. Who was this girl that Anthony had been with this night? She definitely wasn't the same girl who'd called Victoria earlier, because their voices were completely different. The girl who'd called earlier had a very heavy voice, and her English was noticeably broken. She kept mispronouncing words and making popping sounds every time she spoke a word that she could not pronounce. She'd even apologized for not being able to "announce", as she said, a particular word. But this other girl's voice was softer; more feminine, and her English didn't sound broken. As Victoria pondered the thoughts, the tears begin to roll off the side of her face. "It's okay, Mommy," said Alyssa. "GOD will punish Daddy for you. You don't have to cry anymore." How did Alyssa know she was crying again? Alyssa's head was lying on her chest, and she could feel the vibrations and hear the breaths Victoria was taking as she attempted to hold it all in.

The next day, Felicia woke up to the smell of Anthony cooking breakfast. Alyssa was no longer lying on her chest, and Kaleigh was now standing in front of her mother crying. Startled, Victoria looked at the clock. It was a little after eight o'clock, and Victoria wanted to make the nine-thirty service. She hadn't slept much either, because she kept waking up and falling back asleep throughout the night. Victoria jumped to her feet. There was no way she was missing church today. She needed encouragement, and she needed a WORD from the LORD. She reached down and picked up Kaleigh. Bouncing her up and down, Victoria headed straight for the kitchen to hand Kaleigh over to Anthony. She wanted to go and shower first while the children ate breakfast. That way, they wouldn't be late for church, but Anthony had other plans. Victoria walked into the kitchen and handed Kaleigh over to her father.

Victoria: Please feed her. I need to go and take my shower.

Anthony reached for his daughter.

Anthony: Why? Where are you going?
Victoria: Where I go every Sunday, Anthony; to church.
Anthony: I guess I didn't realize today was Sunday. Can you stay home today? We really need to talk.
Victoria: We can talk when I get back home from church.
Anthony: No. I was kinda hoping we could talk now. That's why I'm cooking breakfast. I asked Nahlia to come over and pick up the children, so we could spend today talking.
Victoria: Anthony, Nahlia is not picking up the girls. They are going to church with me. Call her back and tell her thank you, but no thank you.
Anthony: Why? Nahlia's my sister. What? Is she not good enough to babysit our children?
Victoria: Nahlia has a questionable lifestyle, one that I am against, so no. She can't keep the girls, and you already knew I'd say no. So, why try to stir things up a little more than they are by going behind my back and asking your sister to pick up my children?
Anthony: Oh, so they're just your children now?

Victoria: You know what I mean. Don't try to turn this situation around, Anthony. It won't work this time.

Anthony: What happened to Tony? So, I'm back to being Anthony?

Victoria: I don't have time for this right now. I'm going to take a shower, and me and the girls are heading to church. When I come back, the children should be ready for their naps, and we can talk then.

Anthony: There you go putting that stupid church in front of your marriage again. See, that's the problem right now. They come before me, and you wonder why I.....

Victoria: I wonder why you what? Say it. Cheat on me? Anthony, let me say this to you before I go into total ignore Anthony mode. Nobody made you cheat. You made you cheat because that's what you wanted to do. It had nothing to do with me at all. I counsel couples at the church, and that lie is the most common lie told by men who hate the weight of the truth; men who don't want to accept full responsibility for their own actions, so they try to share the responsibility. I have never cheated on you, Anthony. No matter what you did to me, I never stepped outside of our marriage. Was I perfect? No. I had to accept the fact that I am a woman of GOD, and you are not a man of GOD; therefore, we are unequally yoked. When I rededicated my life to the LORD, I had no idea that by accepting HIM, you would end up feeling rejected. And you know what? I'm not even mad at you. I'm hurt, of course. I keep feeling anger towards you as well, but every time anger seeps in, I remember Proverbs 26:11. *"As a dog returneth to his vomit,*

so a fool returneth to his folly." I know what you are, Anthony. I know what to expect from you if I were to stay with you. You'd become faithful for a few months, and everything would go better than good. Eventually, you'd return to your vomit, and we'd be right here in this place again. I choose not to return to this place with you anymore.
Anthony: So what are you saying?
Victoria: I'm saying that I am running late for church, and I need to go and shower. We can finish this conversation when I get back. Please call Nahlia and tell her not to come. Thank you.

Victoria excused herself and went to take her shower. When she got out of the shower, the children were just sitting down to eat. She was irritated but decided to go and get their clothes ready first and then hurry up and bathe each child. Alyssa knew her mom wanted to go to church, so she ate her breakfast quickly. "Alyssa, you don't have to speed eat," said Anthony. "You can take your time." Alyssa nodded her head, but continued to eat swiftly. After she was done eating, Alyssa ran into her mother's room and announced she was ready for her bath.

After bathing Alyssa, Victoria jogged into the kitchen and grabbed Kaleigh. She knew that Kaleigh, being the youngest, was more than likely full. She grabbed Kaleigh and ran into the room to grab her clothes. She then bathed Kaleigh and called Savannah to come in for her bath. Savannah was more of a daddy's girl, and she wanted to stay home with her father, so she ate slowly. "I'm not finished eating," said Savannah. Carrying Kaleigh, Victoria headed into the dining room and noticed that Savannah had eaten half of her food, but was now eating the rest in small bites.

Victoria: That's enough. Get up. You're going to church.
Savannah: But I don't want to go to church. I want to stay here with Daddy.
Victoria: Go into that bathroom and get into the tub right now, or you're going to get a spanking before you leave.

At that, Savannah began to cry and headed towards the bathroom with her mother following. Standing by, Anthony felt the need to intervene.

Anthony: If she said she doesn't want to go to church, you shouldn't force her to go, Vicky.
Victoria: Go to the bathroom now, Savannah! Anthony, I didn't ask your opinion on how to mother my children. I'm not raising low-lives who sleep with married men, so please spare me this argument.
Anthony: I'm tired of you with your judgmental words and your holier-than-thou persona. You're not perfect, Victoria! You got pregnant with Alyssa on a one-night-stand, remember? You used to party harder than me. Now all of a sudden, you think you're a saint when in truth, all you are is an insecure woman who couldn't keep a man if she held him at gunpoint.

Victoria: That's how I know you will not be a part of my future, Anthony. You're still stuck somewhere in my past. Don't you get it? I've moved on from there. Telling the truth is not being judgmental, but you wouldn't understand that. I don't desire to fight with you at all. I don't desire to make this divorce a contentious one. My hope is that we can end this thing peacefully, and you can go and be the shadow in Joel's spotlight.

Anthony: Who said anything about divorce? So you want a divorce now?

Victoria: I really don't want to discuss this right now. I am running late for church, and like I told you earlier, we can discuss this when I get back home. You can utilize this time to see which one of your women will let you come and live with her.

Anthony: What do you mean "live with her"? Victoria, I'm not moving out, if that's what you think. We'll talk this thing out, and if it is decided that we should go our separate directions, you can move to one side of the house and I'll take the other side.

Victoria: Yeah, I bet you'd love that. The ability to still have me and watch me, all the while having the freedom to pursue other women. No, thank you. I have to go and bathe this girl. I'll talk with you later, Anthony.

Anthony reached out and grabbed Victoria's arm.

Anthony: Vicky, it doesn't have to be like this. You are the one making things hard. I'm not going to say that I'm a choir boy or anything, but what am I supposed to do when we are having trouble in our marriage?

Victoria snatched her arm back.

Victoria: Oh, I don't know. I guess you were supposed to fix them. Isn't that what the head of the house is supposed to do? Excuse me. I'm not missing church!

Victoria went into the bathroom and quickly bathed Savannah. When she came out of the bathroom, she was horrified to see that Kaleigh's dress had been soiled. Anthony had given Kaleigh some chocolate candy because he knew she'd soil her pretty white dress. Moving quickly, Victoria changed Kaleigh's dress, and Victoria went to pick up her Bible from the place that she always kept it: on the nightstand next to her bed, but it was gone. "Anthony, where's my Bible?" she asked. She knew that Anthony had moved her Bible in an attempt to keep her from going to church. "I don't know," replied Anthony. Victoria sprinted around the room, and after realizing that her Bible was not there, she picked up Kaleigh, grabbed Savannah's hand and called for Alyssa. As they were jogging out of the door, Anthony stopped Victoria one more time.

Anthony: So, you are going to go to church without your Bible?
Victoria: Oh, Anthony. Darling, I have several Bibles. I have one here in my purse; see? I just prefer the other one, but I'll do fine. You forgot....my dad is the Pastor.

Anthony: Yeah. Well, when you get back, I probably won't be here.

Victoria: That's fine. Just remember to lock the door behind you.

At that, Victoria loaded the children into the car, and off they went to church. Anthony stood in the doorway, surprised at his wife's lack of fear. He'd done everything to stop her from going to church, but none of those things had worked. He went back into the house and called his sister to tell her not to come for the children after all. After he hung up the phone, Anthony's heart became heavy, and fear overtook him. What was he going to do now? He searched his heart for the perfect lie, but nothing seemed good enough. Here he was at a crossroads where he faced the possibility that his wife was about to leave him. The worst of it was that he could not share the blame with her. It was always better to have arguments where he could at least share the blame if he was unable to convince his wife that she was the one at fault.

Frightened, Anthony headed into his bedroom and noticed his phone was vibrating. He hoped it was his wife, but it was Felicia instead. He already had one emotional woman threatening to leave him. He did not want to hear Felicia's complaints as well, so he sent her to voice mail. When the ringing stopped, he noticed that he had twenty-seven missed calls. Fear and anger overtook him as he strolled down his missed call log and realized those calls had all come from

Felicia, and she'd left voice messages after most of the calls. What was she doing? Was she trying to ruin his marriage intentionally? Instead of listening to all of the voice messages, Anthony decided to call Felicia back and end this charade once and for all.

Felicia: Oh, so you finally decide to call me back when I threaten to call your wife, huh?

Anthony: What? You threatened to call my wife? Felicia, I haven't even listened to my voice mail as of yet, but thank you for the warning.

Felicia: So, are you going to tell me?

Anthony: Tell you what, Felicia?

Felicia: Who the other girl is. The one who called your wife.

Anthony: Oh, so you were awake during that call. That means you purposely spoke so my wife could hear you.

Felicia: Does it matter? Aren't you the one who said you'd told the evil witch about me?

Anthony: Yeah, well that's over now. I'm staying with my wife. You showed me a side of you that I didn't even know existed. I thought you were the right one, but if you're willing to call my wife or try to sabotage my marriage, you are definitely not the right one for me.

Felicia: Sabotage your marriage? You're the one having an affair with me, and GOD knows who else. You're the one who told me that your wife was not the right one for you, and that you'd regretted marrying her. You're the one who lies down with me and doesn't even bother to wear protection. You need to be thankful that I honored your request to get on the pill after the first pregnancy.

Anthony: What do you mean first? You mean only pregnancy.

Felicia: No, sir. I'm pregnant now. I stopped taking the pills three months ago because they kept making me sick. And since you'd promised to give me children after you left your wife, I figured that it wouldn't matter if I got pregnant because, according to you, you were planning to leave your wife within the next few months. Am I lying?

Anthony: Felicia, what did I tell you? If you end up pregnant, my wife could get a fault divorce and take everything from me! I told you to be patient, but right when things were looking up for you, you started acting just like her.

Felicia: Patient? Um, Tony; I waited on you for three years! Count them up: one...two...three years! I honestly don't see what the problem is. Y'all are about to divorce anyway, and I'm just two months pregnant, so that gives you seven months to get that divorce before she finds out.

Anthony: Felicia, I'll pick you up on Tuesday so we can go and see Dr. Mengele again. We can fix this problem just like before, and we'll forget about what was said today.

Felicia: Oh no, my friend; I'm having this baby. No more lies and no more secrets. What's your wife's name again? Victoria? Well, I think it's time Victoria knew your secrets.

Anthony: And what am I supposed to do when she takes everything from me? Have you considered that?

Felicia: Have you considered just divorcing her without telling her a thing, and then once the divorce is final, you can

297

introduce your children to their new sister or brother?
Anthony: Felicia, I don't want to fight with you about this.
Are you available now? Let's just go out to eat somewhere
so we can discuss this more.
Felicia: Sure. Meet me at the Meltin' Pot in about an hour.
Anthony: See you in an hour.

At church, Victoria was having a wonderful time. Her father
had preached a message that fed her spirit, and she felt so
at peace. When the praise team got up to sing, Victoria
almost lost herself in the lyrics. She praised the LORD with
her whole heart, and she let the words penetrate her as she
stretched her hands in worship. Alyssa and Savannah were
seated, and both girls watched their mother and other
members stand up to praise the LORD. Kaleigh was with
her grandmother, however. As soon as Victoria had entered
the church, her mother came through to steal her grandbaby, and Victoria was okay with this. After all, being a
toddler, Kaleigh was bursting with energy and did not like to
sit still.

After church service was over, Victoria greeted a few
members and then went to get Kaleigh from her mother, Mrs.
Brenda Davidson. Her mother was in the back hallway
showing off little Kaleigh to some of the members, when
Victoria walked up to her. Noticing that her daughter
appeared stressed, Mrs. Davidson excused herself to walk
with Victoria.

Victoria: Hey Mom. I've come to get Kaleigh. I need to go straight home today.

Brenda: Okay, but is something wrong? Baby, what's wrong?

Victoria: I'll call you later today and tell you, but I really need to go right now. It's been rough, Momma. It's been really rough, but it's a lesson for me.

Brenda: Please come out to eat with me and your father. I just don't feel right about you going directly home. I don't know why. We are heading over to the Meltin' Pot in about fifteen minutes. The kids are hungry and you need a break, sweetie. You don't have to say a word. I see it in your eyes.

Victoria: I'm not that hungry, Momma. I really need to get to the house.

Brenda: Yes, but the children are hungry. Just come out with us and let them eat. After they've had their fill, then you can go home. If you want, I can keep the kids overnight for you and take them to school tomorrow. I have some uniforms for them at my house, remember?

Victoria sighed and thought about it. If she went home, things would likely get loud, and she didn't want to stress the children out. If she went out with her parents, the children could eat and go to their grandparents' house for the night. That would give her enough time to talk with Anthony to see how they could go about filing for a divorce. Victoria wanted the divorce, but she didn't want it to be contentious. She loved her husband, but she was tired of the other women, his lack of respect for her, and more than anything, his lack of respect for GOD. At the same time, her younger brother Caleb and his wife Missy were going to ride in the van with her parents. She hadn't seen Caleb in a year because he'd moved to Texas, and she wanted to spend time with Caleb, his wife, and their new son, Caleb Jr. About forty-five minutes later, they headed on over to the Meltin' Pot after closing up the church.

Victoria decided to drive her own vehicle and trail her parents to the restaurant. As she pulled into the parking lot, she noticed her husband's vehicle parked there. To be sure it was his vehicle, she pulled alongside the car and looked at the mirror. She could see Anthony's identification card hanging from the mirror. Her heart leaped and felt as if it had gone for a swim in her belly. Victoria's parents pulled alongside her, both noticing Anthony's vehicle as well. By the time they'd parked, Victoria was already outside of her car looking panicked. With one hand resting on her stomach, she proceeded towards the restaurant's doors, but Caleb jumped out of his parents' van and ran to get his sister. He wanted to make sure that they entered together. Everyone was sure of what they would see because they knew that Anthony was not a believer. Just as Victoria reached for the door, Caleb intercepted her and stood in front of the door. "Wait on the family," he said, noticing the tears in his sister's eyes. It hurt him to see his sister in that condition. She'd always been there for him when he was down, and now, he wanted to be there for her. Victoria let out a breath as if she was coming back to herself. How far had she let this man drag her down? How long had she been in such a low place? Victoria's parents and children caught up to them, and Caleb's wife made sure Alyssa and Savannah stood with her. Mrs. Brenda held Kaleigh, and Victoria's father wrapped his arms around his daughter as they entered the restaurant. At first, they couldn't see Anthony because the restaurant was a pretty big one, but when the waiter led them to their seats, he ended up walking them right in the direction of Anthony and Felicia.

Anthony looked up and noticed his wife and her family heading directly towards him and Felicia. Everyone's eyes were fixed on Anthony. Like a deer in headlights, he froze with fear. Felicia looked at Anthony, who'd just snatched his hands off of her hands. She followed his eyes and ended up staring Victoria directly in her face. With her golden brown skin and high cheekbones, Victoria looked like a runway model. Amazingly enough, the tables were right next to each other. Caleb and Pastor Davidson made sure that their wives were seated with the children, and they stood guard by Victoria as she put her hands on her waist and began to speak.

Victoria: You know, when I left home earlier, I was so unsure of my decision. I really needed a Word from the LORD about our marriage. But I think I just got my answer.
Anthony: It's not what it looks like. This is a friend of mine.
Felicia: Liar. Excuse me. Let me introduce myself, since he's afraid to do it.

Anthony: Shut up, Felicia.

Felicia: No. You said you already told her, so this shouldn't come as a shock to her. Anyhow, like I was saying, let me formally introduce myself. My name is Felicia, and I am pregnant by this here man that you lovingly refer to as your husband. And for the record, we have been seeing each other for three years, but you should know that because he already told you.

Victoria: Excuse me, ma'am. I don't have any problem with you, nor do I know you. Besides, Tony hasn't told me a thing except he wanted our marriage to work out. But again, I don't have an issue with you. You're just one of the many women he's messed over me with. And pregnant? I offer you my congratulations and my condolences all in one breath. You will learn what I already know.

Pastor Davidson: Wait a minute. I know you. You are on the praise team at Pastor Rochester's church. Pastor Rochester introduced me to you at the Eagle's Eye Conference.

Felicia was humiliated. She immediately recognized Pastor Davidson because Pastor Rochester had spoken so highly of him.

Felicia: Look, I'm not here to make any trouble. I've been seeing Tony for three years now, and he's been promising to leave his wife for three years. I just found out that I was pregnant for the second time by Tony. The first time, he pressured me into getting an abortion, and I did it like a dummy. He invited me here to put that same pressure on me again, but I'm not aborting my baby. The two of you can do what you want with one another, but I'm keeping this baby. Mr. Davidson, my apologies. I did not mean to dishonor you or your family. I didn't even know his wife was related to you.

Pastor Davidson: Yes. She's my daughter. My firstborn, actually. But it doesn't matter who she is or who she is related to. First off, she is the daughter of the Most High GOD, and you should have honored the fact that he is a married man. But it's not all your fault. He bears the bulk of the responsibility. My question is: How can you get up and praise the LORD in dance; even teach a Bible study, and on the sly, you're creeping with the devil? But don't answer that. This is between my daughter and her husband.

Pastor Davidson turned to his daughter.

Pastor Davidson: Vicky, what do you want to do, baby? Tell him what you want.

Victoria: You need to make your way to the house, and you need to remove all of your personal property from my house. I want you out of my house before the close of today, and tomorrow, I am going to file for divorce.

Anthony: Baby, I'm sorry. Please don't do this. Let's just talk about it, okay?

Felicia: Well, I work for an attorney's office, and I know a little something about property. Until an order is placed, you cannot legally put him out of the house. After all, he was the one who purchased the house and the deed is in his name.

Pastor Davidson: No, darling misled soul. That's our house. It's our family house. Did Anthony tell you the house belonged to him? Honey, Anthony couldn't afford a hinge on the door of that house.

Felicia: Wait a minute. That's your family house? It doesn't belong to Tony?

Victoria: No. Tony doesn't own a thing but his underwear. And by the way, you aren't the only woman pregnant by him. Didn't he tell you? I received a call on yesterday from one of his students. It turns out she's expecting a baby as well. He tried to convince her to abort the baby, but she refused.

Felicia turned to Anthony.

Felicia: How dare you lie to me for three years, Tony! Three years?! *Sobs.* And you made me think I was the one? You told me that your wife was a wicked witch who'd tricked you into marrying her.

Anthony: Sit down and shut up, Felicia.

Felicia: No, you shut up. After all I've done for you, this is how you repay me?

Pastor Davidson: By the way, when you come to the school tomorrow, please clean out your desk. You're fired. The university cannot carry the weight of professor-student affairs.

Felicia: Fired? How can you fire him?

Pastor Davidson: Amongst the many things he neglected to tell you, my dear, I hired him. I am the Dean of the university he works....wait, let me rephrase that....I am the Dean of the university he work<u>ed</u> at.

Anthony: Waiter! Waiter! Check, please!

Victoria: How far along are you, Felicia?

Felicia: Two months.

Victoria: Wow! What's the other girl's name again, Tony? Yeah, I think her name is Sherry. Sherry says she's about two months pregnant as well.

Pastor Davidson turned and looked at his son, Caleb. Caleb was holding his cellular phone up, recording the incident.

Pastor Davidson: Caleb, what are you doing?

Caleb: Dad, it's called insurance of the modern-day. You'll thank me later. Believe me.

Felicia: So, is there anything else I need to know, Anthony? Are you really a best-selling author like you said you were? Do you have any assets to call your own? How am I supposed to support this baby? What about your software company?

Victoria: Best-selling author? Software company? *Laughs.* Honey, he's not even an author; I am. I have a software company. As a matter of fact, it's called Vi-Soft. Of course, Vi is short for Victoria. You don't have Internet to check for these things?

Felicia: He told me his books sold only in university stores, and the two of you built that company together.

Victoria: *Laughs.* No, seriously. Anthony has nothing. Zilch. I started Vi-Soft. I'd just launched the company three months before I met Anthony. He doesn't even know how to create software. He helps me to package the software when I get large orders.

Felicia: *Laughs.* This is a joke. A really bad joke. Anthony, you don't even have two nickels to rub together?

The waiter came and sat the ticket on the table, and Anthony got up and left the table. He took the receipt to the front desk where he paid for his food and left. The next day, Victoria filed for divorce. In the divorce, Anthony got nothing but one of the shared vehicles. He continued to be a father to his daughters, and he finally found himself a wife like Joel's wife. It was the sister of Joel's wife, and she was just as understanding as her sister. Years later, when Victoria did remarry, she made sure that GOD was in her marriage. She waited until GOD sent her the husband HE had for her; a man after HIS own heart.

As for Felicia, she went on to have her baby, but her and Anthony's relationship never recovered from the lies. She was surprised and hurt that Anthony had another other woman besides her. To add to this betrayal, the other-other woman was pregnant. Felicia eventually got married some years later, but her marriage ended when she'd discovered her husband's indiscretions. He'd been having an affair with one of her cousins, and this betrayal was too much for her. **The End.**

What happened in this story, and who were the guilty parties? Both Anthony and Victoria were guilty. Victoria met Anthony posing as a sinner. Of course, she was in a state of rebellion, but she knew she would return to the LORD. She went to the "other side" and got herself a husband. After he married her, she then tried to cross back over to what she knew, and you simply cannot do this to people. Every man and woman has the right to serve whomever they want to serve. GOD gave them that free will. Nevertheless, many believing women go after unbelieving men and then try to tow them into the church, kicking and screaming. This is a form of deception because the woman goes in undercover, impersonating a sinner. She then tries to formally introduce her new husband to the LORD, and when he rejects HIM, the problems start. GOD gave us the right to accept or reject JESUS CHRIST as our LORD and SAVIOR. Oftentimes, women marry the men they were supposed to be ministering to or encouraging in the LORD. But we can't say this was an intentional crime; it was a simple case of lack of knowledge.

Anthony, on the other hand, did what he knew how to do. He's a sinner, and sinners sin. They sin against GOD, and they sin against anyone they have access to sin against. Does this excuse what he did to his wife? Not at all. He had to pay for what he did. You see, sinners are often self-worshippers. No, they don't burn candles to themselves and bow down to their own reflections. Instead, they serve the lusts of their flesh. A sinner will always put his flesh before you, because he first put himself before GOD in his own life. A sinner will always love the sin in you and will groom and encourage its growth, but will often discourage the GOD in you and will do any and everything to kick HIM out of your life. It's not uncommon for a sinner to marry a believer and then try to stop them from going to church or try to discourage their worship, just as it is not uncommon for a believer to marry a sinner and then try to stop them from living the sinful life they've grown to love. Of course, we want all sinners to repent and give their lives to the LORD, but this is an act of will. The sinner has to first want GOD, and then the sinner has to repent and turn their heart to GOD. You cannot change who they are, nor can you turn their hearts to GOD. That's why GOD tells us that if we are married to unbelievers, we must remain in subjection to them, so we can win their souls to HIM. This sounds easy until you actually marry a sinner.

Anthony wanted the woman he fell in love with. He wanted the sinner, but he did not want the saint. He is a sinner, and he has a right to be hell-bound if he so chooses. But as women of GOD, we can't go out there and bring sinners home to our FATHER and expect HIM to open the door for us. I know how easy it is. I did it twice because of ignorance, self-conceit and lack of knowledge. It was in the middle of my second marriage that GOD began to truly mature me and open up my eyes. The truth is you cannot teach Ishmael how to be Isaac. You can't talk Ishmael into becoming Isaac. Ishmael is Ishmael. He is not the husband for you. He may look good, and you may think you know him better than anyone else. After all, he told you his deepest and darkest secrets. He looked you deep in your eyes when he told you that he loved you. He even cried in front of you. We'll find any reason to justify sticking around with a man we know we have no future with, but we do it because we try to murder the truth so we can keep hope alive. Nevertheless, the truth shall stand, and hope will fade away when it is not hope in the LORD.

And what about the women who patiently and foolishly play the other woman character? Please know that you are beautiful to GOD, but you have got to learn to see yourself as GOD sees you. When HE looks at you, HE sees a woman whom HE'D love to bless, but you have to first get in HIS will for your life. You can't steal a blessing, but you can snatch a curse. One woman's curse will not be a blessing to you. At the same time, you can't go looking for joy in another woman's pain. Selfishness simply means you are too wrapped up in yourself to care about anyone else, and this means that your heart is far from the LORD. You can sing the sinner's national anthem, stating, "GOD knows my heart" and "Only GOD can judge me," but once you're done singing, look up; you're standing under judgment, and that is no place you want to be. What I found with "other women" is that in 99% of the cases, the women had been hurt by a man themselves. Instead of learning from the situation, they decided to become a virus and help spread the hurt. I played the other woman role once. I was young, naïve and deep in the world, but I truthfully didn't want the guy for relationship purposes. My mind was just perverted then, but that didn't make me any better than the women who actually try to separate marriages for their own selfish gain. I was just as bad.

Being in the world then, I had friends who were worldly; some of which dated married men. What I learned then was that there are different types of "other women." Some of the ones I've met include, but are not limited to the following:

Ms. Low Self Esteem- Most women, if not all, who play the other woman have low self-esteem. The large majority of them <u>speak</u> with confidence, but they aren't as confident as they pretend to be. Ms. Low Self-Esteem wants to feel beautiful and wanted. She's been hurt a lot in her life. She may have been rejected, betrayed or both. In winning, she is made to feel as confident as she pretends to be. Oftentimes, women with low self-esteem just want to win. They often battle with jealousy and envy, but you won't know it by talking with them because again, they speak with a confident tone. False confidence is their cover-up for a broken heart. Any time a woman is overly confident, beware. She's often covering up pain and trying to mask her fear. But if you will watch her eyes around other women, you will notice that she tends to over-analyze them, oftentimes, not liking the prissier ones. She will always like women who are like herself.

Ms. Revenge- I heard a woman say once that some woman had taken her husband, so she was taking another woman's husband. Ms. Revenge has not forgiven a man or some men who have hurt her; therefore, she exacts her revenge on other couples. She will happily be the other woman, but her real plan isn't always to take the husband from the wife and keep him. She just wants to destroy the marriage. She wants to finally win because at some point in her life, she felt like she lost. Ms. Revenge makes many women pay for the hurts other women have made them to endure.

Ms. Gold-digger- Now, a woman after wealth or financial security will date anyone, married or unmarried. She has the spirit of mammon attached to her. Mammon is a spirit that triggers the love of money in a person. Oftentimes, gold-diggers go to the extreme to win what they believe to be a successful man. At any given time, gold-diggers are surrounded by several men, all of which have purposes. Most of the men they are connected to are givers of something. To make matters worse, every man connected to them is not rich or well-off. They simply have jobs or some type of means that the gold-digger considers beneficial to her hunt. A gold-digger will call up these men and have them buy her all types of gifts, but her main focus is the "big fish". That's the guy who has a lot of money, and she oftentimes won't ask him for a red cent initially. That's because she attempts to hide what she wants from him in hopes that he will marry her. All of the expensive attire she wears, in most cases, came from those not-so-wealthy men she's learned to con. Her goal is to look like an independent woman to the successful man so she can officially prey on him with papers in tow.

Ms. Competition- Like Ms. Low Self-Esteem, Ms. Competition is in it for the win. She is oftentimes the girl who was once smart and beautiful. She was the girl who won all of the spelling bees, won or got first runner-up in the pageants, and the girl who ran for student council in high school. Competition is her life; it's what she's good at, and she does not take well to losing. Especially when she feels she should have won. Ms. Competition often compares herself to the wife, stating that she is prettier, she is the better catch, or she is the most logical choice. She spends her life campaigning and is more likely to become bitter than any of her other co-conspirators. Once she's won a man, she will oftentimes toss him away and pursue another unavailable man because she's not happy unless she's competing. You'll notice that with Ms. Competition, she can have a single man who really wants to be with her, but she'd prefer to pursue the married man.

Ms. Menopause- This is the older gold-digger who has grown tired of trying to nab a single man as a single woman. Most of the time, when you're dealing with Ms. Menopause, she will patiently pursue the husband. She may even stick around a few years because she has made an investment into getting him, and she intends to collect on it. Ms. Menopause will oftentimes date men who are younger than she is. Unlike Ms. Competition, she will not bother the wife for years, but if angered, she may become a man's worst enemy.

Ms. No Strings Attached- Oftentimes, Ms. No Strings Attached is married herself. She may invade another woman's marriage just because she wants sex with other men but does not want single men out of fear that they'd get too serious. She wants someone who stands to lose something, just as she stands to lose. Single men are too much of a risk for her. Oftentimes addicted to sex, Ms. No Strings Attached doesn't involve herself emotionally in the relationships. Her goal is not to take the man from his wife; it's just to borrow him. Of course, she has a filthy spirit attached to her, often referred to as the spirit of perversion. Ms. No Strings Attached has been known to break her own rules, and get attached. In such cases, she will intentionally destroy her own marriage to pursue the man she's been cheating with. If rejected, Ms. No Strings Attached may end up with an inmate number.

Ms. Trade-Off- Ms. Trade-Off is also involved in a relationship, but she does not end her relationship with one man until she has another man waiting for her. She likes attached men because she knows they are willing to commit to a marriage. She does not want to run the risk of losing a relationship, only to end up dumped by the man she's seeing. She will often offer to divorce her husband or break up with her boyfriend in the event that the man she's seeing divorces his wife. She's not a stable woman (just like all "other women"). She will more than likely trade off her catch eventually when he is no longer amusing to her.

Ms. Biological Clock- Beware of Ms. Biological Clock. She's been humped; she's been dumped and now, she's done with the games. She wants a family, and she's going to have that man's baby whether he likes it or not. Ms. Biological Clock is often the craftiest of them all. She may pretend not to want children, but in truth, the sound of her biological clock is haunting her by the second. She's likely been with married men before, and she tried to play by the rules, but the rules didn't work for her. None of the men left their wives, so she's developed a new attitude about adulterous relationships. She now believes that she has to to take what she wants in order to win. Her nice days are over, and she's tired of the lies and broken promises. Her baby, to her, proves two things: That woman's husband was sleeping with her, and she has Exhibit A growing in her belly or wrapped up in a blanket. Secondly, the baby is supposed to prove to the man that she was serious about everything she'd said to him. Ms. Biological Clock may act surprised and hurt when she discovers she's pregnant, but make no mistake about it; even though her face looks like it's raining, on the inside, the sun is out and there's a party going on. If the man does not leave his wife, and the wife sticks around, Ms. Biological Clock will often retaliate by dragging them through countless court appearances and always demand more money in child support. She may even attempt to have the wife's earnings reviewed so she can receive more child support. It's not about the money as much as it is about revenge.

Ms. Aspiring Wife- In most cases, Ms. Aspiring Wife is the deadliest of them all. She wants to marry the husband; therefore, she will go to great lengths to get him. She is oftentimes very patient; often waiting years for the husband to leave his wife. There are two categories of Aspiring Wives. The first is the unfaithful Ms. Aspiring Wives. This category of women will engage in multiple relationships at one time because they want to be married. Oftentimes, they fall under the category of Ms. Biological Clock because they have been with one or more married men before and came out of those relationships empty-handed. Now, they are determined to meet somebody's husband at the altar. They may be seeing more than one married man, or in most cases, they are seeing one married man and another single man on the side. They are often more interested in the married man because he has committed to a woman through marriage, so they believe he will have no problem committing to them in marriage. The second category is the faithful Ms. Aspiring Wives. They are the ones who will go to hell's end to win. For them, there is no other alternative. He said he was leaving his wife, so they treat their relationship with him as if he were single. They are most likely to get upset when they find out that the husband and wife are still sexually active than any other category of adulteresses. At the same time, they are most likely to become pregnant or confront the wife because there is no other way for them. He said he was going to leave the wife, and by golly, that's what it has to be! Ms. Aspiring Wife will oftentimes make investments into another woman's husband. She may give him money, buy him clothes and in some cases, buy him a car. She may even move into a bigger house and start preparing for her lover to leave his wife, even when he hasn't promised to leave her. She begins to act like a wife while still a mistress because she is auditioning for the role of wife. She's a very dangerous character if rejected. Ms. Aspiring Wife is known to stalk and even attack the actual wife when reality sets in for her. She is also known to use her car as a weapon against the man who broke her heart.

Of course, there are more categories I'm sure I've missed, but the point is there is no future pursuing the husbands of other women. When I gave my life to CHRIST, I started getting new friends; friends who loved and feared the LORD. I started having loyal-to-GOD friends and not-so-loyal-to-GOD friends. One thing I noticed was that the loyal ones behaved in a very respectful way towards marriages, and they often married some really great men of GOD. Their marriages lasted and withstood the tests of the time, and they learned to be one another's best friend. As singles, they were always respectful of the marriages of other women. They are often uncomfortable being left alone with the husbands of other women and they'd set a bunch of rules for themselves that they followed when dealing with the husbands of other women. The not-so-loyal-to-GOD friends were more likely to be disrespectful of the marriage unit. They were more worldly, and they rarely ever got married. When and if they did marry, it was often to worldly men, and of course, those marriages did not last.

Wait on GOD for your husband. The hardest lesson I've ever had to learn was that even when you are impatient and refuse to wait, you end up married and waiting for your husband to arrive spiritually. Truthfully, that's a LOT harder than waiting on the man to find you, because once married, you will see a physical shell of a man with no pearls of wisdom inside.

One Tear Closer to You

"If you don't get a handle on your emotions, you'll give someone a handle on you."

You said you wanted to be closer to the LORD. You told the LORD that you wanted HIM to remove all of the things in your life that separate you from HIM. But you didn't realize how much walking with the LORD would cost you, so when GOD starts to remove the things, people and mindsets away from you, you run back to what you know and remarry those old mindsets. You run back to the people GOD removed from you to rekindle those flames and re-establish those friendships. You run back and purchase those things or chase behind those things that you thought you lost. But the truth is change oftentimes hurts because GOD is removing everything from you that separates you from HIM. Even though the process can be painful and lonely, it is so very worth it.

Stacy wanted her marriage to Grant to work out, but the marriage seemed to be falling apart over one minor incident that turned into a major accident. Stacy knelt in front of her husband as he sat on the bed, and she began to cry. Grant sat there stone faced and looked at his wife. Tears rolled down his cheeks as he said to her, "Yes, I will go. I won't do to you what you did to me. I will go. My bags are still packed."

Let's rewind to get a better understanding of what happened. It all started off on a Friday night when Stacy invited some friends over to the house. Stacy's best friends Jacqueline, Marian and Piper were all there with their husbands Kyle, Justin and Nathan. Stacy and Grant were now on vacation from work, and Stacy wanted to have a few friends over to eat, drink and play a little pool. Grant wasn't in the mood for company, however, because as a police detective, he'd put in some long hours to finish up paperwork before going on vacation. He wanted to go ahead and pack their bags for their trip the next day and then rest and relax. They were going to be vacationing in Maui, and their plane was to leave at eleven o'clock the following morning. Nevertheless, after trying to reason with his wife, he gave up and decided to go and pack anyway. In doing so, he was not present for the party, which left the other guys feeling unwelcomed. The women were okay, but all of their husbands felt strange being in a man's house when he was in the other room preparing for a trip.

Each man took his wife to the side and voiced his discomfort. Kyle was especially vocal with his discomfort, not just with his wife, but with everyone there. He said to Stacy, "I really hope you guys enjoy your vacation, but I gotta be honest here. I'm not comfortable being in this man's house while he's in the back room. I know he wants to get

318

ready for tomorrow's big trip, and I can understand that, so I think Jacqueline and I are going to call it a night. We'll see you guys when you get back." After Kyle spoke up, the other two men agreed with him, and they all left. Stacy was angered by what she saw as rude behavior on the part of her husband. She looked at the table. Most of the food wasn't even touched.

Stacy stormed into the room where Grant was. He'd just finished packing his last bag and was now sitting on the bed watching television.

Stacy: Really, Grant? That's how you're going to do our company?

Grant: Hello to you too, dear. And what do you mean? You didn't talk with me about having your little party, and I already told you that I needed to pack and get some rest. You wanted a party; you had your party. But I did what I planned to do. I got my bags packed, and now I'm about to get some shut-eye. I suggest you to do the same.

Stacy: You know this wasn't about you wanting to pack or get some rest. This was about you feeling out of control in this situation. Since I didn't ask your highness's permission, you decided to be a no-show to teach me a lesson. Go ahead, Grant! I hope you're happy now!

Grant: Stacy, you can turn this into whatever you want it to be. I'm not about to sit up and argue with you. What I am about to do is get some rest.

Stacy: No. We need to talk about this. Kyle even voiced

319

how uncomfortable he was because the man of the house wouldn't come out of the room. Do you know how that made me feel?

Grant: Good for Kyle. How did that make you feel? Hopefully, it made you aware of your selfish behavior, and you'll think twice about inviting people over without first speaking with me.

Stacy: Oh, I'm sorry. I didn't know I needed your permission to invite people over to my house!

Grant: The last time I checked, it was our house, and yes, you can invite people over if you want. What you can't do is force me to attend. Now, if you really want me to get on that plane tomorrow, I suggest you go somewhere and self-soothe and let me get some rest. This has been a really hard week for me, and I'm not about to spend the whole night arguing with you and then head over to Maui only to argue some more because I'm too tired to enjoy myself.

Stacy: What?! You're threatening not to go to Maui if I don't let you get any rest?! Oh my gosh, Grant! So, that's it? Grant has spoken and now I need to be quiet? If you don't want to go to Maui with me, you don't have to go! Why did I marry such an egotistical, selfish and controlling man?!

Grant: I don't know, but what I do know is I am about to go to sleep. Kyle, Justin and Nathan will get over my no-show, and hopefully; you'll go and pray your way out of this little temper tantrum you're throwing. As for me; I'm about to get some rest, so it's lights out and mouths closed, if you will. Turn off the light for me, Stacy. Please and thank you in advance.

Stacy was overcome with anger. How was she supposed to enjoy Maui with Grant when he was being unreasonable? Just as she was about to speak, she heard her cell phone ringing. "You turn off the lights if you want them off," she said before storming out of the room. Grant's smug look and shrug of the shoulders made her even more upset as she slammed the bedroom door. She walked into the dining room and picked up her cell phone off of the table. It was Piper calling. She was a little upset because her husband, Nathan, had talked about how uncomfortable he was at their house all the way home.

Piper: Hey Stacy. No offense, but the next time you have a gathering at your house, Nathan and I are not coming. He was a little upset as you can imagine. He said he felt like an intruder. Why didn't you talk with your husband before inviting us?

Stacy: I told him when we got off work, but I knew he'd be against the party, so I figured I could just throw it anyway, and he'd enjoy himself as well. I didn't know he'd act like a spoiled one-year-old and lock himself up in the room. I apologize to the both of you for my husband's stupidity, and it won't happen again.

Piper: Okay. But I thought I'd give you a heads-up and say that we won't be at any more of your gatherings. Nathan isn't comfortable, and I was uncomfortable for him. I don't want you to be mad at us when we don't show up next time.

Stacy: Not a problem. My apologies again. Let me go. I'm not feeling so well.

Piper: Okay. Take some Tylenol and get some rest. Goodnight.
Stacy: Goodnight.

When they hung up the phone, Stacy noticed that she had another text message. It was from Marian, and it read, "Sorry about tonight. Hubby wasn't too happy with the way things went down, so next time, please give us a heads-up if your husband is going to be a no-show." Stacy sent a text message apologizing for her husband's behavior, and went to sit on the couch. She was upset, humiliated and angry by everything. Instead of praying about it, she decided to make her husband pay for what he'd done. She went into the bedroom and snatched the covers off of her sleeping husband. Grant woke up and decided not to argue with Stacy, who was now dragging the cover into the living room. He went into the closet and grabbed another comforter. He laid down again and was asleep in less than two minutes.

Stacy couldn't sleep. She didn't even feel like packing her clothes because she was so angry with her husband and so ashamed of how things had went. She would punish Grant, and she would punish him well.

An hour later, Stacy got up to pack her bags. She was still seething with anger because she'd sent a text message to Jacqueline apologizing for Grant's behavior, but Jacqueline did not respond. This was unlike Jacqueline. Ordinarily, Jacqueline would respond to text messages in less than two minutes. This bothered Stacy so much that she ended up sending five text messages to Jacqueline; three of them apologizing for Grant's behavior, and the other two questioning why Jacqueline wasn't answering her texts. Still, she received no response from her friend. She was hurt because Jacqueline was her closest friend. She was the one who encouraged Stacy in the LORD, and she was always there to loan her wisdom when she needed it. Now she was obviously upset with Stacy, and this bothered Stacy. It was now four in the morning, and Stacy had just finished packing. She wasn't sure if she'd packed everything because she was still upset with Grant. She lay down on the couch and pulled the cover over her body. Tears streamed down her face as her thoughts seduced anger, and anger seduced vengeful thinking. Still, she did not pray, nor did she consider that she was wrong.

As she began to doze off, she received a text message from Piper that read, "Are you still up? Can I speak with you?" What did Piper want at this hour? Maybe Jacqueline had called her. Maybe she was having relationship problems. Stacy picked up her phone and called Piper.

Piper: Hello. Are you okay?
Stacy: Yeah. I'm still a little upset though. We're supposed to be traveling in a few hours, and I don't feel like this is going to be a good trip.
Piper: Why is that?
Stacy: Piper, he didn't even apologize or acknowledge that

he was wrong.

Piper: Did you tell him you were inviting us over?

Stacy: I waited until he came home, but that's not the point. He still should have been courteous enough to come and sit with the guys, instead of closing himself up in the room.

Piper: Yeah. Well, maybe he was just tired. Nathan is still upset about it too.

Stacy: Why?

Piper: Nathan originally didn't want to go, but I talked him into it. He wanted us to go out to eat with some of his co-workers, but I told him that you two were traveling and that we really needed to show up.

Stacy: Piper, I am so very sorry.

Piper: It's okay, but I'm not going to lie; it really ticked me off because Nathan argued at me all night long. Where's Grant now?

Stacy: In the bed sleeping like nothing happened.

Piper: So, what are you going to do tomorrow? You're both still going to Maui, aren't you?

Stacy: Yeah, but I'm not excited about it anymore. I don't know what to do.

Piper: You can't let him get away with acting like that, because if you do, he'll start getting really disrespectful towards you and your friends. How do you act in front of his co-workers?

Stacy: Oh, Piper...I make him look great in front of his co-workers. He's invited a few over three or four times, and each time, I played the doting hostess.

Piper: You see, but when your friends come over, he doesn't return the same favor to you. I'm not telling you to do this to Grant, but when Nathan showed off in front of his family, I had to teach him a lesson.

Stacy: What did you do?

Piper: Two years ago, we were at his family's reunion when Nathan decided to raise his voice at me in front of his brothers because I asked him to hold Natalie while I got in the pool with the women. Natalie was about a year old at the time, and I didn't think it would be safe for her to be in the pool with me. I had just learned to swim and didn't want to take the risk. But he didn't want to hold Natalie because the guys were about to engage in a game of football. I asked him if he'd sit this game out because I'd been cooking, cleaning and serving all day. The least he could do was let me enjoy one extracurricular activity, but he decided to be selfish. I asked him two times, and the third time he fired off at me with, "Piper, I told you to keep the baby yourself! Now go and stop bothering me! Sheesh!" I was so angry that I asked another guy standing near him if he'd hold Natalie for me. When he held her, I walked away, and that forced Nathan to have to hold her. I got in the pool and enjoyed myself. For the rest of that day, I did not speak to him, nor was I cordial to anyone else. I was stand-offish, and I answered all questions with a one-word response if I could. Nathan was so embarrassed that he never did that again.

Stacy: Yeah, I need to do something harsh to Grant as well. He's pretty stubborn, but I know what buttons to push to break him.

Piper: Push them, girl. And push them hard. Anyhow, I'd

better let you get some rest since your flight is leaving shortly. Listen....don't let him ruin your trip. You go and have the time of your life and let him think about what he's done.

Stacy: You're right. Operation Teach a Lesson is now in full effect.

Piper: Ha! That's right. Talk to you soon. Bye.

Stacy: Bye.

A few hours later, Grant was standing over his wife. "Wake up. We need to get ready, so we can head over to the airport," he said. "We can stop and grab a bite to eat on the way." Stacy was beside herself. Did he think it was that easy? That they'd head out to Maui, and all would be forgotten? He had a lot to learn, and Stacy decided that she was the one to teach him.

On the road, Stacy did not speak with her husband, even though he'd asked a few questions. He'd asked her if she was sure she'd packed everything; he'd asked her if she'd printed out their boarding passes, and he'd asked her what she wanted to eat, but she did not answer him. Grant pulled up at Stacy's favorite fast-food restaurant. He really wanted to enjoy his trip because he'd been working so hard on the job, and this was an opportunity for him to wind down. Going to Stacy's favorite restaurant was an attempt to lighten the mood, but it didn't work. When they went through the drive-through and Grant asked Stacy what she wanted, she replied, "Nothing. Get something for yourself. I'm good." This bothered Grant because he did not want to throw away his vacation dealing with his wife's negative emotions; nevertheless, he ordered a sandwich, fries and a drink for himself. As they drove off, he began to eat his food. The smell of the food was heavenly, and Stacy found herself wishing she'd ordered something to eat. Hopefully, they were handing out those pretzels on the flight. Sensing that his wife was feeling regretful for not ordering anything, Grant said to Stacy, "One more chance. The flight from LAX to Hawaii is about four or five hours. I can stop at one of the restaurants ahead if you want. If not, we're not turning around." But Stacy was determined to stand her ground. "I'm fine. Let's go to the airport, please," she said.

Grant knew that this trip wasn't going to go as expected. They'd planned this trip for over a year now, but now that the time had come for the trip, Stacy was ready to ruin it to prove a point. Grant was beginning to feel upset as well. Was she really about to ruin the trip of a lifetime just because he didn't attend her party? Was she really willing to go that far?

At the airport, they parked their vehicle and begin unloading their bags. Stacy grabbed her purse and two rolling suitcases and started wheeling ahead of her husband. Grant stopped and stared at his wife.
Grant: Stacy. Stacy! Come here for a minute, please.
Stacy: What, Grant?
Grant: Come here and sit in the car with me for a moment. We have three hours before the flight leaves, so we've got plenty of time.

Stacy: No, I think I'll go on inside.
Grant: Please, Stacy. Come and sit in the car with me. Please.

Stacy turned around and hesitated. In her mind, she felt that now was a good time to explain to Grant the lesson he was being taught. Grant reloaded the suitcases back into the trunk of the vehicle and then met his wife in the car.

Grant: What's wrong with you, Stacy? I have worked my tail off trying to make sure this was a stress-free vacation, but it seems that you've already planned to ruin it. Tell me what's wrong and let's put this behind us now so we can enjoy our vacation.
Stacy: You know what's wrong, Grant. I invited some friends over last night and you made them feel like garbage. Every guy there said he felt uncomfortable because you did not come out of the room. You need to apologize to them.
Grant: First off, I was not wrong because I did not agree to a party. Secondly, you knew we had a flight this morning, and you didn't take me into consideration when you planned that party. Stacy, you work from home, so I'm sure you got plenty of rest, but did you take the time out to consider that maybe I was tired?
Stacy: It doesn't matter, Grant.
Grant: Oh, it doesn't matter?
Stacy: You could have come out of the room and sat with them for an hour or two. That's not asking too much!
Grant: What I can agree with is I should have come out of

the room and at least greeted them. I should have told them that I would not be participating, but I can't take the blame for this one. They are just as much of a victim as I am. You made plans with your girls. You excluded me from those plans, and it did not work out in your favor; therefore, you are the one who owes everyone an apology, including me!

Stacy: I owe you an apology? You know what, Grant? Let's just go on inside and get on this plane. It is very obvious to me that your pride won't let you accept your fault in this. When we get to Maui, we can change our room and get a double bed because there is no way I'm sleeping next to you.

Grant: I'll tell you what. You can get your bags and you're going to Maui alone. I took a vacation to be with my wife and have a good time. If you're telling me that we are going to Maui fighting, and that our vacation is going to be nothing more than arguing and fighting, I'll just stay here. Sometimes, I don't understand you. You prayed and asked GOD to bring you closer to HIM, but now, it seems like you're getting further away from HIM instead. This tells me that you are resisting HIM because you didn't realize how much that shift would cost you.

Stacy: That's not the problem. The problem is you don't like my friends, so you think you will run them away from me by just being rude to them, and I won't stand for this.

Grant: Stacy, could it be that GOD is pulling you away from that crowd? Your friend Jackie is the only decent one in your circle. You said it yourself: You want to be closer to GOD. At the same time, I haven't done anything to you, nor have I done anything against your friends. The problem is you want to be the head of the house, but I'm sorry; that position is taken. Now, I love you and I respect you, but what I will not tolerate is these prep-school tantrums from a grown woman. When you want to talk to me, just talk to me. But raising your voice at me, snatching the cover off me or not speaking to me isn't going to change a thing. You were wrong. It doesn't matter how you slice it; you were wrong! You can tell yourself how right you were all day long, but at the end of the day, you were wrong, and anyone that tells you otherwise is a liar! So, again....it's your decision. We are either boarding that plane as a happy couple going to enjoy a week on the beaches of Maui, or we are a home-bound couple.

Stacy: This is so typical of you. Rather than being a man and apologizing, you try to redirect the blame to me and then threaten to ruin my week if I don't just accept your games. That's it, Grant. I'm going to Maui. You can stay here if you want to. That's totally up to you, but I'm going, and I will enjoy myself with or without you.

Grant: I'm not going to Maui to lay on a beach one hundred feet away from you while you soak in your attitude. You were wrong, Stacy! So, if you're going; get out of the car, get your bags, and have a nice trip.

Stacy's pride got the best of her. She was determined to prove her point, so she put on her sunglasses, got out of the car, and slammed the car's door. Grant popped the trunk from within the vehicle, and Stacy removed her bags and started towards the building. She thought that Grant would change his mind, seeing how hard she was willing to fight for what she believed in, but to her surprise, Grant pulled off.

Everything felt so surreal. Stacy was standing at the desk, handing the flight attendant her ticket. She could not believe that Grant wasn't going to Maui with her, but she did not want to lose this fight. Grant needed to learn a lesson, and Stacy wanted to teach him. Stacy felt somewhat lightheaded because the hurt, anger and reality was all beginning to set in. She now had one hour before her flight was to leave, and she was beginning to feel sick on her stomach. Suddenly, she felt her phone vibrating. Maybe it was Grant. Maybe Grant had a change of heart, realized that he was wrong and decided to board the flight to Maui after all. After removing the phone from her pants pocket, Stacy was upset to see that the caller was not Grant. It was Piper.

Stacy: Hello?
Piper: Hey. Where are you now?
Stacy: Still at the airport, waiting to board the flight.
Piper: Where's Grant?
Stacy: He got upset and went back home. He said he's not going.
Piper: What?! What's his problem now?!
Stacy: Well, I stood my ground and he was like, "I know you're not about to take these problems to Maui with us." I pretty much told him that if he didn't resolve the issue and apologize to you guys, that he wasn't going to enjoy Maui.

So, he elected to leave instead.

Piper: That's my girl. Stacy, you go to Maui and enjoy yourself. You've been planning this trip for over a year now. Don't let him ruin it for you. Do you hear me? Enjoy yourself without him.

Stacy: I will. It's just upsetting that he would go to such great lengths to prove a point. I don't know, Piper. I think he's gone too far this time.

Piper: I totally agree, but just pray about it and let it go. He has to acknowledge that he was wrong before he'll change. Isn't that what the Bible says? That we must confess our sins to one another?

Stacy: Yep. That's what it says.

Piper: He needs to confess to you and us that he was wrong. Nathan got so mad last night that he left and didn't come back until this morning. That really upset me, Piper, because we were starting to clear the air between us again.

Stacy: Didn't you tell me that he stayed out last weekend as well?

Piper: Yeah, but he was mad at me then. This week has been a lot better. Now, it's like we were set back.

Stacy: I'm sorry once again.

Piper: It's okay. Just don't tap out, Stacy. You really need to help Grant to understand that we are your friends, and we have been friends before you even knew him. Friends aren't replaceable, but he is.

Stacy: That's right. I'm so tempted to call him right now to just tell him a piece of my mind, but....

Piper: No. Don't call him! That's what he wants you to do.

Go to Maui and enjoy yourself, Stacy. You deserve it.

Stacy: Yeah, you're right. Let me go. Some people are beginning to stand up, and I want to be at the front of the line.

Piper: Okay. Well, enjoy your trip and I love you. I will be asking GOD to give you traveling mercy.

Stacy: Thank you and love you too. Later, love.

Piper: Later. Bye.

Stacy boarded the flight and went to Maui. In Maui, she was heartbroken. Here was this beautiful paradise, and she didn't have anyone to enjoy it with. When the bell-hop showed her to her hotel room, she was taken aback by how beautiful the room was. Grant had reserved the room, and he'd reserved the best room the hotel had to offer, to Stacy's surprise. He'd even made arrangements to have some white roses laid out on their bed, with a note that read, "Did I tell you that I love you? Let me show you just how much this week." Stacy broke down as she read the card. Had she been unreasonable? Just as she began to cry, her phone rang. Maybe it was Grant.

Stacy: Hello?

Piper: How's Maui, dear?!

Stacy: It's beautiful. Really beautiful.

Piper: Wait a minute. You sound down and out. I know you're not going to let Grant ruin your vacation from over four thousand miles away!

Stacy: Piper, he'd planned this trip beautifully. He reserved

the best room and even had white roses placed on the bed.
Piper: Oh, he probably did that while you were on the plane.
He wanted to make you feel bad for standing your ground.
Stacy: No, he reserved the room months ago. I do know
that much. As for the roses and the note, I don't know when
he ordered them.
Piper: What note?
Stacy: He left a note on my bed that reads, ""Did I tell you
that I love you? Let me show you just how much this week."
Piper: Yeah, he probably called and did that while you were
on the flight.
Stacy: No, I don't think so. But I'll manage. I'll try to enjoy
this week.
Piper: Don't just try. Enjoy yourself. You deserve it, Stacy.
Stacy: I will. I think I'll do a quick tour before taking a nap.
Piper: Okay. Have fun, girl. I'm rooting for you.

After they hung up the line, Stacy decided to tour the hotel to
take her mind off her husband, but nothing seemed to work.
What if she'd thrown away her marriage? And why was
Piper pushing her more towards contending with her
husband, rather than helping her to find a solution? After her
quick tour, Stacy went back to her room and took a nap.
Two hours later, her phone rung and woke her up. She
looked at her cell phone and saw that it was Jacqueline.

Stacy: Hello, stranger.
Jacqueline: Hey, Stacy. What's wrong with you?
Stacy: What do you mean?

Jacqueline: You seemed a little upset when you text messaged me last night.

Stacy: I was just worried. Why didn't you text me back?

Jacqueline: We were at the hospital. We got a call right after leaving your place, and we found out that my mom was in the hospital.

Stacy: Jackie, I'm so sorry. I feel awful. What's wrong with her? Is she going to be okay?

Jacqueline: I hope so. She went into diabetic shock. They scared me so bad when they told me she was in the hospital.

Stacy: I feel like crap. Here I was worrying that you were upset with me because of Grant's behavior, and you were at the hospital. I feel awful.

Jacqueline: No problem. I forgive you. How's Grant doing?

Stacy: I wouldn't know. I went off on him about his behavior and I slept on the couch last night. When we arrived at the airport this morning, I was still upset and he refused to board the plane with me. So, he's at home and I'm here.

Jacqueline: Stacy? Are you serious?! How dumb are you?

Stacy: What?

Jacqueline: I asked you how dumb are you. It wasn't that big of a deal. Really. He was tired. We understood that, and that's why we left. I didn't know why you were even trying to have a party knowing the two of you were leaving in the morning.

Stacy: It just really upset me because I know that Grant doesn't really care for my friends. At the same time, both Piper and Marian were pretty upset. Piper has called me

335

several times to talk about how upset Nathan is.

Jacqueline: I ask you again: How dumb are you? Stacy, you have to understand that Grant is a man of GOD. You said yourself that you'd prayed and asked GOD to bring you closer to HIM. Maybe HE was answering your prayer through Grant.

Stacy: That's almost the same thing Grant said. Oh wow. I really feel awful now.

Jacqueline: You should feel awful. As for Piper; Stacy, why would you listen to Piper of all people? Nathan has been beating her and cheating on her for years. Piper is not happy, and she wants all of us to be just like her...unhappy. I remember she told me that my husband was cheating on me just because he came home late from work one night. Thank GOD, I had the sense GOD gave me to listen to my husband. He was really at work. Another time, she told me that it would be so much fun if we would all leave our husbands and just enjoy single life, travel the world together and just become groupies. Why would anyone listen to the ministry of Piper?

Stacy: She told me to teach Grant a lesson.

Jacqueline: Stacy! No. She wants to teach Nathan a lesson through you and Grant. She's asking you to do what she's too afraid to do in her own relationship. Your marriage is a guinea pig for her. She wants to see you try it out first, and see how it works for you. Don't be so naïve, Stacy.

Stacy: Ouch. I feel like such a fool. I knew about her problems with Nathan. Why did I listen to her?

Jacqueline: That's the same question I want to ask you.

Why would you listen to her? I'm about to hang up this phone now. Call your husband and make things right again. Apologize to him and let GOD do what you asked HIM to do. Let HIM change you and bring you closer to HIM. Even if that means you never talk to me again. I want to see you blessed.
Stacy: Jacqueline, I love you and thank you so much for being a true friend. I will be praying for your mom as well. I know all will be well. Let me call him now. Hopefully, he's not asleep.
Jacqueline: Okay. Goodnight and love you too.

By this time, Stacy felt foolish, awful, sick, angry and desperate. Had she lost her husband over this nonsense? She nervously dialed his cell phone. The first time she attempted to dial his phone, she dropped her cell phone and the batteries came out. Stacy cried as she picked up the batteries and put them back in her cell phone. She paced as she waited on the phone to finish loading. The second time, the phone didn't ring when she called. Instead, there was silence. Angry and desperate, Stacy began to rebuke the devil as she paced back and forward. Finally, the call went through and the phone began to ring. Stacy paced and twirled her fingers as the phone rang and rang again. The call went to voice mail, but Stacy didn't want to leave a voice message, so she called back. Grant still refused to answer his phone. Stacy ended up calling Grant more than twenty times that night, but he did not answer his phone.

Unable to sleep, Stacy pondered what she would do. She decided to book a flight for the morning to see if she could convince her husband to come back to Maui with her. She went into her computer bag and brought out her laptop computer. She managed to book a flight for six o'clock the next morning. With the layovers, the flight would be five hours. She would leave her bags at the hotel and try to convince Grant to come back. She even went ahead and purchased her and Grant's return flights.

That night, Stacy couldn't sleep. She felt so bad for how she'd acted and reacted. Grant had really been looking forward to the trip, and she'd robbed him of it because of her pride. She anxiously watched her cell phone, hoping that Grant would call, but he didn't. And then it hit her. She hadn't prayed at all, so she decided to kneel down and talk with the LORD.

"Dear GOD, I know. I really messed up this time. I don't know what I was thinking. LORD, I ask that you forgive me for my sins. I turn my mind, my heart and my will back to You in total repentance and total surrender. I will let go of the people You want me to let go of. I will embrace Your will for me. Please forgive me LORD, and I ask that You fill my husband with forgiveness towards me. I will glorify Your Name with this situation if You will only deliver me from the mess I've made."

The next morning, Stacy was back on a flight to Los Angeles. She didn't bring anything with her except her purse. On the flight, she quietly prayed some more about the situation. She really wanted to make everything right, but she did not know how Grant would respond. When she arrived at the LAX airport in Los Angeles, her heart felt as if it had dropped into her stomach. Fear overtook her, but she prayed and asked the LORD to remove the fear and fill her faith. She caught a taxi to her home.

Back at the house, Stacy could see Grant's vehicle in the driveway. It was backed in as if he was planning to go somewhere. As she entered the house, an uneasy feeling came over her. What was she about to see? Hearing the door open, Grant came out of the bedroom and was surprised to see his wife. "What are you doing here?" he asked. His voice sounded angry and hurt. Stacy stared at her husband. She loved him so much, and she didn't want to lose him.

Stacy: Can we talk, please?
Grant: Talk about what? We've already talked; I've wasted over two thousand dollars per ticket on a trip, and my vacation was ruined because you thought I was supposed to bow down to your friends. Stacy, go back to Maui. Please. I beg you!
Stacy: I understand you being angry with me. I really deserve it and I'm so so sorry, Grant. Baby, I am so sorry.
Grant: What? You tried to intimidate me into coming, but that didn't work. You tried crying, and you even tried to shift the blame to me. None of that worked. So, now you're trying humility. It's a little too late for that, Stacy.

Stacy: Grant, I ask that you listen to me for five minutes. Please.

Grant went back into the bedroom and sat down on the bed. Stacy kneeled down in front of him, and placed her hands on his legs.

Stacy: Baby, I was stupid and foolish, and I'm sorry. You were right. I asked GOD to bring me closer to HIM. I asked HIM to change my heart, and when those changes started taking place, I guess I got scared. I let pride come in, and I'm really ashamed of how I treated you...my husband. Grant, you are the best husband a woman could have, and I don't want to lose you ever. Baby, I love you with all of my might. I wish I could go back and redo this incident, and I would do it all differently. You were tired; I get it now. It was wrong of me to invite them over without first speaking with you. If you will forgive me and give me another chance, I am recommitting myself to you to be a better wife. Please forgive me, baby. I'm still in transition. Please forgive me.

At that, Stacy laid her head on Grant's legs and began to weep. Grant could not bear the sight of his wife crying. He loved her, but he didn't like her ways. He knew that she was changing to be a better woman, but he also knew he had to stand his ground with her because Stacy could be a little controlling at times.

Grant: Stacy, you really hurt me. You placed yourself before me. You placed your friends before me. Do you know what that feels like? It hurts, Stacy. It's not just upsetting; it's degrading and it hurts. But I'm a man of GOD, so I forgive you. There will be some changes around here, however. This can't keep happening, Stacy. You have got to get a handle on your emotions; otherwise, you are going to tear this marriage down with your bare hands.

Stacy stood up and looked at her husband. She kissed him on his cheek.

Stacy: Baby, I am so sorry. I can't say that enough. I really want you and I to go to Maui and enjoy ourselves. We have six days left to vacation, baby. I really want you to have a good time, and just know that when you are with me, I will have a good time. Please say yes, baby.

Grant: Stacy, I'm not going to Maui. That trip cost too much, and you know I don't like to throw money away. We'll just have to take this as an expensive lesson.

Stacy: Baby, I already purchased the tickets. Please come with me. I won't enjoy the place without you. I'll do anything you want, baby. Please.

Grant: Where did you get money to buy those tickets?

Stacy: I used some of the money I was saving to go to art school.

This hurt Grant. He knew Stacy had been saving for years to go to art school. It was her passion and her heart's cry. Stacy knelt in front of her husband as he sat on the bed, and she began to cry. Grant sat there stone faced and looked at his wife. Tears rolled down his cheeks as he said to her, "Yes, I will go. I won't do to you what you did to me. I will go. My bags are still packed."

Grant and Stacy ended up taking their trip after all. They vacationed in Maui and had a great time together. Stacy got closer to the LORD, and she disassociated from Piper and Marian. She learned to be a Proverbs 31 wife, and a year later, she became the mother of a healthy baby boy.
The End.

What was Stacy's problem? Like many believers, Stacy asked GOD to change her, but when the change began to happen, she started resisting it. Stacy recognized the fact that she was about to lose the lifestyle that she knew, so she tried to breathe life into dead friendships and she expected her husband to do the same. Stacy did not have a handle on her emotions; therefore, the enemy ended up having a handle on her, and he used that handle to control her. Stacy could have lost her marriage trying to prove a point. Let's face it; she was wrong because when we are married, we can't make decisions for our spouses. Any time two people live in one house, they have to learn to live together and respect one another. Instead of respecting her husband, Stacy tried to find a handle on him with which she could control him, but the only handle he had that she could reach was his love for her. People under control often like to control others because they've lost control of their own lives.

All the same, miserable women can't hang around happy women without making them miserable. There are countless women out there who have ended their marriages trying to pacify a miserable and lonely woman who appeared confident but was falling apart on the inside.

Kings always had special advisors to them, and their children had special advisors. No ordinary person could advise the king or any royalty. At the same time, the President of the United States has his own advisory team. We are children of the King of kings; therefore, no ordinary person or people can advise us. An average woman can only teach you how to be average, but if GOD called you to the super-normal, you will need a super-normal advisor.

Many of us pray that GOD brings us closer to HIM and to change our hearts to make us more like HIM. One thing you will discover is that as GOD brings you closer to HIM, you will experience the pain of loss. You'll lose friends, you'll lose old mindsets, and you may even lose your job. No one ever said elevation was easy. Please understand that the anointing isn't free. There's a price you'll pay for that anointing. The pain is intense for some, but not so intense for others. It depends on the relationship each individual has with the things and the people they are being called to let go of. The greater the sacrifice, the greater the journey. Each tear you drop is counted by GOD. HE uses those tears to water your blessings so they will grow. Every tear you cry doing the will of GOD brings you one teardrop closer to the

LORD. *"The LORD is near unto them that are of a broken heart; and saves such as be of a contrite spirit" (Psalm 34:18).* As painful as change can be, it is so very worth it in the end. It's similar to childbirth. *"A woman giving birth to a child has pain because her time has come; but when her baby is born she forgets the anguish because of her joy that a child is born into the world. So with you: Now is your time of grief, but I will see you again and you will rejoice, and no one will take away your joy" (John 16:21-22).*

A mind is like a compass. Where you point it will determine the direction of your day and the direction of your life. If you focus on the wrongs, you will always lose sight of the rights. How your day goes is a direct reflection of what you've placed your sights on. When the husband steps on your foot, it's easy to focus on how you feel. Real strength, however, will cause you to focus on how he feels, because kindness isn't easy to hand out to someone who has hurt you. To get this strength, you need faith. Faith is like a highway to GOD. The distance between you and GOD is equivalent to the amount of faith you have. Many people want to know how close they are to GOD, but the answer is obvious in their faith. How much do they believe GOD? How much a person believes GOD reflects how much WORD they have in them. A person void of the WORD is a person void of GOD, for GOD is HIS WORD.
Some would argue that Grant handled his wife wrong, but he did not. He could have come outside of the room and apologized to the guys, letting them know that he would be

packing for the trip and then going to sleep. But he didn't have to do this because he didn't invite them over. It was just an act of courtesy, but the real villain in this story was Stacy. Piper wasn't so much of a villain. Piper was just another unhappy woman trying to maintain her friend count. Unhappy people love to be surrounded by unhappy people. If you are willing to let them drain you of your joy, you can't blame them for your unhappiness; after all, they didn't steal it from you; you gave it to them. Pay attention to the words your friends constantly say. Pay attention to the moods your friends are constantly in. Pay attention to how your friends are towards you when you are happy. Are they happy for you? Is their happiness genuine, or is it a forced smile designed to cover up their disappointment? When you tell them your good news, do they try to sap you dry by telling you their bad news? Are they distant from you when you're happy, but they are your best friends when you are miserable? It's not that they are trying to be there for you in your hour of misery. Oftentimes, they simply live in misery, and they are glad that you are visiting them there. You have to pay attention to the people surrounding you; otherwise, you'll end up with a ton of friendly enemies who have enough muscles in their faces to make their frowns look like smiles.

Every tear you cry in this walk will bring you one step closer to who you really are, but who you are is hidden in CHRIST. This means that every tear you cry will bring you one step closer to the LORD, if you are standing in HIS will for you. Elevation isn't a bunch of parties where you wake up blessed and lie down on a bed of money. Elevation is the elevator that takes you up towards the LORD, but anything that is unlike HIM cannot ride along with you in that elevator. Therefore, you'll find yourself crying as all of these things, mindsets and people are peeled away from you. But when the hour comes for you to embrace each next level, understanding will be waiting for you, and the joy of the LORD will embrace you.

Don't be afraid to ask the LORD to bring you closer to HIM. After all, you were created by HIM for HIM. You can't make your life about yourself and expect to live in the blessings, joy or peace of the LORD. While you are elevating, continue to pray for GOD'S Kingdom to come, and that HIS will be done on Earth as it is in Heaven.

In Heaven- The principalities like to sit in the heavenly realms. You are basically praying down principalities.

On Earth- You are simply praying that GOD'S will be fulfilled in the realm of the Earth. This tears down the demon who walks the earth looking for someone to devour.

As It is in Heaven- Now you are talking about the throne of GOD. Where the throne of GOD is, there is praise to the Almighty GOD. Where GOD is, there is peace, joy and love. There is no sickness, depression or death in GOD'S presence.

Pray those handles off yourself and grab on to GOD'S unchanging hand. You'll be glad you did.

The Devil's Pacifier

"You cannot marry the Devil and expect the LORD to give
you away."

One of the lessons of life that we all come face to face with
at some point in time is: GOD won't share HIS glory with
anyone. This is one of those statements that religious
people learn to quote but not understand. Let's face it.
We've all been that religious person at some point in our
lives. We religiously said what we knew to be true, but we
still tried to pinch off HIS glory. We even tried to let
someone else sit on HIS throne in our hearts, and when
that failed, we accused the devil of attacking us. The truth
is: You cannot serve GOD and pacify the devil...not even
slightly. Nevertheless, many women still try to maintain
relationships with men who are not their GOD-ordained
husbands, all the while trying to maintain a relationship
with the LORD. They eventually find themselves at a
crossroads where they are made to choose between the
LORD and the men they idolize.

Amanda was married to Cedric, and the two of them had a
son together. Their marriage was only a year old, but it had
already endured some tests that threatened to destroy it.
The issue was that Amanda was a woman of GOD, and

Cedric was a worldly man. Their son was two years old. Of course, he'd been conceived and born before they were married. Why did Amanda fornicate? After all, she was supposed to be a woman of GOD, right? The truth is many Christian women fornicate when they are babes in CHRIST. This means there isn't enough WORD in them to get them to refrain from fornication.

Amanda had given her life to the LORD three years ago, five months before she'd met Cedric. Being a young Christian; however, she dated Cedric the way a worldly woman dates a man. They went out on a few dates, and the relationship eventually became sexual. Not long after they began having sex, Amanda became pregnant with Cedric Jameson, Jr. The couple was ecstatic at the thought of being parents, and Cedric doted on the pregnant Amanda. Amanda wanted to marry Cedric before Junior was born, but her desire to have a big wedding pushed their plans back because they couldn't even afford a small ceremony. The couple ended up getting married on Junior's first birthday, and all seemed well at first.

At the beginning of their marriage, Cedric happily attended church with his wife. He truly did want to give himself to the LORD and embrace life as a Christian, but his struggle was just like everyone else's struggle; it was hard. That's because Cedric wanted the LORD, but he did not read the Bible often, nor did he meditate on the WORD of GOD. Instead, he attended church services, and this just wasn't enough to change his mind. Any time the enemy sees someone who has faithfully served him trying to give their life to the LORD, he will begin to shake up their life. If there is no WORD in them, there is nothing in them to ground them. The WORD of GOD is our substance, and without it, we are like feathers to the enemy; easy to lift, but hard to swallow. We are hard to swallow because GOD protects the baby Christian, giving him or her a period of grace. HE understands that they will continue to make the same mistakes until they have been filled with HIS WORD. Because of this, Cedric was always being shaken up, but he wasn't grounded in CHRIST. Instead, he was grounded in what he knew, and that was to fight, curse or flee. He initially wanted Amanda because he felt she could help him find and root himself in CHRIST. Instead, he ended up helping her to find and root herself in the world.

Amanda really wanted her marriage to work out with Cedric, but she soon learned that when she acted Godly, her husband wasn't so attracted to her. When she behaved in an ungodly manner, her husband seemed to be smitten with her. *"There is difference also between a wife and a virgin. The unmarried woman careth for the things of the Lord, that she may be holy both in body and in spirit: but she that is married careth for the things of the world, how she may please her husband" (1 Corinthians 7:34).*

Slowly, but surely, Amanda began to sin more and more. She would curse often, she surrounded herself with worldly friends, and she listened to music that ministered opposite of the WORD of GOD. Nevertheless, she continued to be a faithful visitor of the church building, and she even attempted to visit GOD in prayer every day. Life seemed good for Amanda for a while until, she discovered that her husband had been having an affair with one of the women she worked with. The pain was intense, but it became even more intense a week after this revelation, when their son was diagnosed with lupus.

The pain was intense, and Amanda felt as if her heart was being ripped out of her. She ended up having a nervous breakdown and had to be hospitalized. While Amanda was in the hospital, she noticed that her husband did not come to visit her often. Instead, he would stop through each day for fifteen minutes or less. Additionally, he was always dropping their son off with Amanda's mother. Any time she called his cell phone, he would not answer. Instead, he would let her calls go to voice mail, and he'd call her back ten minutes to an hour later, claiming that his phone had been in another room.

During this hardship, Amanda began to question the LORD. Why had HE allowed these things to happen to her? Where was HE when she needed HIM the most? Here she was going to church faithfully, and even volunteering to help out around the church from time-to-time, but for what? She ended up being hospitalized for three days and was released on a Tuesday evening.

Once Amanda was released from the hospital, she went home to confront Cedric about his behavior. Here it was that their son was sick, and he had not tried to spend any time with him. Not wanting to stress Junior out, Amanda waited for him to go to sleep before confronting her husband. She told Cedric about his behavior. She told Cedric that she would be seeking a divorce from him because of his affair and his lack of empathy towards his own son. But Cedric's response to her was one she would never forget. He said, "I would like you to divorce me, Amanda. I feel that I can't offer you anything. When you met me, you were in the church and you loved the LORD so much that you did everything to please HIM. Do you remember what you said the first time we slept together? You said you felt so bad that you went home and cried all night. I thought you could help make me a better man, but I was wrong. Instead, I have watched you change your views, and it hurts me to know that I have been the instrument used to help you change your views. Now, where are your prayers going? You drink and party with me. You curse more than I do, and you rarely ever talk about GOD, except on Sundays or whenever HIS Name is brought up. You have become a reflection of me, and it was fun for a while, but what can I offer you except the hell I'm headed to? Do you know why I cheated on you? Amanda, I can't look at you and not feel bad seeing what you have become. I feel responsible for your fall from grace. I feel like you were once an angel, and the devil used me to snip your wings. I knew this marriage wasn't going to work. I know I have to get my life right with GOD, but to tell you the truth, I'm not ready yet.

But what has that gotten me? The doctor is saying I might lose my one and only son; I've watched my wife rapidly decline, and what can I do about it? Absolutely nothing! I don't even know how to pray. I don't even know if GOD would accept any prayers from me because of my lifestyle. So, yes; I do want you to divorce me. If you stay with me, you'll keep coming down where I am, and I'm not going to change any time soon. I can't promise you that I'll stop seeing Wendy. I can't promise you that I'll be here for you forever and ever. I can't even promise you that I'll ever get my life right with GOD. What I can promise you is that if you stay with me, you will regret it."
The End.

What Amanda did was take a husband when she was too young to marry. Sure, we age in the natural, and we may be old enough naturally to get married, but until you are old enough spiritually, you should never walk down anyone's aisle trying to tie any knots. That's because a baby Christian will always choose a husband who is either a baby Christian or someone who is unsaved. Think about it. If you were given the chance to get married when you were eight years old, who do you think you would have married? You wouldn't have chosen a man after GOD'S own heart. You probably would have chosen Barney, Big Bird or some crazy celebrity who fascinated you by wearing a lot of colors. When I was six years old, I had a crush on Boy George, of all people. That's why your parents would never let you be anyone's wife at that age. You had to mature both physically and mentally before you were old enough to legally marry anyone. But there's a whole new level that most people overlook, and that's called spiritual maturity. When you are not spiritually mature, you will meet and marry men who are not fit to be husbands. And when you become their wives, you will find yourself slowly, but surely, trying to appease whatever lusts they have. You will find yourself trying to please the LORD but trying to pacify the devil in the man you chose.

How would you feel if your husband was trying to please you and another woman? The three of you are walking, and he runs between you and her. When he sees that she is upset, he runs over to her aid. When he sees that you are upset, he runs over to your aid. No worries, though. He says to you that you are his wife, so you have nothing to complain about, and you'll be the one to win in the end. But she is going to be coming with you for a while, living in your home, and he'll have to share himself with the both of you until everything he's working for works out in his favor. Would you accept the terms of this agreement? This is what saints do to GOD every day! Many people try to please GOD and the devil. They walk with GOD when they want something from HIM, but they walk with HIS enemy when they want something from him. When they have problems, they run over to the LORD and ask for HIS hand to move in their situations. When all is well, they run over to Satan, but they'll visit the LORD on Sundays and sometimes at night during prayer. GOD doesn't want weekend visits; HE wants full custody. Any time a person straddles the fence, they leave one leg hanging over in enemy territory. Don't think for one second that the devil won't touch you just because you go to church and you shout every Sunday. If anything, he'll want to attack you even more because he loves to make the church look powerless.

A man can get with you, marry you and attempt to serve the LORD with you, but eventually, he will go back to what he loves the most. *"As a dog returneth to his vomit, so a fool returneth to his folly" (Proverbs 26:11).* At the same time, marrying a powerless man spiritually is almost the same as handing Satan the keys to your marriage. *"Or else how can one enter into a strong man's house, and spoil his goods, except he first bind the strong man? and then he will spoil his house" (Matthew 12:29).* It is easier for a sinner to drag a saint down than it is for a saint to pick a sinner up. We can only lift them up in prayer, but you can't carry a man across the finish line. He has to want GOD for himself; he has to cross over on his own because he wants to. There are many men in the world who love to date Christian women, and many of them truly believe that these women can help them to become better men. Instead, they end up losing interest in their wives because going to church, serving the LORD and living a life pleasing to GOD eventually start looking boring to them.

The younger you are in CHRIST, the more you will want to have a man in your life; sometimes, to the point of desperation. That's because we often try to use fill-ins

where we haven't completely submitted ourselves to the
LORD. As you grow up in the LORD, however, you will find
that your desire to be a wife or be involved in a relationship
won't be so intense. Instead, a spiritually mature woman
won't enter any relationship unless she knows for sure that
the man who is wooing her is her husband. A spiritually
mature woman will ignore her flesh to tune into her spirit.
Sure, there are millions of handsome godless men out there
who wouldn't mind visiting church with you from time to time.
If you marry him, he won't be so handsome anymore once
you get to know his heart. One thing you will then find is that
the man you chose has the power to turn your lights on or off
at any given moment. He can decide if your day is sunny, or
if a storm is overhead. In other words, he'll have the power
to say whether you have a good day or a bad day because
he will have direct access to your heart, the very heart from
which the issues of life flow. Any time you serve the wrong
man or the one he serves, he will reward you with sunshine,
but when you get too holy for him, the weather will change in
your relationship and in your life. Your prayer life will get
stronger if you lean on the LORD, because you'll soon find
that you can't fight a devil with words. You need the WORD
of GOD, patience, and every fruit of the SPIRIT.

It's simple, saints. You can't run between the world and the
LORD. You will have to choose whom you will serve. If you
don't, you will have rejected the LORD to accept defeat. You
will have given all of your strength to the powerless, and
when your tests come, you won't have anything to offer but

faithless prayers and complaints. Let the WORD mature you first, and when you are ripe and ready to be a wife, GOD will send your husband to come and pick you. It is then that you will be sweet favor to him and not bitter rottenness to his bones. If you serve the LORD, serve HIM with your choices. Do yourself a favor and wait on GOD; otherwise, you'll end up finding wisdom in pain, gathering knowledge from chaos, and birthing understanding without spiritual anesthesia.

Joshua 24:15- "And if it seem evil unto you to serve the LORD, choose you this day whom ye will serve; whether the gods which your Fathers served that *were* on the other side of the flood, or the gods of the Amorites, in whose land ye dwell: but as for me and my house, we will serve the LORD."
Matthew 6:24- "No man can serve two masters: for either he will hate the one, and love the other; or else he will hold to the one, and despise the other. Ye cannot serve God and mammon."

The Belly of Hell

"Fire is consuming; therefore, hell is never full."

> One thing we all discover in life is that there is much out there for the taking, and no matter how much we take, our lusts can never be quenched. We see billionaires wanting more and more, and we wonder why they aren't satisfied with the big houses, the nice cars and their lavish lifestyles. The truth is that humans are lustful creatures who rarely find satisfaction in just enough or too much. After all, for every big house built, there's a bigger house that towers over it. For every fast car, there is always a faster car. For every handsome man, there is always an even more handsome man alive.

Church-going, curvaceous and spunky were the best words to describe Brooke Meyer. Brooke was both a wife and a mother of two handsome boys whose names were Andrew and Blake. Andrew was thirteen years old and Blake was seven years old. Brooke's husband's name was Brett, and the couple had been married fourteen years.

Brooke was thirty-five years old, but she didn't look a day over twenty-three. A former model and fitness instructor, Brook was a very beautiful woman. Brooke's mother was originally from Nepal, and her father was originally from Germany. With smooth, tan skin like her mother, and grayish-green eyes like her father, Brooke was beautiful to everyone who saw her.

Brooke was accustomed to being the center of attention everywhere she went. She often complained about some of the questions people asked her in relation to her race, but inwardly, Brooke loved all of the attention. When she was growing up, she always excelled in High School, and there wasn't an office that she ran for that she did not win. She'd even won the prom queen title two years in a row while in High School. Now that her glory days were over, Brooke often found herself feeling unsatisfied. Even though her husband was a very successful attorney, he just wasn't cutting it for Brooke anymore. She felt that Brett was predictable and mundane. All he did was go to work, come home, and work some more. Most of his conversations were about court, his clients and the lawyers he often went up against.

One day, Brooke finally got the call she'd been waiting for. A popular airline had accepted her as a flight attendant, and she would be coming to work in five days for her orientation. Brooke was overly excited about the new opportunity, but Brett wasn't so happy because he knew his wife would be away from home most of the time.

For the first year working at the airline, Brooke was

overcome with joy. She loved being a flight attendant for so many reasons, the main reason being the attention she received while working.

It was a Saturday morning when Brooke's life would be changed forever. She was working on a flight headed to Honolulu, Hawaii, when she met Russell Zaleski. Russell was a thirty-eight-year-old frequent flyer who often took lavish trips to and from Hawaii. Russell was seated in first class when Brooke approached him. When his eyes met her eyes, he knew that he wanted her, and bad! She was without question the most beautiful woman he felt he'd ever laid eyes on.

Brooke: Can I get you something to drink, sir?
Russell: Yeah. Let me get a coke...no ice, please.

As Brooke began to pour the drink, Russell could not take his eyes off her. Her beautiful smile made her look like a Miss Universe contestant. Her long, jet black hair complimented her beautiful tan skin.

Russell: I'm sorry to stare, but my goodness, you are absolutely beautiful.
Brooke: Thank you.
Russell: No, seriously. You are the most beautiful woman I have ever laid eyes on.
Brooke: Aw, that's sweet. Thanks.

After pouring Russell's drink, Brooke walked away to serve other customers, but Russell kept his eyes on the beautiful woman who'd just kidnapped his thoughts. He decided to do something big to get her attention. Russell called Brooke back over to his seat, and he placed an order for an eight hundred dollar bottle of wine. Brooke wasn't too amused because she'd seen that kind of spending before, since she'd been working at the airline for over a year. When Russell realized that Brooke wasn't impressed with his purchase, he decided to do something even bigger. He waited another twenty minutes for Brooke to complete her rounds, and he called her over to him again. He'd written a check for $5,000 for Brooke.

Russell: You've been such a great flight attendant, I wanted to leave you with this tip. I just need your whole name to fill it out.

Brooke covered her mouth in shock.

Brooke: Wow! I've never been given such a big tip before! Is this a joke?
Russell: No, it's not a joke. I just want to bless you the way you've blessed me.
Brooke: I am truly thankful...truly, but we aren't allowed to accept tips.
Russell: You just said you'd never received such a big tip before. That means you have received tips. Don't turn me down or I'll be disappointed.

Russell jokingly pouted like a baby and extended the check to Brooke again.

Brooke: Yeah, but it was all cash, so the airline couldn't really track that. A check...I would definitely get fired.
Russell: I won't tell if you don't tell.

Russell winked at Brooke and smiled. Even though Brooke's family was well off, five thousand dollars still sounded good. Since Brett kept such a tight grip on the joint bank account, Brooke thought to herself that taking this money could be a great opportunity go shopping undetected. After all, she had a secret bank account that Brett was unaware of. Finally, Brooke looked around and took the check.

Brooke: Thank you so much!
Russell: You're very welcome. Listen, is there a number I can reach you at? I'd love to get to know you better.
Brooke: Well, I'm married, so that wouldn't be a good idea.
Russell: Oh. So you're married. That sucks. Well, how about this: We can just talk from time to time...You know, as friends.
Brooke: Yeah, but it could still bring trouble in my marriage and yours.
Russell: Actually, I'm not married.
Brooke: Oh.
Russell: Yeah, my job keeps me too busy. I'm always on the go. I'm heading to Hawaii now to record another film.
Brooke: You record films?

Russell: No, I'm not the recorder. I'm actually a stunt double.

Brooke: Really? A real life stunt double?

Russell: Yep...in the flesh.

Brooke: I've never met a stunt double before. What films have you starred in?

Russell: We're actually not allowed to disclose that kind of information because people like to believe that their favorite actors are actually the ones doing the stunts. But I'll tell you on a later date if you give me your number.

Brooke thought about it. Maybe he could help her to get into acting. After all, she had the look, and now she had the connection. Brett wouldn't have to know, and the whole communication could be innocent, she thought.

Brooke: How about this? I don't have a business card on me, so give me your number and I'll call you in a few days.

Russell: Deal.

Russell handed Brooke his business card. The business card didn't list Russell's profession. It only listed his name, office number and cell, along with a picture of him wearing professional attire.

A few days later, Brooke called Russell as promised. Over the next few weeks, their conversations continued to get steamier and steamier, until one day, they decided to give in to their flesh. With the affair now started, Brooke found herself feeling as if she was now where she was called to be. She was now the woman dating a stunt double/ millionaire.

The affair continued for a year, and Russell continued to put pressure on Brooke to leave her husband and their two children. For a while, Brooke offered up many excuses, but all of the lavish gifts and vacations were now hanging in the balance. She wanted to act, and she wanted to be with Russell, so she decided one day to go ahead and leave Brett.

Brett was heartbroken. He loved his wife dearly, and he'd been working hard to buy her that house she'd wanted so badly. Her sons were also heartbroken; nevertheless, Brooke felt like she'd made the right decision. Her plan was to get into acting, make a few million, and then file for custody of her two boys. But things just didn't go as planned.

One week after moving in with Russell, Brooke began to notice his strange behavior. He was always peering out the window, and he demanded that all of her calls be less than thirty seconds long. He said that the feds were tracking him because of the amount of money he had. Because of his paranoia, the couple moved every three months. He also checked Brooke often for hidden wires, and he'd checked their homes for hidden cameras.

After a year of separation, Brett finally filed for divorce.

Brooke hadn't been calling him or their children. He'd hired a private investigator to locate her, and he sent the papers to her new address. Seeing those papers hurt Brooke more than anything she'd ever seen. Russell, on the other hand, was startled that Brett had easily found his address, so he suddenly went and rented a new condominium, and the couple promptly moved out. He also forced Brooke to sign the divorce papers and give up full custody of her sons. By agreeing to these terms, she didn't have to come to court or out of hiding. Three months later, the divorce was final, and Brooke went into a depression.

Over the next two years, Russell became crazier and crazier. He forced Brooke to quit her job so she could be a full-time wife, and he became physically, verbally and emotionally abusive. He continued to brainwash Brooke into believing that the feds were after them, and that she was specifically chosen to carry out a task that would save all of mankind.

Brooke began to notice that she'd never seen any evidence that supported Russell's claim that he was a stunt double. He traveled to Hawaii often, and even though he'd take her with him, he would often leave her at the hotel while he went to work, as he put it. Being the wife of a millionaire wasn't as fun as Brooke thought it would be. It was tiring, it was draining, and Russell was beginning to run her crazy.

One day, the couple was at their new apartment unloading boxes, when Brooke came across some papers. Russell had eaten some bad tacos, and had gotten a bad case of diarrhea as the result. The papers were hidden away in a small box inside of the moving box. Brooke looked around and listened for Russell. She purposely made noise so Russell wouldn't suspect anything. The papers were addressed to Russell from a Psychiatrist by the name of Dr. Richard Jefferson. The diagnosis was also noted on the paper. Russell had been diagnosed with Schizophrenia and Delusional Psychosis. It all made sense now. The trips to Hawaii were to see Dr. Jefferson. Russell was no stunt double; he was a deranged liar. Brooke also discovered that Russell's parents had been paying for the trips, their homes and their lifestyle. His parents were wealthy; Russell was just a spoiled nutcase.

A far cry from the beautiful woman she once was, Brooke managed to leave Russell one Sunday morning when he'd fallen asleep. She tiptoed out of the door and ran for her life. Brooke walked into a nearby church and sat in the audience while the choir sang. For the first time in years, she felt a calming peace come over her. She was now overweight, and her hair was unkempt. It had been five years since she'd seen her sons, and she was sure they wouldn't want to see her now.

After church, Brooke walked up to the Pastor and told him her story. He helped her to get into a shelter for abused and battered women, where she tried to rebuild her life. After two months in the shelter, Brooke finally reached out to her mother and was surprised to hear the joy in her mother's voice. Brooke was sure that everyone hated her by now. Now that she was down and out, she had no one to turn to and no beauty to lean on. Brooke's mother invited her to come and live with her. She told Brooke that she had pictures of the boys, and that they came by once a month to visit her.

Brooke: Do they ever ask about me?

Martha: They used to, but over the years, they stopped. They mention you from time to time...especially Blake. He's almost thirteen years old now, and I can see the hurt in his eyes. Andrew, on the other hand, is better at masking his pain. I think he does it because he wants to stay strong for Blake. Andrew is eighteen years old, and he should be nineteen in a few months.

Brooke: I feel like crap for what I did. I was so stupid, Ma. How could I have been so stupid?

Martha: Are you stupid now?

Brooke: No.

Martha: Okay. Focus on what you are and not what you were.

Brooke: You're right. What about Brett? What's he doing now?

Martha: Brett has remarried, and he has a daughter named Jennifer and a son named Brett, Jr. with his wife. The boys love her. She has been absolutely amazing in their lives.

Brooke felt horrible. Another woman was now sitting on the throne she once called home. Another woman was mothering her sons, and this broke her heart.

Brooke did move back in with her mother. After she'd left, Russell had decided to take his life because he didn't feel that he could live without her. Over the years, Brooke slowly rebuilt her relationship with her sons, but it was never the same again. Both boys loved their mother, but they didn't feel a bond with her. Brooke was never able to rebuild her life the way she once knew it. She ended up working at a local supermarket for the rest of her life.

On a more positive note, she did give her life to CHRIST. **The End.**

Where's the super-good ending? Why didn't Brooke get all her stuff back and end up back in Brett's arms? Why didn't Brooke ever get the relationship back she once had with her sons? Why did she end up working at a supermarket for the rest of her life? We like happy endings because we like to escape real life to live in fantasy, but some mistakes follow us for the rest of our lives. If this truth was told without apology, people would think twice before they made decisions that would affect or destroy their lives. Hollywood tells us that men who cheat end up living pathetic lives, but women who cheat are forgiven and are able to walk back into glory. As women, we tend to empathize with other women, but we aren't so forgiving towards adulterous men. The reality is that Consequence is not gender specific, nor does it care about how pretty you are. There is seed time, and there is harvest. Whatever you are sowing today is what you'll be growing tomorrow.

The story could have been a little easier to digest if Russell hadn't been mentally ill. After all, most women don't have affairs with mentally ill men...right? Wrong. Any man who attempts to date you while you are married has a mind problem. His thinking is wrong because his heart is wicked. Now, he may not be having delusions of people following him, but men who go after married women often have their own special set of issues. For example, a man who took you from another man won't trust you, and he is 90% more likely to be abusive towards you than a man who got you legally. Women who leave their husbands to be with other men eventually learn the very same lessons that men who leave their wives to be with other women learn: It is better to prune your own garden than it is to plant another one.

Brooke wanted more, even though she had far more than most women. There was more to be had, and Brooke wanted it all. Instead, she ended up losing it all. She gave up one of the most precious gifts a woman could have: motherhood. For what? For a chance to live a lifestyle that she felt she deserved because she didn't realize that the flesh is never satisfied because hell is never satisfied.
In marriage, you will find yourself getting bored from time to time because the two of you (husband and wife) will fall into your day-to-day habits. It's normal to want that spark back that you once had, but you can't go and light another man's

fuse when you have a husband at home. What Brooke should have done was talk with her husband about the issues that were present in her marriage.

The issue with Brooke wasn't just that she was bored; the issue was that she was accustomed to being worshipped. She loved and soaked in the attention that others gave her because of her beauty, but one thing about beauty is it fades. Someone who is used to being worshipped has a hard time dealing with reality when it hands them wrinkles, weight and younger competitors to marvel after. That's when you'll start to hear a woman relive her glory days through storytelling.

Don't chase after the vain things in life such as glory, beauty, money or anything that eventually fades away or is spent. Seek wisdom, and wisdom will preserve you, give you long life, and provide for you all the days of your life. A wise woman will always be surrounded by people who love her and want to hear the words that she speaks. An unwise woman will always be surrounded by people who hate her and want to see how cruel Mother Nature can be.

Miranda's Rights

"One woman's dream is another woman's nightmare."

One of the strongholds that many women find themselves under is the stronghold of envy, and another one is jealousy. Of course, most people think the two are the same, but they aren't. Jealousy says, "I want what you have." Envy says, "I want to be who you are," or "I want the relationship you have." Even though both are forms of coveting, they are not exactly one and the same.

The reason women find themselves battling envy and jealousy is because envy first entered mankind through a woman. Of course, it entered the spirit realm through Satan, but on the natural side of things, it entered mankind through Eve. As you can recall, it wasn't the fruit that was the major temptation to Eve. It was what the fruit represented. Satan told her that she could be like GOD, and she could be as a god. He tempted her with envy, whereas she envied GOD in that moment. Jealousy, of course, was revealed when she looked upon the fruit and saw that it was good to eat. In that moment, she was coveting that fruit. She gave in to what she felt, and after she'd sinned against the LORD, she took some of the fruit to her husband. The Bible never says that he was tempted. Instead, he only ate the fruit because his wife gave it to him.

If envy and jealousy could get Adam and Eve kicked out of the Garden of Eden, why is it that many women think there are no consequences for submitting to them now?

Miranda and Nikki had a lot in common. They were both single working mothers who were taking college courses online. Miranda was studying to get her Master's Degree in Speech Therapy. Nikki was studying to get her Bachelor's Degree in Business Administration. The women were neighbors, and even though they didn't really know each other, they would speak whenever they saw one another.

Nikki was fascinated by Miranda because Miranda seemed to have it all together. Miranda was a very pretty woman to Nikki, as well as most people who saw her. She was five feet, three inches tall, and she didn't look as if she'd ever birthed a child. Miranda had big brown, almond-shaped eyes that matched her beautiful honey brown skin. Her shoulder-length hair was always styled beautifully, and Miranda did not wear a lot of makeup. Miranda had one child; a four-year-old daughter named Tamyria.

Nikki was pretty herself. Standing at five feet, two inches tall, she too was petite. She did have a slightly bulging belly; nevertheless, it wasn't too noticeable unless she wore a fitted shirt. With beautiful inset eyes and medium brown skin, Nikki was a looker, and she knew it. Nikki had two daughters: four-year-old Mackenzie and three-year-old Madison. Nikki's on-again off-again boyfriend was named Mac, and he would come and go to Nikki's apartment as he pleased.

One of the fascinating things about Miranda was the fact that she was always on the go. She was always involved in something. She was actively involved in her church, often volunteering for local mission assignments, and she sang in the choir at the church. No one had ever seen a man come to Miranda's house except for Tamyria's father Prescott, and he rarely stopped through. Anytime he did stop over, he remained in the vehicle, and Miranda could be seen bringing their daughter to the car. She always seemed so friendly with Prescott, even though they were no longer together. They would even stand outside his car discussing whatever they were discussing and laughing. This was amazing to Nikki, because every time she and Mac would break up, she would be so angry with him that she would forbid him from coming to her house and seeing their children. Eventually, she'd give in, and he'd start spending the night with her until they were unofficially together once again.

Nikki also had a tough time being faithful to Mac because she knew Mac wasn't a faithful man, and she was searching for a man she could settle down with. To her, Mac was a decent man, but she felt that she deserved better. In her search for a life partner, she dated both single and married men. But she always ended back up in Mac's arms because every other man would stick around for a short time and then find some reason to end their relationship. Nevertheless, as pompous, irresponsible and unambitious as Mac was, he stuck around. At this time; however, they were off again because Mac had found out that Nikki was seeing an older married man when his wife called Nikki's phone to confront her. This was their norm, however. They were always catching one another in lies and affairs, and they'd split up because of these behaviors, but they'd always get back together.

Miranda was a very talented girl. Even though she wasn't a professional hairstylist, she styled her and Tamyria's hair to perfection every day. She also was skilled at making clothes, jewelry and other accessories. Every day, she would leave her house looking great, and Nikki took notice. If Miranda wasn't going to church, she was going to the gym or going to help out with one of the church's drives. Miranda seemed as if she was content with her life just the way it was, and this was really fascinating to Nikki. What made Miranda tick?

One day, Nikki went outside to take out the trash, when she noticed Miranda's door opening. Out came cute little Tamyria first, with her mother's hand on her shoulder. They were obviously going to Wednesday night service at their local church, because little Tamyria was wearing a beautiful blue dress and carrying a little Bible. They didn't seem rushed, so Nikki decided to stop Miranda to ask her a few questions. "Hello. Excuse me. I don't mean to bother you, but who does your hair and who does your little girl's hair?" Nikki asked Miranda. Miranda looked up at Nikki as she opened her car's door. She recognized Nikki from seeing her around, but more than anything, she felt uncomfortable with Nikki. She'd noticed that every time Nikki saw her, she would stare at her, and this made Miranda uncomfortable. Nevertheless, after Tamyria loaded into the back seat and began to lock herself into her booster seat, Miranda began to speak.

Miranda: I do. I do mine and my daughter's hair.
Nikki: Oh wow. You do a really good job. How much do you charge to style hair for adults and for children?
Miranda: I don't do it professionally. I just style mine and my daughter's hair, and maybe my mother's hair from time to time, but that's it.
Nikki: Aw, man. I need a good hairstylist, especially for my oldest daughter's hair. It's too thick, and it's hard to manage for me.
Miranda: You can go up on Eighth Street. There is a salon called Decipher there, and they are really good with natural hair. As a matter of fact, my youngest sister works there, and she's one of the best out there. She's even better than I am. Just look the number up. The place is called Decipher.
Nikki: Okay. Decipher. I'll remember that. Where are you two ladies heading?

Miranda: We are going to church.

Nikki: Oh okay. Well, I'm throwing a party next Saturday, and you are more than welcome to come. I have two daughters that are about the same age as your daughter, so she'd have fun as well.

Miranda: Thanks. I don't really go to parties, but thanks for the invite.

Nikki: Why don't you go to parties?

Miranda: It's pretty complicated, but I'll speak with you on another day. Right now, I need to get on this highway before rush hour traffic lights up. It was nice talking with you.

Nikki: Oh, okay. I'm sorry. I didn't mean to hold you up.

Miranda: No, it's okay. It was nice meeting you. Talk with you soon.

After she left, Miranda felt a little bad. Had she been rude to someone who was simply trying to make small talk? Sure, Nikki made her feel strange by staring at her all the time, but maybe that was just how she was. Maybe she didn't mean anything by it. Miranda decided to go ahead and take her up on her invitation. She would come to Nikki's party and stay for about ten to thirty minutes before leaving just to be neighborly. She didn't want her neighbors to feel that she was too stand-offish.

Saturday finally arrived, and Miranda was preparing to go to the party, when Prescott stopped by to drop off some new shoes for Tamyria. Miranda knew that he was coming by, but she thought he was coming by later that evening since he ordinarily worked on Saturdays. Just as she was removing the pies from the oven that she'd made for the party, Prescott called her cell phone and told her he was outside. Miranda and Prescott had a mutual understanding that he was never to enter her home unless she had company and she invited him in. They were both Christian and did not want to fall into temptation.

When Miranda went outside to get the shoes from Prescott, their daughter ran ahead of her to hug her father. She was always happy to see him stop by but always hurt to see him leaving. Prescott stepped out of the car and picked up his overly excited daughter. After kissing her and showing her the shoes he'd purchased for her, he looked ahead to see Miranda heading towards him. She was always so beautiful to him, and he often wondered how he'd messed up such a great relationship. He also noticed that Miranda was dressed as if she was going somewhere, and so was Tamyria.

Prescott: You look especially lovely today. Do you have a date or something?

Tamyria: No, Daddy. *Whispers:* Remember, I told you I won't let Mommy date anyone but you. I'll cry and scream and make the guy go home. Remember?

Prescott: Good girl.

Miranda: I heard that. If and when I decide to date, you won't be able to stop me, Tamyria. Neither you or your plotting dad.

Prescott: *Laughs.* What are you doing today?

Miranda: *Sighs.* Well, one of the neighbors asked me over to a barbeque slash party. At first, I said no, but later on, I felt bad about it, so I went back and told her I would come. I wish I hadn't done that now.

Prescott: I told you. Always been too nice for your own good. It is better to be friendly and neighborly, but don't get too involved with your neighbors unless you do a background check on them first.

Miranda: Yes sir, Mr. Investigative Reporter. I should have done a background check on you first. *Laughs.*

Prescott: Nope. I'm glad you didn't. If you did, we wouldn't have this beautiful little one. Isn't that right, daddy's little Snookums?

Tamyria: That's right, Daddy.

Prescott: Well, if you don't want to go, just cancel. You don't owe them anything.

Tamyria: No, Daddy. I want to go. Please don't give Mommy any ideas. You know how she is.

Miranda: *Laughs.* I would cancel, but Tamyria really wants to go since the girl has two daughters who are around her age. But when I looked over there earlier, I saw a bunch of guys pulling up, so I'm really not too happy about going now. I figured I'd go in, make an appearance and leave in thirty minutes. I wish I hadn't agreed to this mess. *Sighs.*

Tamyria: I have an idea. Daddy, why don't you come with us so Mommy can feel comfortable?

Prescott: I don't know, baby. It's up to your mother. Do you want me to come with you, Miranda?

Miranda: I don't want to impose on you.
Prescott: No, it's not an imposition. Anything for you.

Miranda looked at Prescott and saw that all-too-familiar sparkle in his eyes. "Okay then," she said. "But behave yourself, Prescott." At that, Tamyria began to clap and rejoice. Miranda told Prescott that she'd be ready in five to ten minutes. He could stand outside with Tamyria and wait on her. She took Tamyria's new shoes in the house while Prescott and Tamyria ran around the yard playing with one another.

Nikki looked out her window. She wanted to see if Miranda was still coming. She saw Prescott in the yard playing with Tamyria. He was such a handsome man. He was tall, handsome and professional looking. His hair was cut low and always trimmed up perfectly. He was well-built with sandy-brown skin and the most kissable looking lips Nikki had ever seen. Normally, he dressed in professional attire, but today, he was casually handsome, wearing a sleeveless shirt that revealed his muscular arms. His blue jeans revealed that he was bow-legged. He looked like candy to Nikki. Miranda was a lucky woman, she thought.

After a few minutes, Miranda emerged from the house with her pies. She handed one to Prescott to carry, and they headed over towards Nikki's house. Nikki was still peering out of her window when they began to head over. On one hand, she was disappointed that Miranda was bringing

Prescott because she'd planned on introducing Miranda to her cousin, Rocky. On the other hand, she was happy to see Prescott coming because she wanted to see if he was as handsome up close as he was from a distance. She then rushed to open the front door as the couple neared her house with Tamyria in tote.

Once they'd entered Nikki's house, Miranda knew she'd made a huge mistake. Even though most of the guests were in the backyard sitting on lawn chairs, the guests who were in the house appeared to be a little rough around the edges. The music was loud and profane, and Miranda couldn't take it. She tried to speak to Nikki, but Nikki didn't hear her initially, so she turned the music down.

Miranda: Thank you for the invite, but we are about to go.
Nikki: Why? You just got here.
Miranda: Yes, but I don't listen to this type of music, and I don't allow my daughter to listen to this type of music.
Nikki: Oh. I'm sorry. I was planning on turning that foolishness off before you came over. That's one of my brother's CDs. I'll change it to something more kid-friendly. Just relax and enjoy yourself.
Miranda: Okay, thanks. We won't be staying long because I have a lot to do today, but I made you some pecan pies.
Nikki: Oh! My favorite! Thank you! And they look so good. Did you make these?
Miranda: Yes.
Nikki: Oh, girl, we are going to be best friends. I have to get

this recipe from you. And who is this guy with you?

Miranda: Oh. Sorry. Where are my manners? Prescott, this is Nikki. Nikki, this is Prescott.

Prescott: Nice to meet you.

Nikki: Nice to meet you as well. Well, come on you guys. Follow me.

Nikki took the pies out of Miranda's hands and led Miranda, Prescott and Tamyria to the backyard through the kitchen. Once in the backyard, dread came over Miranda again as she heard some of the conversations taking place. There was a lot of profanity being spoken, and a few of the girls were up dancing as if they were engaging in sexual activity. Knowing that her guests would be uncomfortable, Nikki yelled out, "Hey y'all! Stop all that cursing! This woman is a Christian woman, and she doesn't want her daughter exposed to that mess! Keisha and Rhonda, stop dancing like that! Y'all can twerk at home!" Miranda felt uncomfortable and out of place. She wasn't being judgmental; she was simply different, and this was not her type of crowd. Prescott kept nudging Miranda as they were led to their seats. He thought it was funny because Miranda was always getting herself into uncomfortable situations.

Tamyria asked her mother if she could go and play with the other children, and she agreed. There were a total of seven children ranging from the ages of three years old to eight years old playing tag. She ran over and stood still waiting for someone to invite her to play tag. Finally, Nikki yelled out to her, "Baby, just start running. You don't have to wait for them to invite you to play. Just start running." That's exactly what Tamyria did. She began to run from the girl who was now labeled "it." One of the girls managed to catch Tamyria, and she tagged her as "it." Tamyria laughed as she chased the other children around, finally catching up to Nikki's daughter, three-year-old Madison. She tagged Madison, but to her surprise, older sister Mackenzie came out of nowhere and pushed her down. After Tamyria had fallen, Mackenzie ran over and kicked her before saying, "You don't touch my sister!" Nikki jumped from her seat and began to yell at Mackenzie. She snatched her by her arm and asked her why she'd pushed Tamyria down. At that, Mackenzie responded, "Because I don't know her, and look at her! She thinks she's better than us! I don't like her." After scolding her daughter, Nikki returned to her seat and apologized to Miranda and Prescott, who were more than understanding. "They're just kids," said Miranda. "Kids play hard."

After the party had died down, most of the people had gone home or went inside the house. Miranda and Prescott had stayed longer than they anticipated because Nikki had spent so much time asking them for help around the party and talking with them. Now that the party had died down, Nikki decided to speak with the couple. She was so very curious about the two. By this time, Mac was there, and he was sitting on a lawn chair next to Nikki.

Nikki: Miranda, I see you a lot of times, and you're always

382

going and coming. What do you do for a living?

Miranda: Well, right now, I work as a substitute teacher over at Roman's Middle School, but I'm also in school getting my Master's Degree in Speech Therapy. This is actually my last year.

Nikki: Oh wow. That's impressive. Yeah, I'm in my second year of college as well.

Miranda: Really? What are you going to school for?

Nikki: Business Administration is what I'm going for now. But I have thought about going into Speech Therapy as well. That sounds like an exciting career.

Miranda: Yeah, it is. I love helping children, and that's what I want to do. So, what about you? What's your name again...Preston?

Prescott: No, my name is Prescott. I'm an Investigative Reporter. I also have my own P.I. Firm where I work as a Private Investigator.

Mac: Aw, man. I knew I shouldn't have come to this party.

Prescott: Why? No, you're cool. With a Private Investigator, we only work when we are hired to do work. We aren't police officers. We don't just go out and arrest people when we see them committing crimes.

Mac: Yeah, you look like one of those Uncle Tom types. I bet you got more money than you can count.

Prescott: I'm not an Uncle Tom. I'm just a regular guy trying to make a living. I'm also a Pastor, so hopefully that mellows it out for you.

Nikki: Mac, shut up! You always have something stupid to say. I'm sorry, y'all. Mac killed all his brain cells three hundred and sixty five joints ago. Right now, he's just the walking dead.

Prescott: *Laughs.* No, it's okay.

Nikki: So, what's up with you and Miranda? I see you coming by her house sometimes, but I never see you going in. I'm not even sure how to read that. I've already figured out that you're Tamyria's father, but I'm confused about the rest.

Mac: I can tell you what happened. She got pregnant and tried to trap him. That's what happened.

Miranda scoffed at Mac and crossed her arms.

Prescott: No. Actually, Miranda and I used to be married to one another. We were young when we got married, and three years later, we got pregnant with Tamyria. We were truly in love when we got married, but things just didn't work out. After the divorce, we were both upset with one another for a few months, but one day, we sat down and talked about it. We decided that for Tamyria's sake, we had to be friends, and not just friends, but best friends. We decided to respect one another and be mature adults for the sake of our daughter. Plus, we are both Christian, so we knew we had to do the right thing.

Mac: If y'all supposed to be Christian, why did y'all get a divorce?

Prescott: We weren't mature Christians then.

Miranda: When I was pregnant, I learned that I was pregnant with triplets. The doctor put me on bed rest because my pregnancy was deemed a high risk pregnancy. Prescott was busy building his career path, and I ended up going into early labor. Two of the triplets were stillborn; only Tamyria survived. I was upset about it, and I blamed Prescott because he was never there. After that, things went downhill.

Nikki: Oh, I'm so sorry to hear that.

Miranda: It's okay. But like he said, we didn't know how to handle all of our emotions at that time, and we ended up divorcing.

Mac: Yeah, that's just like a woman. Blame it on the man! She probably nagged that man to death. That's why he wasn't there.

Prescott: Look, I don't know you, but one thing I won't tolerate is you disrespecting the mother of my child. I respect her, if for no other reason than she is the mother of my child.

Mac: I'm sorry, dude. You got too many muscles for me to be arguing with you. I didn't bring my pistol, so I'll let this one go.

Nikki: Mac, take your stupid, drunk butt home! Always ruining somebody's party! Get! Go home, now!

Mac: I'll leave, but don't call me in the middle of the night talking about you need somebody to cuddle with, cause I ain't coming!

Nikki: Boy, bye!

Not long after Mac left, Miranda and Prescott decided to leave. Nikki's daughters still hadn't warmed up to Tamyria, who was now sitting on her daddy's lap falling asleep. As they headed back towards Miranda's apartment, Miranda thanked Prescott for standing up for her. "You've always been really good to me, and I appreciate the friendship we have, even after everything," said Miranda. "I totally respect you, and I'm glad to be the mother of your one and only child...I hope! You're a really good father." Prescott's heart became warm. Miranda's attempt to add a little humor to the situation hadn't diluted her words. She appreciated him. She respected him, and more than anything, he hoped that she still loved him just like he loved her. "Thank you," said Prescott. "You're a really good mother and a friend, and I'm sorry for not being there for you when you needed me the most. I have never regretted marrying you or having Tamyria with you. You have and will always have a special place in my heart." With that, Miranda hugged Prescott before retreating into her house.

That night, Miranda's thoughts were of Prescott. She'd never really put much thought into the possibility of the two of them getting back together. She'd always seen divorce as final; nevertheless, she'd never dated anyone since their break up. Prescott, on the other hand, had two serious relationships after their divorce, but neither of those relationships worked out. He'd actually proposed to the last one, but broke it off with her after dreaming that when he lifted up her veil at their wedding, she was nothing more than a dark face. She had no features, and she was holding a crystal ball with men inside of it, all screaming in horror. In the dream, Prescott ran away from the altar, and the woman pursued him chanting strange words. Prescott had taken that dream to mean that she was a witch, just as his mother warned him that she was. Prescott's mother always wanted him to remarry Miranda. She was always comfortable with Miranda, and even after their divorce, Miranda continued to visit her and help her when she needed help.

A week later, Nikki stopped Miranda again and wanted to know if she could ride to church with Miranda sometimes. Miranda agreed, and that night, Miranda, Nikki and their children rode together to church in Miranda's car. During the drive there, Nikki and Miranda began to speak.

Nikki: Guess what? The new school term is coming up, and I have decided to major in Speech Therapy. I always wanted to do Speech Therapy, but hearing you talk about it sparked my interest again.

Miranda: That's great, but won't you have to start all over again?

Nikki: Yeah, but I get to keep some of my credits. But it's better if I do what I really want to do than for me to continue going for Business Administration.

Miranda: Yeah, that's right.

Nikki: So, after your graduation, what do you plan to do?

Miranda: I'm still undecided, but I am leaning more towards going back to school to get my PhD in Speech Therapy. I want to open my own practice eventually.

Nikki: Yeah, that sounds great. It's good to see another ambitious black woman. I'm proud of you.

Miranda: Thank you. What about you?

Nikki: I'm not sure yet, to tell you the truth. I'll probably look into starting my own clinic as well. That's always been a dream of mine.

Miranda: That's awesome.

Nikki: Yeah, and I want to get more into church. I want a church boy because they know how to treat a woman from what I hear.

Miranda: Well, not all of them. Devils come to church too. No matter what, you have to ask the LORD to send you your own GOD-ordained husband; otherwise, any man that you meet will be devil-sent and hell-bound, but good to look at.

Nikki: Tell me about it. Mac used to go to church when he was a little boy, but look at him now. I could never see myself marrying him because his only ambition is to be a rapper, which I can tell you ain't gonna happen. I've heard him rap.

Miranda: *Laughs.* Yeah, Mac is a character.

Nikki: What about you and Prescott? Do you think the two of you might get back together?

Miranda: I have no complaints about Prescott. He's a good guy. As far as us getting back together, I don't put much thought into that. If GOD says yes, then we'll get back together. If not, then no.

Nikki: See, that's what I want...that kind of faith in GOD.

Miranda: Yeah, you should just pray for what you want. GOD said you have not because you ask not. That means that anything you don't have, you don't have because you haven't asked for it.

Nikki: Wow, that's deep. Yeah, I'm gonna be praying for a whole lot of stuff tonight then!

Miranda: Yeah, but be careful what you ask for. In order to receive some things, we have to lose some things, and that's not always easy.

Nikki: I don't mind losing. I've been losing all my life, so bring it on. I'm ready to get my blessings too. I need a church home. I think I'm going to join your church when we get there.

Miranda: Yeah, it's a good church, but don't just join the first time you come there. Pray on it first to make sure that this church is GOD'S will for you.

Nikki: Yeah, I will.

Church was good as usual, but Miranda was surprised when Nikki went to the front of the church at the end of service. She wanted to join the church without knowing anything about it.

After church, during the drive home, Nikki continued her line of questioning. Miranda knew that Nikki admired her and was fascinated with her life. At the same time, she knew that it would be dangerous to bring Nikki close to her because she understood the root of Nikki's curiosity. After all, Miranda was a mature Christian, and she did not want to invite problems into her life, or into her daughter's life.

Nikki: Church was really good. I like your Pastor. Prescott said he was a Pastor. Why don't you go to his church? I thought that's whose church we'd be going to.

Miranda: I've been to Prescott's church a few times, but it just felt weird having my ex-husband as my Pastor. I'm still in the same fellowship, just a different church.

Nikki: Where's his church located?

Miranda: Over on Bell Avenue, right behind that Asian market.

Nikki: That's actually closer to the house than your church. I think I might check that one out as well. Wait. You don't mind, do you? I don't want you to think I'm trying to hit on Prescott.

Miranda: Why would I mind? No. You're fine.

At that moment, Miranda realized that Nikki had a thing for Prescott, but she wasn't bothered by it. After all, Nikki was not Prescott's type. At the same time, Prescott was a handsome, successful man of GOD. Who wouldn't be attracted to him?

Nikki made good on her word, and that following Sunday, she went to Prescott's church. She watched as Pastor Prescott ministered the WORD of GOD with confidence and authority. He was so very handsome to her. He was hands-down one of the most handsome men she'd ever laid eyes on. When the "doors of the church are now open" announcement was made, Nikki was one of the first to raise up out of her seat. She jogged down the aisle, hoping to be the first one to get to Prescott. When Prescott recognized her, his spirit was troubled. He knew she was up to no good; nevertheless, he hoped that the WORD being fed there would change her life.

For three weeks, Nikki attended Prescott's church faithfully every Wednesday night and Sunday morning. But she wasn't going to church for the WORD; she was going for Prescott. There was only one problem. She knew that Prescott still loved Miranda, and Miranda still loved Prescott.

One day, she happened to see Prescott out at a supermarket. He was dressed in the same sleeveless top he'd worn to her party, and he was looking better than good. Prescott smiled and greeted her as he knocked on a watermelon to see if it was good. This was her chance. Nikki made her way over to Prescott.

Nikki: You know, you can always tell if a watermelon is good just by shaking it.

Prescott: Really? Thanks for the tip, sister Nikki. I'll keep that in mind.

Nikki: It's actually ironic that I ran into you because I wanted to talk with you.

Prescott: Sure. About what?

Nikki: Is Miranda pregnant again?

Prescott: I doubt it, but why do you ask?

Nikki: Well, I rode to church with Miranda one time, and she was telling me about some boy she had been seeing. I noticed that he comes over to her house sometimes, and he doesn't leave until the wee hours of the morning. Now, she looks like she's pregnant to me. You know us women can tell those things pretty early.

Prescott: Is that right?

Nikki: Yeah. The guy comes by there most times around nine o'clock at night. He's a light-skinned guy with dreadlocks and a red mustang convertible. I've seen him holding Tamyria a few times too. Come to think of it, Tamyria looks just like him.

Prescott: Well, she should look like him.

Nikki: Why is that?

Prescott: His name is Raphael, and he is Miranda's brother.

Nikki: Oh, I guess that's not the guy she's seeing then.

Prescott: Nikki, your forked tongue is going to get you into a place that you don't want to go. Let me share something with you. Miranda and I may not be together, but I know that woman more than anyone knows her. Only GOD knows her better than me. There is nothing you or anyone else can tell me about her. Now, I'm a man of GOD, and I don't entertain gossip, nor will I tolerate the defamation of the mother of my child's good name. If you ever find yourself needing to speak with me, make sure it's about ministry...nothing else. Is that understood?

Nikki: I wasn't trying to be messy. I was just concerned.

Prescott: Have a good day, Nikki. I have some shopping to do.

Prescott walked away, and Nikki stood there frozen in her steps. She felt fear, humiliation and desperation all at the same time. What was she going to do now? It was obvious that she had no chance with Prescott, and she knew that

Prescott would likely tell Miranda of the incident. She rushed home and went to knock on Miranda's door. When Miranda came outside, she was stunned to see the desperation on Nikki's face.

Miranda: Hey Nikki. What's going on?

Nikki: I don't know how to tell you this, but I just ran into Prescott at the supermarket, and he tried to hit on me. I told him that you were my friend, and I could not get with him because you and I are friends. Anyhow, he started cursing me out and even talking bad about you. I'm not going to lie; I ended up cursing him out because I don't play about my friends. I didn't like the stuff he was saying about you, so I let him have it.

Miranda: Nikki, you knocked on the wrong door with that foolishness. There are many things you can tell me in this life, but one thing you cannot do is lie on Prescott to me. I know that man all too well. He didn't curse you out, nor did you curse him out. I knew I shouldn't have gotten even slightly involved with you. I knew something like this would happen.

Nikki: I'm telling you the truth! I have plenty of witnesses at the store that can tell you what happened!

Miranda: Really? Did you get their phone numbers?

Nikki: No, but I'm sure they are still there. We can go there if you want.

Miranda: No thank you, Nikki. Please do not step on my property again with lies and gossip, and never try to defame the name of my daughter's father. He has been nothing but nice to you, and this is just wrong.

Nikki was surprised. Miranda was using some of the same terms that Prescott had used. Their bond was obviously too strong for her to sever; nevertheless, Nikki began to walk back towards her house, swearing at Miranda as she walked away. She thought to herself that maybe Prescott had called and given Miranda a heads-up, but that wasn't true. Nikki was now in her yard screaming obscenities at Miranda and promising to "beat Miranda down" the first chance she got. Miranda went back into her house and closed her door. She was upset with herself for going against her first mind with Nikki. She should have kept her distance, and now she had to see Nikki every day, and her daughter went to the same school as Nikki's daughters. Miranda's lease was almost up for the house she was living in, and she was contemplating resigning it but was having some second thoughts before the incident occurred. She'd prayed on it, and this was obviously the answer to her prayers. Her lease would be up in less than a month, and Miranda decided not to renew it. Still reeling from the incident, Miranda decided to call Prescott.

Miranda: Hey, you got a minute?
Prescott: Yes, of course. Is everything okay?
Miranda: Um, no. Do you remember that girl Nikki whose party we went to?
Prescott: Yeah, I saw her in the store about an hour ago and she...well, let's just say she tried to lie on you.

394

Miranda: I was sure of it. She just came by my house trying to lie on you, and I told her to get off my property with her lies.

Prescott: What happened next?

Miranda: She started swearing at me and threatening me.

Prescott: Have you called the police?

Miranda: No. I'm hoping she'll just drop the matter and move on with her life, but somehow...

Prescott: Somehow, you know better.

Miranda: Yeah. I sensed that she had a crush on you, even at the barbeque. I was sure of it when she said that she thought I was a member of your church, and when she found out where your church was, she told me she was going to go there.

Prescott: Yeah, it's sad. Miranda, you're dealing with a woman who fully envies you.

Miranda: Yeah, I know. What do I do?

Prescott: Just try to stay out of her way. When is your lease up again? You may need to move. That neighborhood seems like it's starting to head in the wrong direction.

Miranda: Yeah, I'm thinking the same thing.

Just as they were talking, Miranda heard the noise of shattering glass. She screamed and the noise woke up Tamyria who started screaming and crying. Nikki had just broken Miranda's window in her bedroom.

Prescott: Miranda! Are you okay? What happened?

Miranda: I think that girl just broke my window or shot

through my window; I'm not sure. I'll call you back. I gotta call the police.

Prescott: I'm on my way! Call 911 now!

After they hung up the line, Miranda called the police and they were on the scene in less than five minutes. Prescott pulled up a few minutes after the police arrived and ran into the house to check on Miranda and his daughter. He found Miranda sitting on the couch, crying and talking to one of the officers. After introducing himself, he sat down next to Miranda and put his arms around her as she told the officer what had happened. Tamyria ran over and jumped into her father's lap. She laid her head on him and began to doze off again. While Miranda was talking, Prescott noticed that she still had the photo of the two of them sitting on her table. The photo was of a pregnant Miranda and a more slender Prescott, before he'd built up so many muscles. After Miranda finished telling the officer her version of the story, another officer came in and said he'd spoke with Nikki, and she claimed that she had not been responsible for throwing a rock through Miranda's window.

Miranda: What does that mean? I know she did it!
Officer Petri: I believe you ma'am. I really do, but right now, it's just your word against hers. We don't have any eyewitness accounts, so we can't arrest her just yet until we have enough evidence to prove that she actually broke your window.
Miranda: How can you guys protect me if you won't arrest

the woman who threw a rock through my window?!

Officer Petri: I'm sorry ma'am. I wish we could do more, but that's the law. Until we get more evidence, it's just your word against hers. Do you stay here alone?

Miranda: Yeah, for the most part, but my brother comes here sometimes whenever he works the graveyard shift. He's not working tonight, and I can't reach him.

Officer Petri: You don't have anyone else who can stay here with you, or maybe somewhere you can go just to be on the safe side?

Miranda: No, I...

Prescott: It's okay, officer. I'll stay here with her tonight.

Miranda: But Prescott, you know...

Prescott: Don't worry. I'll sleep on the couch. I just need to make sure you and Tamyria are okay.

Miranda: Okay. Thank you.

After the officers left, Miranda sat on the sofa and covered her face. She was so tired, but thankfully, the following day was a Saturday, and she was off work. She didn't have any classes to attend either on the next day. Prescott went and sat on the chair right across from Miranda.

Prescott: *Laughs.* Long day, wasn't it?

Miranda: Tell me about it.

Prescott: You always knew how to pick your friends.

Miranda: The funny thing is, I knew that girl envied me. I used to come outside, and I'd see her staring at me, and at first, I thought something was wrong with her mentally. But after meeting her, I realized she had a bad case of envy.

Prescott: Envy-itus.

Miranda: Yeah. Well, it's a real condition, and I surely hate a neighbor of mine had to get infected with it. I like to live in peace...no drama.

Prescott: Yeah, I remember. If I argued at you, you'd get a headache and go and shut yourself up in one of the rooms in our old house.

Miranda: *Laughs.* Yeah, you used to fuss like a woman, though. I have to tell you the truth.

Prescott: What? *Laughs.* No, I wasn't that bad.

Miranda: Oh yes you were.

Prescott: *Laughs.* Jokes aside; can I be honest with you about something?

Miranda: Yes, of course. You know you can tell me anything.

Prescott: Miranda, when we divorced, my whole world changed. For a while, I managed to convince myself that the divorce was your fault; you were being unreasonable, but it finally hit me one day. I wasn't there for you. I was too busy trying to build a career for myself that I tore down our marriage, and for that, I'm sorry.

Miranda: It's okay, Prescott. I've already forgiven you, and I wasn't innocent in it either. I was just so caught up in a whirlwind of emotions I'd never experienced before that I started tearing down my marriage with my own hands. For that, I'm sorry.

Prescott: When I heard that loud sound and you and Tamyria screaming, I felt like I was less than a man. Here I was blocks away from my real family. I was not there to protect either one of you, and had something happened to you, I would have never forgiven myself.

Miranda: What are you saying, Prescott? Because I am so confused right now.

Prescott: I'm saying that I know you are my wife. Miranda, there is no other woman for me out there. I've prayed and prayed for a wife, but I always find myself right back at your doorsteps. I hope this doesn't offend you, but I still love you. *Prescott started to cry as he spoke to Miranda.*

Prescott: I go to bed thinking about you; I wake up thinking about you. I keep my apartment organized the way I think you would organize it. When I get dressed to go anywhere, I imagine that you are reviewing my clothes for me. I can hear your little voice now saying, "That shirt doesn't go with those pants. You're not leaving this house like that; you're making me look bad."

Miranda laughed as tears streamed down her face.

Prescott: Miranda, you are my crown. It doesn't matter what relationship I try to call myself having, no woman can ever be what you are to me. You are my wife, and there is no replacement for you out there. You and Tamyria are the reasons that I smile so hard every day. Even though we are divorced, I work hard so I can make you smile. I want to give you the life that you deserve. When we went to that party together, everything felt so right. It felt natural to be with you. I have never been that comfortable with any other woman; just you. Please say something.

Miranda was quiet for a minute. She cried and covered her mouth as she absorbed the words Prescott had spoken to her. She looked over at Tamyria, who was now stretched out on the couch asleep.

Miranda: Prescott, I will always love you, and you know this. But I don't think it's a good idea.
Prescott: Why not?
Miranda: What we have right now is so good, I wouldn't want to mess it up.
Prescott: Do you love me?
Miranda: Yes, I love you. I told you that.
Prescott: Do you believe GOD?
Miranda: Yes, of course.
Prescott: Then, let us both step out on faith together. Let's not allow fear to keep us apart. It doesn't matter what you say, I love you, and I'm going to pursue you with all my might. I want you in my arms again, Miranda. I wish I could hold you right now. I love you, baby, and I'm not going to give up on us again...ever.
Miranda: I want to come over there so bad and just hug you, but I know that's not a good idea.
Both Miranda and Prescott laughed at the thought. They knew the flesh would get the better of them, and they wanted to do everything the right way.
Miranda: I still love you too, Prescott. I think you know that. I used to tell myself that my husband was out there

somewhere, and one day I'd meet him. But the thought never excited me because the guy I was forcing myself to imagine wasn't you. The thought actually scared me, to tell you the truth. One day, I told myself that if I couldn't have you, I'd just die an old maid. But I'm not going to lie to you: I'm scared, Prescott. I'm really scared.

Prescott: What are you afraid of, baby?

Miranda: I've always loved the fact that we maintained a good relationship after our divorce. What if it doesn't work now? I don't want to bear that kind of pain anymore, and I don't want to hurt Tamyria. She's old enough to feel the effects of a divorce now, and I don't want to take her through that.

Prescott: Miranda, we just have to trust in GOD and stay in HIS will. Back then, we were both immature, and we weren't as grounded in our faith as we are now. We will never divorce again, and I'm sorry for taking you through that. It will work, baby. You will see.

Miranda: You know what's funny? One day, I saw a woman with a beautiful little boy. He kinda looked like you to me...like he could be your son. I realized at that moment that I wanted a son, but I didn't want to have children with any other man. Prescott, I love you with all of me, but I don't know what to do about it. What do we do about it? Do we start dating again, and how long should we date before we are sure that we can really make it work this time?

Prescott: No ma'am. I am a man of GOD; you are a woman of GOD. You know I don't believe in dating. I know that GOD has given you to me as a wife, so we don't have to do as the world does. We just need to make it official once again.

Miranda: What?

Prescott dropped to one knee and pushed the coffee table away from Miranda.

Prescott: Miranda? I spent four years without you, dreaming of no one else but you. I spent four years of my life waking up without you. I don't want to spend another moment away from you. I love you. Will you marry me again?

Miranda laughed.

Miranda: Did you have to say "again"? Yes, baby. I will marry you, and it'll be like this was our first time marrying, because this time, we will do it with CHRIST, in CHRIST. Yes, I'll marry you.

Prescott: When?

Miranda's face turned to shock.

Miranda: What do you mean when you say when? When do you want to get married?

Prescott: I would take you over to the courthouse on Monday morning, but I know we need to do this the right way. Tomorrow is what? Saturday? Let's do it next Saturday? In eight days.

Miranda: Prescott! Are you serious?

Prescott: Yes, it'll be perfect. This way, I can talk with my Bishop and we can make the arrangements. Baby, we don't need some big extravagant wedding. We have JESUS, and HE is all we need.

Miranda: I'm nervous, but okay. Yes! We can do it next

Saturday.

Prescott realized that he'd better get back in the chair and put the coffee table between them. Surprised at his sudden move, Miranda questioned him. "What was that for?" she asked. "You already know," said Prescott. "We are children of GOD, so we don't need to tempt one another just yet." Miranda laughed and Prescott looked at the beauty of her smile. She was such a beautiful woman, and he was excited about the idea of marrying her once again.

The next day, Prescott and Miranda went ring shopping. Tamyria was confused at first when she saw her mother and father trying on rings. "Will I get it a ring too?" asked Tamyria. Prescott and Miranda laughed and told her they would buy her a ring as well. After they'd chosen a ring, they went to Wal-Mart to purchase an inexpensive ring for Tamyria. They got her a ten karat gold little girl's ring that only cost them $39.99. They didn't want to buy anything expensive for her because she was only four years old and would likely lose the ring. They paid to have the ring resized since it was too big for her finger, and they explained to Tamyria that she would get her ring on the same day that they wore theirs.

Later that evening, they all went out to eat together, and they decided to tell Tamyria what their plans were.

Prescott: Daddy and Mommy have some good news for you.

Tamyria: What news do you have? Are you getting me a kitty cat?

Prescott: No. Even better. How do you feel about Mommy marrying Daddy again?

Tamyria smiled and shrugged her shoulders as she shoved the pizza into her mouth.

Tamyria: I don't know. Happy.

Prescott: Well, your mother and I have decided that we are going to get married again next week.

Tamyria smiled again.

Tamyria: Good. Because you know I wasn't going to let Mommy marry anyone else.

Miranda: Excuse me?

Prescott: That's my baby.

Miranda: Oh, but you would have let your daddy marry someone else?

Tamyria: Yes, Mommy.

Miranda: That's not fair.

Tamyria: *Whispers:* Mommy, you know Daddy can't keep a woman. Remember when he wanted to marry that funny-looking woman?

Prescott: What? I heard that. You're not good at whispering, you know. She was funny-looking to you, and you didn't tell me?

At that, Tamyria looked at her dad with a serious face and said, "I didn't have to tell you, Daddy. You dreamed about her and you saw how funny-looking her face was, so you ran away. Remember?"

Suddenly, the table erupted in laughter.

Later that day, Prescott and Miranda went by Prescott's mother's house to tell her the great news. When they arrived, she was sitting outside on the porch in her favorite spot: her rocking chair. Miranda and Prescott exited the vehicle, and Prescott removed Tamyria from her booster seat. Prescott then held Tamyria's left hand while Miranda held her right hand. The scene was so powerful to Prescott's mother that she began to rock harder, and her smile got bigger and bigger. "I knew it! I knew it!" she said. "Finally, GOD has answered my prayers! The two of you are back together again like it was supposed to be!" Prescott looked at Miranda, and Miranda shrugged her shoulders at him while grinning. Tamyria took off running towards her grandmother, and she couldn't wait to share the news. Tamyria said, "Yep, Grandma. They want to get married again, and they asked me for my permission. I don't know why they asked me though. I'm just a kid. Daddy went and bought me and Mommy a ring, and Mommy was crying and smiling at the same time. It confused me, Grandma. Tell them not to be confusing me." While she was talking, Mrs. Prentiss started covering her mouth and crying. She was so very happy. "Grandma? Now, you're doing the same thing Mommy did. I'm confused. Why would you cry and smile at the same time? Which one are you: happy or sad?" Everyone laughed at the inquisitive four-year-old. "Grandma's happy...real happy, baby! And sometimes when people get too happy, they cry."

They went into the house to tell Prescott's father as well. He was bed-ridden and couldn't speak, but the smile on his face let Prescott know that he'd made the right decision. He nodded his head and held his son's hand. He then reached out for Miranda, and when she came, he pulled her close to him and kissed her on her cheek. A single tear ran along the side of his face, and his wife came and wiped it away. She leaned in and hugged her husband, who reciprocated the hug. They were both so very happy.

A week later, the two were married in a small ceremony at the church. Not many people were surprised that the Pastor had remarried Miranda. She was a beautiful woman of GOD who carried herself with such dignity and respect.

After the wedding, Miranda and Tamyria moved into Prescott's apartment with him, and they eventually moved into a larger home. Once the lease was up in her old house, Miranda did not re-sign the lease.

As for Nikki, she went on a campaign trying to destroy the Pastor's good name, but it didn't work because the people who knew him knew that this was not his character. Once Nikki saw that Miranda's house was available for leasing, she broke the lease on her house to move into Miranda's old place. She wanted so bad to be like Miranda. She eventually met a deacon who didn't like Pastor Prescott, and the two of them went on a smear campaign trying to destroy his name. They ended up getting married, and at first, things were looking up for the two of them. They continued to stay in Miranda's old house, and the deacon helped Nikki to get a car similar to Miranda's old car. Nikki tried to channel Miranda's walk, style, and even the way she talked. But one day, everything came crashing down. Nikki flunked out of college because she just wasn't cut out for Speech Therapy. Not long after that, Nikki found out that her husband had been arrested in an area known for prostitution. He'd gone over there trying to pay a male prostitute for sexual favors and didn't realize that the police department was running an undercover sting operation; one that ended up appearing on live television. Nikki ended up testing positive for Hepatitis B, and the couple was evicted from the house when they failed to maintain the monthly payments.

Prescott and Miranda went on to have three more children: two boys and one more girl. Their marriage was a happy one, and they raised their children up with fear and admonition of the LORD.
The End.

Some people would say that it's not nice to have the story end on such a bad note for Nikki and her new deacon husband. Why didn't it end with them getting saved and everything working out for them? Sometimes, the hard truth has to be told. Real life is nothing like Hollywood blockbusters where we leave the theater overjoyed because everyone made the right decisions. There are some people out there who are so anchored down by pride, and so deeply rooted into sin, that they never come to repentance. We wish that they would, but they do not.

What happened with Nikki was common. Sometimes women are fascinated with other women who are not like them, but that fascination can be unhealthy. When they aren't mature in the LORD, they end up walking in full-fledged envy and not even realizing it. Instead, they tell themselves that the object of their envy has done something against them and deserve the wrath they are throwing at them.

Nikki wanted Miranda's life, and she did whatever she could to get it. But understand this: You are anointed to be you, and you can't handle being someone else. It's not even safe to attempt to be someone else, because they are anointed to come out of the trials and tribulations that they endure, but you may not be able to come out of it because you weren't supposed to go through it. There is greatness in every child of GOD, but every woman has her own path designed just for her feet to rest on.

One thing I paid attention to in my own life was the way I felt around my friends. I used to pay so much attention to my friends and their behaviors that I totally overlooked my own feelings and behaviors. I noticed that most of the women who came around me ended up wanting to do some or every thing I was doing professionally, and this became bothersome to me. I didn't understand this because it didn't happen with my male friends. It only happened with the females. One day, a friend of mine was talking with me, and I found myself wanting to try out the field she was in. It seemed fun and fascinating, and it would be something else I could add to my portfolio. Just then, I caught myself. Why did I feel that way? Why was I suddenly thinking about entering a field I'd never considered entering? The LORD then began to deal with my heart, and HE explained to me that this happened because I am a female. Women are receptors, and we will carry and birth whatever gets into us. It wasn't envy, even though it was the very sin that triggers envy: covetousness. Here I was already in multiple fields; what did I need with hers? Absolutely nothing. I then began to understand why many of my female friends were like that. They are all female, of course, and anytime I fed them my information about my business, they ended up pregnant with that knowledge, and they wanted to birth it out. A woman must reach a certain level of maturity before she understands that she cannot wake up from someone else's dreams. At that very moment, I was just beginning to tap into that maturity because GOD had granted me permission to tap into that understanding.

Nikki went and tried to live Miranda's dreams, and she woke up in a living nightmare. She wasn't designed to be Miranda; she was designed to be Nikki. She didn't understand that the blessings weren't in Miranda's life just because she was Miranda; the blessings were the favor of GOD upon

Miranda's life. She thought that if she could be like Miranda, she could have the happiness and confidence she believed Miranda had.

I was conducting research for a business book I was writing, and I ended up finding some research on women in business ownership. I was more than amazed to find that the stats said women were more likely to enter a field just because their friends were in that field. Men are more focused and will stick with a business idea far longer than women. Women tend to try on several business ideas. Why is that? Because we are emotional and unstable sometimes. We are often moved by our emotions and our misunderstandings. A lot of the people who came in contact with me thought that success was in the fields I was in, so they abandoned their own fields to try to tap into my fields. But after a few frustrating tries, they decided that those fields weren't for them. Did this make them bad people? Not at all. They were just at stages in their lives where they needed some extra cash, and they thought those fields were goldmines. They didn't really understand that the blessing was and is upon my life. GOD allowed this to happen to teach them and me a lesson. The lesson is, we must trust in HIM and not our own understandings and devices.

Nowadays, when I come in contact with female business owners, every one of them has a story similar to mine. Every one of them would tell me these horror stories of other women who were pushing up on them, trying to be their friends. In most cases, they allowed these women into their lives and ended up having to pray them out. What I tell people nowadays is to simply be honest with their friends. Let them know what it is they are feeling, because the problem oftentimes is that the person simply does not understand those feelings they are experiencing. And one thing about our emotions is that whenever we feed our emotions with what it wants, we feel better; therefore, we think that we continue to feed them, rather than questioning the content of our hearts.

It's simple. You are you for a reason. Everything you do that lines up with who you are is plugged into your identity and will power you up for the next level. Trying to plug yourself into someone else's identity will only render you powerless.

At the same time, be really careful about women who try to push up on you. In most cases, they see something in you that they want, and this covetousness will eventually turn into envy or jealousy. Never give someone permission to be in your life or in your circle. Instead, if you plan to go far in the LORD, ask the LORD to only allow those around you whom HE would permit to be around you. If you go out there and get friends for yourself, they may stick around for a few years, but if GOD didn't call them into your life, they'll eventually have to leave. In many cases, they won't be so happy about being let go of, and some of them may respond violently.

This isn't just for successful people or people who are heading towards success. This message is for everyone. No matter where you are in this earth, there is someone who feels that they are behind you, and they'd love to get to know you so they can see what fuels you. There are women who want to know how other women got the men they have. There are women who want to know how another woman got the job she has. There are women out there who want to know what is so special about you that you can do or have certain things that they cannot do or have. And these women will push up on you because they want to solve this mystery in their lives. If allowed, they will eventually become an enemy to you because envy can never be anyone's friend.

When Nikki's daughter Mackenzie pushed Tamyria down, she was displaying the very same spirit that her mother was submitted to: envy. One thing about envy is that it often causes people to prejudge others as "thinking they are better than themselves" or "thinking they are pretty." We can never truly say what a person is thinking. Oftentimes, children openly show what their parents are secretly because children are not familiar with discretion. As we grow older, we learn to hide who we are and what's on the inside of us if it is not publicly accepted. If you meet a woman who appears to be nice and holy, but her young daughters are huge gossipers, chances are, the mother is a gossiper as well. Now, this doesn't always apply if the daughters are teenagers or young adults, because they may have picked up gossip through their associations. Nevertheless, young children often pick this behavior up at home, and young children do not exercise discretion.

Always remember that another woman's dream could turn out to be your nightmare. Stay in the will of GOD, for this is your protection.

Her Story- Earlean Johnson

"If the devil ain't mad at you, he must be proud of you."

We are born into this earth as innocent creatures. As newborn infants, we were like Adam and Eve; we knew no evil. We had to rely on our parents to protect and guide us. Our first glimpse of life is often taken while in one of our parents' arms. But what happens when our lives are turned upside-down while we are still innocent? What happens when the building blocks that we are taught to build with are dark and destructible?

Before we realize who we are in the LORD, the enemy recognizes our identities. He knew the season you were to be born. Around the time Moses was to be born, the King of Egypt issued an order to Shiprah and Puah (two midwives) that if any of the Hebrew women were to have sons, they were to kill them, but they were to leave the girls alive. Even though Pharaoh didn't know it, the enemy knew that a Prophet of the LORD (Moses) was about to be born, so he tried to murder him. And of course, we know that not long after CHRIST was born, King Herod issued a decree to have all male children under the age of two in and around Bethlehem killed.

There are many stories in the Bible where the enemy attacked or tried to attack a man or woman of GOD to stop them from fulfilling their purpose in the earth.

The story below is from a woman whom the enemy had a bone to pick with far before she knew what the word "enemy" meant. The story below is the story of Earlean Johnson: an enemy of the enemy.

I was born on July 4, 1977. I was the only girl and the fourth child of my mother. My mother ended up having five children, and they were all boys; all except me. I could tell that I was the apple of my mother's eye.

My mother and father had a volatile relationship. He was an abusive man, and I witnessed them fighting over and over again. My mother did appear to be physically stronger than my father, however. Even though he was abusive, I'd witnessed her getting the best of him many times. One day, she finally got fed up with the abuse, and she left him. Not long after that, she found out that he was married to another woman, even though he was married to her. He had been committing bigamy.

My father was determined to have his cake and eat it too. He refused to let go of my mother, even though she insisted that he leave her alone. He started threatening to take her life, and at first, we were alarmed but not too frightened.

416

One day, I received the call that he'd done it. He'd followed her to a local supermarket and shot her in the back several times. I was nine years old when my mother died, and I was horrified. Over the years, I have heard many stories about what happened that fateful day, but the truth is my mother went to the store with a guy who was a mutual friend of her and my father. They weren't romantically involved, and my father knew this, so that wasn't the problem. The issue was he did not want to lose my mother. Anyhow, my father followed them to the store and confronted my mother in the parking lot of the store. He got into an argument with my mother, and she attempted to walk away from him. He then pulled a weapon and shot her several times in the back, killing her instantly. I knew he'd threatened to kill her many times, but I just hoped it wouldn't happen. The day I got the news that my mother was dead, I was devastated, horrified and of course, in denial. I couldn't believe she was dead. I knew my dad was capable of killing her, but I didn't want to believe that my mother was really gone.

Growing up, I found myself angry at my father. He was eventually convicted of my mother's murder, but he only ended up serving ten years in prison. I felt like he hadn't been punished because while he was in prison, he was often allowed to run errands for the prison. My grandmother ended up raising my siblings and me, and it wasn't easy for her. We were very poor, and we struggled to make ends meet. My grandmother was a widow, so money was tight in the household. Around the age of thirteen, I started going to the cotton fields to chop cotton, so I could help out around the house, and I could buy some of the things I needed for school.

It was hard to forgive my dad for what he'd done. He'd robbed me of a loving and supportive mother, and he'd robbed me of a normal childhood. My grandmother would always tell me that I had to forgive him; otherwise, I wouldn't go to heaven. I wanted so badly to get to heaven that I searched my heart to find a way to forgive him. We were brought up in church, so I'd heard many sermons about forgiveness, and I just decided I would forgive him. My heart wasn't feeling it at first, but I knew that my heart would eventually follow.

When I was a young woman, I ended up meeting a guy who'd swept me off my feet. At that time, I was in high school and called myself in a relationship with another guy, but he hadn't called me in two weeks, so I considered myself single. We'll call the original guy Clyde and the new guy Malcolm. Malcolm was a little younger than I was, but he seemed to be mature for his age. I hadn't had too much experience with boys because I'd been seeing Clyde for a few years, but our relationship was restricted to phone calls only. Malcolm said all of the right things, and he did all of the right things. I didn't know it then, but I was not good with picking men for myself. There was a void in me; a void that was probably created by the absence of my father and the death of my mother.

Malcolm was very attentive at first. He called me a lot, and he wanted to spend time with me, even though it was pretty hard to do so. Not long after meeting Malcolm, my grandmother was involved in a car accident. As a result, she went into a coma and eventually passed away. I was devastated. How was I going to survive without her? I was eighteen years old at the time, and I hadn't had time to prepare for her death. After all, old age hadn't taken her; a sudden and tragic accident had. My world began to spiral downward, but I found comfort in Malcolm's phone calls and in our relationship. He was there for me, and I grieved her passing with him by my side.

When I was nineteen years old, I became pregnant with my son, Malcolm Jr. I was ecstatic! I was pregnant by the man who'd been my first and only lover; a man I loved with all my heart. I thought that it was all destiny. At first, Malcolm wasn't too thrilled about the pregnancy. He was somewhat happy, but he was also afraid of what his mother would say. After all, another girl (we'll call her Sharon) had just had his baby, and his mother had promised to send him away to bootcamp if he'd gotten another girl pregnant. We managed to make it through, and even though his mother was upset at first, she eventually accepted the fact that a baby was on the way and there was nothing we could do about it.

While I was pregnant with my son, Malcolm ended up proposing to me. That was one of the greatest days of my life, besides the birth of our son. I didn't hesitate to say yes, and I couldn't wait to be his Mrs. After my son was born, Malcolm's mother invited me to come and stay in their house with them so she could help me out with the baby. Of course, I happily agreed. This was my chance to be close to the man I loved, and this was my chance to have someone to act as a mother figure to me. My joy was short-lived, however, when a girl started calling the house for Malcolm. We'll call her Penny. Malcolm initially told me that Penny was just a friend, but I was bothered by the fact that she called the house several times a day. I'd spoken with her a few times, and we were friendly with one another at first. One day, I asked her why she was calling so much, and that's when the problems started. She started telling me that she'd been with Malcolm, and she started harassing me. I was a new mother with little experience with men, so of course I didn't know how to process what was happening. I confronted Malcolm about Penny, and he told me:

"She's just a friend."

"She's not even my type."

I believed him because I wanted to believe him. After all, he was the father of my son. For me, it had to work with him. There were no alternatives. From that time on, our relationship began to sink, but I did whatever I could to keep things afloat.

Malcolm had a son who was a little bit older than my son, and I did whatever I could to show him that I loved his son and I would embrace him like I embraced my own son. One day, Malcolm was graduating from high school, and the mother of his son came to the graduation. Once the graduation was over, they began to take photos. His mother asked him to take a photo with his ex-girlfriend, and I became upset. Why was she asking him to take a photo with her and not me? His mother became upset with me because I'd gotten upset about the photo, and she'd pretty much gone off on me. Malcolm was also upset, to the point where he broke up with me. I was devastated. There was no way that Malcolm and I were going to be separate. It had to work because he was the father of my son and the only man I'd ever been with intimately.

During that time, we kept getting back together and breaking up again. While Malcolm Jr. was still an infant, I'd found out that there was another girl who'd given birth to a baby boy, and she said the boy belonged to Malcolm. I didn't want to believe it. When the news came out, Malcolm and I were back together, and to believe that he could cheat on me was to throw a rock at my glass house. Eventually DNA proved that he was the father of that little boy as well. Still, we continued to reconcile and break up again and again.

Malcolm would break up with me and enter relationships with other women. At first, I would wait for him, and I would never tell him that he couldn't have me. After a while, I started having what I referred to as "boyfriends", but they were only temporary fixtures in my life. Whenever Malcolm would come into my life, I'd drop whomever I was with to get back with Malcolm, even if our relationship was just physical but not official.

One day, I found out that I was pregnant again. My son with Malcolm wasn't even a year old, and Malcolm and I weren't officially in a relationship. I remembered my first pregnancy; how supportive Malcolm had been, and I'd hoped he'd be just as supportive. My world was shattered when he asked me what I was going to do about the pregnancy. He didn't want the baby, so I began to panic. I was struggling to take care of the baby I had, and here Malcolm was basically letting me know that I was on my own. I went into a depression, and my fears began to overwhelm me. I made the awful choice to abort my child. At that time, I was three months pregnant. After I aborted the child, Malcolm started acting as if he'd wanted the child. When I told him that I'd aborted the child, he acted surprised and hurt by my decision. To this day, I still regret aborting my baby. That choice has haunted me over the years. I often wonder what the sex of my baby would've been and what my baby would look like now. Malcolm and I continued to have on-again, off-again relationships, and we continued to be intimate with one another.

One day, I found out I was pregnant with my daughter. I was around twenty-three or twenty-four-years old, and I was thrilled. I told Malcolm, and he appeared to be happy as well. We decided to give the relationship another go, and I was happy to have my family back together again. My friends were against my relationship with Malcolm because of our history together, but I wanted to prove them wrong. Malcolm had it in him to be a good man...or so I thought. After I found out that I was pregnant, Malcolm relocated to Atlanta, Georgia. At the time, we were living apart in Greenville, Mississippi. He lived with his mother and stepfather, and I still lived in my grandmother's old home with a few of my brothers. Malcolm asked me to move to Atlanta with him, but I'd just gotten a promotion at work, and I didn't want to move in him as his girlfriend. After all, I was a Christian woman, and I wanted to do things the right way. At the same time, I knew my history with Malcolm. I didn't want to risk going down there only to be sent back home once he decided once again that he didn't want to be with me. I told Malcolm that I was not going to shack with him anymore, so he asked me to marry him. Of course, I agreed. I could not say no to Malcolm.

Before he asked me to move with him, I gave birth to our daughter. We'll call her Olivia. When I was pregnant with Olivia, Malcolm insisted that I have a tubal ligation. He said that he didn't want anymore children. I thought I was okay as well. I had my son and now I had my daughter, so I agreed to have the procedure.

The time came for me and the children to move to Atlanta with Malcolm. I turned in my resignation notice at work, and I began to tell everyone that I would be moving to Atlanta. Most people put on a smile, but they knew Malcolm's history with me, so I received a few "congratulations" and a few disappointed looks. I didn't care. I was going to be with the father of my children. What could be better than that?

There was an older woman working at the store with me. She was a woman of GOD, and I loved her dearly. She was always so positive. I'd never seen her with a frown on her face, and I'd never heard her utter a negative word. One day, she approached me and gave me some news that hurt me deeply. She told me that she'd had a dream about me. In her dream, I was at a crossroads, but I was taking the wrong road; I was taking the straight road. I thought to myself that the Bible tells us to take the straight road. She told me that GOD said I was not to follow Malcolm. She said that GOD had another path HE wanted me to take; nevertheless, I misinterpreted the prophesy because I couldn't imagine life without Malcolm. I went to another woman whom I referred to as my "play mother", and she comforted me by telling me that the enemy could use anyone to speak. She said what I wanted to hear, so I married Malcolm, and I followed him to Atlanta.

At first, things seemed to be looking up. Malcolm rented an apartment, and when I came down to Atlanta, I went straight to work decorating our new apartment. Malcolm told me that he wanted me to be a stay-at-home mother, so I did. I didn't want to do this because I'd been taught to work for what I wanted, but Malcolm said he was going to take care of me, so I honored his request.

One day, we were out in Malcolm's vehicle, and we passed by a Dollar Tree. I asked Malcolm to stop because I wanted to go in Dollar Tree, but Malcolm responded with, "No. You're not going to spend all of my money that I worked hard for." I was bothered by his statement. How dare he tell me not to get a job and then refuse to even let me go to a dollar store! I told him that I would be looking for a job that following Monday so I could make my own money.

Once I started working, Malcolm requested that I pay half of the bills. I was working at a daycare, and I was making half of what he made. During that time, he became more and more verbally and emotionally abusive towards me. He told me:

- I was ugly.
- I was too fat.
- Nothing looked right on me.
- He wanted a divorce.
- He thought we should be just friends.
- Our relationship was more like a partnership than a marriage.
- I was holding him back.
- I would never amount to anything.
- My prayers didn't go any higher than the ceiling.

He also told me not to answer his phone when it rang and not to open his mail. I tried to do whatever he asked of me just to keep peace, but I found myself feeling like a doormat. I wanted him to love me because I loved him, but over time, his words became crueler, and his requests became darker.

He would get off work at eleven o'clock at night, but he started coming home at two and three in the morning. Eventually, he started coming home later and later. He also started asking me more and more for a divorce and telling me that he wanted me to return to Mississippi.

One day, I saw a vision of Malcolm with a girl. I'd dreamed that he'd gone to this girl's house, and her boyfriend answered the door. In my dream, her boyfriend pulled a gun on Malcolm. I told Malcolm about my dream, and I asked him if he was having an affair, but he denied it. Not long after that dream, I received a call in the middle of the night that I had to come and pick up Malcolm. He was at another woman's apartment, and her boyfriend had pulled a gun on him. Malcolm ended up calling the police, and after the police arrived, he called me to come and pick him up because the police were threatening to arrest him. It was the dead of winter and the middle of the night. I was driving a van that I couldn't rely on; nevertheless, I woke the children up, got them dressed, and drove over to that complex to see what was going on. When I arrived there, the police asked Malcolm if he'd told me what was going on. Malcolm then proceeded to tell me that he'd been having an affair; he'd come over to the girl's house, and her boyfriend had pulled a gun on him. I was sick to my stomach. The pain was beginning to become unbearable, and Malcolm had gone too far.
On the way home, Malcolm apologized again and again. He begged me not to leave him. This was a far cry from the

man who'd been asking me for a divorce every day of the week. I was hurt and I was confused, but Malcolm was finally saying the words I wanted to hear him say. He was finally saying that he would be faithful; we were going to start over, and we'd be a family. I didn't know what to do, but I decided to stay and give it one more shot.

Malcolm was on his best behavior for about a week. After a week or two, he started asking me for a divorce again. He started belittling me again. By this time, I knew what that behavior meant. It meant that Malcolm was having another affair. While he was in the shower one day, I decided to go through his phone despite his protests that I was to never touch his phone. While going through it, I found a contact labeled "Naughty Girl." I confronted him, and he told me that the number belonged to Sharon; his first son's mother. Sharon was married at the time, and I didn't understand why he would have her name listed in his phone as "Naughty Girl." Of course, common sense told me that the denotation was sexual. During that time, I became more and more suspicious about his relationship with Sharon. I found his cell phone bill, which I was told to never open, and I opened it. Malcolm had detailed billing, and I couldn't wait to see who he'd been calling. I found that Malcolm and Sharon were talking on the phone every day, several times a day, for hours at a time. I was hurt and confused. Sharon was married to another man, just like Malcolm was married to me. I knew at that moment that they were having an affair, and I confronted Malcolm about it. He denied the affair and ridiculed me for opening his cell phone bill.

By this time, Malcolm was telling me that he did not want me, and he asked me for a divorce every day. Every day, he told me to go back home to Mississippi; every day, he let me know that I was worthless to him. That was the lowest point in my life. I didn't know what to do. I didn't want to return to Mississippi; I didn't want to move back into my grandmother's old house, and I didn't want to admit that everyone was right. Malcolm ended up being deployed to Iraq at that time, and his requests for me to go back to Mississippi had become louder and more heartless. By this time, he was unmerciful with his words. He told me that he wanted me to move back to Mississippi while he was in Iraq. He told me that he wouldn't take care of me and the children if I decided to stay in Georgia. After months of verbal abuse, I finally decided to return home. Malcolm rented a U-haul truck for me, but he didn't give me enough gas to get home. His stepfather ended up giving me the money I needed.

Once I was back at home, I wanted to make sure my name was off the lease. When I called the office, I was told that Malcolm had requested another apartment. He'd told the apartment's office that my family would be moving in with me while he was in Iraq, and he needed a larger apartment. I told them that this was a lie, and I requested that they remove my name from the lease. Not long after that, I found out that he'd moved Sharon and her kids in with him. Of course, we were still married, and I considered getting revenge. I was hurt, and by this time, I wanted to bring Malcolm down; nevertheless, I decided to back off and let GOD deal with him.

The first time he returned from Iraq, Malcolm pretended that everything was all a misunderstanding. I loved him and I wanted to believe him, even though my heart was singing the truth louder than the lies he was telling. After he'd had his fun with me, however, he started singing the divorce tune again.

One day, I'd dropped the children off at Malcolm's mother's house to visit him. I went and picked up a friend of mine, and the two of us went back to her house. We'll just call her Stacy. After Stacy and I hung out at her house, we started riding around town. I received a call from Malcolm telling me to come and pick up the children. He accused me of riding around town with a man. I knew he couldn't be talking about Stacy. After all, she was wearing a long ponytail and makeup. She didn't look like a man at all, but I knew this was just an excuse for him. By this time, I'd dropped Stacy off at home and was headed to Malcolm's mother's house to pick up the kids. When I arrived there, Malcolm came to my car and leaned in through the window. He continued to accuse me of being with another man, and I told him that I'd been hanging out with Stacy. He then started yelling to me that he wanted a divorce, and I told him that I wanted a divorce too. He told me that he would file for custody of the children because he said I was an unfit mother. I had never done anything to make him come to that conclusion. I wasn't a drinker; I didn't do drugs; I wasn't promiscuous, and I took my children with me everywhere I went.

I went into the house to get my kids while he was screaming for me not to get the kids. When we were coming out of his mother's house, my son wrapped his little arms around me and screamed, "Daddy, don't kill my mother!" When I turned around, I saw that he was holding a gun, even though he wasn't pointing it at me. To tell you the truth, I wasn't afraid of him killing me; I was afraid of him killing me in front of my children so I left. I didn't want to take the chance of him shooting me in front of my children, so I honored his mother's request to let her bring the children home later. By this time, my dad had been out of prison for a few years, and we were rebuilding our relationship. I called him and my brothers, and my dad met me at the police department. He'd always expressed regret and sorrow for killing my mother, and I believed this incident hit too close to home for him. He told the police that if something were to happen to me, he would kill Malcolm himself. At that moment, I felt loved by my father. He was finally there for me, even though the circumstances were bad.

Malcolm and I eventually got a divorce. I was hurt because I loved him, but I knew it was for the better. He'd done all he could to destroy me, and I wanted to prove every word he said to be wrong. I ended up going back to college and getting my Bachelor's Degree in Social Work and after that, I went back and got my Master's degree in Psychology. I also recently moved to Texas to start anew with my two children as a single, saved and celibate mother. I am determined to let GOD pick my husband this time. It's been several years now, but I can truly say that I am healed; I have forgiven the people who hurt me, and I am looking forward to all GOD has for me. The only regret I have had was having the tubal ligation. There were times when I thought about having another child (after I'm married, of course). Then again, there are times when I am content with the two I have. Malcolm and Sharon went on to have more children with each other. That's why I warn the women closest to me not to abort their children or have tubal ligation surgeries trying to please the men in their lives. Today, I think about how naïve I was back then, and how easily manipulated I was.

In 2013, my father passed away. Every time he saw me, he saw my mother in me. He was hurt that he'd taken her life, and he asked me over and over again to forgive him. While he was hospitalized, he said something to me that hurt me to the core, however. He told me that my mother had pulled a gun on him, and he'd shot her in self defense. I knew this was a lie, but I wasn't sure if that was the lie he'd told himself or the lie he wanted me to believe. It hurt me so badly that I ended up in the hospital less than a week later with a leaking valve, a heart murmur and high blood pressure. I was only thirty-six years old. This told me that I still had some forgiving to do, and I set out to make sure that every open door to my past was finally closed. I forgave my dad and I forgave Malcolm, but I'm not going to lie and say that it was easy to forgive them. I had to forgive them for me; I had to forgive them for my children, and I wanted to forgive them so my relationship with GOD would not be hindered.

Nowadays, I am a proud mother of my two adoring children, and I have taught them about the LORD, forgiveness and the importance of waiting on GOD.

The End.

As told by Earlean Johnson

Why did the enemy attack Earlean so much? It's obvious. She has an anointing on her life that he wanted to destroy. One thing that a lot of people don't realize is that the enemy doesn't always try to destroy you with incidents; sometimes, he uses those incidents to plant a seed of unforgiveness in our hearts. Unforgiveness is poison to the soul. When a person has an unforgiving heart, the enemy no longer has to attack them. All he has to do is aggravate them.

All the same, we find ourselves in relationships with heartless men who don't have the capacity to love us. Nevertheless, we try to teach them how to love us by being the best women we can, even when they were the worst men we could ever have. As women, we try to be faithful, honest and loving to unfaithful, lying and lustful men. Being faithful to an unfaithful man is like putting diamonds on a hyena.

GOD warned Earlean about Malcolm, but the soul tie was already there. At that time in her life, her relationship with Malcolm was an idolatrous one. Malcolm came before GOD, and any time we make an idol out of a man, our relationship with that man is scheduled for destruction. At the same time, a relationship with Malcolm or men like Malcolm rarely works. There are far too many women in this earth, and any time you have a man with wandering eyes, he's going to try as many of them on as he can. GOD told us to seek first the kingdom of GOD and all its righteousness. HE told us this for a reason. GOD knows that we don't know how to choose men for ourselves. We are carnal creatures, and we will choose men who appeal to our flesh.

We could all come together and bash Malcolm and the men like him, but if we did, we'd only be opening up our hearts to unforgiveness. To bash them means we don't understand what happened; therefore, we are holding them accountable for what they did to us. The truth is that we are just as guilty as the men who betrayed us in most cases. How is that? We entered relationships that we knew GOD didn't want us in. We thought we could make it work. We thought our love was so powerful that it could change the wrong man into the right man. We forgot that GOD loved them first, and HE loved them far greater than we can ever love them; nevertheless, they refused to change for HIM. Who are we that they will change for us?

The enemy fought hard to stop Earlean from walking in her calling. He knew who she was before she knew who she was. She could have easily given up and written her life off as a catastrophe. After all, that's what so many women do once they've been hurt a few times. Many women continue to date the wrong kind of men, and they develop strategies to keep these men at bay. Needless to say, they eventually learn that a man has free will. He will do whatsoever he wants to do, regardless of what a woman thinks or says. At the same time, please know there are some wonderful, GOD-fearing men out there, but there's only one man of GOD for you and I. You are some man's Eve, and he is your Adam. You have his rib, and if you try to fit another man's rib in your life, you will soon find out how painful it is to put a man where he doesn't fit.

Always remember that the wrong man requires a sin offering. He requires you to compromise your faith. The wrong man will always bring a delay to your blessings, and he'll cause you to battle with unforgiveness because he's going to hurt you. That's why it is very important to stand on the WORD and refuse to step down. In doing so, many of the men you would have engaged in a relationship with will not waste their time with you. After all, that's what obedience is designed for. Obedience is designed to keep Satan and his devils away from you. Obedience is designed to protect you from death, sickness, disease, poverty and all the curses of sin. Satan tempts the flesh because he knows that in sin, we have an inheritance. What is that inheritance? *"For the wages of sin is death; but the gift of God is eternal life through Jesus Christ our Lord"* (Romans 6:23).

You can continue to love on a man who doesn't love the LORD, but you will also have a lot of storms ahead of you; storms you wouldn't have ordinarily had to go through. Sure, wives go through trials and tribulations with the right men; nevertheless, those trials aren't usually as hectic and final as the ones executed by the wrong men. One thing about the man GOD has for you is that he has the Spirit of GOD leading him; therefore, when he does wrong, his conscious will bother him. GOD will speak in and to him, and if he doesn't listen, GOD will chasten him. In other words, he's led by GOD and not by the enemy. He will oftentimes find his way back to the right path. Wait on GOD; HE loves you enough that HE waited on you.

Friends Without Benefits

"A one-sided relationship is like having a car with no wheels. Even though it looks like it should be moving, it's going nowhere."

We have all heard the term "friends with benefits", and we all know what the general meaning of it is. The general and modern-day definition is to engage in a sexual relationship with a friend without being titled as a girlfriend. It means the woman has no hope for a future with the man she's sleeping with. Instead, they still refer to one another as friends; nevertheless, the benefit is they are having sex. But let's tell the truth. There's no benefit in submitting your body to a man who refuses to cover you as a husband. There are actually only consequences, and if you count one brief moment of pleasure as a benefit, you have most surely missed the train of wisdom. Just as there are friends "without" benefits amongst men and women, some sister-to-sister relationships are friendships with benefits for one person, but for the other woman involved, it's a friendship without benefits. Allowing one's self to be used for the pleasure of another person is like frying yourself up and placing yourself in a bucket of chicken to be consumed by that person, only to find pleasure in the fact that they said you were good.

Nina pulled her hair back and stood with her legs apart. With her fists clinched, she began to walk in circles around her opponent. Everyone in the neighborhood was there to see this fight. Her opponent has once been her best friend. Her name was Loraine, and she was a giant in comparison to Nina. Some of the people even referred to the battling duo as David and Goliath. Unlike Nina, Loraine appeared confident. She didn't take a fighting position; instead, she stood upright with her fists clinched. Her emotionless face showed no signs of fear or distress. She was ready to put Nina back in line. She was ready to humble Nina.

Let's rewind the story for a little more clarity. Nina and Loraine were both thirty-one years old. Sure, it was a little old for them to be fighting, but this fight had been fifteen years in the making. The two women had been best friends since high school. They'd met when they were both sixteen years old. Nina was new to Chesterfield High School, and she ended up taking Geometry with Loraine. One day, the teacher called on Nina to answer a complex question, and she got the answer right. After that, Loraine began to bully Nina. Nina stood at five feet, three inches tall, whereas Loraine stood at five feet, eight inches tall. Loraine also had a stockier build and was feared by many of the children at that high school, including the seniors, even though Loraine was a sophomore. Nina was also a sophomore in high school, but she'd been held back a year when she was transferred from a high school in Arizona to her new high school in Tennessee.

One day, while at her locker, Nina found herself falling into her locker. She'd been shoved by the one and only Loraine Schaeffer. Angry, she got up to fight Loraine, but Mr. Haversack; the English teacher, was able to intervene and stop the fight before it started. Loraine was suspended for three days, and as a part of her punishment, she'd been forced to apologize to Nina. As a part of Chesterfield High School's bullying policies, both women were forced to sit in a room for an hour to discuss their differences. During that discussion, they both discovered that they could be beneficial to one another. Loraine pitied Nina when she found out that Nina had been the victim of bullying at her previous school in Arizona. She'd moved to Tennessee to live with her father after she'd been attacked at a party by one of the school's most popular football players, Lawrence McGowan. He'd attempted to rape Nina during the party in his parents' bedroom. He'd been dating Nina for a month and had bet some guys that he could have her naked in that time, but it didn't happen. Full of alcohol, the then-drunk Lawrence decided to win his bet by raping Nina. Thankfully, Nina was able to kick him in his groin before escaping. Her bloody nose and swollen lip had assured Lawrence's arrest and future conviction.

Loraine, on the other hand, was just a bully with no friends.

At the same time, she wasn't the brightest bulb in the pack. She struggled with Geometry, Biology, and just about every class there. Seeing how nice Nina was, Loraine decided to befriend and protect her since she felt that Nina wasn't the fighting type. Nina was new to the school and didn't have any friends. She pitied the gentle giant of a woman and decided that she could help Loraine in so many ways. The two women hit it off from that point on, and a friendship was formed that lasted fifteen years. Like most friendly fronts, the friendship was somewhat of a co-dependent relationship. Loraine needed a friend and someone to protect. She wanted to feel needed and loved, and she needed help with her lessons. Nina saw Loraine as a person she could help. She could help Loraine build on her self-esteem, get better grades and maybe, one day, she wouldn't feel the need to bully people. After all, Loraine was not an ugly girl; she just needed a makeover and a friend.

Over the course of their friendship, both women tolerated one another more than anything. Loraine was bothered by Nina's Ms. Fix-It attitude. She was always trying to fix Loraine or make her better. Nina was bothered by Loraine's neediness. She always needed help with something, and she called Nina for every small thing. Nevertheless, the two remained friends until the inevitable happened; Nina ended up getting engaged. It was bad enough that ever since Nina had gotten involved with Chase, she'd slacked up on spending time with Loraine, but to make matters worse; she was not there during the times when Loraine needed her. For example, Loraine had recently started going to community college, and the lessons she had were difficult. She'd called Nina one day to ask for help with some of her homework, but Nina hadn't answered her phone, nor did she return Loraine's call. A few days later, Nina had called her back, but by then, it was too late. Loraine had failed the lesson horribly, and she was not happy about it. She blamed Nina for her bad grade, and the two women had argued, but this was not uncommon for the duo. Nevertheless, Nina was finally tired of the arguing, so she told Loraine that it would be best if the two of them stopped calling one another. Loraine was upset. Obviously, this was Chase's doing. The two women had argued before on several occasions, but Nina had never ended the friendship. To Loraine, Nina needed to be reeled back down to earth; Nina needed to be humbled.

Loraine had a male friend that she often spent time with as well. His name was Jamal, and he'd known Loraine for three years. They'd met one another at a prison where they both worked as guards. Initially, they would just hang out and party with the other guys in the crew. Loraine was always the only woman with the guys; nevertheless, she was drawn to Jamal. He was tall, dark and violent; just the way she liked them. Loraine was still employed at the prison, but Jamal had been terminated after he'd gotten into a fight with one of the inmates. His fighting skills were impressive to Loraine, and she saw him as a man of all men; nevertheless, Jamal said he wasn't ready to be in a committed relationship. He already had two daughters from two previous relationships, and nowadays he just wanted to enjoy a woman-free life. As time progressed, the relationship between Jamal and Loraine turned physical; nevertheless, Jamal always verbalized his expectations beforehand. He always told Loraine that he was not her boyfriend, they were not going to get married, he would see other women, and if she had sex with him, she was fully aware that the relationship was only sexual. They were two friends taking care of one another's needs. Even though Loraine had hastily agreed to those terms, secretly she hoped for more with Jamal. As hard as she appeared to others, Jamal made her feel soft and lady-like.

But it all ended suddenly when Loraine found out that Jamal had started a relationship with a girl named Francine, and he was obviously very serious about her. She'd found this out when she was hanging out with Jamal one day. She'd cooked her famous bacon-wrapped scallops, and the couple was watching a movie together when Jamal's phone rang. Loraine would never forget the look on his face when he looked at the caller identification screen. His eyes seemed to light up, and he sprang up suddenly. Loraine had never seen him be so anxious to take a call before. As a matter of fact, she was used to him being so nonchalant about his calls that while he was with her, she'd only seen him answer the phone one time in three years, and that was the time when his mother was in the hospital.

When Francine called Jamal's phone, Loraine recognized

that Jamal was not withholding himself from entering a relationship; he just didn't want one with her. Jamal sprang to his feet and went into the dining room to take the call. Loraine turned down the television to hear what he was saying, hoping that it was not another woman. She hoped that someone else was in the hospital or maybe someone was calling to offer Jamal a job. The tone of his voice silenced her hopes, however. He sounded as if he was in love. He spoke to Francine with such gentleness; a gentleness he'd never shown to Loraine before. Sure, Loraine had agreed to Jamal's relationship terms, but it was at that moment that she felt something rising up in her. She chewed on her lips as she tried to restrain herself from speaking, but the feelings were too much. When she heard Jamal say, "I love you too," Loraine had what she described as an out-of-body experience. Suddenly, she sprang up from her seat just as Jamal was hanging up the phone.

Loraine: Really, Jamal? So, you're just going to sit here and disrespect me like that in my own home?
Jamal: What?!
Loraine: Yeah, the word is out about you and Francine. You told me that you weren't ready for a relationship, but from what I hear, she has you eating out of her hands. Now, you have the nerve to sit here and talk to the dummy while in my house and in my presence!
Jamal: Loraine, I thought me and you were better than that. Three years of hanging out, and I have never seen you clown. I told you from day one that there was no hope for

you and me. You agreed to those terms, so just spare me the insecure girlfriend drama. After all, you are not my girlfriend or my wife, and you are definitely not my momma.
Loraine: So, it's like that, huh? I'm good enough to screw, but I'm not good enough to be in a relationship with?
Jamal: You said it; I didn't. I see now that this little thing we had; this little friend-with-benefits thing was not a good idea. I never expected you to act like that.
Loraine: So, it's over...just like that? We have one argument in three years, and it's over?
Jamal: Loraine, didn't you hear the terms of our agreement? It never even started.
Loraine: Well, just let the dummy know that I'm coming for her! When I see her, I'm not going to show her any mercy. Tell Francine that Loraine is coming for her!
Jamal: Loraine, the day you put your hands on Francine will be the day you see me like never before. I better not even hear that you have called her, or better yet, that she's getting calls from blocked numbers. The day you try to mess with that woman will be the day you need to go into hiding. You can believe that.

With those words, Jamal exited the door and out of Loraine's life. Loraine was hurt, angry and frustrated. She called Jamal's phone a few times, but he kept sending her to voice mail. Who was this Francine woman, and what was so special about her that he could end their three-year friendship? Even though she wanted to find Francine and confront her, she knew that Jamal was serious. Jamal was even crazier than she wanted to be, and this was one of the things that attracted her to him.

Still angry from the day's events, Loraine decided to take a walk to clear her head. She just could not sit up in that house; she needed to get out.

Her thoughts flowed like a river, and each thought hurt and upset her all the more. How could Jamal do that to her after three years? How could he sleep with her for three years and not feel anything? All the gentle kisses he'd given her had to mean something. What about that time when he'd laid his head on her lap and fell asleep? What about the time when he'd interlocked his fingers with hers as they lay in the bed watching television? What about the time Jamal had displayed jealousy when he found out that one of their old co-workers was calling Loraine? There were so many moments that were precious to Loraine. Did they not mean anything to Jamal?

Loraine's thoughts had overwhelmed her so much that she didn't realize she'd been walking for more than twenty minutes. A familiar voice, however, snapped her out of her thoughts. She could hear Nina's high-pitched voice afar off. She looked up and saw Nina's vehicle parked in front of a house. Nina was unloading boxes from a car. Her laughter roared as she spoke with another girl who was holding the door of the house open for her. She entered the house, but a few minutes later, both she and the other woman emerged

445

from the house, heading back towards the car. They were laughing and talking the way Loraine and Nina used to talk. Loraine felt betrayed as she watched Nina pick up a huge box and attempt to carry it. Suddenly, a man emerged from the house and took the box from Nina. It was Chase, and the woman Nina was helping was obviously Chase's sister because she resembled him.

Loraine stood across the street becoming angrier and angrier at the interaction between Chase's sister and Nina. She decided to confront Nina. It had been three weeks since Nina had abruptly ended their friendship, and now she needed Nina more than ever. Everyone went back into the house, but Nina emerged a few minutes later and headed back to the car. Nina leaned over into the car to grab another box, but suddenly, she felt the sharp pains of something pinching her legs and throwing her forward. Loraine had just tried to slam the car door on Nina's body. Seeing what had happened, some of the guys playing basketball nearby ran over. Most of them knew Loraine and Nina. Nina tried to stand up but was dragged out of the car by her hair. For a brief minute, she didn't know what was going on or who was attacking her. She was dragged a few feet before she was released and then kicked in the head. Looking up, she saw Loraine towering over her. By this time, half of the neighborhood had started making their way to see the fight. "Let her get up first, Loraine," someone had yelled. Staggering, Nina stood to her feet and pulled her hair back into a ponytail. She spread her legs and clinched her fist as

she began to walk in circles around her opponent. She could hear someone saying, "That's David and Goliath, but David don't have her slingshot right about now, so she'd better run." The crowd laughed, and a few more people continued to refer to the battling duo as David and Goliath. Loraine appeared confident. She did not take on a fighter's position. Instead, she clinched her fist and waited for the right opportunity to hit Nina. Suddenly, she heard the sounds of people screaming "no" before she felt a sharp pain, and a force hit her from behind. Loraine fell to the ground, and when she looked up, she could not believe her eyes. It was Chase, and he'd just punched her. He stood over her angrily, looking down at her before some of the guys began to restrain him. One of the guys had even said to him, "Hey man. You're not supposed to hit a woman." To that, he replied, "That is not a woman. And anyone who hits my fiancé is going to taste my knuckles: woman or man!" Just like that, the fight was over. Loraine was too afraid to get up and fight again. She looked up, and Chase's sister was now holding Nina. Nina was crying and staring at her old friend. After fifteen years, she'd never imagined that Loraine could attack her for any reason.
The End.

What happened? Both stories are stories where each person used the other person, but in relationships like this, one person always stands to lose the most, and they are oftentimes the most dangerous of the bunch. Nina saw in Loraine a person she could help, but she did not know that by helping Loraine, she was enabling her to stay in a victim's mindset. Undoubtedly, by helping Loraine, Nina felt needed, and this was enough to make her continue the friendship for fifteen years. Needless to say, even though Nina's help could be seen as a good deed, Nina was also helping herself. Many women find what they see as "projects" or other women they could "fix-up", but these "projects" are oftentimes their own attempts to rebuild their self-worth. Even though they don't mean to hurt anyone with their philanthropy, they often end up on the wrong side of their projects' wrath. This is because everyone is created differently, and any attempt to change them will eventually be met with strife or violence. You may see a woman out there who has a beautiful face, beautiful skin and a nice shape, but the way she dresses takes away from her beauty. Most women who have creative spirits would love the opportunity to give these women makeovers because they think they can change the lives of these women. Instead, they end up offending the very ones they wanted to help because eventually, their fixer-uppers will realize that they are comfortable being just who they are.

Loraine saw Nina as a person who could be her friend and help her with her school work. She also saw Nina as a justifiable reason to use her large size to her ability. She could fight for Nina and protect her from anyone who threatened her. The truth was Loraine was inwardly fighting her own demons, only she was using her flesh to do it. To her, Nina was a friend with benefits. Even after they'd graduated, she could still call Nina up to help her with anything she needed. To Nina, however, the friendship with Loraine became a friendship without benefits for her. She was always giving, and Loraine was always taking. Friendships like that are doomed to end in violence, whether it's violent words or an actual violent act. Both parties were guilty of using one another, but Nina ended up being the person who held the most straws. Her life was in development, but Loraine wanted to stop this development to keep things just the way they'd always been. Loraine needed Nina, but Nina did not need Loraine anymore. Nina wanted to move forward, but Loraine wanted to hold her back. You will find that anytime you end a friendship where you held the most straws, the offed friend oftentimes won't let go so easily. They have more to lose in losing you. A friendship, just like a relationship, should never be unequally yoked.

In the relationship with Jamal, Loraine had availed herself as nothing more than a warm body for him to play with when he was bored. He could enjoy one of the perks of having a wife without actually marrying her. Their friendship with benefits ended up being a benefit to Jamal but a friendship without benefits to Loraine. Sure, she enjoyed pretending that their relationship would go somewhere eventually, but there was nothing in their agreement that benefited her.

And what about her line of reasoning? Jamal had laid his head in her lap and went to sleep before. Jamal held her hand while they were watching a movie before. Jamal used to kiss her gently; Jamal showed jealousy over her, and the list goes on and on. This is the way most women reason within themselves, trying to determine how a man "really" feels about them. If a man loves you, you won't have to look for signs or clues. He will prove his love for you by marrying you. At the same time, any time a woman lies down with a man who has not committed himself to GOD to be that woman's husband, she will always end up being the person holding the short straw. The truth is men are not highly emotional creatures. They are imparters who leave a part of themselves in every woman they lie with. Women are receptors who will receive a part of every man who lies with them; therefore, women have been and always will be more emotionally invested in relationships than their male counterparts. Sure, you'll find plenty of women whose hard words bear witness to the hardness of their hearts. They will proudly tell you that they don't care for men, and they know how to let go of a man should he cross their lines. They will tell you that a man is nothing more than a good time, but when their men leave them, the truth shows up in their attitudes. If you don't care about the man, you won't be mad at him when he walks away. If a woman doesn't care about the guy, she won't make him jump through hoops just to speak with his children. When what a woman says does not match her actions, she is lying. Just like most of you, I've seen women scream out that they don't care for the father of their children or the man whom they'd lain with, but as soon as he was spotted with another woman, their true feelings showed up. They are either chasing after the new woman or trying to fight the man.

Loraine chose to lie to herself because Jamal didn't think enough of her to even lie to her. You'll see that with men often. With some women, they'll be honest because they feel these women have absolutely nothing to offer them but their bodies. These same men will often pretend to be in love with other women who seem to have more standards but aren't as easy to bed. And finally, they will bear all for the woman they feel is worthy of being called a wife. Most women who fit the "worthy of being called a wife" category would be flattered by that statement, but you shouldn't be. If the man who wants to call you his wife is not worthy of being called "a husband" or "your husband", asking for your hand in marriage isn't a compliment. Many women have become so competition-driven that they end up winning losers. It's like being told that you've won a lifetime supply of used paper plates. Eventually, you'll get tired of trying to clean them off, and you'll opt to purchase new and unused ones.

Pray about everyone in your life, and never let a man enter your body who has not already entered a covenant with the LORD to cover you as his wife.

Seasonal Lovers

"Marrying the right man in the wrong season is just as bad as marrying the wrong man in any season."

We often hear about the Ishmaels and the Isaacs. No woman wants to purposely marry an Ishmael. Nevertheless, we rarely hear about people finding their right spouses in the wrong seasons. But it happens, and oftentimes when it does happen, the couple breaks up and never comes back together again because of the damage done during the first trial run.

GOD has designed everything in the earth for seed time and harvest; nevertheless, any fruit that is not ripe will be bitter and not ready for the picking. It may look good while it's green (naive), and you can even give it a little sugar (kisses and lies) to make it taste better, but eventually, what's sweet to the tongue will be bitter to the belly. Even though it got past your tongue; your belly will violently speak out and remind you that what you just took in was not ripe!

"I give myself away. I give myself away so You can use me. I give myself away. I give myself away so You can use me," Antoinette sang as she washed the dishes at her boyfriend

Derrick's house. Derrick sat nearby in the living room. Hearing Antoinette sing reminded him of his mother.

Derrick: Who sings that song?

Antoinette: William McDowell. You mean to tell me you've never heard that song before?

Derrick: I don't think so. Sing it again for me.

Antoinette: I give myself away. I give myself away so You can use me. I give myself away. I give myself away so You can use me.

Derrick: You need to hurry up with those dishes so I can use you some more!

Antoinette: Derrick, be quiet! *Laughs.* No, you know that what we are doing is wrong, and my parents would turn over in their graves if they knew that I was shacking up with a man.

Derrick: Baby, don't start that again. You and I are both happy, and we don't need some piece of paper to validate our love for one another. Besides, I told you....I want to wait until I have enough money to give you the wedding you want.

Antoinette: I know...I know, but it's been three years, Derrick. Nothing has changed yet, and I'm not getting any younger. I want children; I want a house with a big yard; I just want what a married woman has.

Derrick: And I'm going to give you all that and more. Just be patient with me.

Antoinette: You know, Pastor preached on fornication today, and I felt like he was speaking to me. A few times, he even looked over at me, and I just dropped my head in shame.

Derrick: Antoinette, he's just preaching; that's all. If he had been preaching against gambling and looked over at you, it wouldn't have bothered you because you know you don't gamble. Just relax. Can we change the subject, please? Every time we talk about us not being married, you end up mad at me, and I really don't want to ruin tonight. We've had such a good day today. Please, let's not ruin it.

Antoinette: But Derrick, I have one more question, please.

Derrick: What?

Antoinette: Do you love me?

Derrick: Here we go again. Yes, Antoinette; you know I love you. Why are you starting up again? I think I need to leave home on Sundays and come back on Monday morning. Every Sunday after church, you come home feeling convicted. Can we enjoy one Sunday without arguing? Or maybe you need to stop going to church altogether until after we've gotten married. That way, you won't have your weekly cry sessions. I love you, I am going to marry you, and I'm still here. Doesn't that count for something?

Antoinette: I'm sorry. I'm not trying to upset you. It's just that I feel bad when I see my friends getting married and having children. Just the other day, Kelsey found out she was pregnant, and even though I was happy for her, I felt bad for myself.

Derrick: Yeah, but Kelsey doesn't have a man who loves her. Kelsey had sex with a man she barely knew. Now, her child is going to grow up fatherless. Is that what you want?

Antoinette: Of course not, Derrick.

Derrick: Okay, baby. Can we PLEASE just drop this conversation? If this turns into an argument, I'm going to go and get me a hotel room so I can sleep in peace. I have to go to work in the morning.

Antoinette decided to end the conversation. Derrick had actually left one time before after threatening to get a hotel room. He didn't come back until after work the next day. Antoinette remembered how hurt she was at that time and did not want a repeat of that day. It had taken her months to forgive Derrick for staying out that night, so she decided to sit next to her lover and make the best of the evening. Together, they watched a romantic comedy and laughed the night away. They laughed and held hands. Everything felt so right. If only it were official.

The next day, Antoinette came home and found a huge bouquet of roses on the dining room table waiting for her. There was a note next to the roses that read, "I love you, and tonight I want to prove it. Meet me at Brisbaine Park at four o'clock. P.S. Wear comfortable shoes." Antoinette's smile widened as she laid the note back on the table. Derrick was always so unpredictable; so romantic. Her smile got even wider when she walked into the bedroom and saw the huge teddy bear sitting on her bed. Derrick had placed two more bouquets of roses across the teddy bear's lap and covered the bed with rose petals. Today was going to be an awesome day.

When Antoinette arrived at the park, she was surprised to see that Derrick hadn't arrived there yet. She got out of her vehicle and started walking towards their favorite spot. It was a little opening between the trees; somewhere they could be out of sight from other park goers. Antoinette made her way over to a tree where Derrick had carved their name three years ago when they'd first met. She placed her hand on the fading heart and began to run her fingers along the outline of it. She was startled by a man's voice coming form behind her. "I knew I'd find you in this spot," said Derrick. Antoinette suddenly jumped and turned towards her lover. "Boy, you scared me! Please warn me next time," she said jokingly. Smiling and looking exceptionally handsome, Derrick handed her a card. Antoinette was nervous as she opened the card. Maybe this was it. Maybe he was ready to propose to her. When she opened the card, however, she was pleasantly surprised yet somewhat disappointed. The card read, "You've given me three of the best years of my life, and I appreciate you more and more every day. I love and appreciate you more than you know. Yours forevermore. ~Derrick." Antoinette smiled and looked up at her beau. She watched as he sat a small radio on the ground and turned it on. He loaded a CD into the radio, and their song came on. After that, he placed his arms around Antoinette, and the two begin to dance and get lost in the lyrics. What an amazing man he was! Antoinette leaned back to look him in his eyes. His eyes were so full of love. There was no denying it. When he kissed her, his kisses were passionate, loving and almost too good to be true. Day turned into night as the couple danced song after song. Suddenly, a blinding light shined on them, and the sound of a walkee talkee overshadowed the sound of the radio. Dazed, the couple looked up to see a police officer shining his flashlight on them. "And what's going on in here?" asked the officer. Derrick answered, "I'm sorry, officer. We're not doing anything illegal. I was just dancing with my fiancé." His words hit Antoinette in the right way. Did he just say "fiancé"? Antoinette's eyes lit up. "Okay, well, you need to leave this clearing. Some people called and thought some hanky-panky was going on in here. This is a park where children frequent, you know?" said the officer. "I know," said Derrick. "We actually live together, so there's no reason for us to do anything inappropriate outside, but we'll leave." The officer thanked them as he went away. The couple laughed as they headed towards Antoinette's car. Antoinette was surprised when Derrick walked to the passenger's side and opened the door for her. "Where's your car?" she asked him. "How did you get up here?" Derrick smiled and said, "I caught the bus. I wanted to ride home with you because I have one more stop I want to make. Get in." Antoinette smiled and got into the vehicle. She loved to sit on the passenger's side while Derrick drove. While with him, she felt like they were a family. It felt so good to just be near him, smelling his cologne and watching his eyes as he drove towards their destination. Occasionally, he would look over at Antoinette and smile. He would reach down with his right hand and hold her hand.

Finally, they arrived at their destination, and Antoinette couldn't help but be confused. Derrick had taken her to his job, but for what reason? Derrick put his code in and went through the gate. He then pulled up to a fleet of company vehicles and stopped the car. "What's going on?" said Antoinette. "Why are we here?" Derrick didn't answer. Instead, he got out of the car and walked around to the passenger's side. He then opened the door for Antoinette. "Get out," he said with a smile. Confused, Antoinette stepped out of the vehicle. She looked around to see if anyone else was there. Derrick then grabbed his keys, extended his arm, and pressed the remote key on his key ring. Suddenly, one of the car's headlights blinked, and the vehicle's alarm system beeped twice to signal that the car was disarmed. Wait a minute...why did Derrick have the keys and remote to one of the company vehicles? It suddenly hit Antoinette. Derrick had gotten the promotion he'd been striving for. Antoinette screamed with joy, jumping up and down as she spoke.

Antoinette: No!
Derrick: Yes. They confirmed it today. You are now looking at the Director of Product Management at Imotran.
Antoinette: No way! Yay! Congratulations, baby! I'm so happy!

Antoinette jumped on Derrick and wrapped her arms and legs around him. She was so happy, but Derrick had some more news. Worried that she would take the rest of the news the wrong way, Derrick stop smiling and looked at Antoinette. He said, "Wait. Before you get too excited; there is one catch."

Antoinette looked into Derrick's eyes and saw that the joy was no longer there. She lowered herself to the ground and braced herself for his answer.

Derrick: You know with this company. Any time they promote you, you have to move. They won't promote you within the same building.
Antoinette: What does that mean?
Derrick: It means we'll be moving to Michigan.
Antoinette: Michigan?! But Derrick, what am I supposed to do about my job, my family and my friends?
Derrick: Quit your job and find a new one. You can always visit your friends and family on the holidays, or they can visit us. At the same time, I know you'll make new friends.
Antoinette: Derrick, that's a big move you're asking me to make. I can understand if we were married, but we're girlfriend and boyfriend. What if the relationship doesn't work? I've been working at QuickStar Collect for five years. Now I'm supposed to start over somewhere else? It's not that easy for me, Derrick. I don't have a college degree like you do.
Derrick: Relax; relax. Calm down and just trust me, baby. I'm going to take care of you. You've been with me for three years now, going on four years. Have I ever let you down? Have I ever left you, cheated on you or hit you?

Antoinette: Not, but....

Derrick: Well, what makes you think I'll start doing you wrong now? You said it yourself....you're ready for a change. Here's our chance, baby. The world is at our fingertips. We just have to trust GOD and take it. And who knows? Maybe this will be our chance to finally have enough money to have that big wedding with all the trimmings that you want.

Antoinette: Okay.

Derrick: Okay?

Antoinette: Derrick, if you get to Michigan and start doing me wrong, I'll hold your head in the toilet until I stop seeing bubbles. Capeesh?

Derrick: *Laughs.* Capeesh.

Antoinette: *Sigh.* Okay. When's the big move?

Derrick: Next week.

Antoinette: Next week?! Derrick, I don't even have enough time to put in a two weeks' notice, and what about the lease on our apartment?

Derrick: No worries; no worries. My company is going to pay to break the lease, and like I told you, I will take care of you. If you want, you can put in your two weeks' notice tomorrow and take your last week as your vacation week. Didn't you tell me they were pressuring you to take a vacation since the year is almost over?

Antoinette: Yeah. Okay. I'll see what they say.

Antoinette and Derrick went back to their apartment to celebrate the news. Even though Derrick was overjoyed with the news, Antoinette was feeling down. She would have to leave her church, her family and her job. At the same time, Derrick was always putting off marrying her. Sure, he showed her love in so many ways, but the ultimate test of his love was one that he kept putting off taking. But maybe an increase in pay would be just what the doctor ordered to get him to finally marry her.

The following Sunday, Antoinette decided to tell her Pastor about the move. She was nervous, but she didn't want to just leave without telling him. After Sunday service, Antoinette walked up to her Pastor and embraced him. Nervously, she spoke with him and hoped for his blessing.

Antoinette: Pastor. I need to tell you something.
Pastor Ramos: Hey Antoinette. Sure, baby girl. What's up?
Antoinette: I'll be moving to Michigan next week.
Pastor Ramos: That's great! Congratulations. What? Did you get a promotion?
Antoinette: No. My boyfriend Derrick got a promotion, and they are relocating him there.
Pastor Ramos: That's great. I didn't know you lived with a boyfriend. Have I ever met him?
Antoinette: No. He's not the church type. But you'll meet him someday.
Pastor Ramos: Well. Just know that we are here for you if you ever need us and we'll be praying for you. See you soon!

Antoinette was humiliated. Why did he close the

conversation off with "see you soon"? What was he trying to say? Had GOD shown him something? Antoinette opened her car door to find another card on the dashboard. Apparently, Derrick had come by the church and put a card for her in the vehicle. He was such a romantic and dreamy guy. Antoinette opened the card and was taken aback by what it read. It was definitely from Derrick. It read: "Hey my darling. I've been thinking about you and I suddenly realized that I can't live without you. Let's do it. Let's get married. You pick the date and the location and I'm in. Love you. Derrick. P.S. I have a surprise for you when you get home."

Antoinette was overjoyed. Finally! All of her hard work had finally paid off! Even though she'd fornicated, she was finally getting married. Even though her boyfriend was not the church-going type, he loved her and he wanted to prove it! Antoinette was so excited that she stepped on the gas pedal a little too hard heading home. Just three blocks from her apartment, she was horrified by the sight of flashing red lights behind her. This couldn't be happening on the best day of her life! She pulled over and started shuffling through her purse, looking for her driver's license. A minute later, she'd found her license, and an officer was now at her window knocking on the glass. Antoinette let her window down and greeted the officer.

Officer: How are you doing, Ma'am? Are you in a hurry to go somewhere?

Antoinette: Not really. Was I speeding?

Officer: Yes, ma'am. You were clocking sixty-one miles per hour in a forty-five mile per hour zone.

Antoinette: I'm sorry, officer. I didn't realize I was going that fast. Can you please just give me a warning? I'm just leaving church, and I'm supposed to be meeting my fiancé back at the house.

Officer: Ordinarily I could let this go, but you were going sixteen miles over the speed limit, so I'm going to have to issue you a citation, ma'am. May I see your license, registration and proof of insurance, please?

Antoinette handed over the requested materials and watched as the officer headed back to his vehicle. He looked like he'd had one too many doughnuts, Antoinette thought. This had to be the devil attacking her. He obviously did not want her to get married, and the news had undoubtedly put out a fire in hell. As the officer approached her vehicle, Antoinette contemplated offering to pray for him. How dare he let the devil use him like that, she thought to herself. Antoinette let down her window once again, and the officer handed her back her license. "I'm not going to ticket you this time since you're just coming back from church. I will issue you a warning, however. Slow down. Wherever you are going, the building is going to be there whether you get there at five o'clock or five-o-five." Antoinette was elated. She thanked the officer and drove away.

Back at the house, Derrick cooked up a feast for his glowing fiancé. He cooked seafood gumbo, rice, corn on the cob, and he made some homemade yeast rolls. He also made

464

Antoinette's favorite: a strawberry cake with vanilla icing on top. He topped the cake with fresh strawberries and placed strawberries around the cake. It was beautiful. When Antoinette arrived home, she had a glow about her that made him take notice. Her big bright smile lit a fuse in his heart. She told him about her being pulled over and how the officer had let her go with a warning. She was more than happy to see the food, but the highlight of the evening was when Derrick knelt down on one knee and proposed to her. He placed a small diamond ring on her finger, promising to get her a bigger one in a few years. Antoinette happily accepted the marriage proposal, and they set a date for the next year.

A week later, they were living in Michigan, and all was well. Derrick's job paid them more than enough to pay for their new home, and he'd even purchased Antoinette a brand new car with cash. Everything was going great. Antoinette found a new church in the city, and Derrick even joined her a few times in the sanctuary.

Eight months into their new city, the couple was living it up. Antoinette was now working at a collection agency, and the couple tried to keep their relationship exciting by going out on the town once or twice a week. All was well until one day some of Eric's colleagues and superiors were in town for an annual conference. On the last evening of the conference, the crew had decided to meet at a popular Japanese restaurant for dinner. They would all bring their spouses, so of course, Derrick took Antoinette. The evening started off well. Everyone was dressed to impress, and Antoinette sat prim and proper greeting the guests. As the evening passed on, the questions begin to flow. Everyone wanted to know what each worker's spouse did for a living. Mr. Lowell, the Senior Vice President's wife was the first to speak. "Well, I am an Astrophysicist," said Mrs. Lowell. Everyone at the table was impressed. The Regional Sales Director, Tony Parker's wife spoke up and said, "I am a Crime Scene Investigator." Everyone was fascinated with Mrs. Parker's profession as well, and they asked a lot of questions. By the close of the evening, everyone's spouse had proudly spoken of their profession. Everyone except Antoinette and a Sales Manger's wife from Toledo, Ohio. Finally, the Toledo Sales Manager whose name was Tony Segan spoke up on his wife's behalf. "My wife is a stay at home mom," he said. "She's raising our three beautiful daughters." Everyone smiled and told Mrs. Segan that her job had to be the most difficult and highest paying job of them all. Antoinette hoped they wouldn't ask her. She wasn't ordinarily ashamed of her job, but she felt dwarfed in the sea of professional women and men. Finally, one of the women at the table said to Antoinette, "And what do you do? I think you're the only person we haven't heard from." Antoinette pretended not to hear her, but she repeated her question once again.

Mrs. Hamilton: You. I don't know whose wife you are. I'm assuming you're here with Mr. Swinson. What do you do? We haven't heard from you all night.

Antoinette: Who? Me?

Mrs. Hamilton: Sure, darling. Don't be shy.

Antoinette: I work for a collection agency.

Mrs. Hamilton: Oh, that's great. What's the name of the collection agency?

Antoinette: Well, it's a small and fairly new agency. You've probably never heard of it, but it's called Swenton Collections.

Mrs. Hamilton: Swinson Collections? Oh, you guys own your own collection agency?! That's fabulous!

Antoinette: No, it's not our collection agency. It's called Swenton Collections. Derrick's last name is Swin-son.

Mrs. Hamilton: Oh. What do you do there? Are you one of the managers? You look like one of those manager types.

Antoinette: *Clears throat.* No. Actually, I am one of the agents. I just call around trying to collect debts. That's all.

Mrs. Hamilton: Well, that sounds fun. Are you and Mr. Swinson married?

Antoinette: We're getting married in a few months.

Mrs. Hamilton: Oh, that's great! Make sure you send me an invite to the wedding.

Antoinette: I sure will.

At the close of the evening, Antoinette felt drained. She was humiliated and irritated. She thought about shoving Mrs. Hamilton's head through her plate of sushi. When they arrived home, Antoinette took off her shoes and plopped down on the couch. Derrick wasn't so much embarrassed about Antoinette's profession as he was her attitude. Why had she been embarrassed to tell the people what she did for a living? Derrick began to think to himself that Antoinette just did not fit in. She was in an element that she was not comfortable with. Her choice of friends were never corporate types. They were always blue-collared workers who loved to get together and talk about the LORD. From that day on, he began to see Antoinette differently.

A month later, Antoinette was sitting at home. She'd been on sick leave because she'd come down with the flu. Derrick came home from work around eight that evening. When he came in, he didn't greet Antoinette with a kiss or a hello like he ordinarily did. Instead, he took off his shoes, took his briefcase to the bedroom, and began to remove his clothing. Antoinette was sitting on the living room couch, and she wasn't too happy about Derrick's behavior. After all, he'd been acting distant lately. He wasn't kissing her like he ordinarily did, and when he did kiss her, his lips were cold. Nothing like the warm, passionate kisses he used to give her. Instead, she felt like she was kissing a bird's beak after it had been playing in the refrigerator. His conversations were suddenly all about corporate America. He didn't want to talk about life in general like he used to, and he became very short with Antoinette in relation to some of the things she'd say. For example, one day, Derrick was talking about a new product that had been developed for elderly people who stayed at home alone. It was a tool designed to sharpen their memory and alert authorities should their memory slip. They had not come up with a name for the product yet, but Derrick was excited about it. The device was a video surveillance camera that stayed off at all times. Every day the homeowner would have to check in with the device to keep the camera from starting up. They would have to check in twice a day by entering their code. If they failed to enter their code or if they entered the wrong code, the cameras would be activated. It sharpened their memory because they had to remember to check in, and they had to remember the code. It was more of a security device that allowed live monitoring of elderly homeowners who did not want to be put in nursing homes. After Derrick told Antoinette about the new device, she'd responded by saying, "That's not new. It's just an upgrade on many of the security devices already out there." Derrick was turned off by Antoinette's negative feedback. He shot back with, "I don't know why I try to hold grown-up conversations with you. All you want to talk about is soap operas and people."

Now, two weeks after that incident, Antoinette was home with the flu when Derrick came in. She was hoping that her condition would stir up some empathy from Derrick, but it did not happen. She waited for Derrick to emerge from the bedroom after removing his work clothes. Instead, she heard the door shut, and the television came on. What was going on with Derrick? Why was he suddenly so cold towards her? Antoinette's body was sore, but she decided to make her way into the bedroom to confront her fiancé. As she turned the doorknob, she was shocked to see that Derrick had locked the door. She then knocked on the door and waited on Derrick to open it. Finally, she could hear him getting out of the bed to open the door. Antoinette stared at Derrick for a minute as he laid back across the bed.

Antoinette: Why did you lock the door, Derrick?

Derrick: Habit. That's all. Don't read into it, please.

Antoinette: Can we talk?

Derrick: Antoinette, I don't really feel like having one of those long, drawn out talks that go nowhere. Can I please rest up a little? I just got in from work.

Antoinette: Ten minutes. That's all I'm asking.

Derrick: *Sighs.* Okay. Ten minutes it is. What's going on?

Antoinette: Do you remember when you asked me to move down here with you? I told you my fears. I feared that you would change on me, and I didn't want to risk quitting my job of five years if our relationship wasn't going to go anywhere.

Derrick: And what's your point?

Antoinette: My point is you've changed, Derrick. You've changed towards me. It seems like everything I do and everything I say irritates you. Lately, there is no chemistry between us. I don't know what's going on with you. We have less than four months before our wedding, and I haven't seen you prepare for it or talk about it.

Derrick: Yeah, I was meaning to talk with you about the wedding. Antoinette, I don't think now is the time for us to get married. There is just too much going at the company, and I'm going to be nose deep in paperwork for the next nine months or more.

Antoinette: What? Derrick, I knew you were going to do

that.

Antoinette began to cry.

Antoinette: I knew you would do this to me. I should have followed my gut instinct and stayed back in Louisiana. I don't know why I let you talk me into coming down here to be mistreated and then dumped. I loved you with my heart, and this is what you do to me? After all we've been through? All of the years I've put into this relationship. All of the sacrifices I've made for you. And it's all for nothing, right?

Derrick: Look, I don't mean to hurt you. I just think we are two different people heading in two different directions in life. It's not that I don't love you. It's just that....

Antoinette: Let me finish that sentence for you. It's just that your career is budding and I'm no longer good enough for you.

Derrick: It's not that, Antoinette. Let's not be dramatic with this. It just doesn't feel the same between the both of us anymore. There's no spark there. I was thinking......*Sigh*.......I was thinking that maybe we ought to separate for a while. I'll move out, and I'll help you with the bills here, or if you choose to move out, I can help you with the bills at your new place. If you prefer to go back to Louisiana, I'll help you with gas. I'll even help you with the bills there, if you want.

Antoinette sat on the floor and started to weep. What was she going to do? She didn't have any family or friends in Michigan. And here it was: the love of her life was ending their relationship. What was she going to tell all of the people who'd set up their vacations so they could come down to her wedding? How could she face all of the people who'd told her not to go without a ring? More than that, how was she going to raise Derrick's baby alone? She'd just found out that she was pregnant and that she didn't have the flu. Her symptoms were actually from the pregnancy. As she sat on the floor and cried, Derrick sat beside her and began to rub her back as she rocked back and forward. "I'm sorry, Antoinette," he said. "I didn't mean to hurt you. I never meant to hurt you." Antoinette shook her head as she wiped her nose with the sleeve of the jacket she was wearing. "It's okay," she said. "I should have known better. Just give me enough gas to get back to Louisiana. I don't need any more of your money. Just send me back home." Derrick was hurt at her response. He was hoping that she'd be a little more dramatic because that would've made sending her home a lot easier.

Derrick: When do you want to go?

Antoinette: Tomorrow. I don't want to take anything; just my clothes. I'll start packing now.

Antoinette stood up and started towards the closet.

Derrick: But wait. You can't travel with the flu.

Antoinette: It's okay. I don't have the flu. It's just a cold. I'll be okay. Just give me about six hundred dollars for gas, and I'll be okay.

Derrick: What about your job? Don't you want to give a two weeks' notice?

Antoinette: No. I'll be okay. Just get the gas money for me, please.

Seasonal Lovers

Derrick felt horrible as he watched Antoinette pack her bags.
He went into his wallet and took out a thousand dollars and
handed it to Antoinette. She took the money and went into
another room to weep. After she was able to get her
emotions under control, she returned to the room and began
to pack again, not saying a word to Derrick. Derrick asked
her a few questions, hoping to get an angry response out of
her, but Antoinette held her peace and answered each
question calmly as she packed her bags. "This would be a
little easier if you cursed me out or something," said Derrick.
"I know," said Antoinette. "That's why I'm not going to do it."

The next day, Derrick kissed Antoinette's forehead before
heading out to work. "I love you and I will always love you,"
he said to his sleeping ex-fiancé. Antoinette pretended to be
asleep. After Derrick left, she began to load her bags into
her vehicle. Once she'd loaded the last bag, she looked at
her dream house one more time and let the tears flow from
her eyes. She got into her vehicle and headed back to
Louisiana. The drive was a little over fifteen hours long, but
Antoinette was determined to complete the drive in one day.
During the trip, Derrick occasionally called to check in on
her, but she did not answer her phone. Once she'd arrived
in Louisiana, Antoinette went directly to her parents' old
house. One of her sisters and her kids were now living
there. Angela, Antoinette's sister, was surprised to see her
sister standing in the doorway with her bags. She hugged
Antoinette and helped her bring the bags in the house. "Do
me a favor," Antoinette said to her sister. "If Derrick calls,

don't tell him that I am here, and don't tell him anything about me. I'm about to call him one last time, and that's it. I don't want him to know anything about me." Angela agreed, and Antoinette went into her old bedroom to call Derrick back.

Derrick: Hey baby. Are you okay? I wanted to make sure that you arrived well.
Antoinette: Yes, I'm here. You don't have to worry.
Derrick: Antoinette, please don't be mad at me. I never meant to hurt you. It's just that we grew apart.
Antoinette: I know. Have a nice life, Derrick.
Derrick: Wait. Antoinette....

With that, Antoinette hung up the telephone. Immediately, she called her cell phone provider and changed her number. Derrick tried to call her back, but her number was changed. This complicated the breakup all the more.

Week after week went by, and Derrick did not hear from Antoinette. He'd called her sister's house, but her sister said she wasn't living there. He'd called her brother's house, but he was less than friendly and refused to tell Derrick anything about Antoinette. Derrick wanted so badly to remain friends with Antoinette, but she obviously didn't want the same.

Months went by, and still no Antoinette. Before long, four years had gone by, and Derrick had never heard from Antoinette. By this time, he was engaged to a corporate woman named Lori. Even though she fit his mold of what he should have on his arm, the conversations between them were nothing like the conversations he'd once shared with Antoinette. Derrick and his new fiancé always talked about corporate America, and Derrick hadn't realized how tiresome those conversations could be. He missed Antoinette because he knew that she truly loved him. His relationship with Lori seemed more like a partnership with benefits.

On one Wednesday morning, Derrick got the news that he dreaded. His mother was in the hospital, and the doctors said she wouldn't last long. Derrick didn't have any siblings. He was his mother's only child. His dad had died in Vietnam when Derrick was just four years old. His mother had never remarried, and she spent all of her energy and love on Derrick. Immediately, Derrick purchased a plane ticket back to Louisiana. He asked his fiancé to stay behind in Michigan to take care of his house while he was gone, and she agreed.

When Derrick arrived at the hospital, his eyes filled with tears when he saw how tiny his mother had become. She was hooked up to all types of medical equipment, and it was obvious that she wasn't going to last much longer. When Derrick entered the room, his mother opened her eyes and looked at her professionally handsome son. She tried to sit up, but Derrick put his hands on her.

Derrick: No, Mom. Don't move.
Ms. Agnes: Boy, leave me alone! I ain't dead yet! I can still

move. I got plenty of time to be still in my grave.

Derrick: Momma, I'm sorry. I haven't been home in all these years to check on you. Momma, I'm so sorry.

Ms. Agnes: It's okay, baby. You've been busy climbing the corporate ladder.

Derrick: Why didn't you tell me you were sick?

Ms. Agnes: Oh, I'm alright. I didn't want to bother you with my troubles. Your cousin Diana has been taking real good care of me. Where's my Antoinette?

Derrick: Momma, Antoinette and I broke up four years ago. Remember?

Ms. Agnes: You're kidding me. I always knew that girl was too good for you. Where is she now?

Derrick: She came back to Louisiana four years ago. She hasn't called you?

Ms. Agnes: Come to think of it, she did call me a few times. She always checked in on me. I have always loved her like she was my own daughter. Why did you break up with her?

Derrick: It's complicated, Momma. Let's not talk about that right now. Let's talk about you.

Ms. Agnes: I don't want to talk about me! I've been talking about me for seventy-six years now. I want to talk about you and Antoinette. Now, Derrick. Don't tell me you got too big-headed for that girl. Lord, I always knew you'd get too big-headed. Just like your daddy. He got too big-headed for me once too. That was until I set his beloved Buick on fire. That's what humbled him.

Derrick: Momma, you set Daddy's car on fire?

Ms. Agnes: Oh, yes. He got over it though, and you were

born a year later.

While they were still speaking, Antoinette entered the room carrying a bouquet of roses. "I'm here, Ms. Agnes. I heard what happened to you. Are you okay?" Suddenly, Antoinette looked up, and her eyes met Derrick's. Her heart began to flutter, and dread entered her belly. She had hoped that she would never see Derrick again. To be safe, however, she'd left their daughter at home.

Derrick: Hello, Antoinette.
Antoinette: Hi.
Ms. Agnes: Hey, baby! We were just talking about you. How have you and my grandbaby been?

Antoinette's eyes widened. She'd never told Ms. Agnes about having Derrick's baby.

Derrick: Grandbaby?
Antoinette: Ms. Agnes, what are you talking about? What grandbaby?
Ms. Agnes: Oh child, don't play silly with me. I know that's why you've been hiding from the family. I've seen my granddaughter three times in my dreams. She's so pretty. She looks just like you and Derrick.
Antoinette: Um, Ms. Agnes...I don't have...
Ms. Agnes: Don't lie to me baby. Now, the doctors said I'm probably going to die within the next few days, and I'm okay with that. But I want to see my granddaughter one time

before I go. Please don't punish me for what my son did.
Please, baby.
Derrick: Antoinette, do we have a child?

Antoinette's eyes filled with tears. She loved Ms. Agnes, but
she did not want them to know that she'd had Derrick's baby.
Nevertheless, she couldn't let her pass away without seeing
her grandbaby for the first time. Antoinette looked at Derrick
and then at Ms. Agnes, and with her voice trembling, she
said, "I'll go get her." After that, she exited the room, and
Derrick fell into his seat with a look of horror on his face.
Everything was beginning to make sense now. His mind
filled with all types of thoughts. His feelings were all over the
place. Anger welled up inside him as he thought of
Antoinette's deception. Why had she birthed his child and
not told him about it? Why hadn't she told him she was
pregnant? Tears began to stream down his face as he sat in
his seat and let his thoughts overtake him.

Ms. Agnes: Oh, don't you cry now. You're the one who
broke up with that girl and sent her back home like she was
trash. I remember now. I knew she had your baby because
every time I asked her to come to the house, she always
made excuses, and that was not like my Antoinette.
Derrick: Momma, I just can't believe that girl had a baby and
didn't tell me. Why didn't she tell me?
Ms. Agnes: You probably expressed not wanting to have a
baby with her. Did you tell her that?
Derrick: I told her I wasn't ready.

Ms. Agnes: And then you told her that you didn't want her and sent her home. I don't blame her. I wouldn't have told you nothing either!

Derrick: Momma, don't get your blood pressure up.

Ms. Agnes: Baby, I'm okay. I'm just disappointed in you. I'm not mad at her. She did what any mother would do. She was protecting her baby. You don't have a right to be angry with her! You hear me! You don't have the right!

Thirty minutes later, the door opened again, and in came this beautiful little girl holding a teddy bear. With her big brown eyes and cocoa skin, she looked just like a perfect mixture of Derrick and Antoinette. Her long dark hair was pulled back into a long braid. She even resembled her grandmother. Her name was Ivy, and she instantly melted her daddy's heart. Ivy smiled and went directly to her grandmother. Antoinette sat her on the bed, and she hugged her grandmother and then kissed her. "My mommy said that you are my grandmother. You're very pretty. My name is Ivy. What's your name?" Ms. Agnes thanked Ivy and kissed her cheek. Her eyes filled with tears as she beheld her one and only grandchild. "My name is Grandma," she said. Derrick's eyes were fixated on Ivy, but he kept looking at Antoinette. She looked the same, only she'd cut her hair and she'd slimmed down a little; nevertheless, she looked even more beautiful than he'd remembered.

Ivy told her mother that she needed to go to the bathroom, so Antoinette led her into the restroom. Derrick sat in place, still in shock at the day's events. When Antoinette and Ivy emerged from the bathroom, he watched as his beautiful daughter fixed her eyes on him and waved her hand at him. As she attempted to pass by him, Derrick reached out and grabbed her hand. With tears in his eyes, he suddenly hugged his daughter and held her tight. He hugged her so tight that her voice sounded strained when she said, "Mommy, who is this man, and why is he hugging me like he knows me?" Derrick released Ivy and held both of her hands.

Derrick: It appears that I'm your father, Ivy.
Ivy: Mommy? Is this man my daddy?

Antoinette walked over and sat next to Derrick.

Antoinette: Yes, baby. That's your father. I'm so sorry.
Ivy: It's okay, Mommy.

At that, Ivy hugged her father and kissed him on the cheek. "My mommy always told me that you lived in Michigan. Why didn't you come to see me?" she asked. Derrick was relieved that Antoinette hadn't told her anything bad about him. "It's a long story, but I'm here now, and I'll never leave you again." After visiting with his daughter for an hour, Derrick looked at Antoinette. "Can we go somewhere and talk?" he asked. By this time, Antoinette's sister had arrived and was holding Ivy next to Derrick's mother. Antoinette looked at her sister and Ms. Agnes and said, "We'll be right back."

Derrick wanted to go and talk from within his rental car. He wanted to be alone with Antoinette. Once they sat in the car, the two of them remained silent for a few minutes. Finally, Derrick broke the silence.

Derrick: Antoinette, why didn't you tell me that you were pregnant?

Antoinette: I didn't do it to hurt you, Derrick. You always told me that you weren't ready for children yet, and I knew you were tired of me. I'd just found out that I was pregnant the day you asked me to leave. If you remember, we thought I had the flu. It wasn't the flu; I was pregnant with Ivy.

Derrick: And you didn't think that I'd want to know this?

Antoinette: No. Derrick, if I had told you, you would have asked me to get an abortion, and I never wanted to hear those words. How could I tell my child that her daddy asked me to abort her? It's easier for me to tell her that you live in Michigan and let her believe that you wanted her.

Derrick: I never asked you to get an abortion.

Antoinette: But you would have. If you knew I was pregnant, you would have asked me to get an abortion.

Derrick: Okay, you're probably right. But you decided to have the baby, and I'm glad you did. She's absolutely beautiful, but don't you think I would have wanted to be in her life as well?

Antoinette: Derrick, what I did was not about you or me. I was protecting my daughter. You felt that I wasn't smart enough to be with you, and I handled that pain, but I never wanted you to make my daughter feel like she wasn't smart enough. That's my baby, and I could never stand for that.

Derrick: She's my daughter too, Antoinette. I know I was puffed up during that time. I was stupid; I admit that. I was stupid and pompous, and I probably deserve what happened to me.

Antoinette: Probably?

Derrick: Okay, I deserved it. But Antoinette, what we shared was real. I loved you as much as I knew how to love, but that wasn't enough because I didn't have CHRIST in my life at that time. I truly wished you'd told me about Ivy. I've missed three precious years of her life. I've missed those special moments that a dad cherishes. I missed her first words, her first steps; I missed a lot. I didn't get a chance to hear her call me Da-da.

Antoinette: I know and I'm sorry. Like I said, I didn't do this to get back at you or to hurt you. I was protecting my daughter. At least now I can say to her that you never expressed not wanting her. I didn't want to force her on you. Derrick, I never asked you for a dime to help with her. I've never cared about your money. I just want to give my daughter a good life, and I don't need a lot of money to do that. I just have to love her, protect her and teach her about the LORD, and that's what I've been doing. *Sighs.* So, what's next?

Derrick: I would really like to start spending time with her. Antoinette, I don't have any other children. She's my only

child. I can't believe I'm saying this. I have a child. Wow.
Antoinette: Okay. We'll talk more about it, but know this:
The day you hurt my child is the day you'll see me clown.

Derrick reached over and grabbed Antoinette's hand. "I
could never hurt our child," he said. Surprised, Antoinette
removed her hand and opened the car door. "Let's head
back in and check on your mother," she said. "I still don't
know how she knew I had a baby. I never told her that."

Derrick laughed.
Derrick: Obviously, you didn't know mother very well. She
once dreamed that I'd stolen five dollars out of her purse,
and she beat the daylights out of me.
Antoinette: Well, did you?
Derrick: Yep. I was eleven years old, and I was trying to
impress a new girl in our neighborhood, so I stole the money
and went and bought her all the candy she could hold.
When I got back home, Momma came out the door and beat
me like I stole something.
Antoinette: You did steal something.

When they re-entered the hospital room of Derrick's mother,
they were pleased to see Ivy sitting on the bed and singing
to her. Ivy had such a beautiful voice at such a young age.
She was singing her favorite song, and the words melted
Derrick's heart once again. "I give myself away. I give
myself away so You can use me. I give myself away. I give
myself away so You can use me," sang Ivy. Derrick looked

over at Antoinette. He thought to himself that there was no way he would ever let her go again. He was going to do whatever he could to win back Antoinette, and this time, he'd do it the right way.

Derrick's mother lived another nine days before passing away. She was blessed to see her granddaughter every day for those nine days. The day before she left the earth, she looked at Derrick and Antoinette and said, "I'll be gone tomorrow, but I have one favor to ask of the both of you. Take care of my grandbaby, and don't let her see me in that coffin. She's too young to understand. Just tell her that I went to Heaven and I will see her again. Derrick, be a man and take care of your wife. I know you said that y'all never married, but this-here girl is your wife! The season for you to marry was just wrong, but now y'all have to forgive one another and try to make it work. When I get to Heaven, I'm gonna put in a special request for the both of you. Be good to one another. This life on earth ain't that long, but it can be special if you make it special." With that, Derrick and Antoinette cried and held his mother's hands. They both hoped that she was wrong about dying the next day, but Derrick had never witnessed any word his mother spoke falling to the ground.

The next day, Ms. Agnes passed away in her sleep. A few days later, they had her funeral, and the family came together for the reception after the funeral. Derrick was so heartbroken that he couldn't bear being in his mother's house during the reception. Everything still looked put away as if his mother was still there. Some of the family members started questioning where he'd gone, when one of the children there said he'd left crying. Antoinette knew where he'd gone. "I'll be back" she said. "Angel, please watch Ivy for me." Angel agreed, and Antoinette left. She went back to the park where her and Derrick's names were carved on the tree. She knew Derrick had gone there because he said it was the same spot his mother and father used to meet at when they were dating. Even after his father's death, his mother would often return to that spot between the trees where her and Derrick's father's names were still carved in one of the trees not far from Derrick's and Antoinette's name.

When Antoinette went through the opening, she saw Derrick sitting on the ground crying.

Antoinette: She's not here. She's gone to be with the LORD.
Derrick: I know, but if GOD ever let her visit the earth, this is where she'd come.

Antoinette sat on the ground next to Derrick. Derrick asked, "How did you know where to find me?" Antoinette looked at him and didn't speak a word, but he heard the answer loud and clear. "Oh, yeah," said Derrick. "This was our spot too." The two sat there for thirty minutes while Derrick cried. He laid his head on Antoinette's lap and she held him.
Antoinette: It's going to be okay, Derrick. Don't beat

yourself up. Your mother lived a full life, and now she's with the LORD.

Derrick: Antoinette, can I ask you a question?

Antoinette: Sure.

Derrick: Do you still love me?

Antoinette: *Sighs.* Derrick, now's not the right time to discuss feelings.

Derrick: Yes, it is. It's the perfect time, because I need to know. Do you still love me?

Antoinette was quiet for a minute s before answering.

Antoinette: Of course I love you. I will always love you. You were my first love, my fiancé, and the father of my child. How can I not love you?

Derrick: I still love you too. I'm so sorry for what I did to you. I was so stupid.

Antoinette: Derrick, I forgave you before I even left. It's okay. That's over now, and we should just focus on today.

Derrick: Have you ever loved anyone else as much as you loved me?

Antoinette: Why are you asking me these questions, Derrick?

Derrick: Please, just answer the question. I need to know. After our breakup; did you ever love someone else the way you loved me?

Antoinette: Derrick, I never even dated after we broke up. I was too focused on Ivy and school.

Derrick: You haven't dated anyone for four years?

Antoinette: Nope. I'm a mother, Derrick. A mother can't just go out and date random people. I have to focus on Ivy, even if that means I never date or get married. My focus is on GOD and my daughter.

Derrick: That was pretty much the same thing my mother said when she was raising me. A lot of people wanted to know why she never dated again after my father died, but she said that she didn't need any man. She was content with having the LORD and me.

Antoinette: I guess that's why your mother and I got along so well.

Derrick: Antoinette, I know it's pretty tacky of me to be sitting here snotty-nosed and talking to you about us, but I need you to know something. I was a fool to let you go, and I won't rest until I have you in my arms again. I won't rest until you and I are finally married.

Antoinette: Derrick, now is not a good time to discuss this.

Derrick: Yes, it is. There's no such thing as the wrong time to discuss what's right. We have a daughter together, and there's no way I can watch another man raise my daughter.

Antoinette: Don't you have a fiancé back at home?

Derrick: Had. I broke it off with her two days after I arrived here. She got her hands on one of my checkbooks and treated herself to twenty-five thousand dollars of my money. I found out when I went to the bank to take some money out.

Antoinette: You've always been frugal. I bet you knew exactly how much money you had in your account.

Derrick: To the penny. Yeah, I had to do a stop check on that transaction, and I'm filing charges as soon as I get back.

I had one of my colleagues go over there and make sure she was out of my house. He even changed the locks for me. He's a pretty good guy. His name is Jason, and he's Christian. He's the one who helped me to turn my life around. He and his wife Julianne took me into their lives and treated me as if I were their own child.

Antoinette: You gave your life to the LORD? Wow. I know you've been talking about the LORD every day since you got back, but I thought it was just your way of trying to speak my language.

Derrick: Nope. My mother always prayed for me, and of course, you were praying for me. You know, you remind me so much of her. Antoinette, I need you and Ivy in my life. I really do.

Antoinette: Derrick, you hurt me. You really, really hurt me, and I don't want you to hurt my child.

Derrick: How many times do I have to say this? She's my child too. I won't hurt you again. I believe what Momma said. We were meant for one another. We were just trying to make the right thing happen at the wrong time; that's all.

Antoinette: I don't know, Derrick.

Derrick: Do you still love me?

Antoinette: I told you that I do.

Derrick: Then what's the problem? You heard my mother, and she's never wrong. Let's give it one more shot, Antoinette. And this time, let's do it with GOD in the midst. No living together, no fornication, and no kissing until marriage. Can we at least try? You can rest assured that I'll never get the big head again, and if I do, you can set my beloved vehicle on fire.

Antoinette laughed. She truly loved Derrick, and she hadn't imagined her life with any other man. "Okay, we can try," she said. "But only in the LORD. Let's get back to the reception before they think we've eloped." Suddenly, Derrick looked at Antoinette.

Derrick: That's it! We should just elope! Let's run off and get married.
Antoinette: Oh, no. Now, that's going too far, Derrick. Let's just pray on it and wait on the LORD'S answer this time. Don't worry. We don't have to rush things.
Derrick: Okay. I understand, but let me ask you this one question. What if GOD confirms it tomorrow? What if HE says that HE'S in this relationship, and we can marry? How soon would you marry me then?
Antoinette: Let's just see, okay?

Three months later, Derrick and Antoinette got the answer to their prayers. They were married in a small ceremony in Michigan. They flew Derrick and Antoinette's family out to the wedding. They even flew out Antoinette's Pastor to officiate the wedding. Antoinette did not want to live in the old house because of the memories and because Derrick had another woman there, so they sold the house and purchased a new one. Derrick doted on their daughter, and ten months after their wedding, they welcomed their son into the earth. Derrick Swinson, Jr. was every bit of his father's

likeness. From that day on, the couple loved one another as GOD called them to do. Sure, there were disagreements, but their love was always greater than their pride, so no disagreement slept in their house. They always made peace with one another when a disagreement presented itself.
Five years later, they welcomed another son into their family. His name was Tyriq, and he looked more like Antoinette with his big brown eyes, but he had his daddy's smile.

Derrick loved Antoinette because by this time, he'd learned to love the LORD; therefore, he knew the proper way to love his wife. And Derrick always had Ivy to sing to him before she went to bed. Whenever Antoinette told Ivy to prepare for bed, Ivy would always respond with, "Okay, but I have to go and sing Daddy his bedtime song or he won't sleep." The beautiful sound of Ivy's voice could be heard throughout the house singing, "I give myself away. I give myself away, so You can use me. I give myself away. I give myself away, so You can use me."
The End.

There is a quote on the Internet that reads, "A woman's loyalty is tested when the man has nothing. A man's loyalty is tested when he has everything..." (Author Unknown). How true this is! A woman who loves a man will stick by him when he has nothing, but a woman who loves money won't spend time with a broke man unless she thinks he'll have wealth someday. All the same, you can help a man build until he's super-rich, but in the end, if he does not have the

LORD, he will part ways from you...almost guaranteed! Antoinette allowed herself to be used as a helpmate. She set herself up when she allowed herself to be called a girlfriend instead of a wife. What's the big deal? After all, nowadays every guy calls his romantic interest his girlfriend. Nevertheless, search the Bible for the word "girlfriend", and you won't find it. The Bible identifies women as: Maidens (virgins), wives, concubines, whoremongers or widows. All of these other terms that have made their way into our vocabularies aren't actual titles. Girlfriend is not an actual title. It's not even recognized by the law in most states unless you've lived with a guy for five or more years. Even then, it's hard to prove that you are his common law wife. With GOD, however, if the man has not committed himself to the LORD and taken a vow to love you and cover you as your husband, he does not have permission to touch you. If you allow him to do so, you fall under the category of either his wife (illegally), his concubine (when he has several wives), his whore (when you have several husbands) or his widow (if he should die). That's why GOD tells us to seek first the Kingdom of GOD and all of its righteousness. He will then add everything else to us, but of course this is done in due season. If you refuse to wait on your season, you'll end up delaying your progress.

How do you know when it's your season to be found by your spouse? When you don't have to sin to get in. Anytime sin is present, GOD will excuse HIMSELF so that you can find out for yourself that sin does not make a good master. So what was Antoinette's issue? First off, Antoinette should have never lived with Derrick without marrying him. Anytime a man gets husband benefits without being a husband, the chances of him marrying you decrease every day. That's because to men, women are like new cars; they depreciate in value the very minute they are driven. Nevertheless, to husbands, wives are like land; they appreciate if you build the right things on them. That is to say that any relationship not committed or submitted to the LORD will descend over time because GOD did not lift it up. If you want a marriage that works, you must obey GOD entirely. What's the purpose of the wait? Why should you make a man marry you before he beds you? Women date twenty-five or more men on average over the course of their lives. Nowadays, many young people have dated more than twenty-five men before they even finish college. Nevertheless, only one man is going to be your GOD-ordained husband. Everyone else is just an imposter. If you don't wait, you'll end up sleeping with twenty-five or more men while searching for your husband.

Antoinette was obviously not mature enough to be married. How can we draw this conclusion? Because she submitted her body to fornication. It takes knowing the WORD and loving the LORD to truly withhold yourself from a man, especially if you've been sexually active before. That's why GOD said, "If you love me, keep my commandments." It's not religious conviction that will keep you. We know how to shut religious conviction off, and some people know how to drown out the sound of it; nevertheless, love convicts us at such a capacity that we won't feel comfortable doing anything to hurt the person we love. For example, if you are or were married and you loved your husband, you would likely remain faithful to him because you love him. It's funny; we learn how to love and be faithful to men, but the large majority of men and women do not know how to love and be faithful to GOD. Most of the time when we do not love the LORD as we should love HIM, it is because we don't know HIM like we should know HIM. To know HIM, you must know HIS WORD. To know HIS WORD is not just to memorize every scripture in the Bible; it is to believe HIS WORD and establish it as law in your life. You believe that if you ran in front of a moving car, you'd get run over and probably killed, right? Therefore, you have made it a law in your life not to run in front of a moving vehicle. Why did you establish this law? Because of what you believe. GOD wants you to believe HIM, because when you do, you will establish HIS WORD as law in your life. To a baby Christian, the scriptures are nothing more than religious words that tell us how to live...when we feel like it. To a mature GOD-fearing Christian, the scriptures are the very voice of GOD recorded to guide us in life. We must honor and obey HIS WORD, not because we are scared of going to hell, but because we love HIM.

How many times have we been in love with a man and believed every word that fell from his mouth? And when he proved himself to be a liar, like the Bible said he was, we are

493

oftentimes hurt and angry, and we even allow our hearts to become hardened. We often look for behaviors and clues as to how he feels about us. Nevertheless, a <u>man's</u> capacity to love a <u>woman</u> is not enough. He must first love the LORD before he can love not a woman, but <u>his own wife</u>. When a man loves the LORD, his capacity to love is so much greater because GOD lives in his heart. When a man does not know or love the LORD, his capacity to love another human being is dwarfed by his love of himself. Any man who does not have CHRIST will be self-seeking and not worthy of being called a husband. He may do husband-like things and give you some of the biggest smiles you've ever had, but eventually, a dog has to return to its vomit. This means that he will return to what he knows.

Derrick was not the wrong guy; he was the right guy in the wrong season. Derrick was not a bad guy; he was just not ripe yet. I've witnessed men leave women after they (the men) became financially stable enough to choose from a larger audience of women. A godless man who becomes financially stable will oftentimes become spiritually disabled because he will see no need for GOD in his life. *"Like snow in summer or rain in harvest, honor is not fitting for a fool" (Proverbs 26:1).* A lot of women say they want a wealthy man or a man who is a good provider, but what these women don't realize is these types of men have a whole earth of women to choose from in a variety of tongues, races, shades and shapes. Now, if you're found by your GOD-ordained husband in the right season and he's financially stable, you won't have anything to worry about. Nevertheless, if you are found by just another man, don't be surprised when you lose him to just another woman or just another mindset. At the same time, if you are found by your GOD-ordained husband in the wrong season, he won't be any better than a man who is not your GOD-ordained husband. Of course, in Derrick's case, he didn't step outside of Antoinette with another woman; he stepped outside of Antoinette with himself.

I grew up in neighborhoods surrounded by people who believed it was okay to fornicate. I grew up thinking it was okay for a little while because this was the general mentality of the people. One of the things I have witnessed over and over again was seeing women labeled as girlfriends stick with men for years and sometimes decades. They lived with these men; most of them even had their children, but as soon as those men got decent-paying jobs, they began to destroy their relationships. Before long, the men were off in new relationships, while their old girlfriends who'd suffered with them looked for ways to get back at them. Whose fault was that? Can you blame a dog for eating a piece of meat that's within its reach? Sure, many of us came together to bad mouth the men because we didn't know any better. How dare they leave a woman who stuck by and supported them for ten years once they'd finally reached a season where they could pay her back? Nevertheless, the women of GOD need to be educated about the general mindsets of men and how they differ from the mindsets of men of GOD. Television tells us that if we take a broke man and stand by him, when he does find success, he will bless us tremendously for our loyalty. That's a lie from the pits of hell. In most cases, once a man arrives at his successful place, he then arrives at a new mindset; one where his old girlfriend who supported his old mindset is not welcome. The truth is, GOD says to seek first the Kingdom of GOD and all its righteousness! GOD did not say to seek a man first, but when you do get a man before you get to the righteousness, you'll end up being a poor-man's "girlfriend" until he can afford a wife. It's sad to say it that way, but it's the truth. Can we get mad at the men for sinning against us when we are sinning against GOD? No. Sin goes in circles and doesn't stop until it has paid each sinner their due wages. GOD wants you to build up the Kingdom. HE wants you wise so that you'll know the difference between a husband and an imposter. A wise woman has to have an even wiser man.

This story was a love story because the two eventually came back together and made it right; nevertheless, this rarely happens! In most cases, by the time two to four years have passed, both parties would have engaged in one or more relationships where one or more children had been born. Initially, I'd planned for this story to end with them breaking up and never getting back together, but GOD had other plans for this story. The point here is that you can meet the right man at the wrong time and suffer just as much, if not more, pain as a woman who met the wrong man at any given time. This isn't to say to those of you who are still in love with a man from your past that he's the right guy and the season will come around where the two of you will get back together. This is to say that if you stay in GOD'S will, your GOD-ordained husband will find you there. If you get out of GOD'S will, Satan will find you there, and he always has a long line of men who are ready to try you on and toss you back once they've worn you out.

Today, make the commitment to change your mind so that GOD can show you a better life. Don't settle for being anyone's girlfriend. Some women may ask how they should establish a relationship where they can eventually get married, and here are a few pointers that I give to any woman I mentor:

1. If he doesn't love the LORD, he will not and cannot love you with the capacity you deserve to be loved. Don't be unequally yoked with unbelievers, and NO....you cannot save him. You minister to a sinner; you don't date and marry him.
2. Pray about each and every man who attempts to enter your life. Ask GOD to remove every man who is not your GOD-ordained husband and reposition every man who HE sent into your life for other reasons.
3. Do not assume that a man is your husband just because he's cute and GOD-fearing. So many women have met and married religious devils who gave them previews of hell while they were here on earth.
4. Never ever fornicate with a man...ever! If he is your

GOD-ordained husband, he will wait for you, and he will not want to fornicate with you. A man who is not from GOD needs a sin offering; therefore, he requires sex.

5. Never put yourself in the position where you can be tempted to have sex. Let's face it: You're probably not a virgin, which means your flesh may crave sex. If you end up in a man's vehicle on a date, you'll probably end up sleeping with him after the date. Don't worry about being dumped again and again just because you insist on taking your own vehicle. You're supposed to be dumped again and again by the wrong ones until the right one comes along and confirms who you are to him! James 4:7 reads, *"Submit yourselves, then, to God. Resist the devil, and he will flee from you."* This is to say that when you submit to GOD'S will and you resist the devil and every one he sent, the devil is going to get up and run away from you. Would you rather he stick around and put a ring on your finger just because he's cute?

6. Establish a husband hour, and don't allow any man to call you after that hour. It's easy to get "heated" in the flesh when it's late and the two of you are on the phone talking about nothing. Remember that adage: An idle mind is the devil's workshop. For example, friend hours should be from ten in the morning until nine in the evening.

7. Let every man know on the first conversation that you are waiting for your GOD-ordained husband, you do

not believe in premarital sex, and you won't allow yourself to be placed in situations where premarital sex can happen. A lot of times, the Ishmaels won't waste their time with you after that conversation, because Ishmael is a wild man who needs a wild woman.

8. Don't be afraid to let go of the wrong man once you realize that he is the wrong man.

9. When you meet the right man, be sure to stay in GOD'S will so you won't lose him. He's still wrapped in flesh, and he can be tempted. Anytime you sin with a man, you give the devil the keys to your relationship and your life.

10. If the right man breaks it off with you, don't go running into relationship behind relationship trying to teach him a lesson or prove something to yourself and others. Stay put and trust the LORD.

11. When you are a single woman, you need to stay busy in helps ministry. Get into the field and stay there. That's where Boaz will find you. A busy woman doesn't have too much time to think about a man because she's too focused on the LORD. An idle woman has too little time to think about GOD because she's too focused on men.

12. Stay away from ministers who teach you that it's okay to fornicate if you get up and repent. Believe it or not, I had a woman to tell me that she taught this message to the singles who went to her church.

Man-You-Factored

"What looks like a blessing to the unwise is often a lesson in disguise."

Every man that takes a woman as his wife either does so illegally (without the permission of GOD) or legally (with the permission of GOD). Needless to say, a man has to have a woman's permission to be in her life. The issue is: Most men who audition to be in your life are not your GOD-ordained husbands. Instead they are illegal lovers who have scattered their seeds amongst the many women who have given them husband-benefits without the titles. A man who is given the benefits of marriage without actually bringing his bride before the LORD is not GOD-approved. He has learned the language of a liar, often perfecting his skill on lost women who have been abandoned by their previous lovers. He impersonates a good man; he impersonates a blessing; he impersonates a husband; he even impersonates a man of GOD! His lies have to be even better than the men before him because the more lovers that his target has had, the harder her heart is; nevertheless, he comes prepared. All he has to do is get her to lie to herself. She has to psych herself into believing that he is the one she's been waiting for. He has to get her to make him an important factor in her life. He doesn't add value to her life; instead, he takes away from her value; nevertheless, if she believes that he will eventually become the husband she wants, she'll invest into the relationship. After he has robbed her of her trust, her chastity and her self-worth, he will move on to any other woman who will accept his manufactured lies and factor him in as an important asset to her life.

Chelsea worshiped the ground Billy walked on. He was handsome, smart, loving, and he was her husband. She would do almost anything to please him and to keep him. Billy was a firefighter with aspirations of being a model. His Caribbean blue eyes and sandy-colored hair were complimented by his pearly-white teeth and deep dimples. Billy worked hard to stay fit as well. Chelsea was a looker as well, but she felt especially privileged to have Billy. After all, most of the women in her city wanted Billy, but she held the papers to him.

Not only was Billy super-handsome, but he was also a regular church-goer. He often volunteered to help around the church, and he was known for his charitable deeds around the community. He'd once rescued an old woman from a fire, and someone took a flattering photo of him carrying the damsel in distress to safety. Men flocked to him for advice, admiring his strong voice and strong approach to life. His wife was in full submission to him, and the future looked so very bright for him.

One Thursday evening, Billy was at the fire station about to get off work. Chelsea was at home cooking a new dish she felt he'd love. She was also wearing a satin pink gown, and she'd taken the time out to adorn her body with makeup and Billy's favorite fragrance. She'd ran run his bath water and laid his clothing out for him. She wanted him to know that he'd made the right choice in marrying her. Chelsea thought that by going that extra mile, her husband would always be happy and content with her.

Chelsea didn't have a job because Billy made it very clear from the start of their relationship that he did not want his wife to work. He wanted to be the provider, and he wanted his wife to be at home, cooking and taking care of their children. When Billy met Chelsea, she was in college. She finally graduated with a Bachelor's Degree in Accounting; nevertheless, she was content with not working. She did, however, finish school at her mother's urging. After all, when Billy met her, she was in her final year and final semester. She stayed home and made sure that everything was always perfect when Billy came home.

Billy and Chelsea had been married for two years, and they didn't have any children because Billy said he wanted to start buying a house before he became a father. Chelsea reluctantly agreed to this, but her Christian background and beliefs forbade her from taking birth control pills.

Nevertheless, Chelsea got on birth control, and she took her pills faithfully.

Now, it may sound as if Chelsea was at Billy's beck and call, but she was not. Even though she loved Billy, she was often argumentative towards him because she felt that she was giving more than she was receiving. Billy always knew how to calm his raging wife down. He would always go outside and pick a wildflower wherever he found one and bring it in to his wife. He would also apologize for upsetting her, even though he would firmly stand his ground when he felt he was right. His apologies were never for his decisions; he only apologized about his decisions being upsetting to Chelsea.

The food was almost ready, and Billy still wasn't at home. He'd gotten off work more than an hour ago, and Chelsea was starting to become angry. Where was he, and why hadn't he called to say that he would be late? Chelsea went to check her cell phone. Maybe Billy called and she didn't hear her phone, she thought. But that wasn't the case. She called Billy's phone, but there was no answer. Upset, she waited five minutes and then called again. She wanted him to come home while his bath water was still warm and his food was fresh out of the oven; nevertheless, she didn't get through to her husband. She decided to calm down and finish cooking the food. After all, being late and not answering his phone was not out of character for Billy, but something about this day made her stomach turn in knots.

Finally the food was ready, and Chelsea's anger slowly turned into worry. Where was Billy, and why wasn't he answering his phone? And why was she having a dreadful feeling in her stomach? Chelsea went to check the temperature of the bath water, and it was still somewhat warm. While she was in the bathroom, she heard the living room door open. Finally, Billy was home. Chelsea walked into the living room and nothing could have prepared her for what she saw. Billy was standing there with a black eye that was so swollen; it looked as if it had turned inside out. His bottom lip was also swollen, and his hair and clothes were covered in grass. He'd obviously gotten into a fight, and he'd obviously lost the fight. Chelsea ran over to Billy, but he extended his hand to keep her at a distance. "Don't touch me," he said. "I'm fine. I just need to lie down."

Chelsea: Baby, what happened? No. You need to go to the hospital!
Billy: I've already been in the hospital, and I'm fine. I took off the covering they put on my eye because it was irritating my eye, but I'm fine. Please just leave me alone. Please.
Chelsea: Baby, please tell me what happened?
Billy: I forgot to duck. Now, can I please go and lie down?

Chelsea was horrified, but she did not want to continue to pressure her husband with questions. She figured he would tell her what happened to him once he'd settled in.

Chelsea: I ran your bath water and the food is ready.

Billy: Okay. Thank you. I'm not hungry right now though, but I can use a bath.
Chelsea: Okay. Your clothes are already in the bathroom.

Billy went into the bedroom and removed his clothes, then headed into the bathroom to take a bath. Chelsea sat on the couch confused and worried about her husband. Who could intentionally harm such a wonderful pillar of society? Who could disfigure such a beautiful man?

Chelsea went into the kitchen and decided to bring Billy's food into the bedroom. She set up the breakfast tray on the bed and placed the food on the tray. To Chelsea, this was another opportunity to show her unfailing love, loyalty and support. She wanted to nurse her husband back to health. When all was well again, he would appreciate her all the more, she thought. Chelsea walked back into the kitchen to grab a cup and the pitcher of sweet tea she'd made. She almost collided with Billy coming back into the bedroom. Billy looked at the tray table on the bed and then back at his loving and supportive wife.

Billy: Thank you, baby. You've always been there for me when I needed you the most. I know you're probably confused about everything that happened, and I will tell you about it later. Right now, I'm a little upset, and I'm sorry if I'm a little testy. I've obviously had a bad day, and I just want to get some rest. Food is the last thing on my mind right now. Please understand.

Chelsea: It's okay, baby. I'll take it back to the kitchen. I just wanted to make sure that you were okay. It hurts me to see you hurt.

Billy: I know, and that's why I love you. Do me a favor and pray for me; okay?

Chelsea: You know I will, baby.

Billy: Oh and one more thing. Once the swelling goes down on my eye, I'm ready. I'm finally ready.

Chelsea: Ready for what?

Billy: I'm ready to make you a mother. I want you to have my children, Chelsea, and I want to give them to you quick.

Chelsea: Oh wow. I'm ready to give you children too, baby. I know that you will make a great father.

Billy: And I know that you will make a great mother. Let me get some rest. I love you, baby.

Chelsea: I love you too.

Chelsea stood on her tip toes and kissed Billy on his cheek. Billy stopped and looked at his wife, but his swollen mouth made it almost impossible to kiss her back, so he went to bed. Chelsea returned to the kitchen to eat and wash dishes. Afterward, she took her bath and headed into the bedroom to go to sleep. After saying her prayers, Chelsea turned on the lamp on her side of the bed to read her Bible. She leaned over to kiss her husband one more time, but her eyes suddenly caught sight of a bruise on his face that was beginning to turn purple. The bruise was obviously a set of teeth marks. Who'd bitten her husband, and why did they bite him?

The next morning when Chelsea woke up, she noticed that Billy was not in the bed, and the house sounded eerily silent. Chelsea arose from the bed and began to call Billy's name, but he didn't answer. She went throughout the house looking for her husband, but he wasn't there. Finally, she opened the front door and saw that Billy's car was gone. That dreadful feeling came over her again, and she went directly to the gun case. Once she'd opened the case, she noticed that Billy's revolver was gone. Frantic, Chelsea began to call Billy's phone, but he didn't answer any of her calls. What should she do? If she didn't call the police, Billy may be lying somewhere hurt, or he may hurt someone. If she did call the police, and Billy's not hurt, he would be upset with her. Chelsea picked up the phone again and called Billy's cell phone, but this time, she blocked her number. To her surprise, Billy picked up the phone and started screaming.

Billy: Listen you crap ball! I'm standing outside your house right now! Come on outside and be a man this time! Come on and fight me like a man! And tell your wife to stop calling my phone! I've had my fun with your wife, and let me tell you, she hollered like a pig at the slaughter! And you know what...I had her over one hundred times! Last week, I had her in your bed when you were out of town! Are you angry yet?! Come on outside! I'm ready for you this time!
Chelsea: Is that true, Billy?
Billy: Chelsea?
Chelsea: Is it true?

Billy: Why did you block your number, Chelsea?

Chelsea: Is it true, Billy? You're outside some man's house ready to fight him over his wife?

Billy: I will explain it all when I get home.

Chelsea: No. Explain it to me now, Billy. So all this time I've been going above and beyond the call of duty to make you happy, and this is what you've been doing behind my back?

Billy: I have to go. I'll talk with you when I get home.

Billy disconnected the phone line, and Chelsea collapsed to the floor in anguish. The pain was intense, but Chelsea tried to bottle it in. She'd been so good to her husband, and at that moment she realized that it was all for nothing. Chelsea got up off the floor and went into the bathroom. She considered slitting her wrists, but what would that solve? Billy would end up playing the victim and getting tons of remorse. Chelsea decided to hold it in and prepare breakfast for her husband. She went into the kitchen and started Billy's favorite breakfast: egg whites, toast and turkey bacon.

Thirty-minutes later, Billy came home and to his surprise, his wife didn't utter a word. She didn't ask any questions or give him any attitude. It was hard to read the expression on her face because she didn't look angry, nor did her tone sound negative. She spoke as if it were just another day, and this scared Billy.

Chelsea: Your breakfast is ready. Go ahead and wash up

so you can eat.

Billy: Okay. Thanks. Chelsea, don't you think we need to talk about my bruises and today's conversation?

Chelsea: It's not necessary, baby. Let's just enjoy today.

Billy: Oh no. Did you poison my food?

Chelsea looked at Billy, but there was no sign of emotion in her eyes. She took the fork on Billy's plate and shoved some of his food in her mouth so that he could see that it wasn't poisoned. She then gave him an unopened container of orange juice with a glass she'd just rinsed out. Billy was still confused and a little afraid.

Billy: Okay, this is weird. Anyhow, there's this woman named Brandy, and she works over at a bar I drop in from time-to-time. Brandy told me she was having marital problems one day and asked if she could have my phone number just for a little counseling. At first, when she started calling me, everything was good. She told me that she believed her husband was cheating on her, and she asked me for some advice. So anyway, I advised her to pray about it and seek answers from the LORD, but little did I know that she was eying me. Her husband found her phone and some text messages we'd sent to each other, and I guess he took them out of context. The next thing you know, he started calling and threatening me. It turns out she told him a bunch of lies about her and me to make him jealous. She even told him that we'd been having an affair, and I'd slept with her over one hundred times. So after he called me yesterday, I

called her, and I was like, "Brandy....what's going on and why is your husband calling me?" She started telling me all of things she'd told him and saying that she told him all those things to get back at him. I told her...I said, Brandy...I am a happily married Christian man. You can't involve me in your marital problems, but she started crying and telling me that he'd been beating on her and their child. After I straightened her out, she got mad and started saying she was going to tell her husband all kinds of lies about me and her. She even had the nerve to say that she was going to call you with that mess. Can you believe that? Well, yesterday, I stopped by the bar to straighten her out, but I didn't know her husband was there. He snuck up on me and broke a bottle of beer over my head. The next thing I knew, I was on the ground getting punched and kicked by three dudes. The police was called; the guys were arrested, and I ended up in the hospital. All because of a bunch of lies. When you called me private, I thought you were him, and I said all of those things to get under his skin, but they weren't true.
Chelsea: Okay. As long as you're okay; that's what matters.

Billy was surprised at Chelsea's response. So much so that he was afraid to eat, sleep or even get too relaxed around Chelsea. That day ended up being worse than Billy had anticipated because his wife showed no signs of grief, anger or curiosity.

The next day, Billy was off to work again, and Chelsea sent him off the same way she always did. After Billy was gone,

Chelsea went online to burn a little time. She logged onto Facebook and saw that she had an inbox message. The message was from a woman named Brandy! Her profile picture displayed a picture of her with a lollipop in her mouth. She was a pretty woman but obviously very worldly. Chelsea opened the message, and to her surprise, there was a picture of Billy wearing nothing but what looked like an Indian skirt. He was standing in a bedroom obviously waiting on something. Suddenly, another message came through with another photo attached. This time, Brandy was in the photo with Billy. By this time, Billy was sitting on the bed and Brandy was standing in front of him. She was wearing a red bra and panty set, and she had one finger on Billy's mouth as if she were trying to silence him. The final and most heartbreaking photo came through, and this was obviously a photo of a different day. Billy was sitting at Brandy's table, and she was sitting on his lap feeding him. A few more people were in the photo, some of them being Billy's co-workers. Everyone looked so happy, and Billy appeared to be smitten. Nevertheless, even though the photos hurt Chelsea, she didn't respond to the sender, nor did she mention the photos to Billy. She tried to brush them off and focus on saving her marriage. In her mind, she was obviously slacking somewhere, and this caused Billy to go out and have affairs. So Chelsea became even nicer to Billy. She even stopped having those occasional arguments with him. She would always respond, "You're right; I'm wrong, and I'm sorry."

As the months went on, Billy became more and more worried about his wife. She was obviously suppressing her feelings, and he knew this was unhealthy behavior; nevertheless, he didn't know what to do about it. Everything always appeared normal at home, but it didn't feel normal to Billy. Chelsea did everything in her power to keep peace in her home. She read her Bible, she prayed, and she tried to remain a humble wife to her husband.

One day, Chelsea was working on her garden, when a beige Ford Focus pulled up. The vehicle pulled into her driveway and parked. Chelsea looked to see who the two occupants were in the vehicle. Finally, a man got out of the vehicle, but he was focused on the woman in the passenger seat. He was obviously irritated with her and trying to get her to step out of the car, but she refused. The man made his way over to Chelsea as Chelsea stood to her feet. He introduced himself as Brock and said his wife's name was Zoe. Brock's low hair cut, broad shoulders, and even the way he stood up let Chelsea know that he was a military man, more than likely a Marine.

Brock: Hello. My name is Brock, and that's my simple-minded wife in the car, Zoe. Anyhow, is Billy home?
Chelsea: No. Billy's at work? I'll let him know you stopped by.
Brock: You must be his sister.
Chelsea: No. I'm his wife.
Brock: Not possible. No man with a wife as pretty as you

could ever consider cheating on his wife.

Chelsea: Excuse me?

Brock: I'm sorry, ma'am. I'm getting ahead of myself. What I came by to do was to ask Billy face-to-face to stop calling and texting my wife Zoe. You see, I just got back off tour duty in Iran, and I decided to surprise my wife. I didn't tell her I was coming back early. When I got home, I found your husband's vehicle in my driveway. When I went into the house, however, I didn't see him, but I noticed that my back door was open. Thankfully, I managed to get his tag number, and I had an officer friend of mine run a check on the tag, and it came up to Billy Southwell. Of course, with this being a small town and all, I knew who Billy Southwell was. My wife claims that nothing was going on between them until I read some steamy text messages on her phone and even found a half-naked picture from your husband in her text messages. I text messaged him and told him to never contact my wife again, and he's been texting me back and forth for the last hour. I decided to come over here and confront him man-to-man. I don't do text messages like some high school cheerleader. I'm a grown man. Right now, I'm taking that simple-minded woman in the car to see an attorney so we can start the divorce proceedings, but I wanted to see Billy first to ask him if she could stay with him, because she's getting out of my house today!

Chelsea: I'm sorry to hear that. I'll tell Billy you stopped by, and I'll give him the message for you.

Brock: Please do, and ma'am...don't lower yourself for a guy like Billy. He's doing half the married women in town.

Chelsea apologized again to Brock, and he left. She went back to gardening, but she couldn't find peace. Billy was doing half of the married women in town? That would explain why he's always talking to some man's wife, claiming to be advising them. The sweat ran down Chelsea's face as she dug the dirt with the trowel. She didn't realize it, but she was now stabbing the ground with the gardening tool with force. She went back into the house, took a shower, and decided to tell Billy what happened but to remain calm about it.

When Billy got off work, he could feel that the atmosphere in the house wasn't a good one. Nevertheless, Chelsea had cooked one of his favorite dishes, and the couple ate together as if all was well. After Billy finished his supper, Chelsea told him about Brock and Zoe's visitation. Billy was beside himself with fear and anger. He tried to explain Zoe away as just another woman he was trying to help. She was just another woman with an insecure husband. This time, Chelsea wasn't buying his lies; nevertheless, she remained quiet. She'd never really bought into any of his lies; Chelsea was just the type of woman who suppressed everything. Of course, Billy was becoming more and more concerned, even offering to go to couple's counseling with his wife, but Chelsea declined.

The final straw came one day after Billy got off work. It was a Wednesday evening, and Billy had just gone into the bathroom to take his shower. Ordinarily, he would take his phone in the bathroom with him, but because he'd had such a grand day that day, he forgot his phone. He left his phone on the dining room table. Chelsea was putting Billy's supper on the table when the phone started to vibrate. It was an incoming text message. With overwhelming curiosity, Chelsea decided to read the text. She peeped down the hallway and listened closely for any clues that Billy was out of the shower, but he'd just gotten in, so she knew she had about thirty minutes before he got out. Chelsea opened the text message, and it was from a number that was all too familiar to Chelsea. It was one of the women she'd befriended at a Christmas party some years ago. The fire department that Billy worked at had thrown a Christmas party, and one of the firemen came there with his wife, Audrey. The fireman's name was Bryan. Bryan and Billy were close friends, so Chelsea became close friends with Audrey, the fireman's wife. As Chelsea read the text message, every bit of pent up rage began to well up in her. The text message read: *Hey, I tried to call you. He got called in to work tonight. Hope you can come over and put my fire out.*

Chelsea was boiling with fury, but she tried to remain calm. She knew that Billy would see she'd read his text message since it was no longer under new text messages. She decided to text Audrey back. Her text to Audrey read: *Sorry, I got a text message from you, but it was empty. Please resend the message.* Audrey took the bait and resent the message verbatim. Chelsea took a snapshot of the previous message, deleted it and waited for her husband to emerge from the bathroom.

When Billy got out of the shower, his food was on the table ready for him. Chelsea then told Billy that his phone had vibrated. Billy picked up his phone, read the text message and then looked at Chelsea. "Hey. They are a little short-staffed down at the station tonight, and they are asking me if I would come and put a few hours in. I need to run, and I'll be home before sunset. Can you make my plate to go?" Chelsea nodded at her husband and went to prepare his plate for him. She thought about every way imaginable to torture her husband but concluded that the best torture would be to actually confront him at the scene of the crime.

After Billy took his food, he kissed his wife on the cheek and left. Once Billy was gone, Chelsea downloaded the image of the message, enlarged it and printed it. She then waited fifteen minutes and got into her vehicle. She drove down to the fire station and knocked on the back door. Amazingly enough, Bryan came to the door.

Bryan: Hey Chelsea. What are you doing here?
Chelsea: Is Billy here?
Bryan: No. I don't think so.
Chelsea: Okay. I need to show you something.

At that, Chelsea handed the printed document to Bryan. "What's this?" he asked. Chelsea was silent, and Bryan read the text message. Bryan's face turned blood red as he read the message. He then looked at Chelsea and asked her, "Did this message come in tonight?" Chelsea nodded her head. "Okay," said Bryan. Bryan headed back into the station, grabbed his keys, and left. Chelsea trailed him there and pulled in behind him. She could see her husband's vehicle parked on the opposite side of the road. She exited her vehicle and walked in the house with Bryan. The adulterous duo were in the bedroom having their fun with one another. They did not hear the living room door open, but they had no choice but to hear the bedroom door being kicked until it broke from its hinges and fell. When Bryan and Chelsea entered the bedroom, both Billy and Audrey were naked and covering themselves with a bed sheet. The fear sucked the life out of their complexions. Bryan then brandished a hunting knife and attacked Billy viciously. Billy screamed in pain as the knife penetrated his stomach and then sliced through his hands and arms over and over again. Audrey sat there crying and covering herself, begging for her life. Chelsea stood there and watched the attack unfold. Billy pleaded with her for help, but she didn't move. Her face remained emotionless as she watched her husband get brutally attacked. Billy then managed to wrestle the knife out of Bryan's hand and knock Bryan onto the floor. With a small window of escape, Billy muscled his way free from Bryan and then ran to his vehicle. Bryan did not pursue him, however. Instead, he picked up the fallen knife and began to brutally stab his wife. Chelsea called out Bryan's name again and again. She did not want him to kill his wife, but

Bryan continued to punch and slash his wife until the knife broke. He then began to strangle her until her body went limp. With his rage appeased, Bryan then made his way into the living room and sat on the couch, waiting for the police to arrive. He was covered in blood, and his face was stoic. Chelsea went and sat next to him to wait on the police as well.

Meanwhile, Billy sped home to call the police. He'd left his phone in the house while trying to get away, but he managed to grab his keys because he always left them hanging by the front door. As Billy neared his home, he noticed that his street was blocked off, and firemen were standing in front of his blazing house. Chelsea had set their house on fire before leaving. Wounded and naked, Billy stumbled out of the vehicle and ran up to an officer on the scene. The officer immediately began to call an ambulance when he saw Billy approaching him. Billy told him to get some officers out to Bryan's house. He told the officer the address and kept screaming over and over again, "He's killing her! He's killing her! And he's going to kill my wife!" Paramedics covered Billy's naked body and had to wrestle him into the ambulance. He wanted to go back to Bryan's house with the officers, but of course, he needed medical attention, and the officers made sure he got it.

Back at Bryan's house, the officers had arrived and subdued Bryan and Chelsea. They found Bryan's wife in the bedroom, and thankfully she was still alive. She'd played dead so that Bryan could stop strangling her.

Chelsea was charged with arson, and Bryan was charged with two counts of attempted murder. Billy and Audrey recovered from their wounds, but the slashes on Billy's face permanently disfigured him for life. Audrey was able to make a full recovery, and she credited her survival to the LORD. "When I saw my husband attacking Billy, I told the LORD that if HE spared my life, I would turn my life over to HIM and I would never do anything like this again," confessed Audrey as she testified in front of her church one day.

During the trial, the town's people came out in numbers to support both Chelsea and Bryan. Chelsea ended up pleading no contest to the charges. A sympathetic judge gave her time served for the three months she'd spent in jail and placed her on probation. Bryan pleaded not guilty by reason of insanity. Several of the men in town testified about having discovered that Billy had affairs with their wives. Some of the women testified to having had affairs with Billy. The witness who turned the tide was Bryan's now ex-wife. She took the stand in his defense. She said, "The man I saw in that bedroom that night was not my husband. He looked like my husband; he had Bryan's body, but he was not Bryan. I don't want him to go to prison because of something I did. Please. He's suffered enough. I did him wrong, and it woke up something that was in him. I can truly say that I have forgiven him, and I ask the court to forgive him as well. He's such a wonderful man if you know him. He took care of our children with such a passion. He was always helping someone out. He once carried an old lady across the street because she was having trouble crossing it. Yes, what he did was wrong, but it wasn't him that did it. What I saw in his eyes was darkness. My husband wasn't there that night, but his body was. We have two children together, and it would crush them to see their daddy go to prison. At the same time, they have just started the healing process and began to forgive me for destroying our family. Please don't make them go through this process all over again. I don't know if they could survive it one more round. Please find him not guilty. That's all." By the time Audrey was finished speaking, the jury and every soul in that courtroom was in tears. The jury came back with their verdict in less than an hour: not guilty by reason of insanity. The crowd outside cheered as the verdict was read.

As for Billy, he moved away from that town out of humiliation. He never forgave his wife for telling Bryan about him and Audrey. Billy and Chelsea divorced, and Chelsea moved to California to pursue an acting career. She ended up starring in a few Christian films before remarrying and settling down with her movie producer husband. Chelsea had to learn the value of expressing how she felt, and she had to truly accept JESUS CHRIST as her LORD and SAVIOR before she was able to fully heal and be taken as a wife.

Bryan received treatment at a local psych ward before being released less than a year later. He too moved away and

decided to go back to school to become an attorney.
The End.

Now, this was one of those stories that would bother anyone who thinks it should have all happened a different way. Why couldn't the story read that Chelsea confronted her husband, and he repented and eventually turned his life over to the LORD? Why did it have to read that Bryan attempted to take two lives that day? Why had Chelsea set their house on fire? After all, this is a Christian book, right? It should have been nicer. That's the issue with so many believers today. We want to ignore what's really going in the world and just concentrate on all of the good things happening in our lives. Because of this mindset, so many people end up losing their lives. People aren't being told the whole truth a whole lot. Many storytellers feed grown people fairy tales because many people don't handle the truth well. We've become so comfortable with lies that we've lost sight of the truth. Stories like these happen in every state in the United States everyday. But that's not the message here.

What was Chelsea's problem? It's simple; Chelsea made an idol out of Billy. She made a factor of a man she shouldn't have allowed into her life. She worshipped the ground he walked on. She loved him so much that she would do anything for him. She counted herself blessed because of Billy's exterior; nevertheless, she made several attempts to turn a blind eye to his ugly interior. Chelsea kept trying to respond to who she wanted Billy to be, but eventually, she had to confront who Billy really was. Billy was a man who loved to commit adultery against his wife, and he loved the wives of other men. Sure he went to the church, but what does that mean? His fruit displayed the nature of his heart. Billy was an evil man who did a few good things and got attention, not so much for the deeds, but because of how he looked. He fit into the fantasies of most of the women who saw him, including Chelsea.

Billy would seem like a catch to most women. He has a decent job, he's super-handsome, he is a regular church-goer and philanthropist...he was just the epitome of perfection to those who did not know him. He didn't want his wife to work; instead, he insisted on taking care of her. Most of us would melt if a man told us to sit at home and let him take care of us. But here's the thing. Every man who says that is not saying it for the right reasons. Some men are good, and they simply want to provide for their wives, and that's the way GOD designed it to be. But there are some men who do this for self-glorification and to strip the woman of any power she might have. It's sometimes done to keep the wife at bay because a woman who cannot take care of herself will often stay with a man who is mistreating her when she can't afford to leave him. That's why you have to wait on the LORD to send you the husband HE designed for you; otherwise, you will likely end up in the arms of a man who uses your dependency as a power switch. GOD does not want you to depend on anyone but HIM. In addition, don't get caught up in all of the external things. It is better to be in the arms of your average-looking husband who truly loves you and loves the LORD with his whole heart than it is to be in the deceptive grips of some beautiful devil you married who loves himself more than he loves you or the LORD. Any time a woman marries a man who loves himself more than he loves the LORD, he will require that she love him more than she loves the LORD. If she dares not to do so, he will leave her to find a woman who will worship him.

All too often, women marry men who shouldn't have been a factor in their lives in the first place, but just like men, we tend to be visual creatures. We are also creatures with vivid imaginations, so we take what we see and create an imagination of a perfect life with the person in our sights. We consider the people we want in our lives as long-term fixtures who will stick around and be the character we've imagined them to be. We then factor them into our hearts as permanent fixtures; people whom we feel we can't live without. This means that the man you have chosen for yourself is a man-you-factored as important. You weren't supposed to get in a relationship with him, but you did because you created a need for him in your heart, and then you allowed your thoughts to be powered by that need. Even if a man is in church, it doesn't mean that he is in CHRIST. Some people are wolves in sheep's clothing. The Bible warns us about them, but can you resist the wolf when it looks a well-cut-out model? Can you resist the big bad wolf when he makes good money? Answer the questions honestly to yourself, and then pray for deliverance if you know you'd fall in the flesh for the flesh. Remember 2 Corinthians 11:14, and it reads: *"And no marvel; for Satan himself is transformed into an angel of light."* Satan can come to you looking like an angel. Some men can come to you looking like beautiful heroes designed to save you from your dire situation and then turn around and be the very thing you need to be rescued from. There are so many women out there who appear to have the perfect relationships. Every time you see them with their boyfriends or spouses, they are holding hands and smiling. Every Facebook photo of them shows them lovingly embracing one another. If you are easily fooled, you'd think they hit gold in their sin, but they did not. Now, there are some people out there who love the LORD, and you can see their love for their spouses in their eyes, so don't get them mixed up with the fakers. But there are some people who put on a front because it gets them an audience, and they can live vicariously as the characters they pretend to be, even if for but a few minutes. If you believe them and go out and sin your way into a relationship, you'll eventually become their best friends when you share with them how bad your beau is doing you, and they surprise you by telling you how bad their beau is doing them.

Here are some truths that every woman needs to know:

1. **The wrong man can love you; howbeit, in his own capacity.** A man who does not truly love the LORD does not have the capacity to love a wife. He has just enough love left to share with you, but a husband

drenches his wife with his love because he's so full of GOD.

2. **The wrong man can marry you.** Understand that men don't always marry for love, just like all women don't marry for love. Some men marry women because they have stuck by them throughout all of the foolishness they've taken them through. They know they can count on these women to endure every hurt they issue out to them over the course of their marriage. At the same time, some men can marry you because they actually do believe they love you; nevertheless, GOD is love. Therefore, if they don't know and love the LORD, they can't truly know and love you.

3. **The wrong man can do the right things sometimes.** This needs to be showcased in bold red lettering. The wrong man can treat you like a princess and serve you like a queen, but eventually he'll return to his vomit.

4. **The wrong man can say the right things many times. Satan is a liar and he is the author of a lie.** Now, Satan has plenty of children out there; both men and women, and they can lie so well that they start to believe themselves. And here's the funny part. Sometimes a liar thinks he's telling you the truth because he does not know the truth.

5. **The wrong man can look good on your arms.** How many times have we seen the photos of people who look so good together, only to find out that their

relationships needed a facelift? This generation of young adults is very visual, but they are blind. They can't see the truth because they cover their eyes with lovely lies, and they make these lies their truths. Let's face it. You can meet a super-handsome man who looks better than any man you've ever seen, and he can still be an Ishmael!

6. **The wrong man can give you children.** He's got his man parts, and if they work, they will work. There are many men who'd love to toss their seeds at you before fleeing the scene. To them, children are nothing more than another notch on their belts until the child support payments are due. All the same, there are men who will truly believe that they love you, and they'll want to give you their child to seal your relationship with them. Even if a child or multiple children are born to these unions, the strength of the union is tested the same way GOD-ordained marriages are tested. That's when the relationships end and the bitterness begins.

7. **The wrong man can stand up for you.** When we were younger, we were so easily flattered by even the little things. If someone bothers us and our beau sticks up for us, we suddenly feel loved, appreciated and secure. But fighting or standing up for you isn't always a sign that he loves you or that he's the right one. Sometimes, the reasons for standing up are personal and have nothing to do with you. I remember when I was about eighteen years old, and I

called myself having a boyfriend from a nearby state. I was sitting in the living room with my door open when he called one day. While talking to him, one of my friends stopped by who happened to be a guy, and he peered in through the screen door. Like he always did, he referred to me in a profane way jokingly. We would often call each other names because that was our mindset back then, and we thought it was funny. My then boyfriend heard the guy and got upset. He demanded that I hand the phone over to him, and I did. He threatened my friend, and I felt so loved. How dumb was I? That answer came months later when he started threatening me. About two years later, I had a boyfriend who beat up a guy for touching me. I felt so special because at that time, I was super-naive, broken, worldly and lost. What I didn't realize was that he wasn't fighting for me; he was fighting because he had been disrespected. I was nothing more than property that he was claiming.

8. **The wrong man can invest money into a life with you.** Some men get a kick and a boost out of doing nice things for the women they are dating or sleeping with. Just because a man pays a bill for you or buys something for you doesn't mean that he's the right guy or even that he loves you. In many cases, the man is simply renting the woman until he finds a woman worthy buying.

9. **The wrong man can stick around for years, decades and even a lifetime.** A man can love you at

his own capacity, but this isn't enough to make him stick around or even marry you. Nevertheless, when you are the best candidate that he's run into, he can and will stick with you for years, decades and even a lifetime. But if someone else comes along who appears to be a better candidate, you're history.

10. **The wrong man can pray for you.** Every man who prays is not a man of GOD. Every man who prays is not praying to GOD, even though he says HIS Name. Every man who prays is not a perfect fit for you. Some men of GOD can pray for you because they really like you and want you to be their wife; nevertheless, if GOD says no, your yes won't matter.

The next time you meet a guy and he appears to be perfect for you, pray about him. As a matter of fact, pray about every guy who enters your life. If a man tries to get to know you better, always refuse to sin with him, and be sure invite him to church with you often. The quickest way to run off a devil is to start acting like an angel.

The Sin-Finder

"Satan goes about seeking whom he may devour. An ungodly man looks for women he can season with sin and feed to the enemy."

Men are natural hunters. It's how GOD made them. But a Godly man will seek a Godly wife and then seek to know her more over the course of their marriage. He will encourage her in the LORD because he will recognize that the closer his wife is to the LORD, the more she grows and the more there is to discover about her. An ungodly man, however, seeks wives who are awaiting their GOD-sent husbands. His goal is to impersonate the husband; oftentimes by impersonating a man of GOD. After he has nabbed one of these women, he has no problem marrying her. Needless to say, after the marriage he does not seek the good in her, he will begin to seek the sin in her; oftentimes rewarding her when he finds the sin and punishing her when he does not.

"Keep talking! I'll come over there and shove your head through your own door!" shouted Lindsey as she was being lifted and carried back into the apartment she shared with her husband, William. Lindsey was in the middle of yet another shouting match with one of her neighbors, an older woman named Etta Morgan. The two women had argued twice before because Ms. Morgan kept calling the police when William and Lindsey's weekly parties would get too loud. Since then, every time Lindsey saw Ms. Morgan outside of her apartment, she would threaten the elderly widow. William laughed as he carried his wife back into their apartment. He sat her down on the couch, smiled at her, and said, "You're a wild woman. Try to calm down sometimes, baby. Don't go over there and beat the old woman up. She already got one leg in the grave!" Lindsey smirked and rolled her eyes. "Well, I'm gonna help her get the other one in there if she keeps messing with me!" Lindsey's voice sounded serious but comical. Charged up by his wife's latest behavior, William looked at his wife and smiled. "I know what you need to calm you down," he said. "Any time my baby starts getting rambunctious, it means I've been neglecting her."

Lindsey was so happy to see her husband pleased with her behavior. This was a far cry from the way he'd acted at the beginning of their marriage. Having been raised in the church, Lindsey was initially a very respectable woman with aspirations of starting her own ministry. But she met and fell in love with William because of his non-traditional approach to life and his rebellious attitude. William didn't mind going to church, but to William, the church had to play by his rules. In the beginning of their marriage, they'd argued a lot because William wanted to surround Lindsey with men and women she ordinarily wouldn't associate with. He wanted to play music that Lindsey ordinarily didn't listen to, and he wanted Lindsey to have a few alcoholic drinks with him from time to time. After Lindsey had put up some resistance, William would punish her by sleeping on the couch, refusing to speak with her and emotionally starving her of affection. But Lindsey noticed that when she'd gotten upset and cursed William out once, he responded positively. He said, "Oh, there she is. My baby knows she can be feisty when she gets upset. Yes ma'am; I'm sorry." After that, Lindsey found herself cursing more and sinning more because William would always reward her with good days when she did. It wasn't long before Lindsey completed her transition from being a GOD-fearing woman to a William-fearing woman. She feared losing William. She feared upsetting William, and she feared disappointing him. *"There is difference also between a wife and a virgin. The unmarried woman careth for the things of the Lord, that she may be holy both in body and in spirit: but she that is married careth for the things of the world, how she may please her husband"* *(1 Corinthians 7:34).* Nowadays, Lindsey was a cursing, drinking and partying woman who went to church when she felt like going. She had the husband, the house and the three children she'd always wanted. Sure, she had to make some adjustments to her life's plan, but she did, and she was comfortable with her new life.

Saturday nights were party nights at the Hanover household. A few of William and Lindsey's friends would come over, and they'd drink and dance the night away. The couple had just moved into their new apartment a few months ago, only to discover that the residents at Brooklyn Heights Apartments were nothing like the residents at the apartments they'd moved from. Not only had Mrs. Morgan called the police on the couple a few times, some of the residents had confronted the couple about their loud parties.

One day, Lindsey got the news that her father had just passed away. Lindsey was hurt and upset. Why hadn't anyone told her that he was sick? After all, he lived just thirty-five minutes away; she could have easily visited him. Lindsey's father was a man of GOD. He'd raised his family in the church, and he lived a life of fear towards GOD so that his family could see the benefits of serving the LORD. Of his eight children, only two had strayed away from the truth. His younger son had starting hanging around a bad crowd and gotten addicted to crack cocaine some seven years ago; nevertheless, he'd surrendered his life back to the LORD and gotten off the drugs. He was now a minister, husband, father and community activist. As soon as he'd started getting clean, Lindsey met William, and she started down the wrong path. Her father, brother and family members tried to intervene, but Lindsey threw some harsh words at them, moved away, and changed her number. She hadn't talked with her family members for six years, and William felt especially honored that she would defend him and his lifestyle to the point where she'd abandoned her family. Now, some six years later, a cousin of Lindsey's had found her on Facebook and told her about her father's death.

Disgusted that her family hadn't reached out to her to let her know that her father was sick, Lindsey told her cousin that she would not be attending his funeral.

That night, Lindsey found herself thinking about her childhood and all of the wise things her father used to say to her. She remembered how he would carry her in his arms, and how he loved to sneak up on her and scare her anytime she got lost in her imaginations. One particular memory stood out the most. It was the one where Lindsey was just seventeen years old, and at her mother's urging, her father had finally given her permission to date. Her first date was a boy named Carlos Nichols. Carlos was an all-around bad boy, but he was the most popular guy at school. When Carlos came to the house to pick Lindsey up, her father took her into another room and said to her, "Now, Lindsey. I understand that you're young, and that's why I don't want you dating, but I'm only giving in because your mother is on my back about it. The type of men you bring home reflects a lot on your mental age and maturity. It's very obvious to me that you are not mature enough to date; otherwise, you wouldn't bring a rebel into your family's home. You've got little sisters who look up to you, and let me tell you this...those types of men aren't interested in loving you. They are interested in seeing how much fun you can be to them. Their whole world centers around themselves. You're nothing more than another notch on his belt; another diamond to sparkle in his earring. I know you think you can make a decent man of him, but know this: You don't have the power to change a man, because GOD gave him the power of will, and he can choose to be whatever he wants to be. That boy chose to be the way he is. It's up to you, however, to decide if he gets to be self-seeking, disrespectful and arrogant in your life. Choose wisely. Even though GOD will and does forgive us for our sins when we confess them and repent of them, the consequences of our choices will sometimes continue to haunt us for the rest of our lives."

Lindsey's eyes watered as she reminisced of that conversation and the many conversations she'd had with her father. Suddenly, she was feeling regretful about having abandoned him. He had always been her hero, and no matter what she'd done, he was always there to encourage his daughter in the LORD. Now he was gone, and she didn't have another opportunity to tell him that she loved and appreciated him. All the same, he'd never even met his grandchildren because Lindsey had walked away from him and the family when her relationship with William was still new.

While Lindsey mourned her father, William found himself becoming more and more aggravated by her. He wanted to have a great evening. He was hoping to invite some people over and party all night long, but now he had to deal with a grieving wife who was sitting in his apartment grieving a man who didn't even like him. William's thoughts upset him all the more; nevertheless, he managed to remain calm. He went into the other room and stayed on the computer all night long. He came to check on his wife one time, pretending to be supportive, but in truth, William didn't care that Lindsey's father was dead. Lindsey's children stayed away from her as well. She had twin sons named Marquise and Marq, who were five-years-old. Her three-year-old daughter's name was Lina. After William explained to the boys why their mother was grieving, they both became upset with her for crying about a man who didn't like their father. Lina always followed the lead of her brothers; therefore, she didn't go to check on her mother either.

Over the next few days, Lindsey found herself having a change of heart. There was no way she could miss her father's funeral. She'd already missed the last six years of his life on earth, and she didn't want to bury his body without seeing it one last time. She'd also noticed that her family remained distant from her for those few days. She'd taken off work using her bereavement time, and no one seemed to be speaking to her. No one but Lina, and even Lina would become distant when in the presence of her father and brothers. Lindsey felt hurt and betrayed by her family, so she decided to confront William and tell him about her plans.

William was sitting in the living room reading a book to Lina when Lindsey interrupted.

Lindsey: William, can I speak with you for a minute?
William: Sure. What's up?
Lindsey: Alone, please. I just put the children's food at the

table. Take Lina into the dining room so she can eat with her brothers, please.

Lina: Can he PLEASE finish reading me the book first?

Lindsey: Lina, go into the dining room and eat...now!

Lina rolled her eyes at her mother and scooted off her father's lap. She headed into the dining room and began to eat with her brothers.

Lindsey: What's wrong with you and the kids? My father died, and I've been grieving, but it feels like I'm being punished for grieving my father.

William: Nobody's punishing you, Lindsey. The kids are just upset that you would cry over a man that hated their father...that's all.

Lindsey: He wasn't just a man; he was my father. And how would they know how he felt about you unless you told them?

William: Well, I told them because they are old enough to understand right from wrong.

Lindsey: Okay, and please help me to understand what I did wrong.

William: Lina, I planned to have a great week with you and the kids, but you have been moping around the house for the last few days. How do you expect everyone to act?

Lindsey: Supportive. That's what I expect. My dad did not hate you. He just didn't like your lifestyle, that's all. And no matter what he did, he was still my dad!

William: Oh, so you are going to stand here in my apartment and defend the man?

Lindsey: Your apartment? William, you're not even working! That little unemployment check isn't even enough to pay the light bill. Your last job was a part-time minimum wage job that you managed to keep for what, six months? So spare me the talk about "your" apartment.

William: See, I knew this was going to happen. As soon as your family comes barging into our lives, you start defending them and tearing down your own family. I will move out of "your" apartment tomorrow since it's "yours"!

Lindsey: William, that's not even fair! I'm grieving my father right now, and all you can do is think about yourself?! You're turning my kids against me because I have the nerve to love my daddy in your presence?! You need to calm down and rethink what you're doing. You can't destroy this family over something so trivial.

William: I'm not destroying this family. You are. And what's next? You're going to end up telling me that you want to go to his funeral?

Lindsey: Why not?! He's my father!

William: That's it. I'm leaving.

Lindsey: What?! You're leaving me because I want to go to my father's funeral?

William: No, I'm leaving you because you're being stupid and tearing this family apart. I'll be back tomorrow to get the rest of my things.

At that, William grabbed his keys and left. His sons sat in the kitchen looking at their mom with anger in their eyes.

Lina, on the other hand, was more sympathetic towards her mother. She saw that her mother was crying, and couldn't bare the sight of her crying. She came and hugged her mother, trying to comfort her, but Lindsey was overcome with hurt. She'd just lost her father, and here it was that her husband was threatening to leave her as well.

After Lindsey managed to calm down, she made sure the children did their homework, bathed, brushed their teeth and went to bed. Her thoughts were all over the place. She knew that if she did not go to her father's funeral, William would forgive her and come home. If she did go to her father's funeral, William would probably never come back. Her father's funeral was in two days, so she had two days to make her final decision.

Suddenly, there was a knock on the door. Lindsey thought it was William, but why would William be knocking? Maybe he was trying to be obvious in his attempts to show that he now viewed the apartment as "her" apartment. When Lindsey looked out of the peephole, however, she did not recognize the woman standing in the doorway. Once she opened the door, she saw the old woman who lived next door standing off to her left pulling the arm of the angry woman standing in front of Lindsey. The woman was about Lindsey's age, and she'd obviously come ready for a fight. A few feet back was a tall man leaning against a tree.

Samira: Excuse me. Are you the woman who's been

threatening my elderly mother?

Ms. Morgan: Yep. That's her, but Samira, just leave it alone. Let's go and let the LORD handle this.

Lindsey: I haven't threatened her. I just yelled at her.

Samira: Oh, so telling her that you are going to shove her head through her own door isn't a threat?!

Lindsey: Look, I don't have time for this right now. My father just died, and I'm just not in the mood.

Ms. Morgan: Samira, let's just go. Leave it alone!

Samira: How can I have empathy for her dead father when she doesn't even respect my living mother?! Excuse me. I don't know what your name is, but if you even lay a finger on my mother, I'm gonna come over here and make you taste the leather in my shoes!

Ms. Morgan: Samira! Stop and let's go!

Samira: If you even threaten my mother again, I'm going to jail. My mother has been living here for eight years with no problem! I moved her over here because this was a safe, quiet area, but ever since you and your husband moved in, there is no peace over here! My momma is too old to be fighting you, but rest assured...I don't mind! And I got something for your husband too!

Lindsey: Listen, don't come to my door threatening me! I don't know who you are, but I'm not the one!

Samira: What are you going to do? I'm right here in front of your door, and I'm not going to trade words with you for long. Like I said: Keep the peace over here and leave my momma alone! Because if I have to come back through here one more time, I'm not going to say a word! It's going to be you, me and these leather boots!

After saying what she had to say, the woman walked away, and Lindsey stood in the doorway staring as she entered her mother's apartment being pulled on by her mother. Suddenly, the man leaning against the tree spoke up and said, "Tell your husband the same goes for him. We don't play about our mother!" Lindsey closed her door, fearing what could happen next. Here these two people were defending their mother, and she'd abandoned her father; a father who was only trying to protect her. Lindsey sat on the couch and began to cry. She cried all night long until she fell asleep on the couch.

The next morning, Lindsey got up and got her children ready for school. It was now Friday, and her father's funeral would be the next day. William still hadn't come home, however. Lindsey fed the children and took them to school. Once back at home, she tried to reach her husband again and again, but he'd turned his cell phone off. That's when it dawned on Lindsey. If she gave in to William's desire, she would never forgive herself. It was hard enough dealing with the fact that she'd abandoned her father for six years, but she couldn't bear the thought of missing his funeral. William would just have to self-soothe.

Lindsey spent that day preparing her clothes and her children's clothes for the funeral. All day, William did not call, nor did he come home. When the children came home, the twins were still upset with their mother, and this hurt Lindsey to her soul. Here it was that her own children were against her because of their father. She suddenly realized that she'd been against her own father because of their father. She was suddenly made aware of the pain she'd caused her father. Lindsey cried, but she wouldn't back down. She scolded her sons for mistreating her, and she told them that they would be going to their grandfather's funeral the next day, whether they liked it or not. Marquise began to cry because he felt like his mother was running his dad out of their lives. Lindsey spoke with him, but he wouldn't understand anything she said. He was being just as unreasonable as she'd once been to her own father.

The next day, Lindsey arose early to prepare the children and herself for the funeral. She'd been in touch with her cousin on Facebook and gotten the location and time of the funeral. Right when she was about to leave, William suddenly came into the house. He saw that his wife and children were dressed to go to the funeral. That's the reason he'd come home. He wanted to make sure that Lindsey did not take their children.

William: So, I guess you're still going?

Lindsey: Yes, I am.

William: Well, you can go, but the children are staying here with me.

Lindsey: William, why are you giving me such a hard time? Don't you think you're being insensitive?!

William: You can shut up and do what you want, but my children are not going to that funeral. That's that!
Lindsey: They are going, and I suggest that you get out of our way. I don't want to be late for my own father's funeral!

William was about to speak, when suddenly there was a knock on the door. He opened the door, and there stood a police officer who began to read William his rights. It turned out that William had been involved in a hit-and-run accident the night before over on Cleveland Street. When the officer said that he'd hit a car on Cleveland Street, Lindsey's eyes grew big. Cleveland Street was where one of William's old mistresses lived. She was even more upset to hear the details of the accident. He was trying to back out of the woman's driveway when he accidentally hit a parked police car sitting on the other side of the road. Instead of stopping, William had taken off, but some bystanders were able to get his license plate number as he drove away. Lindsey thought the mistress, whose name was Annetta, had been old news. After all, the affair had taken place three years prior to this incident, and for three years, she hadn't heard Annetta's name or even suspected that he was still seeing her. Humbled, William began to plea with his wife to come down to the station to bail him out. He promised her that it was all a misunderstanding, and that he would explain the details to her once she'd bailed him out. Lindsey looked at her husband and said, "No. I'm going to my father's funeral. I will deal with you when I get back." The children cried as they watched their father being led away in handcuffs;

nevertheless, Lindsey was determined to see her father one last time. She loaded the children into the car and headed to the church.

Lindsey's family was so elated to see her. Her mother had aged, but she still looked the same. She hugged her daughter and cried, not letting go of her daughter for more than five minutes. Her father still looked the same, however. It was as if he hadn't aged. Lindsey apologized to her family, and they all loved on one another. The children were able to see their grandfather's body, and the children were relieved to meet their family. The family wasn't as bad as their dad had told them they were.

While at church, the pastor gave a powerful sermon. It was a sermon that Lindsey felt hit close to home. She knew then that she had to return to the LORD. She recommitted her life to CHRIST at her father's funeral. There wasn't a dry eye in sight as Lindsey rededicated her life to the LORD. When everyone saw little Lina go to the altar, they were really overtaken with joy. "I want JESUS too," she told the pastor. "Do you think HE wants me?" Everyone's eyes filled with tears and some people even awed when they heard the question. "Of course JESUS wants you," said the pastor. "HE loves you and HE has always loved you. No matter what happens, HE will always continue to love you." Lina smiled and said, "Okay. I love HIM too." Marq finally got up and approached the altar. When Marquise saw that his brother was heading to the altar, he too got out of his seat and approached the altar.

Later that day, Lindsey's family showed her and the children pictures of Lindsey growing up and pictures of Lindsey's father over the years they'd missed. With teary eyes, Lindsey said to her mother (Hilda), "I hate myself for abandoning him. Why was I so stupid? He never even got a chance to see his own grandchildren." Lindsey's mother grabbed her hand, smiled, and said to her, "He saw his grandchildren, baby. You know your dad wasn't technically savvy, but he was determined to see you and the grandchildren, so he opened up a Facebook account under another name and sent you a friend request. He would log on every day to see your posts and look at pictures of the children. He even spoke to you many times on there."

Lindsey: What? What's his name on Facebook?
Hilda: Pastors Promise.
Lindsey: What? That's Daddy? Pastors Promise is Daddy?! He used to always comment on my posts and every picture I put up of the children. We even stayed in contact via inbox. He was like a personal counselor to me. I even told him that he was like a father figure to me. Oh my goodness! That was Daddy?!

Lindsey's voice quivered and her eyes filled with tears as her mother told her of how excited her dad was after every conversation he had with her. He kept fathering her even when she'd walked away from him. Lindsey told her family that she would never go away from them again. Her children even loved the family. She ended up staying the night at her family's place before returning home.

On Sunday evening, Lindsey returned home. She knew that William was still in jail because he'd been arrested on a Friday. He would likely be arraigned and released on Monday. Lindsey prepared herself emotionally for his wrath, because she knew he would do everything in his power to hurt her once he got out.

Monday evening, William came home, but he was too afraid to be angry with his wife. After all, he'd been caught at his mistress's house, and he didn't want to end up losing Lindsey. Lindsey questioned her husband, and of course, he told lies behind lies to cover up his deeds. He didn't; however, bother her about having gone to her father's funeral because he was too afraid of upsetting her. With her new-found dedication to the LORD and the rekindling of her relationship with her family, it was only a matter of time before William left Lindsey. Nine months later, he moved out because Lindsey no longer wanted to have parties; she'd stopped cursing, and she'd started going to church. She was now teaching her children about the LORD, and the new Lindsey was a turn-off to William. After getting hired at a factory in a nearby city, William moved out of the house, abandoning his wife and children to live a sinful life.

When William moved out, Lindsey didn't feel the hurt most women feel when losing a husband. Instead, she felt relieved. She felt so relieved that she logged onto Facebook and went to Pastors Promise's page and inboxed him a message. "Hey Dad. It's me again. I wanted to tell you that I love you, and it finally happened the way you said it would happen. I remember one day you told me that if I served the LORD with my whole heart, the devil would get up and run away from me. He finally did, and I am so thankful. William left yesterday, and the house feels so much more peaceful without him. I didn't realize just how evil that man was. I wish I'd listened to you, Daddy, but like Momma told me...I can't beat myself up because you wouldn't like that. You know; she's doing good now too. I'm going to be moving back to the city in about a month, and we'll be staying with Momma for a while. I'll take real good care of her for you. Your grandchildren love and adore her. The twins ask about her every day and when I told them we were moving in with her, they danced all over this apartment. Thank you for teaching me about the LORD. I wish you could write me back, but I'm going to ask the LORD to make sure you get this message. Hopefully, HE will let you respond and send the message to me through an angel. I love you, Daddy, and I will write you again soon. P.S.: I was looking through my page one day, and I found an old post of mine that you'd responded to. In the post, I was ranting and complaining about how much it had been raining lately. I said that I wished the rain would stop, and you responded by saying, "The rain comes to help things grow. Without the rain, the sunshine would kill us. Without the rain, there would be no winds. Without the rain, nothing would grow." You then said, "Some people believe that the rain is the teardrops of the angels. They cry because of the ways of mankind, but more than that, they cry so that we can live." Daddy, I believe that you are with them now, and since it's raining outside today, I am going outside without an umbrella, and I'm going to enjoy the rain. I love you, and if you cry, be sure your tears fall on me. I love you."

The End.

What happened to Lindsey is actually very common. An ungodly man will always try to take you away from your first love. He envies the relationship you have with the LORD, and he will not allow you to put GOD before him. An ungodly man will always feed the sin in you and starve you of affection when you try to be a Godly woman. Even if he met you in the church, he will still not be happy with you being a woman after GOD'S heart. He wants a woman who will serve his lusts, his devils, and his ideas of what a wife is and what a wife does.

Lindsey didn't realize it, but she came to a crossroads where she was given the opportunity to make a choice. She would have had to sacrifice her relationship with William to stay in the LORD, or she had to sacrifice her relationship with the LORD and her earthly family to follow after William. She chose William, and William proved to her that an ungodly man never makes for a good husband. It doesn't matter how good you are to an ungodly man, he will remain ungodly unless he chooses to submit himself to the LORD. Women often complain that they've done everything for the men in their lives, and no matter what they did, those men did not reciprocate their love, honesty and loyalty. What these women fail to realize is that these men failed to reciprocate GOD'S love, honesty and loyalty far before they'd met them. A man who is not loyal to GOD is always loyal to the enemy. Even in choosing William, Lindsey found out that no amount of love from her could make William be a good man to her. As women, we often think that if we are faithful and loving to our spouses, they will be loving and faithful to us, but this just does not happen with an ungodly man. Ungodly men tend to have entitlement complexes. They oftentimes believe that you're good to them because you're supposed to be good to them; nevertheless, they aren't good to you because they deserve to be good to themselves. William found in Lindsey a woman who was willing to give it all up to be with him, and of course to him that meant she deserved his hand in marriage. Why is this hard to grasp for many women? When you tolerate a bad man, he just might marry you just because you're one in a million to him. The women before you tossed him like a cigarette butt at a biker's convention, but you stuck around throughout all the garbage he took you through. Because of that, he figured you could live in the funk he called life.

You'll find a lot of married women who have husbands like that. Anytime these women act sinfully, their husbands reward them and shower them with attention, affection and gifts. When these women act Godly, their husbands punish them by becoming verbally, emotionally and sometimes even physically abusive towards them. An ungodly man's greatest weapon is his love or what we believe to be his love. He will give and withdraw his love at the drop of a hat because he's learned over time that women don't function well in environments where they feel unloved, ignored and unappreciated. He knows that by withdrawing himself, he could run his wife to the brink of insanity. He could then lay out the terms for her of what she needs to do to get back in his good grace. These women can't have too many conversations about the LORD with their husbands. They can't tell their husbands how much they love the LORD. They can't talk too much about what the LORD has done for them in front of their husbands. Instead, they have to engage in fleshly conversations with and around their husbands in order to keep their interest.

When Leslie experienced her own children turning on her, she began to understand how much she'd hurt her father by turning on him. Another lesson here is how much we hurt our FATHER in Heaven when we turn on HIM for men. We actually turn on the Creator for the created! How dumb is that? That's like killing the only hen alive to get to the eggs. It's a cycle that we all go through. We betray the FATHER to get to a man, and that man betrays us to get to someone or something else. It's a cycle that can only be stopped when we learn to be loyal daughters to our FATHER in Heaven. That's when we will be found by loyal, Godly men. In the meantime, we shouldn't even think about dating because we will always attract what we are. If we are not loyal, we will attract unfaithful, unreliable and untrustworthy men. That's when we'll sit up and complain about how good we've been to a man and how bad he did us in return. Doesn't GOD have the right to establish that same complaint against us? Look at how good HE'S been to us, and how disloyal we've been to HIM in return. Then, we have the nerves to complain when someone comes along and treats us like we treat the FATHER. You have to see it that way so that you can get the lessons from what you've been through, grow from them and don't repeat the errors.

Know this: You can go out there and get yourself any man you want. GOD gave you free will. But don't let the devil lie and tell you that you can get the man first, take him to church, and he'll finally change to become that GOD-fearing rebel that you want. Rebels aren't GOD-fearing, and GOD-fearing men aren't rebels. You can't find a perfect mixture of sin and sainthood and call it your husband. If you go out there and get an ungodly man, you're going to have to be an ungodly woman to keep him. In most cases, you'll eventually lose him when you start rededicating your life to the LORD. Isn't it better to just wait and get it right the first time than it is to enter bad relationships that end in pain, only to still have that wait in front of you? Either way you choose, you will still have to wait.

Your Godly husband will lead you further in the LORD; an ungodly man will lead you further away from HIM. Take your own personal stand for righteousness and wait on GOD. If you do, you will end up being a rare jewel, and rare jewels can only be afforded by the men GOD has enriched. This means that an uncommon woman will end up with an uncommon man, and every other woman will stand in awe. Sure, people may laugh at you initially. They'll scoff at you for waiting, talk about you, and spread lies about you. They will flaunt their men in your face and try to get you to believe that they found a blessing in their sin, and they are nothing but liars in disguise! There are no blessings in sin! Believe me...I searched sin high and low looking, but anytime you enter sin, you'll come out with a sinner. Anytime you enter dark places, you'll come out with blind men who want to lead you. *"And he spake a parable unto them, Can the blind lead the blind? Shall they not both fall into the ditch?" (Luke 6:39).*

Demotion For Promotion

"A treasure isn't valuable because it's pretty. It's valuable because it's rare."

Because of sin, man's perception of life, direction and GOD has been perverted. Oftentimes what we see as good is really evil. What we see as love is really hatred, envy, strife or obsession. What we see as elevation is actually demotion. What we see as an attack is oftentimes a chastening. What we call intelligence is actually foolishness to GOD. Our perception has been clouded, and we now fly through life upside down, praying against what we should be praying for; opposing people we should be supporting, and judging people we should be encouraging. This is why we NEED the WORD of GOD to get us through this life; otherwise, lack of knowledge, ignorance, and deception will cost us the freedom that CHRIST has availed to us.

"Spatial disorientation is a condition in which an aircraft pilot's perception of direction does not agree with reality" (Reference: Wikipedia.org).

I remember watching a show on television about plane crashes. A pilot had crashed a plane and killed everyone on it. They believe, based on the black box's recordings, that he was suffering from spatial disorientation. When his plane began to descend, he thought he was actually ascending, so he pressed the accelerator and crashed the plane. The copilot warned him, but he would not listen.

This is similar to how sin has perverted man. Oftentimes, we are heading in the wrong direction, but as long as we've got religion and supporters, we will continue to fly upside down, thinking that we're going up when we're really going down.

"Excuse me. Where did you get those shoes from?" asked a voice coming from behind Mikayla. Mikayla was walking through the mall, heading towards the exit. She was running late for church, and this wouldn't be so bad if she wasn't the pastor. Mikayla turned around and saw the petite young woman standing behind her. The young woman was beautiful; nevertheless, she appeared to be wearing gray contact lenses and a long curly wig, and her arms were covered in tattoos. "I got them from Pete's Shoes. Do you know where Pete's is located?" asked Mikayla. "They are a new store, and they've got some really cute shoes." The young woman's face remained serious; nevertheless, her tone was friendly. "Thank you. Yes, I know where Pete's is." After Mikayla and the young woman parted ways, Mikayla couldn't help but think about the girl who appeared to be a lost soul. If only she knew how much GOD loves her, she would probably come out of hiding and show the world how beautiful she really is, thought Mikayla.

As Mikayla exited the mall, she saw the girl again, and she was leaving the mall as well. As the girl exited the door, Mikayla watched as she stopped another woman. Was she just walking around stopping people? What was her story? Mikayla walked towards her car, pushing her way through the cold, heavy winds that were pushing against her. It was mid-November, and the pre-effects of winter had hit Annapolis, Maryland, without mercy.

Once in her car, Mikayla let out a long sigh. It was so cold, and she was eager to feel the car's heater. After starting the car and adjusting the temperature controls, Mikayla began her long drive to the church. Her church was located in Dover, Delaware, which was about an hour and a half drive from Annapolis.

Mikayla loved the long drives because the drives gave her time to think and unwind. During this particular drive, however, her mind went back to the girl she'd met in the mall. What would make a beautiful woman want to be who she is not? What would make her covet another woman's gray eyes, long hair and naturally rosy cheeks? What would make a woman want to cover herself with tattoos? What kind of hurt had this girl endured? Mikayla was a little disappointed in herself as she began to think how she wished she'd stopped and ministered to the girl. The opportunity was there, but she had been in such a rush that she blew it.

While Mikayla was parking, her phone suddenly rang. It was her husband Walter, and he was calling from the house phone. This disappointed Mikayla because Walter was supposed to be at the church as well.

Mikayla: Hello. Why are you at home?
Walter: Why shouldn't I be at home?
Mikayla: We have Bible Study tonight, Walter!
Walter: Since when did we start having Bible Study on Tuesday?
Mikayla: What do you mean on Tuesday? Today is Wednesday.
Walter: Mikayla, check your phone. Today is Tuesday. Don't tell me you are at the church right now.
Mikayla: Oh my goodness. Yes, I am. I just pulled in. I was wondering why the parking lot was empty. I thought today was Wednesday.
Walter: Yeah, that's why I was calling you. I was wondering where you were. When you left the house, I thought you were going to the mall and back. I just looked at the clock and realized that you've been gone for three hours. That's why I started to get worried.
Mikayla: I'm sorry. That job has been overworking me, and I've been trying to clean out the church building. I'm praying

hard that they go ahead and approve us for that new building.

Walter: It's okay. Where are you now?

Mikayla: Dover...at the church. I told you that already.

Walter: Oh well. I guess I'd better go and get me something to eat then. I was over here dreaming about your chicken casserole.

Mikayla: Tell Jessica to cook some casserole for you. I taught her how to cook it, and sometimes I think she makes it better than me.

Walter: No thank you. She's mad at me because I told her that she was too young to date, so I don't think it's a good idea to have her cook anything right now. She's in her room right now pouting.

Mikayla: I'll talk to her when I get home. Let me let you go. This traffic is heavy, and I need to stay focused.

Walter: Okay. Love you.

Mikayla: Love you too. Bye.

Walter: Bye.

After hanging up, Mikayla started the long drive back towards her house. Even though she was somewhat disappointed for getting her days mixed up, she was happy for the opportunity to enjoy another long drive. During these drives, Mikayla would visit her thoughts, pray and listen to music.

After Mikayla arrived home, Walter told her that her job had just called before she came in. It turned out that Mikayla was supposed to work that day, but she had been a no-call, no-show. This was the second time she'd forgotten to go to work. Panicked, Mikayla called her job and told them she was on her way. She still had two hours left on her shift, so Mikayla decided to go in, tell the truth and humbly apologize to her manager.

Once at work, Mikayla was summoned to the manager's office where she was promptly terminated from her job. Her manager brought up the previous time that she'd forgotten to come to work and another two times where she had been tardy, all within a six month span. Mikayla tried to reason with her manager, but she was unmovable. Wrought, Mikayla left and drove home in tears. She prayed and prayed about her manager, because she felt that the woman was letting the enemy use her.

Later that day, a friend of Mikayla's called to tell Mikayla about a problem she had been having with one of her sisters. Her friend's name was Deena, and Deena was also a pastor who lived in a nearby city. Deena was bothered by the fact that her sister's daughter was pregnant. Her sister's daughter was fifteen years old, and they'd just found out that she was pregnant. Deena felt like her sister (Dawn) was responsible for her daughter's pregnancy because of her sister's past. When Dawn was younger and first had her daughter, she had been a wild woman. As a matter of fact, when Dawn was pregnant with Kia, she wasn't sure who Kia's father was. After Kia was born, her mother had a string of relationships that all ended badly. Dawn didn't give her life to the LORD until Kia was twelve years old; nevertheless, Deena felt that Kia's pregnancy was Dawn's fault. If only Dawn had let Deena raise Kia like she'd asked her, none of this would have happened...at least that's what Deena believed. While speaking, Mikayla sympathized with her friend and agreed with her wholeheartedly. She then told Deena about the events of her day. The two women stayed on the phone for more than an hour, and before hanging up, they decided to come against the works of the enemy. After all, he had to be attacking them....right?

Deena also had a daughter, but she was thirteen years old, and her name was Kesha. Kesha was Deena's only daughter, and she made sure she raised Kesha in the church. Kesha was an honor roll student, and she always exceeded in everything she did. To Deena, Kesha was proof that she was a good mother.

After hanging up the phone line, Mikayla and her husband decided to go to bed. While asleep, Mikayla began to dream. In her dream, she was walking around an empty warehouse that was full of boxes. In each box, there were pillows of a different color. As Mikayla looked at the labels, she noticed that each box was being shipped to the same address. Some of the boxes were big and some were small. Some of the pillows were beautiful, and some were not-so-nice to look at; nevertheless, every box was being shipped to the same address. There stood one lone box, however, and it was sealed shut. Out of curiosity, Mikayla grabbed a box cutter sitting nearby and opened the box. Inside the box were four different but extremely pretty pillows, and each pillow had a label on it; howbeit, on each label was a different address. This didn't make sense to Mikayla, so she looked at the label on the box. The label on the box showed a different address than the labels on the pillows, and the address was different than the other boxes that were in that warehouse. What did this mean?

Suddenly, Mikayla woke up. She sat up in her bed and tried to figure out what the dream meant. She came up with several possibilities, but none of them could explain the foreign box with four different pillows in it. Baffled, she told Walter about her dream, but he couldn't interpret it either. Walter was in the bathroom, brushing his teeth and getting ready for work. After speaking with him, Mikayla decided to make breakfast for him and the children. She wanted to make her family's favorite breakfast, so she made Eggs Benedict and strawberry fruit smoothies. With three teenagers in her house, Mikayla knew that she had to make sure she made plenty for the family. Mikayla had two sons: eighteen-year-old Sterling and seventeen-year-old Dwayne. Her one and only daughter was fifteen years old, and her name was Sharise.

When the breakfast was ready, everyone loaded into the kitchen to retrieve their food, but no one showed any signs of joy. Everyone seemed rushed and unconnected. Mikayla was bothered by her family's behavior. What was wrong with them? Why had they all gotten their food to go? Why hadn't anyone thanked her for the wonderful breakfast, and why hadn't anyone kissed her goodbye? She decided to call her daughter's cell phone after she left.

Mikayla: Sharise, is there something wrong with you and your brothers?

Sharise: What do you mean? What did we do wrong?

Mikayla: Y'all didn't sit down to eat, nor did you kiss me goodbye when you left.

Sharise: What's new, Mom? You never cook breakfast and you never see us off, so what do you expect?

Mikayla: Sharise, you know I have been working to make a better life for you and your brothers. It's not that I didn't want to be around you guys; I was gone because I was working.

Sharise: No problem. The next time you make breakfast, we'll all get together and write you a thank you letter.

Mikayla: What?

Sharise: Love you, Mom. I'm at school now. Gotta go.

At that, Sharise hung up the phone. Still bothered, Mikayla decided to call her husband's cell phone.

Mikayla: Walter, what's going on?

Walter: What do you mean, Mikayla?

Mikayla: Neither you nor the kids took the time out to eat your breakfast at home, and you didn't thank me for the breakfast. A little appreciation would have been appreciated.

Walter: Mikayla, it's been about three years since we sat down and ate breakfast, or haven't you noticed?
Mikayla: Three years?
Walter: Yeah. Where have you been? The twilight zone?
Mikayla: I guess I was getting up too early to go to work and then church, so I wasn't aware of that.
Walter: Yeah. There are a lot of things you are unaware of.
Mikayla: What does that mean?
Walter: We'll talk later. I'm at work now, standing in front of the time clock. Gotta go.

At that, Walter hung up the phone, and Mikayla was even more confused. What had she missed, and why was her family so disconnected from her? Mikayla decided to go to the grocery store to purchase something to cook later that day. While at the grocery store, she saw a little boy lying on the floor crying. He was about six years old, and his desperate mother didn't seem to know what to do. She tried to pick him up, but he kept screaming and crying. Mikayla thought to herself what she would do to that little boy if he were her son. She shook her head in disgust as she passed by the now-emotional mother. She had actually sat on the floor with her son and started crying. She was cradling him and trying to calm him down. "What's this generation coming to?" Mikayla said under her breath. "The new generation of parents are awful."

When Mikayla was checking out her groceries, she could still see and hear the little boy screaming and crying. The cashier looked over at the woman who was now carrying her screaming son and said, "It's really sad."

Mikayla: Yeah. If he were my son, I would give him something to cry about. That's what's wrong with these children today. Too many of the parents are trying to be their friends to the point that they forgot discipline is an important part of parenting.
Cashier: No. The mother works here. Her husband was in the military, and they just found out that he was killed in Afghanistan yesterday. The store collected money for her, and she came by to pick it up. Her son is actually well-behaved; he's just grieving.

Mikayla felt awful. She'd judged this scene, and it wasn't as it appeared. A son had just lost his father, and she'd judged the situation without knowing it.

As she was walking out of the store, she got another call from her friend Deena. This time, Deena was crying and speaking a little too fast for Mikayla to understand.

Mikayla: Deena, I don't understand what you are saying. Calm down and tell me what is wrong. Take a deep breath and calm down.
Deena: Okay....okay. It's Kesha.
Mikayla: Deena, what happened to Kesha?!
Deena: Nothing. Do you remember that I told you that Dawn's daughter Kia was pregnant?

Mikayla: Yeah.

Deena: Well, the story is starting to unfold now. I let Kesha go to a birthday party last month at a classmate's house. It was a sleep over, and the parents had assured me that there would be no boys there; only girls. I still wasn't too comfortable since I didn't know the parents, so I asked Dawn if Kia could go with Kesha to the party. At first, Dawn was against it, but I talked her into letting Kia go. I felt that because Kia was older, she would help keep Kesha in check. Well, I got a call a few minutes ago that some boy had been arrested. It turns out that he was at the party and he raped Kia. She didn't have sex with him after all. He raped her, and that's how she got pregnant!

Mikayla: Oh, I am so sorry! Deena, I am so sorry. Is she okay?

Deena: Yeah, but guess what else? From the news I'm getting back now, Kesha was drinking at the party, and she apparently had sex with that guy's friend. The guy who raped Kia thought that Kia was going to put out because she was with Kesha, and Kesha had put out. Now the school nurse is telling me that my baby might be pregnant as well! Mikayla, she is only thirteen years old! Thirteen!

Mikayla: Deena, calm down until you get the whole story. It might be some kind of mix-up. Where are you now?

Deena: I'm on my way to the school to pick up Kia and Kesha. One of the ladies at the school suggested that I take them to see some girl who counsels and ministers to young girls who are sexually active and rebellious.

Mikayla: The school actually recommended a minister to

you?

Deena: No. The secretary suggested it. She said she knew the girl, and the girl had helped her daughter out when her daughter became pregnant. She called the girl for me, and she was in her office and available. She does the work for free, so I'm on my way. Her office is about three blocks away from your house.

Mikayla: Okay. I can meet you there. What's the address?

Deena: I'll text it to you when we hang up. I need to go now.

After they hung up, Mikayla headed over to the office to meet Deena. When she arrived at the office building, she saw Deena's car parked, and Deena and the girls were still in the car. Deena was talking to the girls, but when they saw Mikayla, they pointed to her, and everyone started to exit the vehicle. They walked up to this building that had a lot of doors. They were looking for Suite B1, and they finally found it. They knocked on the door, and a few seconds later, a woman came to the door and opened it. The first thing Mikayla saw was the woman's arms. They were covered in tattoos. Mikayla's eyes finally met the woman's eyes. She was the woman from the mall! The very woman that Mikayla thought was a lost soul. The young woman's name was Diamone, and she looked to be only about twenty-one years old.

Diamone: Hey! I know you! Didn't I see you yesterday at the mall?

Mikayla: Yeah! Oh wow! How are you? You asked me

about some shoes I was wearing, right?
Diamone: Yep! Small world we live in.

The woman ministered to both Kia and Kesha, and Mikayla was surprised to hear her story. Diamone was twenty-six years old, and she was a former sex abuse victim. She had been molested by her father since she was four years old; she had been abandoned by her mother at six years old, and she'd lived a life of pain, heartache, betrayal...and finally, CHRIST. She talked about how her pain had led her down a dark road. At fourteen years old, she'd started selling her body for money. At sixteen years old, she began to get tattoos on her body to represent every man she'd slept with. It was her way of keeping a record. Her eyes were naturally gray, and she happened to like wigs. Mikayla felt horrible. She'd prejudged this woman! She'd seen the exterior of the woman and judged her as lost without first knowing the heart of the woman underneath the rough exterior or her story. Mikayla confessed to the woman that she'd prejudged her and felt pretty bad. "It's okay," said Diamone. "You're not the first person, and you won't be the last to do so. The good thing is you recognize that you made a mistake, so you probably will think twice before passing judgment next time. I get that almost everywhere I go. I've had people trying to minister to me every time I walk into a conference, a new church or go anywhere near leaders. I have to explain to them that I am a pastor too. That's why I don't regret my bad upbringing. It forced me to get to know people from their hearts and not from their exteriors. Where I'm from, you'd better know the heart of a man if you want to survive. That's why GOD sent me to the girls I minister to. There are so many people who wouldn't give them a second look. They'd judge them as lost causes, and they wouldn't even try to help these girls. Instead, they are too busy helping the sheep who are not lost. But it's good that you got a chance to see me and hear my story. If it changed your perception, it also changed how you will minister to those who look like me. After all, they can be saved. They just need people who love them enough to reach into what they don't understand to pull these girls out."

After the meeting, Mikayla was amazed at what she'd found out. It turned out that Kesha (Deena's daughter) had been having sex since she was twelve years old, but before the rape, Kia had been a virgin. Both she and Deena had judged Kesha as the good one and Kia as the bad one. They both felt horrible, and they both apologized to Kia again and again.

Mikayla went home and decided to speak with her own daughter. After all, Sharise was fifteen years old, and she wanted to make sure that her daughter wasn't sexually active. When Sharise arrived home, Mikayla spoke with her and was hurt to learn that Sharise was sexually active and had been sexually active for a year. She was also hurt to find out that Sharise had tried marijuana a few times, she'd gotten drunk a few times, and was now trying out a relationship with a girl. She also learned some hurtful things about her sons.

Mikayla talked with her children, prayed for them, and decided to spend more time focusing on the hinges that were loose in her own house, rather than trying to fix what looked broken in someone else's house. She learned to not be judgmental of others and to look at the fruit of a person and not their exterior. Not long after that, she got the call she'd been waiting for. She'd been approved for the loan to get the new church building, and she was excited. With her new lessons, she became a better minister, and she became a better shepherd.

She was also given revelation about the dream she'd had. All of the boxes were different sizes and the pillows inside each box were different colors, shapes and sizes; nevertheless, they were going to the same place. That is to say that many of GOD'S children are different. We come in a variety of shapes, colors, sizes and backgrounds; nevertheless, we are all headed towards the same Heaven. The one box that was sitting alone, however, was heading towards a different place, but there were four pillows inside that lone box. Each pillow had a different address on it. This represented the individuals who think they are going one place, but are all headed in the same direction....towards the fiery pits of hell. Even though they looked like the pillows in the other boxes; their destinations were not the same.

Over the years, Mikayla was help able to guide every one of

her children back to CHRIST.
The End.

One of the problems that's common in the church today is that a lot of leaders are pastoring the sheep they know, but they won't go out looking for the lost sheep. So many leaders walk about in the flesh, looking at the exterior of a person and not the heart of that person. You will find that some of the people with the roughest exteriors have a heart for GOD underneath all that's visible. They were once dark souls, lost in the ocean of sin, but GOD called them out. If you talk with many of them, you will find that it took a peculiar leader to reach them because so many church leaders were too afraid to minister to them. They didn't give them too much attention because they secretly wanted these people to get out of their churches. They wanted nothing to do with anyone who looked dangerous, and they missed many beautiful opportunities to win souls for CHRIST. That's why GOD has started cleaning up so many people who were once prostitutes, drug addicts, drug dealers, gang members and every rough character under the sun, and HE has started sending them out to get the sheep that other people were afraid to approach. Some of the most powerful leaders today are the ones who have come from some of the roughest backgrounds, and their stories are without boredom. Many of them could write books and create movies on the things that happened to them and shame any Hollywood motion picture on the market. *"But their scribes and Pharisees murmured against his disciples, saying, Why*

*do ye eat and drink with publicans and sinners? And Jesus
answering said unto them, They that are whole need not a
physician; but they that are sick. I came not to call the
righteous, but sinners to repentance" (Luke 5:30-32).*
What happened to Mikayla? In trying to find the lost souls,
she'd become lost herself when she started walking after the
flesh and leaning to her own understanding. She'd prayed to
get into another church, but any time we pray for something,
we have to complete a course of learning so that we can
embrace the new knowledge GOD has availed to us. Before
Mikayla could be promoted, she had to be demoted...at least
by her own view. You see, what Mikayla saw as an attack
was her being prepared to walk into the realm of answered
prayers. She'd prayed for a new church building, and she
lost her job. Maybe GOD wanted her to minister full-time to
HIS people. When she thought she was confused about the
days, the truth was that she was just positioned in the right
place at the right time to get new understanding. She forgot
her work schedule because she was on GOD'S schedule.
Oftentimes what we see as opposition is actually us being
positioned for our blessings. But because we think up is
down and down is up, we cry wolf and try to stop what we
perceive as an attack. The real attack is oftentimes us being
judgmental.

Deena had also judged her sister and her sister's daughter
because she measured herself as a better mother today
than her sister was yesterday. She hadn't realized that her
daughter was sexually active, whereas her sister's daughter

was not. She'd gotten raped and had become pregnant as a result of the rape. She then learned that her daughter was possibly pregnant from consensual sex. What's the message here? Never ever judge another person or their children. *"For with what judgment ye judge, ye shall be judged: and with what measure ye mete, it shall be measured to you again"* *(Matthew 7:2).*

When I was a young girl, all the way up until I was a teenager, I remember knowing people who were very judgmental of me and my siblings. Some of them would even scold my mother for letting me wear makeup at the age of sixteen or for other privileges I had that they felt I shouldn't have had. I was upset because, even though my parents were strict, they were beginning to let me stretch my legs a little as a teen, but I didn't have as much leg room as most teens. Anyhow, I remember sitting by and listening to one woman scold my mother about how she was raising me. My mom decided to stop taking us over to her house, and not too long after that, we started getting news that her children were having children...and they were younger than we were! Another individual accused me of being pregnant when I was just entering puberty. She'd drawn a conclusion in her mind about me because I was sick, and she told my mother and everyone who would listen that I was pregnant, promiscuous, and would probably catch HIV by the time I was thirteen. I wasn't sexually active; I was being molested. Over the years, I listened to that woman accuse me again and again of being who I was not, but of course, she paid no attention to what was going on with her own daughter. I even had a neighbor who just did not like me because I wasn't in church. She would often tell me that she's going to take me to church with her, and I agreed. This woman spent three to four days a week in church, but she couldn't reach a lost soul because she was too busy judging when she should have been ministering. Her children ended up further in the world than I was.

What's the point of these stories? At a very young age, I had a thirst and a hunger for CHRIST, but I was lost. Many people who judged me missed the opportunity to lead me back to the LORD. Instead, they ridiculed me, gossiped about me and waited for me to fail. They spoke word curses over me; curses that would never take root because of the GOD who called them liars! And every one of their children fell into the same pit they'd dug for me with their words. So the message is...GOD needs ministers, not judges. HE is the only Judge; nevertheless, we were given the right to judge the church, not the world! Sometimes, children can get lost, but all they need is someone to minister to them and show them the way back to the LORD. Like I said, if anyone had come along and invited me to church with them, I would have happily gone. I was so impressionable, and I wanted GOD so much, but I didn't know how to find HIM. I didn't know how to serve HIM, and I thought HE didn't want to hear from me because of how bad I'd been. After all, that's what I kept hearing again and again.

I'm thankful all of that happened, because it taught me not to judge people. I think everyone needs to get that lesson. Do I judge people? Sometimes I may see someone and draw a conclusion, but I always repent of it, and I make an extra effort to speak to that person or maybe hold a conversation with that person. What I have witnessed is that in doing so, I have found that many people I would have thought were lost were not lost. There are two stories that I like to share with people, and the first one happened in a check-out line at Wal-Mart one day. There was a woman standing in front of me, and she looked like she was a woman of GOD. The way she was dressed and her whole demeanor made me think she was GOD-fearing. She kept looking back at me grinning, and finally, I greeted her and said something about the weather. She smiled, opened her mouth, and started cursing up a storm. She was so calm and relaxed, and she felt comfortable cursing the weather out to me.

Then there was the time when I was at the mall with my husband, and we saw a man covered in tattoos. He had tattoos all over his body, including all up his neck. I thought he was a racist because his head was shaved, and he looked like my perception of a racist. He was trying on shoes, and I decided to greet him but stay away from him. He then started telling my husband and I how comfortable some shoes were, and that they were on clearance. Before I knew it, he started talking about his love for JESUS CHRIST and what church he went to. I had to learn to stop letting my eyes tell my understanding what to believe. In order to minister to GOD'S people, you have to preach with your eyes shut and listen with your heart. I have met so many lost sheep who were hungry for CHRIST, and heard many horror stories of how they'd been judged by the traditional church folks. It's pathetic, because many of the lost are still lost, while many churches are having concerts, not revivals. That's why so many people are navigating life upside down, and so many leaders are flying downward, but they think they are ascending. *"Not every one that saith unto me, Lord, Lord, shall enter into the kingdom of heaven; but he that doeth the will of my Father which is in heaven. Many will say to me in that day, Lord, Lord, have we not prophesied in thy name? and in thy name have cast out devils? and in thy name done many wonderful works? And then will I profess unto them, I never knew you: depart from me, ye that work iniquity"* (Matthew 7:21-23).

Finally, always make sure that your home is in order before you complain about the disorder of someone else's home. Until we get this understanding and stop acting like the Pharisees and the Sadducees, we will keep getting the same results. Sure, you have to teach against sin, but remember: the sinner is not the sin. The assignment is to get the sinner to renounce the sin and to teach them to submit their bodies as living sacrifices to GOD. You demonstrate this through love. No, you don't hang out with the lost; you minister to them. You don't allow your children to hang around the lost; you teach them to minister to them, love them and not to judge them. A child who is being judged oftentimes knows that he or she is being judged, and this does nothing to help

576

them; it only diminishes their self-esteem, and it helps to usher them towards the devil.

Remember, what you see as up is sometimes down; what you see as good is sometimes bad, and what you see as love is sometimes hatred in disguise.

"But God hath chosen the foolish things of the world to confound the wise; and God hath chosen the weak things of the world to confound the things which are mighty; And base things of the world, and things which are despised, hath God chosen, yea, and things which are not, to bring to nought things that are: That no flesh should glory in his presence" (1 Corinthians 1:27-29).

Spiritual Pedophile

"You can't raise a man of GOD."

This corrupt flesh of ours keeps getting us in trouble. We see this beautiful man standing before us, and we would love for him to be our man of GOD. The problem is he's just a man. He hasn't graduated to being a man of GOD yet. Many times, he hasn't even enrolled in the classes; nevertheless, he looks too good to let by. He flirts with us, and our minds go in every direction they can go in. We want him, and we want him bad; so what do we turn to? In most cases, we turn to our imaginations. In our imaginations, he becomes this strong and loving soul who's been hurt, betrayed, misunderstood and under-appreciated. Then we come in with our love, and we remain faithful to him; we understand him, and we appreciate him because we see the value in who he is. Every woman before us had to be three shades of crazy to let him go. In our imaginations, he will rescue us from every hurt, void and danger around us. That is, until we end up saying, "I do" to a man who has grown up naturally, but spiritually, he's still a baby. Many times, he hasn't even been born again yet. A mature woman of GOD who takes a babe in CHRIST or a man who has not been born again is a spiritual pedophile.

Dorothy found herself getting lost in Julian's eyes as they danced the night away in her back yard. Dorothy met Julian at a Run for Cancer event, and the two of them hit it off immediately. After a little flirting, Julian had finally asked Dorothy out on a date, and she happily accepted. On their first date, they'd gone to dinner and a movie. Now, they were on their second date at her house. They'd just enjoyed a candlelight dinner in the backyard, and now they were dancing the night away. Dorothy was a woman of GOD. She knew the truth, and she spoke of GOD in almost every sentence she uttered. She served on the ministry team at her church, and often volunteered around the community to help out with charitable projects. Julian was not a man of GOD. He believed that GOD existed; nevertheless, he only attended church on what he saw as religious holidays. He was very much community-oriented, however, often loaning himself to the various charitable events that were held in his city. To Dorothy, this was enough. He loved people, so obviously, that made him a Christian...right?

The date was very romantic, and the couple found themselves losing track of time as they danced and kissed one another. When Julian tried to take the kissing a step further, Dorothy pulled back. "I'm a Christian," she said. "I don't believe in sex before marriage." Her words killed Julian's mood. How could she stand there and kiss him the way she was kissing him, and then refuse to finish off what she'd started? Noticing the shift in Julian's mood, Dorothy invited him into the house, where she started telling him why she believed what she believed. She asked Julian if he knew what fornication truly was and what it would do to a human being who engaged in it. Julian did not answer her. Instead, he looked at his watch and excused himself from the date. Dorothy never heard from him again.

A few months later, another man was eying Dorothy. His name was George, and he sat in the church with his eyes fixed on Dorothy. The pastor was preaching, the people were praising, and everyone was happy; nevertheless, George wasn't caught up in the joy of it all. He saw the very thing that made his heart leap, and that was Dorothy.

George came to church every Sunday, and so did Dorothy. They were both faithful service attenders, and they were both single. Dorothy had never really paid too much attention to George, even though she could feel his eyes on her every Sunday. Dorothy did find George to be a handsome man; nevertheless, she went to church to praise the LORD and congregate with other believers. She never saw the church as a meeting ground for couples.

Dorothy was a professional photographer, and George knew this. So one day, he decided to schedule a photo session with her. After church service, George approached Dorothy.

George: Excuse me, beautiful woman. I don't mean to bother you, but is it true that you are a photographer?

Dorothy: Oh, hey George. Of course. You know that.

George: I wasn't sure. I want to see about scheduling a photo session with you for my business portfolio. Is there a number I can reach you at?

Dorothy: Sure, let me get my business card for you. Here it is. Call the number on the back of the card. The number on the front is an old number.

George: Will do. What are your business hours?

Dorothy: You can call me anytime between eight o'clock in the morning until around ten o'clock in the evening on any day of the week.

George: Ten o'clock? Won't your husband be upset with you getting calls that late?

Dorothy: Funny, George. Just call the number on the card when you're ready.

George: Okay. Will do.

Dorothy knew that George was attracted to her; nevertheless, she wasn't sure if he was in a relationship with someone else or not. At the same time, George was relatively new to the church. He'd only been attending Wakefield New Covenant Ministries for a little over three months, and Dorothy didn't know what to make of him. All the same, it felt great to be pursued.

Two days later, on a Tuesday morning, Dorothy received a call from George. Dorothy was awake, preparing to go out and photograph a couple, when she received George's call. He wanted to schedule a photo session for the next day, and Dorothy had one opening at three o'clock the following evening. Truthfully, this was George's way of asking Dorothy on a date; one that he knew she would accept.

The next day, George came to Dorothy's studio dressed in all white attire. Dorothy couldn't help but to take notice of how handsome he looked. His low hair cut and perfectly trimmed goatee framed his oval face with perfection. Dorothy found herself getting swept away in her thoughts. What if he was the husband she'd been waiting for? What if his pursuit of her was GOD-ordained? She danced with her thoughts, hoping against hope that George's new membership at her church was arranged by GOD. All the same, there was a feeling in her spirit that she did not like. There was an uneasiness in her about George, but Dorothy managed to convince herself that this uneasiness was just butterflies in her stomach.

While at the studio, George waited for Dorothy to finish the session she was doing with a newlywed couple. He admired Dorothy's style and how involved she was with her clients. George sat on a stool near the door and watched the session until it was complete. He was truly impressed with Dorothy's work and her professionalism.

After the couple left, George walked over to Dorothy while she was transferring the new photos onto her computer.

George: Hi.
Dorothy: Hey, George. How are you?
George: I'm great. I didn't know you were such a good photographer. If I had known, I would have called you a long time ago.
Dorothy: Thanks. I love photography. I guess that's why I put my heart into it.
George: Great. Well, I can't wait to see how you take a plain guy like me and make him look great.
Dorothy: You look good on your own, George. You already know that.
George: Wow. Thanks. I learned something new today.
Dorothy: Sure you did.

The session turned out to be a complete success. George was a man full of jokes, and he kept Dorothy laughing throughout the session. He was also very photogenic.

After the session was over, George began to flirt with Dorothy even more. He asked to take her out on a date, and at first, she was a little reluctant to accept. After a few more jokes, however, Dorothy accepted George's invitation to go out the following Friday evening. On Friday, the date went well, and the couple continued to date for a year.

While Dorothy was dating George, she wanted to keep their relationship private and away from the ears of the church because George was not where she was spiritually. She realized that he was a babe in CHRIST, and she felt like no one would understand their relationship. George also wanted the relationship to remain private, but for very different reasons. George tried on many occasions to seduce Dorothy into having sex with him, but she refused. She was determined to remain celibate until marriage, and that she did. George's failed attempts made him a little more determined to have Dorothy as his wife, and two years after they'd started dating, they were married in a small ceremony at Dorothy's grandmother's house.

The marriage started off well. George doted on his new wife, often buying her roses, cards, balloons and other gifts of endearment. One of the issues that Dorothy noticed right away was that George was on the perverted side of thinking. He wanted forbidden sex, and he seemed to be addicted to sex. At first, Dorothy thought it was just a newlywed phase, but six months into their marriage; she realized that George's mind, and his day-to-day thoughts, were consumed with anything sexual. Another issue she had was that George slowly began to pull out of church. He started speaking reproachfully about the pastor of that church, and he seemed to go from being a babe in CHRIST to being an unbeliever. George's lifestyle reflected that he was a man of the world, and he wanted nothing to do with the church.

Dorothy became more and more worried about her marriage. She knew that being unequally yoked was forbidden by GOD. She knew that a house divided would not stand. She knew that George's ways would eventually cost them their marriage, so she started having in-home Bible study with her husband. This would be a great idea for married couples who both wanted the WORD, but George resented Dorothy's attempts to disciple him. He also resented her attempts to minister to him every time he did or said something she considered to be evil. Slowly, George's feelings for his wife began to fade. She became more of a pest to him as he witnessed what he felt was her attempt to mother and pastor him.

It was a typical Thursday afternoon, and the couple had now been married for two years. George was outside washing his car, and Dorothy was in the living room taking a nap on the couch. Suddenly, Dorothy was awakened by the smell of smoke and the sound of the smoke alarm. She jumped out of the bed and ran into the hall way. It was evident that the smoke was coming from the kitchen. Covering her nose, Dorothy headed into the kitchen and noticed that George had turned some oil on to cook, and he'd obviously forgotten about it. Dorothy covered her arm with a towel so the rogue grease would not pop her as she turned the stove's eye off. She then turned on the stove's fan, pushed the skillet off the burner, opened the back door, and opened some of the windows in the house. Upset, Dorothy headed outside to confront her husband.

Dorothy: George! George!
George: Here I am. What's up?
Dorothy: Are you trying to kill me? Why did you turn some

oil on and not watch it?!

George: Oh, I forgot about it. Did you turn it off?

Dorothy: No, I turned it up. What do you think?! Of course I turned it off! Why did you do that?

George: I simply forgot.

Dorothy: Yeah, but that could have killed me. That's not a simple mistake, George.

George: Look, I said I forgot! What's done is done, so go in the house, shut up, and go back to sleep or something!

Dorothy was upset by her husband's words and tone, but she decided to go back in the house to see about getting all of the smoke out of the house. Lately, she had been arguing with George less and less, and he seemed to argue more with her as she followed the lead of the LORD.

George was still reeling from Dorothy's tone. How dare she come at him like that! George continued to wash the car, but his thoughts of his wife became darker and darker. This was a woman he was no longer attracted to. This was a woman who had her head in the clouds, or at least that was what he believed. She needed to be humbled. She should have been happy to have him, but no; she had the nerve to confront him about a simple error. George's thoughts continued to upset him all the more until he'd finally enraged himself enough that he felt he could not contain himself. He angrily threw down the water hose, jogged into the house, and went into the kitchen where he knew Dorothy would be. Without warning, he pinned Dorothy up against the wall, holding her by her neck. "Don't you ever raise your voice at me again! You need to be happy someone wants you with that face!" With those words, George released Dorothy, grabbed his car keys and left. Dorothy stood against the wall, frozen in shock. She didn't understand what had just happened or what could have made George so angry. Dorothy began to cry and pray to the LORD. The enemy obviously had her husband in his grips, and Dorothy prayed fervently for his release.

A few days later, George and Dorothy were cuddled up on the couch and watching television, when George suddenly became irritated with Dorothy. She was chewing gum and leaning a little too close to his ear. Dorothy had no clue that she'd infuriated her husband until he suddenly pushed her face so hard that she bit her tongue and fell off the couch. "Stop chewing in my dag-on ear!" screamed George as he got up and went into the other room. A few minutes later, Dorothy followed George into the room to try and figure out what had upset him.

Dorothy: Can we talk?
George: You got a mouth, so obviously you can talk.
Dorothy: George, what have I done wrong to you to make you be so cruel to me?
George: You're just irritating, Dorothy.
Dorothy: I don't understand.
George: You wouldn't understand. You're too simple-minded. To tell you the truth, I'm not even sure if I'm

attracted to you.

Dorothy: What would you like from me, George? If you're not attracted to me, why don't you just divorce me?

George: I definitely see that in our near future.

Dorothy: Why is that, George? What have I done to you? Why do you let the devil use you like that?

George: Dorothy, I don't want to hear any religious talk right now! Can't you see that I don't want to be bothered with you?!

Dorothy: George, the Bible says that you should not mistreat your wife or your prayers will be hindered.

George: Do you ever see me praying? Get out of here!

Dorothy: I'll leave, but can we at least talk about what's going on for five minutes?

George: Dorothy, you have until the count of three to get out of that doorway before you find yourself with a black eye. One...two...

Dorothy walked away with tears in her eyes. She truly loved George. How could he be so evil towards a woman who loved him so much? How could he not see how much he was hurting her? Why didn't he care that he was hurting her?

Over time, Dorothy tried everything she could think of to usher George towards change. She even invited people from varying religions into her home to speak with him. Even though she did not believe their doctrines, she knew that every one of those religions encouraged men to stay with their wives and to be better husbands. Nothing Dorothy could think of worked. She read the Bible to her husband and not with him because he wasn't interested in reading the Bible. She tried to convince him to come to church with her, but this rarely worked. She tried to pepper their conversations with talks about what was right and wrong, and this only irritated George.

That cold and inevitable day came, however, when George couldn't take it anymore. One day, he beat Dorothy worse than he'd ever beaten her, and the next day, he moved out. He felt that Dorothy brought out the worst in him, even though Dorothy was trying to bring out the best in him.

While the couple was separated, George often called Dorothy to ask for money. He knew that his wife loved him, but he also knew that he did not love her back. Dorothy searched George's heart with many words for any sign of love but could not find it. Anytime she saw him, she searched his eyes for any sign of compassion, but it was not in him. She couldn't find his love for GOD, and she could not find his love for her. All she could find was hatred, idolatry, selfishness and conceit in George's heart. After being separated for three months, Dorothy finally filed for divorce, but she did not get the response from George that she'd expected.

Dorothy had finally come to the conclusion that her husband did not love her. She finally accepted that she'd married the wrong man, and since he only called her when he wanted something, Dorothy assumed that George would be happy about receiving the divorce papers. She was wrong. Immediately after receiving the divorce papers, George began to harass and stalk his wife. He came to her job and sat in his car, often watching her as she went to work and got off work. He made sure she could see him because he wanted to scare her. He would show up at her house and just sit in his car. He'd even come into the house a few times while Dorothy was not at home. He would leave subtle clues around the house to let her know he'd been there. For example, he once took the comforter off the bed; he turned on the heater even though it was mid-summer; he left the television set on once; and finally, he'd used her bathroom one time and neglected to flush the toilet. The bathroom incident was the final straw. Dorothy finally decided to call the police. Initially, she thought his stalking behavior was a sign that he did have some feelings for her, but she eventually had to accept the truth: George was not stalking her because he loved her; George was stalking Dorothy because he was angry that she had been the one to file for divorce and not him. After all, he'd managed to convince himself and Dorothy that he was too good for her. For Dorothy to file for the divorce was a slap in the face for George's dignity because it signaled that her mind was beginning to change, and she was beginning to take back some of the power he'd stolen from her.

George was eventually arrested for stalking but was only

given thirty days in jail. While he was incarcerated, the divorce was finalized, and Dorothy moved to Pennsylvania.

While in Pennsylvania, Dorothy met a man named Doyle. Doyle was new to the church that Dorothy was now a member of. His wife had just passed away a little over a year ago, and he was trying to give his life back to the LORD and show his children a better route to take in their lives. His wife had been addicted to heroin and had been killed while trying to steal heroin from another addict.

Doyle had two children. He had a four-year-old son named Ned, and a two-year-old daughter named Allie. When Doyle met Dorothy, he initially thought she was a GOD-send. She was a woman of GOD with no children and a decent job. Who could ask for more?

After dating Dorothy for five months, Doyle invited her to come and live with him and his children. Dorothy refused his invitation, citing that she was celibate and did not believe in sex before marriage. Because of her stand, Doyle married her, and the couple remained married for only nine months before Doyle filed for divorce. He felt that Dorothy was too judgmental, and that she'd belittled him and his children one too many times.

After the divorce was finalized, Dorothy was back out on the prowl.
The End.